AMERICAN HISTORY
After 1865

By

Ray Allen Billington (1903-1981)
SENIOR RESEARCH ASSOCIATE,
HENRY E. HUNTINGTON LIBRARY

And

Martin Ridge
SENIOR RESEARCH ASSOCIATE,
HENRY E. HUNTINGTON LIBRARY
and PROFESSOR OF HISTORY
in the CALIFORNIA INSTITUTE OF TECHNOLOGY

LITTLEFIELD, ADAMS
QUALITY PAPERBACKS

LITTLEFIELD, ADAMS QUALITY PAPERBACKS

a division of Rowman & Littlefield Publishers, Inc.
8705 Bollman Place, Savage, Maryland 20763

British Cataloging in Publication Information Available

Library of Congress Cataloging in Publication Data

Billington, Ray Allen, 1903–1981.
American history after 1865.
A Littlefield, Adams quality paperback.
Includes bibliographical references and index.
1. United States—History—1865–
I. Ridge, Martin.   II. Title.
E661.B55   1981   973.8   81–17134
                                   AACR2
ISBN 0–8226–0027–7

1169 9152

Printed in the United States of America

About the Author

Ray Allen Billington: Senior Research Associate, Henry E. Huntington Library. Formerly taught at Clark University, Smith College, and Northwestern University where he was William Smith Mason Professor of History. Has been president of Organization of American Historians, American Studies Association and Western History Association.

Publications: *The Protestant Crusade, 1830-1860* (Macmillan, 1938, Quadrangle, 1963); *Westward Expansion: A History of the American Frontier,* (Macmillan, 4th edn., 1974); *The Far Western Frontier, 1830-1860,* (Harper 1956); *The Westward Movement in the United States* (Van Nostrand, 1959); *The Historian's Contribution to Anglo-American Misunderstanding* (Hobbs, Dorman, 1966); *America's Frontier Heritage* (Holt, Rinehart & Winston, 1966); *The Genesis of the Frontier Thesis* (Huntington Library, 1971); *Frederick Jackson Turner: Historian, Scholar, Teacher* (Oxford, 1973; Bancroft Prize winner, 1974); *America's Frontier Culture* (Texas A&M Press, 1977). Co-author: *The United States: American Democracy in World Perspective* (Rinehart, 1947); *The Making of American Democracy* (Rinehart, 1950); *America's Frontier Story* (Holt, Rinehart & Winston, 1970). Editor: numerous books, including *The Histories of the American Frontier Series* (Holt, Rinehart & Winston, 1963-   ).

Martin Ridge: Senior Research Associate, Henry E. Huntington Library and Professor of History, California Institute of Technology. Formerly taught at Westminster College, San Diego State University, and Indiana University. He has been editor of the *Journal of American History.*

Publications: *Ignatius Donnelly: Portrait of a Politician* (University of Chicago Press, 1962; Phi Alpha Theta Prize Winner, 1963; and Pacific Coast Branch of the American Historical Association Prize Winner, 1963); *An American Dilemma* (University of Southern California Press,, 1981). Co-author: *California Work and Workers* (Harr-Wagner, 1963); *The American Adventure* (Lyons and Carnahan, 1964); *America's Frontier Story* (Holt, Rinehart and Winston, 1970).

How to Use This Outline

Every student of history should have two objectives in mind : to *understand* man's past, and to *interpret* that past in the light of present-day experience. *Understanding* is possible only when the record of man's multitudinous activities is first freed of unimportant details, then arranged in an orderly pattern. When this has been done the student does not have to memorize a mass of unrelated facts ; instead he can follow the course of history as he would a proposition in logic, reasoning from related event to related event. *Interpretation* is possible only when the student is sufficiently well versed in both past history and present-day problems to recognize the relationship between the two.

The purpose of this history in outline is to make easier the understanding and interpretation of America's past between the Civil War and the present. With this in view, several unique features have been introduced :

1. All factual details have been eliminated save those considered essential by most teachers. In addition, the most important information has been emphasized by underlining the basic facts, names, and dates.

2. Material has been systematically arranged in outline form, with headings and subheadings printed in **bold type.** By following the phrases in **bold type** through a section or a chapter, the student can construct a brief and easily memorized outline of any subject.

3. Each chapter concludes with a section interpreting the material, and showing the connection between events discussed there and modern America.

The careful student who wishes to benefit most from these features should follow a standard procedure in studying for any examination. First, he should read thoroughly and carefully the text and collateral material assigned in the course he is taking, making notes on the outside reading. Then he should study this outline, noting that certain facts and interpretations are in both the text and the outline, while others are in the text alone. These latter are less essential than the former, but should be remembered if possible.

Next, the student should prepare an outline of this outline by copying out the topics in bold type in the chapter or chapters he is studying. This is recommended because most of us have visual memories; by writing something down we store that information in our minds. Moreover, that skeleton outline, which will fill less than a sheet of paper, will be easy to remember. Having learned that outline thoroughly, the usual student in an examination will be able to recall the more detailed treatment of the subject in this fuller outline, and from that most of the subject matter in the text. He should also pay attention to the names and events underlined, remembering that those are of such importance that they appear commonly on examinations.

Finally, having learned the factual story, the student should study the interpretative sections carefully, seeking to supplement them from his own knowledge of the past and present. By thinking about the material in this way he will not only achieve better understanding, but will be equipped to apply his knowledge in his own life.

Two other features of this history in outline are designed to help the student. At the end of each chapter is a section entitled "Additional Reading" which lists eight or ten of the most useful books on the subjects considered, together with brief comments indicating their nature and point of view. These bibliographies should help the student select, from the longer lists given in most texts, the few books that are essential if he wishes to do further reading. Finally, the volume ends with a section in which various types of examination questions are discussed and a number of sample questions given. The student should study carefully those questions pertaining to the section of the subject on which he is to be examined, and if possible should write out answers to several of them. By comparing his answers with the corresponding sections of this outline, he will be able to realize and correct his own defects before taking an actual examination.

R. A. B.

Contents

CONTENTS

AMERICAN HISTORY
After 1865

CHAPTER I

The Reconstruction Period
1865-1877

ℭ THE RECONSTRUCTION PROBLEM
A twofold problem faced the United States when General
Robert E. Lee's surrender (April 9, 1865) ended the Civil
War: 1) how could the eleven Confederate states be restored
to their former position in the Union; and 2) how could the
economically prostrate South be rehabilitated? Northern
politicians were largely responsible for attempts made to
solve the first problem, while Southerners were primarily
concerned with the second. Hence the story of Reconstruction must be divided into two parts, one dealing with political
events, the other with social and economic progress.

I. POLITICAL RECONSTRUCTION. The triumphant North was called upon to decide whether the defeated
southern states should be kept perpetually subservient, restored to their full rights in the Union, or readmitted with
limited self-government. Divergent opinions among the
victors made the solution difficult.

**A. Factors Influencing the Formulation of a Re-
construction Policy.** The task of restoring the Confederate
states to statehood was complicated by several factors:

1. The Constitutional Factor. Northerners before and
during the war had held that secession was illegal and that
the rebellious states were still in the Union; Southerners had
maintained their legal right to secede. With the war over,

1

Southerners were anxious to return to the United States as soon as possible, yet to do so they must adopt the Northern view. Northerners, on the other hand, wishing to inflict penalties on the Confederates, were forced to accept the South's contention and argue that secession was legal. Both sides found this transition difficult.

2. The Economic Factor. This influenced opinion in two ways: 1) The war had cost the North heavily. The Union war debt amounted to almost $3,000,000,000, and casualties to 360,000 persons. Many Northerners were determined to make the Confederates pay for these losses, while Southerners, convinced that their cause was both legal and just, refused to do so. 2) Northern industrialists, irked by the South's prewar record of aiding agriculture at the expense of manufacturing, were determined to keep the section politically subservient. Only in this way, they felt, could they secure the tariffs, sound-money laws, easy credit, and government bounties needed for business expansion.

3. The Social Factor. Humanitarians in the North viewed political reconstruction as a means of forcing the South to accept the principle of racial equality. Like the industrialists, they favored a program that would allow the federal government to dominate the Confederacy until that section granted political and social equality to the freed slaves and economic privileges to the poor of both races. They also wished to punish the plantation owners for keeping Negroes in bondage.

4. The Psychological Factor. The hatred bred of war did not die easily. Northerners insisted that Southerners be punished; Southerners were in no mood to accept the olive branch from their victorious enemies. Some Confederates fled to Mexico, England, or Canada, while those who remained were suspicious and distrustful. Cooperation under these circumstances was difficult.

5. The Political Factor. The Republican Party viewed the northern victory as its personal triumph. Its leaders felt that their party should be rewarded by perpetual political dominance; the future of America would be threatened, they believed, if the secession-minded Democrats ever regained supremacy. Hence they weighed the political as well as the social effect of each Reconstruction law before Congress, favoring only those that promised to weaken the Democrats and strengthen the Republicans. This narrow policy led to a division within the party, for most Northerners were more concerned with the restoration of the Union than with political quarrels. One faction, the *Moderate Republicans* under the leadership of Presidents *Abraham Lincoln* and *Andrew Johnson*, favored a mild policy toward the South. The other, the *Radical Republicans*, wished to adopt a harsh policy aimed at perpetual political subservience for the section. Its leaders were Charles Sumner, Benjamin Wade, and *Thaddeus Stevens*. The battles between these factions complicated the legislative process throughout the period.

B. The Stages of Political Reconstruction. The story of political Reconstruction falls into four stages: 1) the period before Lincoln's assassination on April 14, 1865; 2) the years between 1865 and 1866 when President Andrew Johnson tried to carry out his own policy; 3) the period from 1866 to 1868 when the Congressional Reconstruction policy was formulated; and 4) the period after 1868 when southern opposition gradually negated the Congressional measures.

1. The Lincoln Reconstruction Plan.

a. FEATURES OF THE PLAN. Abraham Lincoln, whose love of Union transcended sectional hatred, held throughout the war that the southern states could not legally secede, nor did he deviate from this stand as peace approached. Using his power as commander in chief, he issued a proclamation on *December 8, 1863* which established a procedure for political Reconstruction. This provided: 1) that all Confederates except prominent military and political leaders could regain citizenship by taking oath to support the Constitution and the *Thirteenth Amendment* abolishing slavery; 2) that when 10 per cent of the number of people in each state who had voted in the election of 1860 met these requirements they could set up a government which would be recognized by the President. This was the *Presidential Reconstruction Plan*, or *Ten-per-cent Plan*. During 1864 Lincoln used it to set up state governments in Tennessee, Louisiana, and Arkansas.

b. CONGRESSIONAL REACTION. Congress refused to accept the President's moderate program, for the radicals feared that it would not secure equality for the Negroes, punishment for Confederate leaders, or continued victories for the Republicans in southern states. Their reply to Lincoln was the *Wade-Davis Bill* (July 8, 1864), which provided: 1) Congress rather than the President would administer the Reconstruction program; 2) a majority of the population of each southern state, rather than 10 per cent, must take an oath of allegiance before a government could be established; 3) high Confederate officials and military leaders were disenfranchised; 4) slavery was abolished; and 5) Confederate debts were repudiated. Lincoln disposed of the Wade-Davis Bill by a pocket veto, but Congress answered with the *Wade-Davis Manifesto* (August 5, 1864), which castigated the President for usurping congressional authority. Lincoln's political skill might have averted the growing conflict, but his assassination on April 14, 1865, ended hope of compromise.

2. The Johnson Reconstruction Plan.

a. CHARACTER OF JOHNSON. Andrew Johnson, a War Democrat who had been Lincoln's running mate in the election of 1864, had neither the political acumen nor the popular backing to battle the congressional radicals. Moreover, the President's murder convinced even moderate Northerners that the South must be punished severely.

b. THE JOHNSON PLAN. Despite these handicaps, the *Johnson Reconstruction Plan* was based largely on Lincoln's policy. Announced during his first weeks in office, it: 1) proclaimed a general amnesty for all Southerners except Confederate leaders and those whose wealth exceeded $20,000; 2) recognized the governments of Virginia, Tennessee, Arkansas, and Louisiana as constituted under Lincoln's Reconstruction Plan; and 3) informed the remaining southern states that they could re-enter the Union when they had repudiated their war debts, abolished slavery, disavowed their ordinances of secession, and ratified the Thirteenth Amendment. By December 4, 1865, when Congress met, all the southern states save Texas had fulfilled these terms and were ready to be readmitted.

3. *Congressional Reconstruction Policy.* When Congress convened it refused to seat representatives from the reconstructed states, holding that the southern commonwealths had reverted to territorial status by seceding, and were now under complete congressional control. Instead, a radical Republican *Committee of Fifteen,* made up of members of both houses and dominated by Representative Thaddeus Stevens of Pennsylvania, began formulating its own reconstruction policy.

a. EARLY CONGRESSIONAL STEPS.

I. *Freedman's Bureau.* A bill (February, 1866) extended the life of the *Freedman's Bureau,* a wartime agency that had cared for freed slaves. The measure was vetoed by Johnson, but a later bill embodying the same features was passed over his veto on July 16, 1866.

II. *Civil Rights Act.* This measure (April, 1866) forbade the states to discriminate against Negroes, guaranteed persons of color the equal protection of the laws, and decreed that cases rising under the act be tried in the federal courts. It was passed over Johnson's veto.

III. *Fourteenth Amendment.* Fearful lest the Civil Rights Act be declared unconstitutional, radical Republicans

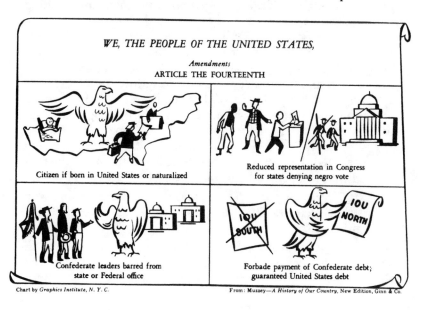

WE, THE PEOPLE OF THE UNITED STATES,

Amendments
ARTICLE THE FOURTEENTH

Citizen if born in United States or naturalized

Reduced representation in Congress for states denying negro vote

Confederate leaders barred from state or Federal office

Forbade payment of Confederate debt; guaranteed United States debt

Chart by *Graphics Institute, N. Y. C.*   From: Muzzey—*A History of Our Country,* New Edition, Ginn & Co.

formulated the *Fourteenth Amendment*. This provided that:
1) all persons born or naturalized in the United States were
citizens with full rights; 2) southern states must grant Negroes the vote or suffer the loss of a portion of their congressional representation; 3) former Confederates could not hold
office until pardoned by Congress; 4) the Confederate war
debt was repudiated; and 5) the measure be enforced by
Congress rather than the President or the courts.

b. CONGRESSIONAL ELECTIONS OF 1866. These elections allowed the people to choose between the *Presidential
Reconstruction Policy*, which allowed the southern people to
shape their own institutions, and the *Congressional Reconstruction Policy*, which gave control over the South to Congress.

I. *The Presidential Campaign.* The presidential cause
was handicapped by two things: 1) In most districts the
choice was between a radical Republican and a copperhead
Democrat, forcing even moderate Republicans to vote the
radical ticket; 2) Johnson conducted an inept campaign for
his candidates, making immoderate speeches and sinking to
vituperation rather than stressing issues.

II. *The Congressional Campaign.* The radicals campaigned astutely, appealing to patriotic instincts and hushing
basic questions. Moreover, they were aided by three developments in the South: 1) A bloody *race riot* in New Orleans
(July, 1866) convinced northerners that the ex-slaves must
be protected. 2) *Black Codes* adopted in most southern states
indicated that Southerners intended to reduce the Negroes to
a status resembling slavery. These codes regulated the social
and economic status of freedmen, even providing that "va-
grants" could be fined $50 and, if unable to pay, apprenticed
for six months. 3) The persistence with which southern
states elected former Confederate leaders to office demonstrated that the people had not learned the lessons of war.

III. *Results of Elections.* The radical Republicans won
a sweeping victory, which they interpreted as a mandate for
their program.

c. CONGRESSIONAL RECONSTRUCTION PLAN (March 2,
1867). This measure, adopted after the elections: 1) ruled
that no lawful governments existed in any of the southern

states save Tennessee; 2) divided the South into five military districts under commanders who were instructed to protect life and property; and 3) decreed that no state could return to civilian rule until its voters, both white and colored, framed a constitution that guaranteed Negro suffrage and was acceptable to both Congress and the people. Each must also ratify the Fourteenth Amendment.

d. ENFORCEMENT OF CONGRESSIONAL RECONSTRUCTION. Recognizing the doubtful legality of their plan, radical Republicans took steps to insure its administration by Congress rather than the courts or the President.

I. *Denial of Court Authority*. An act of March 7, 1868, denied the Supreme Court jurisdiction over the Reconstruction acts. The radicals believed this necessary as the Court had, in two cases, threatened the constitutionality of the measures: 1) in *Ex Parte Milligan* (1866) it had ruled that military trials were illegal in areas where civil courts were functioning; and 2) in *Ex Parte McCardle* (1868) it had accepted jurisdiction in the case of a Mississippi editor who had been convicted by a military tribunal.

II. *Denial of Presidential Authority*. Two acts of March 2, 1867, removed administration of the Reconstruction Act from the President: 1) The *Army Appropriations Act* decreed that military orders could be issued only by the general of the army; 2) The *Tenure of Office Act* prohibited the President from removing any federal officials without Senate consent. Together these laws vested control of the military districts in *Edwin M. Stanton,* a radical Republican who was Secretary of War, and prevented Johnson from dismissing Stanton.

III. *Impeachment of Johnson.* Still fearful of the President, the radicals laid plans to impeach him. Their opportunity came on February 21, 1868, when Johnson dismissed Stanton. Three days later the House voted to impeach Johnson for violating the Tenure of Office Act and for other "high crimes and misdemeanors." He was tried before the Senate, and escaped conviction by only one vote. Although vindicated, Johnson's power was so weakened that he accomplished nothing in his remaining months in office.

e. ELECTION OF 1868. Calling themselves the National

Union Republican Party, the _radical Republicans_ nominated General _Ulysses S. Grant_ for the presidency, before adopting a platform that lauded congressional reconstruction and promised payment of the national debt in gold. The _Democrats_, seeking a _"New Departure"_ to win votes, nominated Governor _Horatio Seymour_ of New York, and endorsed the _Ohio Idea._ This promised repayment of federal bonds in "greenbacks," or paper money, rather than in gold, a proposal designed to appeal to debtor elements among eastern workers and western farmers suffering in the postwar deflation that began in 1867. Grant was victorious by an electoral vote of 214 to 80, although his popular majority was only 300,000 votes. The votes of 700,000 Negroes elected him. The result was no mandate for radical policy.

4. Failure of Congressional Reconstruction.

a. ENFORCEMENT OF CONGRESSIONAL POLICY. Even before Grant's election, Johnson faithfully, if unwillingly, carried out the Congressional Reconstruction Act. By the spring of 1868 all states but Texas and Virginia had adopted constitutions. The Mississippi constitution was rejected by the voters, but the other seven states set up governments which ratified the Fourteenth Amendment, and in June, 1868, were readmitted to the Union by Congress. The _Fourteenth Amendment_ became effective in _July, 1868._ Thus only three states—Mississippi, Texas, and Virginia—were under military rule when Grant took office. Radicals decided that these states should not be admitted until they had ratified the _Fifteenth Amendment,_ which forbade the states to deny the vote to any citizen because of "race, color, or previous condition of servitude." All three did so by 1870.

b. SOUTHERN OPPOSITION TO CONGRESSIONAL RECONSTRUCTION. Between 1870 and 1877 the center of the conflict over Reconstruction shifted to the South. There two factions contested for control of each state: 1) Democrats seeking to re-establish white supremacy, and 2) radical Republicans determined to secure equal rights for Negroes. In this group were Negroes, northern _carpetbaggers_ who had come south to lead the freedmen, and southern _Scalawags,_ or whites who had deserted to the Republican camp.

This faction was backed by radicals in Congress who were always ready to pass laws for its support.

I. *Reasons for Republican Defeat.* The white Democrats were eventually triumphant in this contest. This was because: 1) The Reconstruction legislatures lost support by accumulating huge debts and by increasing taxes from fourfold to fourteenfold. Many of their expenditures were legitimate, for the cost of physical reconstruction was heavy, interest rates high, and the dollar inflated. Yet tax increases are never popular. 2) Many carpetbaggers and scalawags were corrupt. They, rather than the Negroes they led, were responsible for most of the dishonesty that discredited the Reconstruction legislatures. 3) The traditions of white rule and local rule were too strong in the South to be broken easily. 4) A rising conservative class, made up of landholders and businessmen, was soon powerful enough to spearhead an attack on radical policies. These *Bourbons* wanted to keep the Negro subjugated in order to assure a cheap labor supply as well as white supremacy. Moreover, knowing they were in the minority, they sought to secure political supremacy for their class by driving a racial wedge between the lower classes.

II. *Form of Southern Opposition.* Opposition to radical rule in the South took two forms: 1) In states where whites were in a clear majority—as Tennessee and North Carolina—Democrats regained control of the state government by legal means; 2) In others, where federal troops remained to enforce racial equality, extralegal devices were employed. Most effective were secret societies—such as the *Ku Klux Klan* and the *Knights of the White Camelia*—to intimidate the Negroes. Their program of terrorism kept Republicans from the polls, allowing the Democrats to recapture the legislatures. Congressional radicals attempted to suppress these societies by passing the *Force Act* (1870) and the *Ku Klux Klan Act* (1871). These gave the President power to: 1) suspend the writ of habeas corpus; 2) supervise congressional elections; and 3) employ troops to assure Negroes civil and political rights. Their enforcement led to the suppression of the secret societies by the end of 1872.

c. END OF CONGRESSIONAL RECONSTRUCTION. By 1872 the United States was tired of radical Reconstruction policies. In the election of that year the Republicans divided, with one faction advocating the end of congressional control of the South. Although the radicals re-elected Grant by a narrow majority, they realized that they must change their program. This was done in 1872 when an *Amnesty Act* restored the franchise to almost all Confederates. As a result, white Democrats gradually regained control of the southern states. By 1877, when *Rutherford B. Hayes* was inaugurated as President, only South Carolina and Louisiana remained in radical hands. In both these states two governments existed, one representing a minority group of carpetbaggers, scalawags, and Negroes backed by federal troops, the other based on white supremacy and supported by nearly all whites. President Hayes, convinced that the radical governments did not represent the majority will, withdrew the troops in *April, 1877*. Democrats immediately seized control. Political Reconstruction was ended, with the radical program completely rejected.

II. SOCIAL RECONSTRUCTION. The economic and social rehabilitation of the South was as much a part of Reconstruction as the political revival of the area. That significant progress was made was less the result of the ill-directed efforts of radical Republicans than of the labors of Southerners themselves, principally the freed slaves and small farmers.

A. The Plight of the South.

1. The Economic Problem. The South was in a desperate situation when the Civil War ended. Livestock had been slaughtered. Fields were left barren by marauding troops, or neglected because farmers had no seed to plant. Plantations and homes were destroyed, or were decaying away. Many principal cities had been bombarded into rubble. Railroads were torn up, bridges destroyed, and the entire transportation system was in confusion. With the collapse of Confederate money, finances were chaotic. Not a bank or insurance company was solvent, while the securities in which thousands had invested their savings were worthless. All goods had to be imported from the North on credit, at exhorbitant interest rates.

2. *The Social Problem.* Schools and churches were closed everywhere. Four million freed slaves, suddenly endowed with legal and social privileges for which they had not been trained, must adjust themselves to freedom. Many, intoxicated by release from bondage, wandered about the countryside. Others waited for the government to give them the "forty acres and a mule" that rumor told them would be theirs. For a time all work was at a standstill as Southerners wrestled with the problem of devising a new labor system and an economy suited to freedom.

B. The Economic Revival.

1. *Agricultural Readjustment.* The first need was to revive agriculture. At first landowners tried to operate plantations with gangs of hired Negro workers, but this was contrary to the whole spirit of emancipation. Gradually, *share cropping* and *tenant farming* were introduced. These methods were necessary in a region where workers lacked means to buy their own farms, but the Negro share croppers were little better off than under slavery. Living in shacks, and working long hours in cotton fields, they were always in debt to landowners and storekeepers.

2. *Breakup of Plantations.* Gradually, however, the more energetic climbed upward economically as they accumulated capital needed to buy land. Their opportunity came when heavy taxes levied by Reconstruction governments forced plantation owners to throw their holdings on the market. Between 1860 and 1880 the number of farms in the South doubled, while the size of the average farm decreased from 335 acres to 153 acres. This land redistribution benefited the Negro less than the small farmers and former poor whites. During the Reconstruction period this group laid the economic basis for its later political supremacy.

3. *Results of Agricultural Changes.* The whole South benefited from the displacement of plantation agriculture by small-scale farming. By 1870 the yield per acre was greater than at any time before the war. By 1879 the cotton crop was greater than in 1860, while the value of minor crops now surpassed that of cotton.

C. The Social Revolution. The democratizing influence of land redistribution was paralleled by social gains for the hitherto underprivileged classes in the South, both white and colored. The Reconstruction legislatures were responsible for this improvement. Their Negro members, thirsting for means of self-improvement and conscious of the needs of the lower class, passed dozens of progressive laws. In many states roads were built, public buildings improved, taxation systems modernized, poor relief inaugurated, and land distributed to the needy. More important were their educational innovations. Nearly all "carpetbag" legislatures established compulsory free schools for the children of both races. The program for human betterment outlined during these years has not yet been fully achieved in the South.

III. THE BALANCE SHEET OF RECONSTRUCTION. An assessment of the results of the Reconstruction policies adopted between 1865 and 1877 indicates that the era's legacy to the future contained both harmful and beneficial features:

A. Harmful Results.

1. Less Intelligent Leadership Was Provided for the South. The disenfranchisement of the Confederate military and civil leaders forced members of this well-educated group into oblivion. Their eclipse elevated the former small farmers and poor whites to positions of political and economic supremacy. The vision of these men was cramped by a background of poverty and ignorance, while their hatred of Negroes accentuated the race problem.

2. The Racial Issue Was Sharpened. Southern whites thereafter associated Negroes with carpetbaggers and scalawags whose reign had produced corruption and fraud. Hence they concluded that Negro participation in politics was dangerous, and systematically restricted voting to whites.

3. The South Became Unnecessarily Economy-Minded. Shocked by the expenditures of radical Republican legislatures, Southerners concluded that good government and economy were synonymous, even though social gains must be sacrificed.

4. One-Party Government Was Fastened on the South.
The Reconstruction legislatures convinced southern whites
that the Republican Party was the party of "niggers" and
corruption; thereafter no self-respecting white man would
vote anything but the straight Democratic ticket. From 1876
to 1916 that party was completely supreme below the Mason-
Dixon Line; not until 1928 was there any serious deflection
in the *"Solid South."* The harmful results were noticeable
both locally and nationally:

a. LOCAL RESULTS. One-party rule stifled democracy
in the South. Two competing parties would have bid for
support by broadening the voting lists, promising social legislation, and campaigning for progressive measures dear to
the people. With only one party in control, voting lists were
contracted by depriving Negroes of the franchise, while the
South lagged behind other sections in social legislation, education, and other measures to benefit the masses.

b. NATIONAL RESULTS. These were of two sorts: 1)
One-party rule prevented an alliance of lower-class elements
in the South and West. Hence northeastern industrialists,
with their opposition divided, were able to control the government through the late nineteenth century. 2) The Democratic Party was burdened with a conservative wing which
blocked much progressive legislation, particularly during the
twentieth century when the remaining members of that party
followed a liberal course. This was the case especially as
conservative Southerners, elected time and again without
opposition, gained control of many congressional committees
through seniority, then used their powerful positions to
frustrate the majority will.

5. Sectional Hatred Was Increased. Southerners hated
the North for its radical policies and Negro rule; Northerners hated the South for its insistence on white supremacy.
The wartime wounds would have healed much sooner had
they not been inflamed during the Reconstruction period.

B. Beneficial Results.

1. The Redistribution of Property forced on the South
by the Reconstruction legislatures ultimately benefited the
entire section. Wealth was more equitably spread, crops
diversified, and agriculture placed on a sounder basis.

2. The Educational System and Social Legislation proposed by the radical governments, although not achieved at the time, laid a basis for many of the gains made since.

3. Reconstruction Was Less Brutal Than It Might Have Been. No Confederate leader was executed, almost no land confiscated, and few Southerners punished. Although the radical policies seemed harsh to Southerners, they were far milder than those adopted in other countries following civil wars. As the South awakened to this fact, its resentment was slowly forgotten, allowing the two sections to merge into one during the late nineteenth century. By 1898, when Congress removed the last political disabilities from ex-Confederates, the animosities of the Civil War were all but forgotten.

Additional Reading

Both Rembert W. Patrick, *The Reconstruction of the Nation* (1967), and Avery Craven, *Reconstruction: The Ending of the Civil War* (1969), are brief syntheses embodying the findings of the latest research. John Hope Franklin, *Reconstruction: After the Civil War* (1961), and Kenneth M. Stampp, *The Era of Reconstruction, 1865-1877* (1965), explore the era competently. All these books, which stress social as well as political events, reveal the social gains made in the South under the Radicals. Their contributions are more fully explored in Hans L. Trefousse, *The Radical Republicans: Lincoln's Vanguard for Racial Justice* (1969), and Robert Cruden, *The Negro in Reconstruction* (1969). The best exploration of the complex issues that shaped the nature of Reconstruction policies is Herman Belz, *Reconstruction and Union: Theory and Policy during the Civil War* (1969), while the effect of the courts is shown in Stanley I. Kutler, *Judicial Power and Reconstruction Politics* (1968). A stimulating reappraisal of President Johnson's role is Eric McKitrick, *Andrew Johnson and Reconstruction* (1969). Paul Buck, *The Road to Reunion* (1937), traces the evolution of forces helping to reunite North and South. One of the best books on social and economic developments is still Allan Nevins, *The Emergence of Modern America* (1927).

Chapter II

The Economic Revolution
1865-1890

❲ THE INDUSTRIALIZATION OF THE UNITED STATES

The most important force reshaping American politics, diplomacy, life, and thought in the late nineteenth century was industrialization. Between 1865 and 1890 the United States changed from an agricultural country to an industrialized nation, fully adjusted to a machine civilization. This transformation can best be shown statistically: [1]

	1860	1890	% of Increase
Population	31,450,000	62,600,000	99
Number of farms	2,000,000	4,500,000	120
Number of factories	·140,500	355,400	153
Value of farms	7,980,500,000	16,100,000,000	101
Value of factories	1,000,000,000	6,500,000,000	555
Value of farm products		2,500,000,000	
Value of manufactures	1,900,000,000	9,400,000,000	394
Industrial workers	1,300,000	4,200,000	223

These figures spelled out a revolution in every phase of life. The history of the period, outlined in the following chapters, is largely a history of the changes wrought by the mechanization of American society.

---

[1] All figures are in round numbers to facilitate memorizing.

I. CAUSES OF THE ECONOMIC REVOLUTION.
Many factors were responsible for this rapid transition from an agricultural to a machine civilization.

A. Plentiful Raw Materials. The rich natural resources of the East had scarcely been tapped by the pre-Civil War generation, while still greater riches waited exploitation in the West. _Lumber_ could be obtained from the virgin forests that covered the Great Lakes country, the Rocky Mountains, the Pacific Northwest, and parts of the South. The United States contained about half the world's _coal_ reserves, concentrated in a belt running west from Pennsylvania. _Iron ore_ was found in Pennsylvania and Alabama, but especially in Minnesota and Upper Michigan. The _Mesabi Range_ of Minnesota by 1900 furnished one-third of all ore used in the United States, and one-sixth of the world's supply. Lake steamers, carrying the ore to the coal fields of Pennsylvania, Ohio, and Illinois, produced such steel cities as Detroit, Toledo, Cleveland, and Gary. _Oil_ was found beneath Pennsylvania and later in the Southwest. _Copper_ from Michigan supplied industry until the 1880's when the mines of Montana and Arizona assumed supremacy. _Silver_ from Colorado and Nevada, and _gold_ from California and South Dakota were also used by industry. _Lead_ was plentiful in Colorado, Missouri, and Illinois.

B. Available Capital. This came from two sources:

1) _Foreign capital,_ especially from England, Holland, and Germany, financed many industries. Investors there were eager to finance American industries partly because higher interest rates were paid, and partly because the United States bought more abroad than it sold there. The difference, which was owed foreign capitalists, was reinvested in this country. Foreigners owned $3,300,000,000 in American securities in 1900. 2) _Domestic capital_ was made available with the decline of commercial activities. High insurance rates on American vessels during the Civil War allowed England to capture much of the carrying trade of the Atlantic basin, while the steam-driven steel vessels perfected by British shippers after the war proved more economical than the wooden sailing vessels of the United States. American ships, which carried 66 per cent of American commerce in 1860,

carried only 9 per cent in 1900. Hence money formerly invested in commerce flowed into industry. As factories expanded, more and more capital was created for reinvestment.

C. Available Labor. This came from two sources:

1. From Within the United States. The millions of Civil War soldiers seeking jobs were soon supplanted by workers released from the farms. Improved agricultural machinery allowed the nation to produce all food necessary with constantly fewer men. To give one example: In 1830, 183 minutes of labor was needed to produce a bushel of wheat, in 1900 only 10 minutes. Between 1870 and 1890 better farm machines freed 4,430,000 men from agriculture for work in industry.

2. From Abroad. Between 1860 and 1900 almost 14,-000,000 immigrants reached the United States. This influx was caused by overcrowding at home, a desire to escape military service, religious or racial persecution, and the liberalization of European laws forbidding emigration. Equally important were the attracting forces: the demand for cheap labor in the United States, and the activities of shipping and railroad companies who advertised for immigrants.

a. THE OLD IMMIGRATION. At first, immigrants came from northern and western Europe, especially Great Britain, Germany, and the Scandinavian countries. Most of these, with the exception of the Irish, migrated to the West, where many settled in Chicago, Cincinnati, St. Louis, Milwaukee, and other cities. There they were available as factory workers, as were the Irish who concentrated in the eastern cities.

b. THE NEW IMMIGRATION. Beginning in the 1880's the bulk of the immigrants came from southern and eastern Europe. The Italians, Poles, Russians, Austrians, and Jews who made up this "new immigration" had no money for farms; instead they sought jobs as unskilled workers in steel mills, mines, manufacturing plants, and railroads. Accustomed to low living standards, they were willing to work for poor pay amidst intolerable working conditions. About one-third were *birds of passage* who intended to return to the Old Country with their savings.

c. MINOR IMMIGRANT GROUPS also contributed to the labor supply. French-Canadians from Quebec flocked into New England's textile mills, while Mexicans filled the cities of California and the Southwest. Peasants from China and Japan helped build the western railroads before forming colorful "Chinatowns" in cities everywhere. As all sought jobs, factory owners could bid the price of labor down to a point, in real wages, never known in the United States.

D. American Ingenuity. Mechanical and managerial skill allowed industrialists to offset their greatest handicap: competition with cheap-labor areas abroad where living standards were lower. This was done by:

1. Mass Production Techniques were employed so successfully to meet the artificial demands created by the Civil War that they spread to most industries in the postwar era. By using the *principle of interchangeable parts* (standardized units that could be fitted together interchangeably), American manufacturers could produce more cheaply than European, despite higher labor costs. These same devices were not adopted abroad, where tradition hindered innovation.

2. Inventions to improve manufacturing processes or supply more items for production were patented in large numbers; between 1865 and 1900 the number issued was 638,000, while in the whole period between 1790 and 1865 only 62,000 inventions were patented. Included in these were: the *typewriter* (1867) by Christopher Sholes; the *linotype* (1886) by Otto Mergenthaler; the *incandescent lamp* (1880) by *Thomas Alva Edison;* the *telephone* (1876) by *Alexander Graham Bell;* the *Bessemer Process* for making steel (1864) by Henry Bessemer and William Kelly; the steam turbine (1882); the *dynamo* (1880) by Thomas A. Edison; the Westinghouse air brake (1872); the railroad "parlor car" (1864) by George Pullman; the automatic coupler (1871); the refrigerator car (1875); the electric railroad (1870-1880) by Thomas A. Edison and Stephen Field; and wireless telegraphy (1896).

E. Broadening Markets. Within the United States was the largest area in the world over which goods could flow without encountering barriers in the form of differing currencies, customs barriers, or trade regulations. This _domestic market_ expanded steadily during these years because of: 1) _Improved living standards_ which accompanied industrialization. Realizing that wealth could be acquired by bold plunging rather than careful saving, Americans generally lived above their immediate means, thus consuming more goods than Europeans. 2) _Railroad building,_ which increased the mileage of American lines from 30,626 in 1860 to 163,597 in 1890. Each mile of track laid expanded manufacturers' markets. At the same time _foreign markets_ were opened by the steam-driven, iron ships that came into general use after 1860.

F. Encouragement from the Government. The prevailing political theory of _laissez faire_ held that the government should not interfere in industry. This allowed businessmen to pay low wages, charge high prices, employ corrupt practices, and enter into monopolistic combines without interference by state or national governments. At the same time federal laws were passed to aid industry. These included high protective tariffs, land grants and loans to railroads, and acts requiring shipbuilders and railroads to use American-made materials.

G. Leadership Was Attracted. The ablest men of the generation were attracted into industry rather than politics. _Andrew Carnegie, John D. Rockefeller,_ and _Charles Schwab_ were industrial geniuses who in an earlier generation might have become outstanding statesmen. In this period their thirst for power could be better satisfied in business than in government.

II. THE DUAL REVOLUTIONS. The two fields most affected by the revolution in economics were production and distribution.

A. Production. In the field of manufacturing three significant developments occurred after the Civil War:

1. Growth of Heavy Industry. The so-called heavy industries (iron, steel, machinery) developed more rapidly than the light industries (textiles, food processing) that had dominated the nation's economy before the Civil War. Of these the _steel industry_ was most important. Its rapid growth began in the 1880's when the *Mesabi Range* of Minnesota was opened to provide cheap iron ore. At the same time the perfection of the *Bessemer* and *open-hearth* processes for converting iron into steel reduced the price of steel from $300 to $35 a ton. The industry centered about Pittsburgh, where the coal and limestone needed for smelting were plentiful. Lake steamers brought ore from Minnesota to this point. By 1900 two-thirds of the nation's steel was produced there, with lesser centers at the lower end of Lake Michigan (near the coal beds of Illinois) and in the Rocky Mountain area. The leading steel producer was *Andrew Carnegie,* a Scottish immigrant who formed the Carnegie Steel Company in 1892. This produced one-fourth of the nation's steel. In 1901 Carnegie sold out his interests to a group of financiers headed by *Elbert H. Gary* of Chicago and *J. P. Morgan* of New York, in the merger that resulted in the *United States Steel Corporation,* capitalized at $1,400,000,000. By this time the United States was the world's leading steel producer, with a capacity double that of England.

   2. Geographic Dispersion of Industry. Before the Civil War, manufacturing was concentrated in the Northeast. While that section still retained its industrial supremacy, industrialization spread to the West and South:

   a. THE WEST. The industries centered there were related to the agriculture that was the section's principal interest. They included firms producing farm machinery, furniture, building supplies, flour, meat, and steel. Production was centered about Chicago, with lesser centers at St. Louis, Cincinnati, Minneapolis, and other cities.

   b. THE SOUTH. Before the Civil War the South produced only 8 per cent of the nation's manufactured goods. Ingredients for manufacturing were plentiful, however: 1) *Raw materials* existed in the form of cotton for textiles; iron ore and coal in northern Alabama, where Birmingham was founded as a steel city; tobacco in North Carolina; and lumber in the lower South to supply the nation when the forests of the Great Lakes were exhausted. 2) *Labor* could be recruited from the ranks of former slaves and poor whites at lower wages than in the North. 3) *Capital* was provided by many small investors who believed that the South was defeated in the Civil War by its lack of industries. Determined to change this situation, and influenced by such slogans as "Bring the mills to the cotton," they scraped their savings together to purchase stock on the installment plan. The result was the gradual creation of the *New South* which by 1900 produced half the nation's cotton textiles and boasted an industrial investment of $1,000,000,000. Industrialists, or Southern Bourbons, controlled the section as had great planters a generation before. The lot of the common people was not greatly improved, for living conditions in "mill villages" were no better than on barren fields, yet industrialization helped heal the breach between North and South by giving the two sections common problems and objectives.

3. Growth of Monopoly. Before the Civil War most factories were owned privately, by partners, or by small corporations. Combination began when the *Panic of 1873* inaugurated a period of fierce competition between the many small businesses. To escape price cutting, owners first used the device of *pooling,* through which the several manufacturers of a product entered into a "gentleman's agreement" on the price to be charged or the geographic area in which each would sell his goods. In the 1880's pools gave way to *trusts,* formed when previously competing firms handed over their stock to a board of trustees. The first important trust was the *Standard Oil Company* as it was reorganized in 1882 by John D. Rockefeller. This not only monopolized most of the nation's oil distribution, but was in a position to demand *rebates* from railroads in return for its business. When competitors were bankrupted by this or similar tactics they were absorbed by the Standard Oil Company. The success of Rockefeller's trust inspired many imitators; before the close of the century 5,000 competing firms were merged into 300 trusts, each enjoying a virtual monopoly. Among these were: the United States Steel Corporation, the American Sugar Refining Company, the United States Rubber Company, the American Tobacco Company, the Amalgamated Copper Company, the Pullman Palace Car Company, and the International Harvester Company. While they allowed industrialists to enjoy the economies of large-scale production and distribution, their monopolistic character tempted manufacturers to charge excessive prices.

B. Distribution. A revolution in both internal and external transportation occurred between 1865 and 1890, as railroads and steamship lines opened new markets to manufacturers.

1. Internal Transportation. Railroad mileage in the United States increased from 35,000 in 1865 to 200,000 in 1900.

a. EASTERN RAILROADS. Although the eastern railroad network was marked out before the Civil War, two significant developments occurred:

I. *Improved Facilities* transformed the eastern railroads from unreliable carriers into today's efficient systems. This was accomplished by laying thousands of miles of track reaching to every hamlet, as well as by adopting a uniform gauge which allowed cars from one road to be used on others. Equally important were such inventions as George Pullman's "palace car" (1864), George Westinghouse's automatic air brake (1872), the refrigerator car (1875), the block signal system, and automatic coupling. Faster and heavier locomotives steadily increased the speed and comfort of travel.

II. *Railroad Consolidation* united the many competing lines into a few giant systems. The pioneer was *Cornelius Vanderbilt,* who employed a fortune made in commerce to create the *New York Central System.* By 1900 this road extended from New York to Boston, Cleveland, Detroit, Chicago, St. Louis, Cincinnati, and Indianapolis. The *Pennsylvania Railroad* in the meantime expanded west and south to Chicago, Baltimore, and Washington. A third eastern railroad, the *New York and Erie,* was the victim of two unscrupulous financiers, Daniel Drew and *Jay Gould,* whose stock manipulations drove the line into bankruptcy in 1875. Its period of expansion did not begin until 1894 when it was reorganized by J. P. Morgan. Similar combinations consolidated most of the eastern railroads by 1900.

b. WESTERN RAILROADS. At the close of the Civil War

the Far West was without transportation. During the next thirty years a number of transcontinental lines united the Pacific and Atlantic.

I. _Problems of Western Railroad Building._ In the Far West the lack of population to provide way traffic discouraged private railroad builders until the federal government came to their aid with land grants and loans. _Land grants_ consisted of outright gifts of land along the right-of-way, varying from ten to twenty square miles (sections) for each mile of track laid. Between 1850 and 1871 Congress gave railroads 131,350,000 acres, while western states added 49,000,000 acres to this amount, a total area more than the size of the state of Texas. The railroads sold this land during the next few years, at an average price of $5 an acre, sometimes realizing enough to pay total construction costs.

II. _The First Transcontinentals._ Demands for a Pacific railroad mounted after the Gold Rush of 1849 peopled California. Sectional jealousies halted construction until the secession of the southern states, when lines were begun utilizing the four best routes:

1) **The Central Route** from Chicago to San Francisco through South Pass was used first. Two lines were chartered in 1862, the _Union Pacific Railroad_ to build westward from Omaha, and the _Central Pacific Railroad_ to build eastward from the Pacific. Each was given twenty sections (square miles) of land for each mile of track laid, as well as substantial loans. Both employed construction companies to do the actual building, the _Crédit Mobilier_ for the Union Pacific, the Crocker Corporation for the Central Pacific. As these were owned by the same men who owned the railroads, the profits from the excessive sums they charged for building found their way into the pockets of the promoters. Thus the Union Pacific cost $50,000,000 to build, but the Crédit Mobilier charged the company $94,000,000, with the difference going to the men who controlled both companies. Despite this graft, the railroads were pushed to completion rapidly after the close of the Civil War released men and materials for their use. The Central Pacific used Chinese labor to build eastward over the Sierra Nevada Mountains and across Utah. The Union Pacific, employing Irish workers, winged

across the plains and through South Pass. On May 10, 1869, the two met at _Promontory_, Utah.

2) The Northern Route from Lake Superior to Portland, Oregon, was followed by the _Northern Pacific Railroad_, which was chartered in 1864 and reached Bismarck, North Dakota, before the Panic of 1873 halted construction. The road was reorganized in 1881 by _Henry Villard_ and completed in 1883.

3) The Thirty-Fifth Parallel Route was used by the _Atchison, Topeka and Santa Fe Railroad_, which received a land grant from Congress in 1863. Guided by _Cyrus K. Holliday_, it reached California in 1883 over a route that crossed Kansas, passed through Santa Fe, New Mexico, and bridged the Colorado River at Needles, California.

4) The Southern Route along the thirty-second parallel was granted the Texas and Pacific Railroad, organized in 1871 to build to California, where it would meet the tracks of _Southern Pacific Railroad_, a line operated by the same promoters who controlled the Central Pacific. When the Texas and Pacific went bankrupt, the Southern Pacific built eastward to El Paso, Texas, where it joined eastern lines in 1882.

III. _Later Railroads._ After 1883, when the first four transcontinental lines were completed, numerous other roads were built into the Far West. These included the Chicago, Burlington and Quincy Railroad, the Kansas Pacific Railroad, and the _Great Northern Railroad_. The latter, built by _James J. Hill_ along the northern border of the United States, was forced to create way traffic as it went to offset the lack of a land grant. By 1893, when its tracks reached the Pacific at Tacoma, Washington, Hill had scattered farms, towns, and ranches over its entire route, bringing prosperity to the Northwest as well as to the Great Northern Railroad.

2. External Transportation. The tonnage of the American merchant marine shrank from 2,500,000 in 1860 to 800,000 in 1900, due largely to the failure of shipbuilders to shift from wooden sailing to steel steam-driven vessels. During this period the carrying trade passed into the hands of British, German, and Dutch companies, which offered cheap transportation on fast steam-driven steel ships. These superior carriers brought markets in Europe, Africa, and Asia nearer to manufacturers than domestic markets had been a generation before.

III. IMPACT OF THE ECONOMIC REVOLUTION ON AMERICAN LIFE. When the Civil War began, the Americans were an agricultural people, provincial in viewpoint, unaware of the world around them, distrustful of strong government, and culturally immature. Before the close of the century they had become an industrial people, international in viewpoint, imperialistically minded, and culturally awakened. The following chapters show the way in which these changes were brought about by industrialization. The principal results of the revolution in economics, however, may be briefly summarized:

A. Social and Intellectual Readjustments.

1. The Decline of Individualism. The most important social effect of the mechanization of American life was the increased interdependence of the people. Several factors were responsible:

a. ECONOMIC FACTORS. Industrialization welded the United States into a compact economic unit, with each person dependent on many others for his livelihood. No longer could men be self-sufficient farmers or craftsmen; instead they became closely meshed cogs in the industrial machine. This tended to lessen sectional antagonisms created by the Civil War.

b. SOCIAL FACTORS. Life became more impersonal in the machine civilization. Instead of laboring lovingly to create a finished product, workers in mass-production industries were responsible for one small operation and never had the satisfaction of seeing the final fruit of their labors. At the same time, the gap between employer and employee was widened by the spread of corporate ownership. Employers were now managers responsible to boards of directors or stockholders who were too far distant from the workers to be bothered by a social conscience. Nor could individualistic workers bargain collectively with a corporation. The rapid growth of labor unions followed this realization.

c. URBAN FACTORS. As men concentrated about machines, cities became dominant units in American life. Long a rural people, Americans were forced to adjust themselves to an urban existence. This created problems that remained unsolved at the end of the century: of low living standards, of slums, and of poverty. The concentration of people in cities, however, stimulated cultural development.

2. The Decline of Laissez Faire. The decline of individualism was accompanied by an important shift in political thought. Traditionally wedded to a laissez-faire philosophy which held that the function of government was to protect life and property without interfering in economic affairs, Americans gradually became aware that this negative policy allowed industrial monopolies to overcharge consumers and stifle smaller competitors. Reasoning that only a return to free competition would end these evils, they called upon the government to force monopolies to break down into competing units. Thus they accepted a new political philosophy; government, they believed, should act positively to assure fuller lives for its people.

B. Economic Changes. Industrialization forced various segments of the population to reassess their roles in society:

1. The Farmers, long accustomed to dominating the nation, were forced into a subsidiary role as industrialists gained control. Their rebellion launched the agrarian uprisings of the last quarter of the century.

2. Workers, powerless to bargain individually with corporations, formed labor unions to press for more pay, shorter hours of work, and better working conditions. A smaller number, losing faith in an economic system that rewarded them so poorly, joined radical parties to express their discontent.

3. Humanitarians were not only concerned with the plight of the poor, but were fearful lest the decline in economic democracy would lead to a decline in political democracy. Their attack on the "gospel of wealth" underlay the political changes of the twentieth century.

C. Political Changes. A transformation in the nature of both politics and diplomacy resulted from industrialization:

1. The Degradation of Politics. As America's ablest men were drawn into industry, political offices in cities, states, and the nation were filled with second-raters, many of them corrupt. The resulting wave of fraud shocked the world.

2. Rise of Imperialism. As the United States became the world's leading producer of manufactured goods the people demanded colonial possessions such as those owned by European powers. The wave of imperialism that swept the nation at the close of the century was traceable to this attitude.

Additional Reading

Robert H. Wiebe, *The Search for Order, 1877-1920* (1967), is a brilliant brief interpretation, essential to understanding the relations between politics and economics. Less interpretative but an excellent survey is John A. Garraty, *The New Commonwealth, 1877-1890* (1969). Extremely useful also in explaining economic growth are Samuel P. Hays, *The Response to Industrialism, 1885-1914* (1957), Thomas C. Cochran and.William Miller, *The Age of Enterprise* (1942), and Edward C. Kirkland, *The Coming of the Industrial Age* (1960). A series of stimulating essays applying new economic theory to industrial development are in Robert Higgs, *The Transformation of the American Economy* (1971). Important studies of business leaders include Allan Nevins, *Study in Power: John D. Rockefeller* (1953), and Joseph F. Wall, *Andrew Carnegie* (1970). Southern economic growth is explained in C. Vann Woodward, *Origins of the New South, 1877-1913* (1951.) P. A. M. Taylor, *The Distant Magnet* (1971), is the best brief interpretative history of immigration, while Oscar Handlin, *The Uprooted* (enlarged edn., 1973), provides color and understanding. That immigrants who went west were "upraised" rather than "uprooted" is demonstrated in Andrew Rolle, *The Immigrant Upraised: Italian Adventurers and Colonists in Expanding America* (1968). Oscar O. Winther, *The Transportation Frontier* (1964), deals generally with western railroad building, while the most important railroad is expertly described in Robert G. Athearn, *Union Pacific Country* (1971).

CHAPTER III

Closing the Frontier
1865-1890

¶ THE SETTLEMENT OF THE TRANS-MISSISSIPPI WEST

At the beginning of the Civil War the settled areas of the United States extended through the first tier of states west of the Mississippi. Beyond lay an unoccupied domain of plains, mountains, and deserts, broken only by islands of settlement in California, Oregon, Utah, Texas, and a few other spots. This whole region was peopled before 1890, when the director of the census announced that an unbroken frontier no longer existed. So rapid was the westward movement of people that between 1870 and 1900 more land was settled than in all the previous history of the United States. This affected every phase of life during these years and into the twentieth century. The frontier advanced in a series of well-defined waves.

I. THE MINING FRONTIER. The California gold rush of 1849 lured 100,000 men to that state. For the next decade they sought wealth in the streams flowing westward from the Sierra Nevada Mountains, but after 1858, when all possible mining sites were appropriated, they fanned out to seek gold elsewhere. The result was a series of "strikes" throughout the West, each followed by a "rush" to that section of the country.

A. Advance of the Frontier.

1. The Colorado Rush

a. THE RUSH OF THE '59ERS. Gold was discovered near present-day Denver in 1858 by a party of prospectors under W. Green Russell. News of the strike, carried east in exaggerated form, led to the *Pike's Peak Gold Rush* of 1859. Most of the 100,000 men who reached Colorado soon returned east after failing to "strike it rich," but those staying on discovered "pay dirt" in a number of streams. Gradually a stable population was built up.

b. EVOLUTION OF GOVERNMENT. As the number of settlers increased, the Pike's Peak country underwent a transformation typical of all mining areas:

I. *Mining Camps.* The first stage began when law-abiding elements in each mining camp held a mass meeting that adopted laws concerning the size of claims that could be staked out, the punishment of criminals, and the like. Usually a committee of judges was elected to enforce the laws in these primitive democracies.

II. *Vigilance Committees.* When these crude legal systems proved incapable of curbing the gamblers, gunmen, and desperadoes attracted by the easy money, a group of the more substantial miners usually formed a *vigilance committee* to cope with the lawbreakers. Working in secrecy, they singled out the principal offenders for a quick trial that usually ended with an execution. A few examples of this sort were enough to restore order to the community.

III. *Permanent Government.* The miners were never satisfied with these extralegal governments, and as soon as possible attempted to establish relations with the United States. In Colorado the prospectors met in November, 1858, to demand admission as the *Territory of Jefferson.* Congress was unable to act on the petition until the secession of the southern states, when the Territory of Colorado was created. Colorado was admitted to statehood in 1876 after further discoveries of gold and silver at Leadville and Cripple Creek increased the population.

2. *The Nevada Rush.* Prospectors on the eastern slopes of the Sierra Nevada Mountains discovered gold near the Carson River valley in 1858. That autumn the fabulously rich *Comstock Lode* was found; during the next twenty years this vein yielded up gold and silver worth

$300,000,000, while the principal mining camp at *Virginia City* was transformed into a thriving metropolis. Nevada was admitted to statehood in 1864.

3. The Northern Rockies. Prospectors working northward from California discovered gold in the *Fraser River* district of British Columbia, then worked their way eastward making strike after strike. The rush into *Idaho* began in 1860 with discoveries on the Clearwater River, followed by others on the Salmon and Boise rivers. Idaho could be admitted as a territory in 1863. In the meantime, gold was discovered in *Montana* during 1862. The principal rushes to that region occurred in 1863 and 1864 when towns such as Bozeman and Helena were established as mining camps. Montana became a territory in 1864.

4. The Black Hills Gold Rush. The last great rush was to the Black Hills of South Dakota, where gold was reported by a military expedition in 1874. During the following year 15,000 miners invaded the region, most of them living about Custer City and Deadwood. In those mining camps the "wild west" had its last stand; there Billy the Kid earned his fame as a gunman while Calamity Jane gained nation-wide notoriety. Order was gradually restored, particularly after the *Homestead Mining Company* took over control of the region.

B. Results of the Advancing Mining Frontier.

1. Settlement of the Far West. Although few of the prospectors participating in each rush stayed on, a stable population gradually formed about each mining camp. This was composed of miners, workers in rock-crushing mills, and farmers attracted by the prospect of high food prices. Hence many of the least attractive regions of the West, from the agricultural point of view, were settled and obtained territorial organization.

2. Improvements in Transportation. The peopling of isolated areas in the Far West aroused a demand for better transportation. This was first met by stage coaches operated over regular routes by government-subsidized private companies. Most famous of these was the *Butterfield Overland Express*, which used the southern route between the Mississippi Valley and California from 1857 to 1861, then moved northward to the South Pass route. The same pass was employed briefly in 1860-1861 by the *Pony Express,* which carried mails to California in ten days. Although the completion of the California telegraph in 1861 doomed the Pony Express, stagecoaching remained profitable for several years. Between 1862 and 1866 this phase of transportation was dominated by *Ben Holladay,* who controlled 5000 miles of express routes. Overland freighting, another profitable enterprise, was monopolized by the firm of *Russell, Majors and Waddell,* which at one time owned 3500 wagons and employed 4000 men. The coming of the railroads in 1869 doomed both the express and freight businesses.

II. THE INDIAN PROBLEM. The advance of the mining frontier alarmed the Indians of plains and mountains, who felt that they must fight to retain their hunting grounds. The result was a series of wars that ended only with the red men herded onto a number of small reservations.

A. The Early Wars, 1861-1868. Two wars followed the Colorado Gold Rush:

1. The Cheyenne-Arapaho War began in 1861 when the tribes' Colorado lands were overrun by miners. For the next three years the Indians raided stagecoaches, mining camps, and immigrant parties. The climax came in 1864 when the red men, having sued for peace, returned to their camp on Sand Creek in eastern Colorado. There they were attacked by territorial militiamen under Colonel J. M. Chivington. Almost 500 were killed in the *Chivington Massacre.* This brutal act aroused many more Indians to opposition.

2. The Sioux War, which began in 1865, was caused by: 1) resentment over the Chivington Massacre; 2) anger at the defeat of the Minnesota Sioux in a minor war just fought in that territory; and 3) an attempt by the federal government to build the *Powder River Road,* or *Bozeman Trail,* from Ft. Laramie, Wyoming, to Bozeman, Montana. This highway, which ran through the Indians' favorite hunting grounds, was designed to connect the Montana mines with the East. Rather than surrender this spot, the Sioux took to the warpath. Between 1865 and 1867 war raged along the whole western plains area.

3. The Congressional Peace Commission. The commission was appointed in 1867 to end the war and introduce a new Indian policy. This policy was based on the belief that war was inevitable as long as Indians occupied lands wanted by whites; peace could be maintained, the commissioners believed, only by settling the red men on reservations where they could learn farming and prepare for eventual assimilation. Two reservations were created:

a. OKLAHOMA RESERVATION was set aside for the southern plains tribes as well as for the _Five Civilized Tribes_ who had been moved to the area from the Southeast before the Civil War. Eventually 75,000 Indians from twenty-two tribes were settled there.

b. BLACK HILLS RESERVATION, in western Dakota, was assigned to the Sioux. At the same time, smaller reservations were created in Colorado, Utah, Montana, and elsewhere for lesser tribes. Several wars were fought between 1868 and 1874 before the Indians could be herded onto these reservations.

B. The Later Wars, 1875-1890. Indian resentment at reservation life was responsible for a series of wars fought between 1875 and 1890. These forced another shift in Indian policy.

1. The Sioux War of 1875-1876. This was touched off by the Black Hills gold rush into the Sioux reservation. A number of the Indians under Chiefs _Sitting Bull_ and Crazy Horse were finally surrounded by federal troops on the Little Big Horn River in southeastern Montana, but were defeated only after destroying a small detachment of soldiers under _Colonel George A. Custer_ at the _Battle of the Little Big Horn_. Most of the Sioux surrendered a short time later, although Sitting Bull and a few others fled to Canada.

2. The Nez Percé War (1877) was fought in the Pacific Northwest by the Nez Percé tribe under _Chief Joseph_. After heroic resistance the Indians were finally defeated and assigned a reservation in Oklahoma.

3. The Apache War (1871-1885) was fought against the Apache Indians of New Mexico and Arizona under their great chief _Geronimo_. Eventually the shattered remnants of the tribe were assigned small reservations in the Southwest.

4. The Ghost Dance War (1890) occurred on the Black Hills Reservation, when Indian resentment at unjust treatment by the government was whipped to war pitch by religious revivalism. The massacre of some 200 Sioux at the *Battle of Wounded Knee* ended the uprising.

C. Federal Indian Policy. The continuing wars convinced Congress that a new Indian policy was needed. Reformers insisted that assimilation would be hurried if the natives were treated as individuals rather than in tribal units. Through the 1880's steps were taken to break the power of tribal chiefs, while educational opportunities were provided for younger Indians. The policy was climaxed by the passage of the *Dawes Severalty Act* (1887), which provided that all tribal lands should be divided among the Indians, with each receiving an adequate farm. As the Dawes Act was applied to tribe after tribe the reservations were broken up and the Indians absorbed into American society. In 1924 Congress bestowed citizenship on all of them.

III. THE CATTLE KINGDOM. Indian removal opened the Great Plains to the cattlemen. Cattle to stock this giant pasture were available in Texas, where they had multiplied rapidly after being introduced by the Spaniards. By the close of the Civil War 5,000,000 longhorns could be purchased for $3 or $4 a head, while similar beeves brought $40 a head on the northern market. This price differential was responsible for the spread of the cattle kingdom.

A. The Long Drives. These began in 1866 when drovers started northward from Texas with 226,000 cattle, in bands of 1000 head each, bound for the railroad at *Sedalia,* Missouri. Few reached their destination, for the resistance of Missouri farmers, and the difficulty of driving wild cattle across the rough Ozark Plateau, proved to be nearly insurmountable obstacles. To overcome these an Illinois meat dealer, *Joseph M. McCoy,* in 1867 built a new terminal point for the Long Drive at *Abilene,* Kansas, on the Kansas Pacific Railroad. In the next four years 1,500,000 cattle were driven over the *Chisholm Trail* to that town. After 1871 most of the drives were to

Ellsworth or Newton, Kansas, and after 1875 to Dodge City, Kansas. In all, some 4,000,000 cattle reached those _cow towns_ between 1867 and 1879.

B. Spread of the Cattle Kingdom. The Long Drive was economically wasteful, as cattle lost weight on the trail. Hence many longhorns driven northward were used to stock the northern range. Ranches soon covered Kansas and Nebraska, then spread westward into Colorado, where a million cattle were grazed by 1869. The occupation of Wyoming and Montana followed during the next decade. The cattlemen made no attempt to buy land, pasturing their stock on the public domain. Having no recourse to law, they worked out a rough system of justice which was backed with the universally worn Colt six-shooters. A herder who appropriated a spot along a stream was understood to have a "range right" to all land running back as far as the "divide" that separated one waterway from another. The roundup was introduced to separate cattle that drifted across these imaginary "range lines," while cowboys guarded the herds to keep them on their own ranges.

C. End of the Open Range. High profits led to an overstocking of the range during the 1880's; returns of 30 and 40 per cent attracted so much eastern capital that more cattle were introduced than could be fed on the dwindling grass supply. Attempts to limit grazing were made by cattlemen's organizations such as the _Wyoming Stock Growers' Association,_ but with little success. An excessively cold winter in 1886-1887 and a series of dry years thereafter killed off thousands of beeves and ruined hundreds of ranchers. Those ranchers who survived retreated to the High Plains of the West, where they bought land, fenced their fields, and provided for winter feeding of hay or grain.

IV. THE ADVANCE OF THE FARMERS. The last western area to be occupied by farmers was the Great Plains province, which was settled between 1870 and 1900.

A. Opening the Great Plains. The advancing agricultural frontier was halted by the semiarid Great Plains until man-made inventions made their conquest possible. Before they could be farmed, cheap fencing had to be perfected, farm machinery and agricultural techniques improved, and a land system devised.

1. Fencing. This was needed as each advance of the farmers was made at the expense of cattlemen whose herds trampled crops; the wooden fences used in the East were too expensive in this treeless area. The problem was solved by an Illinois farmer, *Joseph F. Glidden,* who in 1874 began manufacturing *barbed wire fence.* By 1880 he was producing 600 miles daily.

2. Farm Machinery. As the lack of rainfall reduced the productivity of the Great Plains, each farmer had to till many acres to produce the same crop that could be grown on a few acres in the more humid East. Labor-saving machinery was necessary for him to do this in the short planting and harvesting seasons. This was provided by many inventors. In 1868 *James Oliver* patented the *chilled steel plow;* by 1873 sulky gang plows allowed the farmer to ride and plow several furrows at once. *Grain drills* for planting were in use by 1874, and the hay loader was invented in 1876. Reapers for harvesting grain were already known, but they were not satisfactory in the West until 1878 when the twine *binder* was introduced. The *header,* which cut the heads from grain while leaving the stalks standing, was added in the 1880's. Threshing machines were also improved during that decade by the addition of blowers and steam power. These inventions allowed a farmer to work only three hours to produce an acre of wheat in 1890, while in 1860 sixty-one hours were required.

3. Scientific Agriculture. Farm experts devised two ways to use the semiarid land of the Great Plains:

a. IRRIGATION was used in some areas where water was available from underground wells or mountain streams.

b. DRY FARMING was employed elsewhere. The farmer plowed deeply to bring subsurface water upward, then created a dust mulch on the surface to prevent evaporation. Progress in scientific agriculture was made possible by government aid. The *Morrill Act* (1862) offered land grants to states that founded agricultural schools, while the *Hatch Act* (1877) subsidized state experiment stations to carry on agriculture research.

4. The Land System. A satisfactory land system was essential to the advance of the frontier. This was apparently provided by the *Homestead Act* (1862), which offered every actual settler 160 acres of government land free of charge. Actually the Homestead Act did not solve the West's problem.

    a. DEFECTS OF THE HOMESTEAD ACT. The law was poorly suited to the Great Plains, where a farmer needed either from 360 to 640 acres if he intended to practice extensive agriculture, or from 40 to 60 acres if he planned to use irrigation.

    b. SPECULATIVE ACTIVITY. Despite the Homestead Act, speculators continued to control the best land in the West. They obtained this in several ways:

    I. *Loopholes in the Land Laws.* The Homestead Act applied only to surveyed land; speculators moving ahead of surveying parties could pre-empt the best sites. Others hired dummy entrymen to take out homesteads on choice locations. About 100,000,000 acres were obtained by speculators in this way.

    II. *Railroad Land Grants.* The railroads received 181,000,000 acres of land, most of which was desirable, as it was near transportation facilities. This was sold at an average price of $5 an acre.

    III. *Grants to States.* Under the Morrill Act (1862) the states were given 140,000,000 acres of western land as endowments for agricultural schools. This land was then sold to speculators.

    IV. *Reservation Lands.* As reservations were taken over by the government, the former Indian lands were sold, usually in large blocks to speculators. Not until 1887 did the Dawes Severalty Act rule that Indian lands must be sold in 160-acre plots to actual settlers. In the meantime 100,000,-000 acres were disposed of to speculators.

    c. RESULTS OF DEFECTS IN LAND SYSTEM. While speculators secured 521,000,000 acres of land, homesteaders obtained only 80,000,000 acres. Thus most farmers were still required to pay high prices for their western farms.

B. Occupation of the Northern Plains.

1. Reasons for Settlement. Despite the defects of the land system, the Great Plains were peopled rapidly after

1870. This was because:

a. SURPLUS POPULATION had piled up in the Mississippi Valley, held back for a generation before 1870 by the hostile environment of the Plains.

b. RAILROAD ADVERTISING. Nearly all land-grant railroads set up bureaus of immigration to dispose of their lands. These advertised for immigrants throughout the East and Europe, provided free transportation and loans to prospective farmers, and did much to publicize the West everywhere.

c. ASSURED MARKETS for western produce attracted farmers. The northern plains were ideally suited to growing hard spring wheat, while hard winter wheat could be grown from Kansas southward. Mills to turn this wheat into flour by the efficient *New Process* method of milling were built at Minneapolis, Kansas City, and St. Louis during the 1870's. This process employed a succession of rollers, each set closer together than the last, to reduce the grain to flour gradually.

2. *The Advance of Settlement.* Population moved out first over Kansas and Nebraska, following rivers and railroads westward; both states were filled by 1880. Another stream of settlers turned northward to settle Dakota territory, where giant *Bonanza Farms* established by railroads in the Red River Valley after the Panic of 1873 demonstrated the richness of the soil. Wyoming and Montana, although less well suited to agriculture, also attracted pioneers during the 1880's. A demand for statehood from all of these newly settled regions was met in 1889 when Congress admitted North Dakota, South Dakota, Montana, and Washington to the Union. Idaho and Wyoming objected so strenuously to their admission that they were added a year later. These six states were known as the *omnibus states* because they were admitted by an "omnibus bill" rather than individually.

C. Occupation of the Southern Plains. The peopling of the northern plains left only the Indian Territory (Oklahoma) without white settlers.

1. *Opening the Indian Territory.* As the country about Oklahoma was occupied, pressure was exerted on the government to open this region to homesteaders. This pressure came from two sources: 1) the railroads that penetrated the

area and were eager to develop agriculture there, and 2) frontiersmen who wanted to obtain land before all the West was settled. The latter were known as _Boomers_. Led by _David L. Payne_, the Boomers invaded the Indian Territory by force during the early 1880's, only to be driven out by federal troops. Congress, sensitive to this pressure, in 1885 authorized the Indian Office to secure title to two parts of the Indian Territory not actually occupied by any tribe, the _Cherokee Outlet_ and the _Oklahoma District_, a triangle of land in the center of the territory. When this was done, the President announced that the Oklahoma District would be opened to settlers at noon on April 22, 1889.

2. Settlement of Oklahoma. When the deadline arrived, 100,000 Boomers lined the edge of the Oklahoma District, held back by troops who guarded the border. At noon officers sounded bugle blasts and the greatest land rush in history was on. By nightfall the whole district was settled, including the cities of Guthrie and Oklahoma City. During the next few years other reservations were opened as the Dawes Severalty Act was applied to tribe after tribe. Oklahoma became a state in 1907.

3. Settlement of the Southwest. The last two states in the Southwest, New Mexico and Arizona, entered the Union in 1912. Both were notable for their progressive constitutions, which provided for the initiative and referendum, direct primaries, short terms for elected officials, women's suffrage, limited executive power, and even—in the case of Arizona—the popular recall of judges. With their admission as states the political organization of the nation was completed.

V. THE CLOSING OF THE FRONTIER. The director of the census announced in 1890 that a frontier no longer existed. While much unoccupied land remained in the West, the areas of settlement were so broken that for the first time in history no line could be drawn separating occupied and unoccupied regions. This important date marked the close of one era in the nation's development.

A. Effect of the Closing of the Frontier. After three hundred years of expansion, the American people were forced to adjust themselves to a closed-border existence. This had important effects on their economy and psychology.

1. Economic Effects. These were lessened by the fact that the westward movement went on despite the "end" of the frontier. The West was only thinly settled before 1890, while improved agricultural methods continuously opened areas considered unfertile. Hence four times as many acres were homesteaded after 1890 as before, and between 1900 and 1920 a million Americans moved on to the Prairie Provinces of Canada. Despite this, the approaching end of the era of cheap lands stimulated a rush of farm buying which sent the price of agricultural lands up 118 per cent between 1900 and 1910. At the same time the price of farm produce rose sharply, reaching a peak during World War I. This advance was not due to the closing of the frontier, but to: 1) gold discoveries that inflated currency, 2) lagging farm production because of drought during the 1890's, and 3) new industrial uses for corn and cotton. Yet the rising commodity and land prices stimulated two developments:

a. AGRICULTURAL SPECIALIZATION. As land prices mounted, farmers tended to plant only the one crop best suited to their soil, thus obtaining the higher returns needed to carry their heavy investment. By 1920 the one-crop system was firmly planted in South and West. The South specialized in cotton, the upper Great Plains region in spring wheat, the lower Great Plains in winter wheat, the Iowa area in corn, and the urbanized portions of Wisconsin, Illinois, and southern Minnesota in dairy products. This system reduced the self-sufficiency of farmers, and endangered their security in periods of drought or depression.

b. FARM TENANCY increased as eastern capitalists, seeking a sure investment, poured money into land. By 1920, 40 per cent of the farms of Iowa and 50 per cent of those of Illinois were owned by absentee landlords.

2. Psychological Effects. For two centuries Americans had believed that the United States was prosperous because cheap land drained surplus labor westward, thus keeping wages and living standards high. Now they had to learn to live within closed borders. The results were two-fold:

a. THE CONSERVATION MOVEMENT of the early twentieth century was based on the belief that natural resources could no longer be squandered as in the past.

b. THE QUEST FOR SECURITY became of paramount concern to the people and their government. Woodrow

Wilson, Theodore Roosevelt, and Franklin D. Roosevelt built their political programs on the belief that government must provide its citizens with the social welfare and economic opportunity formerly provided by cheap land.

ADDITIONAL READING

A survey of the period is in Ray A. Billington, *Westward Expansion* (4th edn., 1974), while excellent interpretative essays are in Robert V. Hine, *The American West* (1973). The best survey of mining activity is Rodman W. Paul, *Mining Frontiers of the Far West* (1963); the same author's *California Gold* (1947) stresses the economic impact of the rush of the '49ers. On transportation from stagecoach to railroad the most useful survey is Oscar O. Winther, *The Transportation Frontier* (1964); although Raymond W. and Mary L. Settle, *Empire on Wheels* (1949), should be consulted on overland freighting. Dee Brown, *Bury My Heart at Wounded Knee* (1971), is a popular history of the Indian wars as viewed by the Indians; for the northern wars it should be supplemented with the excellent Robert M. Utley, *The Last Days of the Sioux Nation* (1963). William H. Leckie, *The Buffalo Soldiers* (1967), and Arlen L. Fowler, *The Black Infantry in the West, 1869-1891* (1971), describe the important role of Negro soldiers in the Indian wars. Aspects of the evolving Indian policy are the theme of Robert W. Mardock, *The Reformers and the American Indian* (1971). The highly readable history of the cattle industry in Ernest S. Osgood, *The Day of the Cattlemen* (1929), should be supplemented with Lewis Atherton, *The Cattle Kings* (1961), which shows that ranchers rather than cowboys were the true heroes of the West; W. Turrentine Jackson, *The Enterprising Scot* (1968), which traces the flow of British capital into ranches and mines; and Robert R. Dykstra, *The Cattle Towns* (1968), which strips the ranching frontier of much of its false romance. Philip Durham and Everett L. Jones, *The Negro Cowboys* (1965), shows that more than one-fifth of the cowboys were black. Walter P. Webb, *The Great Plains* (1931), is a classic interpretation of the settlement of the region, which is described in Gilbert C. Fite, *The Farmers' Last Frontier, 1865-1900* (1966).

~~~~~~~~~~~~~~~~~~~~~~~~~~~~~~~~~~~

CHAPTER IV

Business and Politics
1868-1890

~~~~~~~~~~~~~~~~~~~~~~~~~~~~~~~~~~~

ℂ BUSINESS CONTROL OF POLITICS

The years from 1868 to 1890 were the most drab in the nation's political history. At no time during this period did the parties take clearcut stands on the vital questions facing the people; instead they obscured major issues while giving voters a choice between nonentities for elected offices. This was because the true political rulers were captains of business who had no wish to solve the pressing problems facing the United States: the relations of capital and labor, the threat of industrial monopoly, the tariff issue, the farm problem, and the role of the nation in world relationships. Instead, their sole concern was to perpetuate a laissez-faire system that left them free to amass profits, at the same time winning special favors from the government for business.

I. THE GRANT ADMINISTRATION, 1869-1877. The degradation in politics was shown in the administration of _Ulysses S. Grant._ Inexperienced politically and blindly worshipful of anyone who had made money, Grant became the tool of unscrupulous industrialists and scheming grafters, although he was personally honest. Of the second-raters in his cabinet only his Secretary of State, _Hamilton Fish_ of New York, had any ability.

A. Domestic Problems. In addition to the problem of Reconstruction (see Chap. I) Grant was forced to deal with the currency situation, tariff revision, and civil service reform.

1. The Currency Problem. In 1868, $400,000,000 of the legal-tender *greenbacks* issued during the Civil War were still in circulation. Their inflationary effect was favored by farmers and debtor groups, but opposed by business leaders, who demanded that Congress take steps to redeem the greenbacks in gold, thus placing the country on a firm gold basis. For a time Grant seemed to side with the inflationists in this controversy, particularly in his handling of the Supreme Court in the *Legal Tender Cases.* In the first of these, *Hepburn v. Griswold* (1870), the Court held that greenbacks were not legal tender for obligations entered into before they were issued, and even questioned their constitutionality. When Congress increased the number of judges from seven to nine, Grant named two additional justices favorable to greenbacks. Hence in the second case, *Knox v. Lee* (1871), the Court reversed itself to hold Greenbacks constitutional. Business pressure finally prevailed when Congress passed the *Resumption Act* (1875), which provided that after 1879 all greenbacks would be redeemable in gold.

2. The Tariff Problem. High protective tariffs had been enacted during the war as part of the general taxation program. Instead of lowering duties after fighting ended, Congress responded to pressure from lobbyists and between 1867 and 1870 raised levels on numerous items. Western dissatisfaction was so great that Republican leaders, fearing defeat in the election of 1872, pushed through a general 10 per cent reduction in the *Tariff of 1872.* No sooner was the law passed, however, than the Panic of 1873 created a need for additional governmental revenue. To obtain this the *Tariff of 1875* restored high duties once more.

3. Civil Service Reform. Grant's mediocre appointees aroused such resentment that the President in 1871 asked Congress to provide that certain offices must be filled by qualified candidates selected through competitive examinations. This system, which was already in use in Europe, had been advocated for some years by a group of reformers under *Carl Schurz.* Congress adopted such a law in 1871, but it was never enforced.

B. The Election of 1872. Grant's sorry record

aroused such dissatisfaction that the Republican Party split over his renomination. Reformers under _Carl Schurz_ broke away to form the _Liberal Republican Party_ with _Horace Greeley_ of New York as their standard bearer. Greeley's long association with such eccentric causes as vegetarianism and temperance alienated many people, while his advocacy of protective tariffs made him unacceptable to Democrats. The Democratic Party, however, reluctantly accepted Greeley as its candidate. The _Republicans_ nominated _Grant_ on a platform that praised high tariffs and paid lip service to civil service reform. He was re-elected by an electoral vote of 286 to 62, receiving 56 per cent of the popular vote.

C. Panic and Corruption. The little popularity that Grant had enjoyed declined rapidly during his second administration. This was due largely to the Panic of 1873 and the evidences of corruption that came to light.

1. Panic of 1873. The wartime boom came to a sudden end in September, 1873, when the failure of a leading investment house, _Jay Cooke and Company,_ touched off a major panic. Stocks were dumped on the market, banks and factories closed, and business failures multiplied. Within a few months the nation was almost paralyzed economically, with 3,000,000 persons unemployed. Hard times continued for five years.

2. Corruption. A series of revelations during Grant's second administration laid bare a record of fraud and corruption that involved many of the President's close friends and even came close to the President himself.

a. THE GOLD CONSPIRACY. Two unscrupulous financiers, _Jay Gould_ and _James Fisk,_ decided to "corner" the nation's gold supply, drive the price up, and then sell out at a profit. To make this possible, Gould convinced Grant that the farmers would benefit if the government withheld its gold from the money markets for a time. Then, with the support of certain treasury-department officials, Gould and Fisk began buying metal in September, 1869. In four days they ran the price up from 140 to 163. Then, on Friday, September 24, the Secretary of the Treasury began selling gold once more. The effect of that _Black Friday_ on business almost resulted in a premature depression.

b. THE CREDIT MOBILIER SCANDAL. The builders of the Union Pacific Railroad created the Crédit Mobilier as a construction company to build the road, then awarded it such profitable contracts that the railroad nearly went bankrupt while the Mobilier paid dividends of several hundred per cent. Fearing the exposure of their scheme, the backers of the Mobilier placed blocks of their company's stock in the hands of several Republican congressmen, using _Oakes Ames,_ a congressman from Massachusetts, as their agent. A congressional investigation eventually exposed the whole unsavory affair.

c. THE SALARY GRAB. In March, 1873, Congress doubled the salary of the President, and increased the salaries of congressmen by 50 per cent. Grant signed the bill but public indignation forced the next Congress to repeal the law.

d. THE SANBORN CONTRACT. A deal between the Secretary of the Treasury and J. D. Sanborn, a minor politician, allowed the latter to collect $427,000 in unpaid taxes, keeping half the sum as his commission. An investigation showed that most of this sum was used to pay Republican party workers.

e. THE WHISKEY RING FRAUD. This involved a ring of liquor dealers in St. Louis who defrauded the government of millions in excise taxes through connivance with treasury officials and even with the President's personal secretary. Grant was hurt rather than shocked by this revelation, and went so far as to defend his secretary against investigators.

D. Foreign Problems. The constructive foreign policy of Grant's administrations was not shaped by the President but by his able Secretary of State, _Hamilton Fish_ of New York.

1. Territorial Expansion. This was begun under William E. Seward, Secretary of State under Lincoln and Johnson, who in 1867 purchased _Alaska_ from Russia for $7,200,000 and annexed the Midway Islands west of Hawaii. Seward also tried to buy the Danish West Indies (Virgin Islands) from Denmark, but the Senate refused to ratify the agreement. Grant was eager to add _Santo Do-_

mingo to the United States, largely because American specu-lators with interests there convinced the President's secretary that this was advisable. Ignoring the State Department, Grant sent his secretary to negotiate a treaty of annexation. This was defeated in the Senate, largely through the efforts. of *Charles Sumner.*

2. Relations with England. Hamilton Fish's expert diplomacy allowed the peaceful settlement of two conflicts with England.

a. THE FENIAN UPRISING. Irish patriots in the United States planned to use ex-Union troops for the conquest of Canada, which would then be returned to England in ex-change for Ireland's independence. With an army of 1500 Irish soldiers, they crossed the Niagara River in 1866 and fought an engagement with Canadian militiamen before flee-ing back to New York. The United States curbed further attempts at invasion but never reimbursed Canada for losses suffered in this attack.

b. THE ALABAMA CLAIMS. The United States charged that British negligence allowed the Confederate cruisers *Alabama, Florida,* and *Shenandoah* to put to sea during the Civil War, thus making England liable for all damage the three ships did to American shipping. Extremists on both sides frustrated early attempts to settle the issue; an arbitra-tion treaty drafted in 1869 was defeated in the Senate when Senator Charles Sumner charged that England's action had prolonged the war two years and cost the United States $2,000,000,000. Canada, he suggested, should be offered in payment. In contrast, Hamilton Fish worked quietly with British diplomats to arrange the *Treaty of Washington* (1871). England expressed regret for her action and agreed to submit the question of damages to an international tri-bunal. This tribunal eventually awarded the United States $15,500,000. The settlement was a triumph for the cause of arbitration and a landmark in international law.

II. THE HAYES-ARTHUR ADMINISTRATIONS, 1877-1885. Hard times after 1873, combined with the dis-closures of corruption in Grant's second administration, threatened to defeat the Republicans as the election of 1876 approached.

A. The Disputed Election of 1876.

1. The Party Conventions. The *Republican* convention was split between "regular" Republicans who supported either Grant or *James G. Blaine* of Maine, and "liberal" Republicans who favored *Rutherford B. Hayes* of Ohio, a colorless three-time governor of the state who stood for honest government and civil service reform. Middle-roaders in the party, realizing that Grant's unsavory reputation must be offset, finally cast their votes for Hayes, giving him the nomination. The *Democrats,* determined to make reform the campaign issue, chose New York's progressive governor, *Samuel J. Tilden,* as their candidate. Tilden enjoyed a national reputation as a reformer for his part in overthrowing the notorious *Tweed Ring* which had fleeced the taxpayers of New York City. He was essentially a conservative, however, favoring "hard money" as did Hayes.

2. Results of the Election. Tilden won 184 electoral votes to 165 for Hayes. Twenty electoral votes were in dispute, however. These were from South Carolina, Louisiana, and Florida—where Republican-dominated election boards, refusing to accept the apparent Democratic majorities, certified that the states had gone Republican—and from Oregon, where, on a technicality, the Democratic governor had replaced one Republican elector with a Democratic one. Each of these four states submitted two sets of returns, one giving Hayes the vote, the other Tilden. If all twenty disputed votes were awarded Hayes he would have the 185 electoral votes necessary for election; if only one went to Tilden then Tilden would become President.

3. The Election Commission. The problem of deciding which candidate should have the disputed votes was complicated by the fact that the Senate was Republican and the House Democratic. They finally agreed on an *Election Commission* of fifteen, with five members from the House, five from the Senate, and five from the Supreme Court. Seven were to be Democrats and seven Republicans, while the fifteenth was Judge Davis of Illinois, who was nonpartisan. At the last minute Judge Davis resigned from the Supreme Court to enter the Senate, and a Republican judge was named in his place. By an eight to seven vote the Commission gave all twenty disputed votes—and the election—to Hayes. The justice of the dispute is hard to determine. Tilden had a popular majority of 250,000, but many southern Negroes who would have voted for Hayes were kept from the polls by force.

B. Problems of the Hayes Administration.

1. Civil Service Reform. Hayes' principal ambition as President was to end the *spoils system* through which men were named to government offices because of their political loyalty rather than their merit. His efforts were frustrated by both his own cabinet and Congress. Despite instructions from Hayes, only *Carl Schurz,* the Secretary of the Interior, and *John Sherman,* the Secretary of the Treasury, filled their departments without regard to the political allegiance of the appointees. Congressional opposition to reform came into the open when Hayes removed from office *Chester A. Arthur,* collector of the port of New York, who was a political friend of Senator *Roscoe Conkling.* The Senate refused to confirm the President's nominee for the position, even though his qualifications were unquestioned, because its members resented interference with their control of political spoils. Their attitude doomed effective civil service reform for the time.

2. Resumption of Specie Payments. The Resumption Act of 1875 provided that after January 1, 1879, all greenbacks were to be redeemable in gold; that is, that anyone could take a greenback to the Treasury Department and exchange it for a gold dollar. In anticipation of this day the government had accumulated a gold reserve of $100,-000,000 by selling bonds for gold. As $400,000,000 in greenbacks were in circulation this was deemed sufficient to satisfy all who cared to make the exchange. Actually few did so, and the greenbacks continued to circulate on a gold basis.

C. The Election of 1880.

Hayes' refusal to run for a second term gave the "regular" Republicans, or *Stalwarts,* a chance to reverse the trend toward reform. When supporters of U. S. Grant and James G. Blaine could not agree, however, the convention nominated a dark horse, General *James A. Garfield* of Ohio, who was affiliated with the "liberal" or _Halfbreed_ faction of the party. His humble birth in a log cabin and his military record were counted on to attract voters. To appease the Stalwarts, _Chester A. Arthur,_ the New York spoilsman, was nominated for the vice-presidency. The _Democrats,_ seeking to regain popularity in the North, selected as their candidate a Union general, _Winfield S. Hancock_ of Pennsylvania. Their campaign stressed the need for civil service reform. Returning prosperity after the Panic of 1873 doomed their chances, and Garfield was elected by an electoral vote of 214 to 155. His popular vote, however, was only 7000 more than that for Hancock.

D. The Triumph of Civil Service Reform.

1. Garfield's Appointments. True to his Halfbreed principles, Garfield followed Hayes' example in attacking the spoils system. When he named an efficient administrator as collector of the port of New York, the senior Senator from that state, _Roscoe Conkling,_ resigned in protest, as did the junior Senator, Thomas C. Platt (who was thereafter known as "Me-too" Platt). Both hoped to be vindicated by re-election, but, to the amusement of the nation, the New York legislature refused to return them to Washington. Garfield also showed his honesty in handling the _Star Route Frauds._ These involved contracts to carry the mails over western routes where stagecoaches or riders were used instead of railroads. Investigation showed that the contracts were awarded only after substantial bribes to many influential men, including the secretary of the Republican National Committee. Yet the President disclosed the fraud fearlessly, forcing the guilty parties out of office.

2. Assassination of Garfield. After only four months in office Garfield was shot by a crazed office-seeker. This focused attention on the need for civil service reform, but few expected progress under the new President, _Chester A. Arthur,_ a leading Stalwart and proponent of the patronage system. To the delight of the people the responsibilities of office sobered and changed the former spoilsman. One result was an effective civil service law.

3. The Civil Service Law of 1883. In his messages to Congress in 1881 and 1882 Arthur pleaded for civil service reform. His pleas fell on deaf ears until the *election of 1882* returned a Democratic majority to the House. Then both parties joined in adopting the *Pendleton Act* (1883). This authorized the President to appoint three civil service commissioners with power to conduct competitive examinations for officeholders in branches of the public service that were "classified" by the President or Congress. Only a few offices were classified at first but each succeeding President extended the list, partly to protect his own appointees against removal by the next executive.

III. THE ADMINISTRATION OF GROVER CLEVELAND, 1885-1889. By 1884 the time was ripe for a Democratic victory because: 1) the Civil War generation was passing from the scene, making less effective the Republican device of winning votes by *waving the bloody shirt,* or boasting that they had saved the Union; 2) the Republicans were still believed to be the party of fraud and corruption; and 3) the emergence of the *Solid South* guaranteed the Democrats a sure block of votes.

A. The Election of 1884.

1. The Republican Candidate. Stalwarts, revolting against Arthur's reforming record, nominated *James G. Blaine.* Although Blaine's long service in Congress and as Secretary of State made him the leader of the party, he was handicapped by two things: 1) his affiliation with the Stalwart wing of the party damned him in the eyes of all reformers; and 2) he had in 1876 used his political influence to obtain a land grant for an Arkansas railroad, receiving in return the privilege of selling the road's bonds at a high profit. Proof of this transaction was contained in letters that he had written to one James Mulligan. When Blaine obtained these letters by a ruse, the *Mulligan Letters* became an important issue in the campaign.

2. The Democratic Candidate. The Democrats were encouraged to nominate a reforming candidate when liberal Republicans, led by *Carl Schurz* and George William Curtis, announced that they would bolt their party if a suitable choice was made by the opposition. Although derisively labeled *Mugwumps* by the Stalwarts, these progressives promised to control the election. Hence the Democrats selected *Grover Cleveland,* whose reforming activity as mayor of Buffalo and governor of New York had won him national fame.

3. The 1884 Campaign and Election. Despite the clear-cut division between the two candidates, two minor issues helped decide the election. 1) Cleveland was charged with having fathered a seven-year-old illegitimate child in Buffalo. He admitted the truth of the charge, but announced that he had done everything possible financially to rectify a moral error. Republican emphasis on his immorality, however, doubtless influenced many middle-class voters. 2) Just before the election Blaine was visited by a delegation of Protestant ministers whose spokesman, Dr. Samuel Burchard, referred to the Democrats as the party of *"rum, Romanism, and rebellion."* Blaine's failure to refute this insulting phrase cost him the votes of many Roman Catholics, particularly in New York, where Cleveland's popular vote was only 1149 more than Blaine's. The importance of these minor issues was revealed by the closeness of the final vote. Cleveland's plurality was only 23,000 and the electoral vote 219 to 182. The Democrats won control of the House but Republicans still dominated the Senate.

B. Reform Under Cleveland. Fundamentally conservative, Cleveland was interested in increasing the administrative efficiency of the government. This, rather than a desire to improve the welfare of the people by positive action, accounted for most of the laws that he sponsored.

1. Civil Service Reform. Cleveland's belief in civil service was demonstrated when he added 12,000 offices to the classified list, yet members of his party exerted great pressure on him to place Democrats in office, pointing out that loyal politicians deserved some reward after being out of power for twenty-four years. Cleveland responded reluctantly but completely; by the close of his term two-thirds of the nonclassified offices were held by Democrats. This cost him the support of many reformers.

2. Pensions. During the Civil War Congress had authorized pensions for Union soldiers suffering disabilities while in service, and for widows and children of veterans. Those unable to obtain benefits under this law usually asked their congressmen to introduce private pension bills, which were always passed without question, even though the applicant had no legal claim to a pension. The 500,000 members of the Union veterans' organization, the _Grand Army of the Republic_ (G.A.R.), served as a pressure group in behalf of such laws. Cleveland offended this organization and all veterans by: 1) rigorously scrutinizing all private pension bills and vetoing hundreds where no disability claim was warranted; 2) vetoing a _Dependent Pension Bill_ (1887) which would have granted pensions to all disabled veterans, whether or not their disabilities were suffered while they were in the armed services; and 3) ordering the return of captured Confederate flags to their original states. The uproar resulting from this last step was so great that Cleveland withdrew his order and the flags remained in the North until 1905, when they were returned by a Republican Congress—without uproar.

3. Conservation. Cleveland's Secretary of the Interior uncovered a record of fraud in the disposal of the public domain. Acting vigorously, the President forced the return of lands illegally granted to railroads, lumber and mining interests, and cattlemen. In all he restored 81,000,000 acres to the public domain.

C. The Tariff Issue. This was the most important problem faced by Cleveland.

1. Background of the Problem. The Tariff of 1875, which continued the protective principle accepted during the Civil War by leveling 40 per cent duties on imports, was not questioned until the 1880's, when a new problem emerged.

a. PROBLEM OF THE SURPLUS REVENUE. Beginning in 1880 the federal government each year took in $100,000,000 more than it needed for operating expenses. This was highly undesirable, for in those days government funds were stored in vaults rather than banks. As money was removed from circulation, business suffered the effects of deflation. All agreed that the surplus was bad, but the government faced difficulties in either spending the excess sums or stopping their flow into the treasury.

ɪ. _Spending the Surplus Revenue._ The surplus could be spent in only two ways, neither desirable: 1) By paying off the national debt. This debt was largely in the form of government bonds which were held by national banks. As these banks issued paper money (national bank notes) on the basis of the bonds they held, any sudden repurchase of the bonds by the government would dangerously contract the currency. 2) By spending money recklessly through *pork barrel* bills to improve rivers and harbors. Cleveland was too honest to sanction such waste.

    ii. *Preventing the Growth of Surpluses.* Equally impossible was the task of stopping money from flowing into the national treasury. This money came from two sources: 1) excise taxes on liquor and tobacco, which moral reformers insisted on retaining; and 2) the tariff, which businesses demanding protection wanted to keep high.

    b. REPUBLICANS AND THE TARIFF. President Arthur recognized the seriousness of the problem and named the *Tariff Commission of 1882* to recommend some means of dealing with the surplus revenue. Although the Commission was packed with protectionists—its chairman was secretary of the National Association of Wool Manufacturers—it recommended a general reduction in duties to the 20 per cent level. When Congress undertook to carry out its suggestions lobbyists swarmed in to plead for their special interests. The resulting *Mongrel Tariff of 1883* differed little from the Tariff of 1875, but did stamp the Republican Party as favoring high levels.

2. Cleveland and the Tariff.

    a. ATTITUDE OF DEMOCRATIC PARTY. While southern and western Democrats generally favored lower tariffs, a strong group of eastern Democrats under *Samuel J. Randall* of Pennsylvania were archprotectionists. Their influence was shown in 1884 when Representative W. R. Morrison of Illinois tried to push through a 20 per cent reduction. Forty-one Randall Democrats joined with Republicans to defeat the measure.

    b. TARIFF MESSAGE OF 1887. Cleveland made up his mind slowly on the issue, but by 1887 he was convinced that the surplus revenue could be wiped out only by lowering duties. In 1887 he devoted his entire presidential message to the subject, asking Congress to enact a lower tariff as the only way to deal with the surplus. Cleveland knew that any measure would be defeated in the Republican Senate, but he hoped the Democratic House would favor reduction, thus providing an issue for the election of 1888.

c. RESULTS OF TARIFF MESSAGE. Cleveland's plan succeeded. The _Mills Bill_, providing for wholesale reductions, was adopted by the House with only four Democrats in opposition. In the meantime, Senate Republicans under _Nelson W. Aldrich_ met the challenge by proposing even higher tariffs. As neither bill could pass, there the matter rested until the election of 1888.

IV. THE ADMINISTRATION OF BENJAMIN HARRISON, 1889-1893.

A. The Campaign of 1888. The _Democrats_ renominated _Cleveland_ and pledged themselves to carry out his program. The Republican nominee was _Benjamin Harrison,_ an Indiana lawyer with few attributes for the office. Capitalizing on manufacturers' fears of tariff reduction, Harrison's supporters raised a vast campaign fund from industrialists. This, plus a solid G.A.R. vote against Cleveland, gave Harrison the election. His popular vote, however, was 100,000 less than Cleveland's. Both houses of Congress were Republican by narrow majorities, with "Czar" _Thomas B. Reed,_ Speaker of the House, in a position to push through a legislative program.

B. Minor Political Issues.

1. Civil Service. Harrison, ignoring the civil service laws, filled government offices with party hacks. His commissioner of pensions, for example, remarked on taking office, "God help the surplus revenue." Harrison did name the youthful _Theodore Roosevelt_ to the Civil Service Commission.

2. Pension Legislation. A _Dependents' Pension Act_ similar to the one vetoed by Cleveland was adopted by the Republicans in 1889. This provided pensions for all Union veterans suffering any physical or mental disability, no matter how or where contracted, as well as increased allowances to widows and children of veterans.

3. The Federal Elections Bill. This measure, which was designed to restore the vote to southern Negroes, gave the federal government a measure of control over national elections. It passed the House but was defeated in the Senate. The results were the opposite of those sought by Republicans, for the southern states responded with still more discriminatory laws. All provided for literacy tests for voters, limiting the franchise to those who could read and interpret a section of the state constitution. As these tests eliminated many poor-white voters, they were soon displaced by laws restricting voting to descendants of those able to vote before 1867. Until 1915, when these _grandfather clauses_ were declared unconstitutional by the Supreme Court, they remained on the statute books of most southern states.

C. The Tariff Problem. Republicans set out to devise a tariff that would continue protection but cut down the surplus revenue. Their answer was the _McKinley Tariff_ (1890), which raised duties to such high levels that imports virtually ceased, thus lowering the amounts received from customs duties. The bill also placed raw sugar on the free list. As sugar imports had paid duties of $50,000,000 yearly, about half the surplus revenue was eliminated by this one item. Louisiana sugar growers were placated by a bounty of two cents a pound, which cared for still more of the surplus. At the insistence of Secretary of State _James G. Blaine,_ the McKinley Tariff contained provisions designed to stimulate trade with Latin America. These included: 1) placing molasses, tea, coffee, and other items on the free list; and 2) authorizing the President to impose duties on these items whenever another nation levied unjust duties on American goods. This backhanded reciprocity aroused only resentment in Latin America. Popular reaction to the higher prices resulting from the McKinley Tariff was expressed in the _Congressional elections of 1890._ Three-fourths of the Representatives elected were Democrats, while even William McKinley of Ohio, the author of the bill, was defeated.

V. THE BANKRUPTCY OF POLITICS. Why was the political record of the postwar years so drab? And how did this record influence the future?

A. Reasons for Political Degradation. The principal reason for the lack of progress was the failure of the political parties, both Republican and Democratic, to provide the people with a means of expressing the majority will. Neither developed any clear-cut program on major social or economic issues; instead, both became loose confederations or local machines bent only on seizing power. For this two things were responsible: 1) Local politicians, who were in real control of the parties, were too afraid of offending their constituents to take an open stand on any important question; 2) Party lines did not accurately reflect the basic issues. This was shown in the tariff controversy where eastern Democrats voted with eastern Republicans for protection, while even western and southern Democrats fought for high duties on goods produced in their districts. This allowed organized minorities to win political victories that did not reflect the will of the people.

B. Lessons for the Future. Astute political observers who were in their youth during those years—men such as Theodore Roosevelt and Woodrow Wilson—saw the solution to the problem. Among parties constituted as were those of the United States, strong executive leadership was necessary for positive results. Cleveland, although by no means an outstanding leader, demonstrated this when his dramatic tariff message of 1887 temporarily welded his party together on this issue. The statesmen whose forceful leadership made the Progressive Period possible learned their lesson during this period.

ADDITIONAL READING

Politics between 1876 and 1896 are briefly but competently surveyed in John M. Dobson, *Politics in the Gilded Age* (1972). Robert D. Marcus, *Grand Old Party: Political Structure in the Gilded Age, 1800-1896* (1971), and H. Wayne Morgan, *From Hayes to McKinley: National Party Politics, 1877-1896* (1969), explore the subject in greater depth. The most recent biography of Grant is John A. Carpenter, *Ulysses S. Grant* (1970), which is just but not overly sympathetic. Allan Nevins, *Hamilton Fish* (1936), is still essential for an understanding of Grant's foreign policies. C. Vann Woodward, *Reunion and Reaction* (1951), is the standard study of the manner in which economic forces influenced the election of 1876. Standard biographies of some of the political leaders include: Harry Barnard, *Rutherford B. Hayes and His America* (1954); R. G. Caldwell, *James A. Garfield* (1931); George F. Howe, *Chester A. Arthur* (1934); and Allan Nevins, *Grover Cleveland* (1934). A briefer study of Cleveland is H. S. Merrill, *Bourbon Leader: Grover Cleveland and the Democratic Party* (1957), while Rexford G. Tugwell, *Grover Cleveland* (1968), is generally unsympathetic. Party manipulation is explained in L. D. White, *The Republican Era, 1869-1901* (1958) and George H. Mayer, *The Republican Party, 1854-1964* (1964).

CHAPTER V

The Assault on Laissez Faire
1868-1890

❨ THE REVOLT AGAINST RUGGED INDIVIDUAL-
ISM

Despite the barren political record of the postwar era, the basis for reform was laid during those years. Those responsible were farmers and workers who, driven to rebellion by the growing power of Big Business, organized to support a new theory of government. They held that the state should assume a positive role in men's lives. If railroad rates were too high, they argued, the government should protect shippers by forcing roads to lower their charges; if a business became so monopolistic that it could charge unreasonable prices, it should be broken down into competing units. The gradual acceptance of this theory revolutionized political thought, for Americans had long maintained that private property was immune to governmental interference.

I. THE ATTACK ON THE RAILROADS.

A. The Granger Movement. The theory of government regulation was first advanced by the most individualistic of all Americans—the farmers. They were goaded into action by deep-seated discontent with the status quo.

1. Causes for Agrarian Unrest. Agricultural prices broke sharply in 1868, then tumbled further downward after the *Panic of 1873*. This was due to overproduction, for new farming areas opened in Canada, Australia, Argentina, Russia, and India flooded the world's markets with produce. American farmers insisted, however, that the cause was not overproduction, but underconsumption. If easterners purchased food according to their full capacity to consume, there would be no surpluses. They did not, it was maintained, because prices were kept high by middlemen who exacted too high a profit for transferring goods from producer to consumer. Chief among these were:

a. RAILROADS. Farmer grievances against western railroads were many: 1) As monopolies they charged all the traffic would bear. In proof of this, farmers cited the lower rates on eastern railroads where competition existed. 2) The land-grant railroads were looked upon as speculators which withheld territory from settlement for selfish ends. 3) The long-and-short-haul device was resented. By this railroads charged more for a short haul in areas where they enjoyed a monopoly than for a long haul where they faced competition. 4) The roads were charged with granting rebates to large shippers, giving free passes to politicians, and corrupting state legislatures.

b. GRAIN ELEVATORS. As only one elevator existed in each farm community, farmers had no choice but to sell their grain in a monopolistic market. Most elevator operators kept their prices in line with national prices, but they were charged with corrupt methods of grading and weighing grain that cheated farmers.

c. MANUFACTURERS. Farmers believed that monopolistic corporations producing farm machinery and other necessities charged prices that bore no relation to production costs.

2. The Advent of the Grange.

a. ORIGINS OF THE GRANGE. The farmers' answer to the problem of monopoly was to win political control of state legislatures, then pass laws regulating freight rates and elevator charges. Seizing on a social organization, the _National Grange of the Patrons of Husbandry,_ which had been organized in 1867 by _Oliver H. Kelley,_ a clerk in the Department of Agriculture, they joined in such numbers that by 1874 the Grange had 1,500,000 members. Grangers soon dominated the legislatures of Illinois, Wisconsin, Iowa, and Minnesota.

b. THE GRANGER PROGRAM. The Granger legislatures adopted a twofold program:

I. _Rate Regulation_ was the weapon used against railroads and grain elevators. Laws were passed setting maximum rates for carrying or storing grain, and commissions were established to enforce the measures.

II. _Cooperative Buying_ was employed to lower the price of goods purchased. By pooling their orders farmers found that they could buy farm machinery for about half the retail price. Thus encouraged, they began establishing cooperative grain elevators, insurance companies, flour mills, banks, and factories. Most of these failed because of inadequate managerial skill and cut-throat competition from industrialists.

3. The Granger Cases.

a. LEGALIZATION OF RATE SETTING. Railroad and elevator operators insisted that the Granger Laws violated the _Fourteenth Amendment_ by depriving them of property without due process of law. Their objections led to the _Granger Cases_ (1876-1877). In the most famous of these, _Munn v. Illinois,_ the Supreme Court passed on an Illinois statute setting rates for storing and handling grain. The Court upheld the law, stating that property was no longer completely private when it was "affected with a public interest." This occurred when it was "used in a manner to make it of public consequence, and affect the community at large." Elevators, railroads, gristmills, and the like were defined as "clothed in a public interest" and hence subject to regulation.

b. THE PROBLEM OF INTERSTATE COMMERCE. In a second group of cases, of which _Peik v. Chicago and North Western Railroad_ was the most important, the Court not only applied this doctrine to railroads, but held that the Granger Laws did not violate the _interstate commerce clause_ of the Constitution which gave Congress sole authority over commerce between the states. Until Congress acted, the Court ruled, the states were free to adopt legislation necessary to the welfare of the people.

c. RESULTS OF THE GRANGER CASES. These decisions marked the first successful attack on the doctrine of laissez faire in post-Civil War America. They laid the basis for all subsequent state regulatory activities, and eventually for the federal regulation of interstate carriers. Despite this success, the Grange declined rapidly after 1877, partly because its success convinced farmers their battle was won, partly because its cooperative ventures collapsed. The railroads soon reverted to their old practices.

B. The Advent of Federal Regulation.

1. Undoing the Granger Laws. With the decline of the Grange and the growing conservatism of the Supreme Court, the Granger Laws were virtually nullified in two important cases:

a. THE WABASH CASE. In the case of *Wabash, St. Louis and Pacific Railway v. Illinois* (1886) the Court reversed its decision in the Peik Case, ruling that states had no right to fix rates on shipments passing beyond their borders. In effect this ended state regulation, for nearly all traffic crossed state lines.

b. THE MINNESOTA RATE CASE. In the case of *Chicago, Milwaukee and St. Paul Railroad v. Minnesota* (1889) the Court decreed that the reasonableness of any rate set by a state commission was a matter to be determined by the courts. This allowed railroads to protest any rate, then fight the matter through the courts for years before a decision was reached.

2. Demand for a Federal Law. If the states could not regulate railroad rates, progressives agreed that the federal government must do so. Its power was clear under the *commerce clause.* This was emphasized in two Senate committee reports:

a. THE WINDOM COMMITTEE (1874) recommended that the United States build and operate competing railroads to force private lines to keep their rates down. At the same time a bill authorizing federal rate regulation was passed by the House but defeated in the Senate.

b. THE CULLOM COMMITTEE (1886) disclosed that railroads were guilty of *pooling* tactics: that is, that competing lines formed pools to set high rates or end competition in a region. As three-fourths of the roads were interstate carriers that could not be regulated by the states under the Wabash Case decision, the committee recommended immediate federal regulation.

3. The Interstate Commerce Act (1887) was passed by Congress in response to this demand. It: 1) established an *Interstate Commerce Commission* of five to enforce the measure; 2) required railroads to post their rates publicly and decreed that these must be "reasonable and just"; 3) forbade such practices as pooling, rebates, and rate discrimination among shippers; 4) prohibited higher charges for a short haul than for a longer haul over the same line; and 5) authorized the Commission to investigate complaints against railroads and hand down rulings which would be enforceable through the courts.

4. Failure of Federal Regulation. The Interstate Commerce Act was rendered ineffective by judicial hostility. As the Commission could enforce its rulings only through the courts, their friendship was essential. Instead, they handed down hostile decisions in fifteen of the sixteen cases tried before 1905. The decision in one of these, the *Maximum Freight Rate Case* (1897), ruled that the Commission did not have power to fix rates, while another, in the *Alabama Midlands Case* (1897), virtually nullified the long-and-short-haul prohibition By 1900 the act was noneffective.

II. THE ATTACK ON INDUSTRIAL MONOPOLY. Big business was subjected to an attack from: 1) labor unions, and 2) reformers who demanded governmental regulation.

A. The Organization of Labor. The ineffectual local trade unions of the prewar era were transformed into powerful national unions during these years. This unity was forced on the workers by the problems they faced in an industrialized America.

1. Causes for Labor Unrest.

a. Rise of Corporations. These ended all personal relationships between employers and employees, as corporations were governed by distant boards of directors who were in no position to look after the welfare of workers. Managers of corporations, moreover, were primarily interested in producing profits for stockholders rather than in protecting the rights of laborers in their factories. Workers therefore felt that they must protect their own interests.

b. Mechanization of Industry. As machines took over the tasks formerly performed by men, individual skills became less and less important. This tended to place workers at the mercy of employers who no longer had to placate the small number of skilled artisans available for a particular trade. Instead, they could draw upon the inexhaustible pool of unskilled or semiskilled labor provided by immigration. To protect their jobs laborers felt that they must organize.

c. Nationalization of Industry. This made competition among workers nation-wide; industries could take advantage of cheap labor wherever it existed rather than depending on a local supply. At the same time the power exerted by national business organizations suggested that national labor organizations could wield a similar influence.

d. Working Conditions. Wages did not increase as rapidly as living costs during this period. In 1890 the average pay for unskilled workers was $10 a week, and for skilled $20. This did not allow an average family to exist unless the wife and children also worked, as was usually the case. Hours of labor were from ten to twelve each day, six days a week. Factories were badly lighted and ventilated, with no attempt made to guard employees against dangerous machinery. Compensation for death or injury were virtually unknown.

e. Need for Organization. Workers could not turn to politics to obtain better conditions as had farmers. This was because the doctrine of laissez faire was so entrenched that any demand for the federal regulation of industry would have been ineffective. Workers felt that they must protect themselves, and that this could only be done by forming nation-wide unions strong enough to combat nation-wide corporations.

2. *Stages of Organization.* Labor organization went through three stages between the close of the Civil War and 1890:

a. THE NATIONAL LABOR UNION. This was established in 1866 by a combination of local craft unions, reform groups, and trades assemblies. Built on the "federal" principle, its individual unions continued their separate existence but sent delegates to national conventions where a common policy was shaped. This policy embraced such diverse objectives as the eight-hour day and producers' cooperatives. The National Labor Union collapsed after the Panic of 1873 because its leaders failed to realize that the worker did not want idealistic panaceas but better wages, hours, and working conditions.

b. THE KNIGHTS OF LABOR.

I. _Rise of the Knights of Labor._ Formed in 1869 by _Uriah S. Stephens,_ a Philadelphia tailor, the Knights of Labor attempted to unite workers of all skills, colors, and creeds into _One Big Union_ that could wrest from employers a more equitable share of the nation's wealth. It gained membership rapidly, especially after the _Panic of 1873,_ but its golden period did not begin until 1878 when _Terence V. Powderly,_ a Pennsylvania machinist, became Grand Master. Although Powderly was an idealist who believed in long-term objectives rather than strikes, the Knights under his direction won their first great victory in 1884 when a strike on the Missouri Pacific Railroad forced a restoration of wage cuts. This brought the Union such prestige that its membership grew to 700,000 by 1886.

II. _Decline of the Knights of Labor._ The union's decline began in 1886 and was caused by two events: 1) the failure of a strike against the Texas and Pacific Railroad; and 2) the _Haymarket Riot_ in Chicago. This followed a nation-wide strike on May 1, 1886, for the eight-hour day. In Chicago the strike was supported not only by the Knights but also by a handful of foreign-born anarchists who preached the forceful overthrow of the government. When one of their number was addressing strikers at the McCormick Harvester Works on May 3 the meeting was charged by police, who killed several workers. The anarchists called a protest meeting at Haymarket Square the next evening. Although the 1500 people attending were orderly, a column of police marched into the square just as the meeting was breaking up. Someone threw a bomb into the column, killing seven of the police and wounding sixty more. Public resentment was so great that seven anarchists were sentenced to death on the grounds that they had advised violence, even though no one could show that they were connected with the bomb throwing. Anarchism and labor were now so associated in the popular mind that the Knights declined rapidly in membership. Skilled workers especially withdrew to protect themselves from *blacklisting* by employers. This was done by sending names of union members to all factories employing men of their skills. They could then not find employment anywhere in the country.

c. THE AMERICAN FEDERATION OF LABOR. Formed in Pittsburgh in 1881, the A.F. of L. did not become important until it received the influx of skilled workers who deserted the Knights of Labor after 1886. This new organization was composed of self-governing craft unions, united on the federation principle through an elected governing board which set national policy. Membership was restricted to skilled workers who were as much interested in protecting themselves from the competition of the unskilled as in protecting labor from capital. The objectives of the organization were completely realistic; disregarding long-term panaceas, the A.F. of L. worked for an eight-hour day, a six-day work-week, better wages, job tenure, and the abolition of child labor. It sought to obtain these ends by using the *strike* and the *boycott*. This practical program, combined with the excellent leadership of its long-time president, *Samuel Gompers* (1885-1924), won the A.F. of L. 500,000 members by 1900. These were successful in winning the *closed shop* (plants hiring only union workers) and the abolition of *yellow-dog contracts* (labor contracts forcing workers to agree they would not join a union), as well as better pay, shorter hours, and better working conditions in many industries. Yet by its nature the A.F. of L. excluded 90 per cent of the American workers who did not have the craft or skill to qualify for membership in one of its affiliated unions.

3. Industrial Strife. Moderate as were the demands of organized labor, public opinion and employers were so hostile that those demands could be achieved only after a long period of industrial strife. Between 1881 and 1900 strikes numbered 24,000 and involved 128,000 establishments. Several attracted national attention:

a. THE RAILROAD STRIKE OF 1877. Protesting wage cuts following the Panic of 1873, railroad workers went on strike, then attempted to stop the roads from operating. The conflict was so bitter that federal troops were called out to quell riots in Pennsylvania, Maryland, West Virginia, and Illinois. The greatest disorders occurred at Pittsburgh after militiamen killed twenty strikers. Some $5,000,000 worth of property was destroyed before the strike was broken, the workers returning at the lower wages set by the railroads.

b. THE HOMESTEAD STRIKE (1892). This was staged at the Homestead, Pennsylvania, plant of the Carnegie Steel Company in July, 1892, following a company threat to cut wages and smash the Amalgamated Association of Iron and Steel Workers. When workers picketed the plant, Carnegie's lieutenant, _Henry C. Frick,_ imported 300 guards from the Pinkerton Detective Agency. As the _Pinkertons_ landed from barges they were captured by a mob and run out of town, several on both sides being killed in the process. Frick's appeal to the state for aid resulted in an invasion of militiamen that turned Homestead into an armed camp. The strikers held out for nine months, but when public opinion turned against them they resumed work at company terms. The strike crushed the Amalgamated, leaving the steel industry unorganized for forty years.

c. THE PULLMAN STRIKE (1894). A drastic wage cut at the Pullman Palace Car Company of Chicago following the Panic of 1893 led to a strike of the _American Railway Union_ under the leadership of _Eugene V. Debs._ This soon spread to other railroads when trainmen were discharged for refusing to operate trains carrying Pullman cars. As bitterness increased, mobs representing both contestants did $80,000,000 worth of damage in the Chicago area. This led the railroads, operating through the _General Managers' Association,_ to appeal to President Grover Cleveland for protection despite the insistence of Governor _John P. Altgeld_ of Illinois that the situation was under control. Cleveland responded, even though the Constitution stated that federal soldiers could be sent into a state only at the request of the governor or legislature, justifying his action on the grounds that the army was needed to safeguard the mails. The 2000 troops that arrived on July 3, 1894, soon broke the strike. One far-reaching result was an extended use of the federal *injunction*. Such a writ was issued against Debs, ordering him to do nothing that would prolong the strike. When he disregarded this order he was tried for violating the injunction and sentenced to six months in jail. The Supreme Court upheld his conviction in the case of *In Re Debs* (1895). The decision gave employers a new weapon against all strikers who interfered with interstate commerce.

4. Results of Labor Organization. Apparently, labor made few gains during the period; public opinion and the courts remained hostile to unions while the mass of workers was still unorganized. Actually, some progress was made:

a. ATTITUDE OF EMPLOYERS. A few employers realized that industrial peace could be secured only by co-operating with unions. These firms showed a willingness to bargain collectively with workers or to submit disputes to impartial arbitration; they also set up old-age pension plans, death benefits, and profit-sharing programs. Among the corporations adopting such an attitude were the Pillsbury Mills, the Baltimore and Ohio Railroad, and one hundred others.

b. ATTITUDE OF GOVERNMENT. National laws favorable to labor included: 1) an act (1868) setting the eight-hour day on public works; 2) the creation of the Bureau of Labor (1884); 3) the prohibition of the importation of contract labor (1885); 4) an act (1892) establishing the eight-hour day for all government employees; and 5) the Erdman Act (1898) providing for the arbitration of disputes on interstate carriers. State laws of the same nature were also passed, although most were disallowed by conservative courts. Massachusetts established a ten-hour day for women and children in 1879 and other industrial states soon followed. Acts were also passed to assure better working conditions. At the end of the century, however, 70 per cent of the men still worked from ten to twelve hours a day, six or seven days a week.

B. Trust Regulation. During the postwar years the federal government made its first attempts to regulate business as well as transportation. While these were largely unsuccessful they set a pattern that changed the whole nature of American life in the twentieth century.

1. Background of the Problem.

a. GROWTH OF INDUSTRIAL MONOPOLIES. Public sentiment against monopolies, or *trusts,* began to develop in the 1880's, following the formation of the <u>Standard Oil Company</u> and other giant combinations (See pp. 21-22). The Standard Oil trust particularly was singled out for attack. In 1882 this company owned fourteen other companies outright, as well as holding a majority interest in twenty-six others. All were operated by nine trustees who held the stock of the individual companies, the stockholders receiving in return "trust certificates" which entitled them to a share in the profits. The oil trust was so successful that before 1887 others were formed in cottonseed oil, linseed oil, lead, whiskey, sugar, and other products.

b. OBJECTIONS TO THE TRUSTS. It was charged that these trusts: 1) set high prices which had no relation to the cost of production; 2) forced producers of raw materials to sell at a low price as they controlled the market; 3) ruined small businesses by obtaining rebates from railroads in return for their business; 4) mistreated workers by <u>blacklisting</u> those who joined unions, thus denying them a chance to obtain other jobs where they could use their skills; and 5) bribed legislatures to obtain special favors from state and national governments. This was especially the case after 1886 when the Supreme Court, in the case of <u>Santa Clara County v. Southern Pacific Railroad,</u> ruled that corporations were "persons" within the meaning of the <u>Fourteenth Amendment,</u> and hence that states could not deprive them of "life, liberty or property without due process of law." In effect this ruling forbade the states to tax or regulate corporations without the approval of conservative federal courts.

2. Demands for Trust Regulation. It was popularly believed that the public could be protected only by forcing the monopolistic trusts to break up into competing units. This could best be accomplished by the federal government through the use of its power over interstate commerce; Congress could forbid monopolies to ship their produce across state lines. A demand for federal action was voiced in the 1880's by: 1) an Anti-Monopoly Party which in the 1884 election won few votes but called attention to the problem; 2) popular writers who attacked the trusts in books and magazine articles; 3) farmer and labor organizations which demanded reform; and 4) state legislatures which passed laws forbidding agreements that would restrain free competition. Fifteen such laws were passed in 1889 and 1890.

3. The Sherman Antitrust Act (1890). This important measure, passed by Congress in response to popular pressure, provided: 1) that every contract, combination, or conspiracy in restraint of trade among the states or with foreign countries was illegal, and 2) that any person who monopolized trade or commerce among the states or with foreign countries was guilty of a misdemeanor and subject to a fine of $5000 and one year's imprisonment.

4. Failure of the Sherman Antitrust Act.

a. DEFECTS OF THE ACT. The measure was so loosely worded that it proved unenforceable. Thus, although trusts were forbidden and disappeared rapidly, they were replaced by *holding companies,* through which a single corporation owned and voted the controlling shares of the stock of a large number of companies. Organizations of this character proved immune to federal attack.

b. HOSTILITY OF THE COURTS. Conservative federal courts removed most of the teeth from the Sherman Act by defining "trade" narrowly. The outstanding example was the decision in *United States v. E. C. Knight Company* (1895) which held that an exchange of stock which gave the E. C. Knight Company control of 95 per cent of sugar refining was not an act of "trade" and hence not forbidden. After this rebuff, government attorneys made few attempts to enforce the law. Only eighteen suits were brought between 1890 and 1900, and some of these were designed to restrain labor unions rather than industries.

c. Growth of Corporations. Encouraged by the courts' attitude, industry organized more rapidly after 1890 than before. Between 1860 and 1890 twenty-four combinations were formed, capitalized at $436,000,000; between 1890 and 1900, 157 were created with a total capitalization of $3,100,000,000.

III. GOVERNMENT AND BUSINESS: AN APPRAISAL.

A. Results of the Attack on Laissez Faire. Big business ruled America in 1900 as it had in 1870, but by that time business was bigger and the rule more complete. Farmers were still at the mercy of monopolistic railroads, workers (other than a few skilled craftsmen) were unprotected by effective organizations, and both industry and transportation were dominated by a few individuals who held the real reins of government. Equally important was the fact that the courts still placed property rights above human rights on their scale of values.

B. Results of the Attack on Big Business. A generation of agitation bore some fruit, however. Farmers and workers had demonstrated that they could unite for a common end; only time was needed before their organizations would give them a more equitable share of the national wealth. Even more important was the fact that the Interstate Commerce Act and the Sherman Antitrust Act demonstrated the federal government's power to take positive steps in behalf of the general welfare of the people. Later generations of lawmakers had only to improve these basic measures to make them effective instruments for human betterment.

Additional Reading

John G. Sproat, *"The Best Men": Liberal Reformers in the Gilded Age* (1968), analyzes social ideas and politics during the post-war period, while essays edited by H. Wayne Morgan, *The Gilded Age,* (1970), incorporate the latest research on the relationship between politics and reform. Daniel Aaron, *Men of Good Hope* (1951), deals with specific reformers. Sidney Fine, *Laissez Faire and the General Welfare State* (1956), explores the changing patterns of reform thought as they responded to industrialism. Solon J. Buck, *The Agrarian Crusade* (1921), deals briefly with the

Granger movement, but should be supplemented with George H. Miller, *Railroads and the Granger Laws* (1971), which shows that much of the so-called "Granger legislation" dealing with regulation was the result of efforts of small-town merchants. Norman J. Ware, *The Labor Movement in the United States, 1860-1895* (1929), is still helpful on the Knights of Labor; briefer accounts are in the many general histories of labor of which the most useful is Philip Taft, *Organized Labor in American Industry* (1964). This same author has produced the standard history of the American Federation of Labor in *The A. F. of L. in the Time of Gompers* (1957), and *The A. F. of L. from the Death of Gompers to the Merger* (1959). Samuel Yellen, *American Labor Struggles* (1936), describes conflicts during the period.

CHAPTER VI

The Urban Impact
1870-1890

❰ THE CITY IN AMERICAN CIVILIZATION
The city was a product of the machine age. As men left
their farms to cluster about factories, more and more they
felt the impact of an urban environment which reshaped their
lives and their thought. Some found in the city an inspiration for cultural expression. The remarkable progress in
literature, music, art, and architecture was traceable to the
urbanization process. Others were aroused by the evils and
sin that centered in the cities; the reform movements that
flourished in the late nineteenth century all stemmed from a
desire to wipe out the poverty, slums, and immorality which
appeared in magnified form among city dwellers. The important changes that occurred in American society during
these years were largely the products of urbanization.

I. THE RISE OF THE CITY. In 1860 one in every
six Americans lived in cities (compact units of 8000 inhabitants or more); in 1890 three out of every ten. New York
was the largest with 2,500,000 inhabitants, but both Chicago
and Philadelphia had more than 1,000,000, and St. Louis,
Boston, and Baltimore more than 500,000. Others were
growing rapidly: Kansas City and Detroit grew fourfold
between 1860 and 1890, Cleveland sixfold, and Los Angeles
twenty-four fold.

A. Reasons for Urbanization.

1. *Economic and Social Factors.* Industrialization was

principally responsible, as men grouped themselves around machines. Also important were: 1) railroads that allowed large populations to be fed and supplied with fuel; 2) the influx of immigrants; and 3) the exodus of men from farms as declining profits and labor-saving machinery released agricultural workers.

2. Physical Factors. Cities could not become important until mechanical devices allowed men to live in large groups. Sewers, garbage disposal plants, and trolley cars were not romantic, but they were indispensable.

a. TRANSPORTATION. Horse cars, in use before the Civil War, were first displaced by cable cars, invented by Andrew S. Hallidie and installed in San Francisco in 1873. These gave way to electric *trolley cars,* which were developed by Frank J. Sprague and used in Richmond, Virginia, in 1887-1888. New York opened its first *elevated railroad* in 1878, and Boston the first *subway* in 1895. Bridges to span rivers on which cities were built were also essential. The leading builder was *John A. Roebling* who, with his son Washington A. Roebling, completed the *Brooklyn Bridge* in 1883. This was the engineering marvel of the age.

b. LIGHTING. Gas lights were gradually displaced by *arc lights,* invented by Charles F. Bush of Cleveland in 1878. The *incandescent lamp,* perfected by Thomas A. Edison in 1880, solved the problem of home lighting.

c. PUBLIC HEALTH. Public water works, garbage disposal plants, and efficient sewage systems were gradually developed, helping solve the problem of contagious diseases. Equally important was the announcement of the germ theory of disease by *Louis Pasteur* of France. This allowed doctors to check the epidemics that had previously wiped out city populations.

II. WEALTH AND POVERTY. The rise of the city called attention to the growing gulf between rich and poor that accompanied industrialization. This discrepancy, made clear by the spreading slums in urban America, aroused humanitarians to strenuous efforts that were designed to restore economic democracy in the United States.

A. The Gospel of Wealth. Industrialization increased the national wealth from $16,000,000,000 to $65,000,000,

000 between 1860 and 1890, but was also responsible for the uneven distribution of that wealth. Nine per cent of the people owned 71 per cent of the nation's money by 1890; at the other extreme 88 per cent of the families owned only 14 per cent of the wealth. This inequality was defended by spokesmen for the gospel of wealth, of whom *Andrew Carnegie* was the leader. In magazine articles and books they argued that: 1) the fortunate few deserved extra compensation for making the United States the world's leading nation; 2) all eventually benefited as wealth seeped down to the masses; and 3) the concentration of riches supported education and culture.

B. The Problem of Poverty. The concentration of wealth meant that millions of city-dwelling Americans would live in poverty. In spreading slums, tenements housed masses of workers amidst unhealthy conditions; the death rate among New York's 1,500,000 tenement dwellers was 62 per 1000 while elsewhere the rate was only 20 per 1000. By 1890, 10 per cent of all the population lived in slums. Their plight was revealed by such widely read books as Jacob A. Riis, *How the Other Half Lives* (1890), and John Spargo, *The Bitter Cry of the Children* (1906). Aroused by such revelations, humanitarians suggested numerous panaceas:

1. Social Reformers. One group sought to remedy the plight of the poor by social action.

a. ORGANIZED CHARITY. Reformers launched a threefold attack on the problem: 1) *State boards of charities* were created to supervise local almshouses, orphanages, and insane asylums. Massachusetts created such a board in 1864, and half the states had imitated its example by 1900. 2) The Society for the Prevention of Cruelty to Children was organized in 1874 to campaign against child labor and similar evils. 3) *Social Service Centers* were set up in slum areas. These provided pleasant recreational surroundings for youth and adults, as well as club facilities, training in arts and crafts, education, and the like. The most famous was *Hull House* in Chicago, founded in 1889 by *Jane Addams.* In all, one hundred were established between 1886 and 1900.

b. PRISON REFORM. To assure more equitable treatment for those driven to crime by poverty, reformers developed the theory, then novel, that prisons should be used to regenerate rather than punish lawbreakers. The theory was first applied at the New York *Elmira State Prison,* opened in 1877 under the direction of *Zebulon R. Brockway.* Youthful offenders were separated from hardened criminals, sentences reduced for good conduct, a parole system installed, and educational opportunities provided. The example was imitated in other prisons before 1900.

c. RELIGIOUS INSTITUTIONS. The Young Men's Christian Association (1851), the Salvation Army (1879), and the city mission (1887) sought to combine social and religious regeneration.

2. Critics of the Social Order. Those not satisfied with these palliatives analyzed the nature of the social structure in their effort to reform society. In this group were social critics, utopian novelists, and political radicals.

a. SOCIAL CRITICS. Of the many who suggested social readjustments, none was more prominent than *Henry George.* In his *Progress and Poverty* (1879) George argued that as land was the basis of all wealth, its unequal distribution forced the many who owned no land to slave for the few who did. This situation could be remedied not by a redistribution of property, but by a *single tax* on land to replace all other taxes, thus depriving owners of unearned profits stemming from the increase in land values. George's book sold 2,000,000 copies before 1905, and almost elected its author mayor of New York in 1886.

b. UTOPIAN NOVELISTS. Of those who used fiction to picture the ideal society of the future, the most outstanding was *Edward Bellamy,* whose *Looking Backward, 2000-1887* (1887) described the United States as it would be in the year 2000. All production facilities were owned by the people through their government. The greater efficiency resulting allowed much leisure time, which was used for cultural advance. The book sold 400,000 copies in ten years, while one hundred and fifty *Nationalist Clubs* were formed to advocate Bellamy's system.

c. POLITICAL RADICALISM. Anarchism and socialism were advocated in the late nineteenth century.

I. *Anarchism.* This flourished briefly in the 1880's, largely among immigrants from southwestern Europe, where the philosophy had many followers. Anarchists, through such journals as *The Alarm* (1883), advocated a forceful overthrow of government and the substitution of a ruleless social order.

II. *Socialism.* German and French immigrants introduced Marxian Socialism to the United States just after the Civil War. They advocated an orderly change to a system of government ownership of facilities for production and distribution, with the nonprofit-making exchange of commodities. The Panic of 1873 gave them sufficient strength to form the *Socialist Labor Party* (1877), but membership was confined largely to immigrants. American labor, capitalistic in philosophy, wanted a larger share of profits rather than any change in the system. Not until the close of the century was discontent among workers widespread enough to foster a native socialist movement. Formed in the 1890's by *Eugene V. Debs*, the *Socialist Party* polled 95,000 votes in the election of 1900, and nearly a million in the election of 1912. Many were the protest votes of middle-class intellectuals, but more were cast by workers who no longer felt that the United States was a land of infinite opportunity.

III. THE REVOLUTION IN RELIGIOUS THOUGHT. Urbanization and the concentration of wealth posed a problem for churchmen. Accustomed to dealing with a rural, middle-class society, they were forced to revise theology and remake the churches as social institutions under the impact of industrialization.

A. Theological Readjustment. American Protestantism traditionally based its teachings on the assumption that the Bible must be literally interpreted. This belief suffered a threefold attack after the Civil War.

1. The Attack on Orthodoxy.

a. THE EVOLUTIONARY HYPOTHESIS. The English scientist, *Charles Darwin,* in his *Origin of Species* (1859) and *Descent of Man* (1871), showed that life forms had evolved slowly from primitive ancestors, rather than being created suddenly as stated in the Book of Genesis. After the death in 1873 of *Louis Agassiz,* the Harvard biologist who was the last scientific opponent of Darwinism, all scholars accepted the hypothesis, while intelligent laymen were won over by such popularizers as _John Fiske_.

b. THE HIGHER CRITICISM. New methods of historical scholarship devised in Germany allowed scholars to subject the Bible to scientific criticism. This demonstrated that the Scriptures were not written at one time and under one inspiration, but were the product of many peoples who displayed the weaknesses and ignorance of all human beings. This was as shocking to the orthodox as the doctrine of evolution.

c. THE STUDY OF COMPARATIVE RELIGIONS. The sympathetic study of other religious systems disclosed that Christianity was not alone in prescribing an enlightened moral code. The people learned of other religions through such best-selling books as James Freeman Clarke, _Ten Great Religions_ (1871)

2. _The Theological Revolution._ For a time the churches resisted this assault by ridiculing or denouncing evolution and the higher criticism. As popular acceptance of the new theories spread, however, they were forced to adjust themselves. Leadership was supplied by progressive clergymen such as the Reverend _Washington Gladden,_ Congregational minister of Columbus, Ohio, and the Reverend _Henry Ward Beecher,_ Congregational pastor of Brooklyn, New York, who found no basic antagonism between the scientific concepts and the basic principles of Christianity. By the end of the century theological schools were teaching evolution and the higher criticism. This change was strenuously resisted by an orthodox minority, giving rise to a conflict between _Modernism_ and _Fundamentalism._ The center of fundamentalist thought was in rural areas of the South and West, although such revivalists as the Reverend _Dwight L. Moody_ attacked modernism in the Northeast.

B. Social Readjustment. The churches faced two problems as social institutions: 1) How could they combat the growing secular trend, and 2) Should they follow rich or poor as the redistribution of wealth divided the classes.

1. _The Secular Trend._ Churches lost membership rapidly as secular interests occupied more and more of men's

time. The need for recreation in a speeded-up industrial society also lessened interest in worship. Although the churches did all in their power to combat this trend they accomplished little, as shown by the gradual secularization of the Sabbath day.

2. Wealth or Poverty? As the gulf between rich and poor widened, the churches at first followed the wealthy, building their edifices in upper-class neighborhoods and neglecting the slums. Ministers adopted such an unsympathetic attitude toward labor that workers felt unwelcome in many churches.

3. The Social Revolution. The solution of their dual problem—reversing the trend toward secularization and winning the workingmen back to the churches—was devised by such progressive clergymen as the Reverend *Washington Gladden* and the Reverend *Josiah Strong.* They proposed to make Christianity a part of the everyday life of the people, not simply a brief Sabbath episode. To this end they urged ministers to side with labor in the conflict with capital, to denounce the *"tainted money"* of corporations, and to make their churches into attractive social institutions. The latter was accomplished by adding reading rooms, club rooms, gymnasiums, and the like. These *socialized churches* gained membership far more rapidly than the nonsocialized churches, encouraging imitation. In line with this trend was the rise of a new religion, *Christian Science,* under the guidance of *Mary Baker Eddy.* By promising physical as well as spiritual salvation it appealed especially to urban workers. Even more indicative of the new religious spirit was the formation of the *Society of Christian Socialists* (1889) by clergymen who believed that the teachings of Jesus led directly to socialism. Efforts of this sort did much to restore the influence of the churches by 1900.

IV. THE REFORM MOVEMENTS. Urbanization accentuated the evils that had long troubled reformers, thus heightening the effort to stamp out political inequalities, the liquor traffic, and racial prejudice.

A. The Struggle for Women's Rights. Women had few legal or economic rights in 1865. Long considered creatures of the home, they were believed unequal to the task of competing in a male world.

1. The Basis for Equal Rights. Changed economic and social conditions stemming from industrialization prepared women for political equality:

a. ECONOMIC ACTIVITIES. Industry allowed women to demonstrate their ability by working in gainful occupations; between 1870 and 1900 the number employed increased from 1,800,000 to 5,300,000. These gains were made possible by inventions that allowed emancipation from the drudgery of the home: prepared foods, commercial bakeries, kitchen implements, and improved washing and ironing facilities.

b. SOCIAL ACTIVITIES. Women did yeoman service in social agencies. They also showed their organizing skill by forming women's clubs; the first was founded in 1868 and by 1889 the clubs were numerous enough to unite in the General Federation of Women's Clubs.

c. INTELLECTUAL ACTIVITIES. Women's colleges were opened at Vassar, Smith, and Wellesley between 1865 and 1875, with others following rapidly. More significant was the spread of coeducation, especially in the state universities. By 1900 about 70 per cent of all colleges admitted women. Thus trained, they were able to enter such professions as teaching. Two of every three teachers were women by 1900.

2. The Campaign for Equal Rights.

a. STRUGGLE FOR LEGAL EQUALITY. State after state liberalized its laws to allow women to own property, retain their earnings, make contracts, and sue or be sued. By the end of the century this battle was won.

b. STRUGGLE FOR POLITICAL EQUALITY. Agitation for the right to vote was carried on by such reformers as *Elizabeth Cady Stanton* and *Susan B. Anthony*, who organized the *National American Woman Suffrage Association*. By 1895 sixteen states allowed women to vote in school elections and four on taxation bills. *Wyoming* (1890) was the first state to grant full political equality; three other western states followed before 1900. Some sentiment developed for a constitutional amendment to bestow the franchise on women, but this was not secured for another generation.

B. The Attack of the Liquor Traffic. The rising power of the liquor industry, as shown through the _Whiskey Ring_ (see p. 44) strengthened the hand of reformers seeking prohibition. As support mounted, they organized the _Prohibition Party_ (1869) and the _Women's Christian Temperance Union_ (1874), the latter with _Frances E. Willard_ as its guiding spirit. _The Anti-Saloon League_ (1895) was designed to coordinate the efforts of smaller temperance societies. These organizations agitated for expensive licenses for saloons, school education against drinking, and complete prohibition. By 1890 seven states had passed dry laws, while smaller areas elsewhere banned liquor sales under local option. Yet the per capita consumption of liquor trebled between 1860 and 1900.

C. The Problem of Racial Minorities. Two minority groups felt the lash of discrimination: the Negroes and recent immigrants.

1. The Negro Problem. Southern states were left free to handle the Negroes after 1877 when federal troops were withdrawn. Their answer was a _Jim Crow_ system of segregation with separate schools, railroad cars, and the like. This was upheld by the Supreme Court in the _Civil Rights Cases_ (1883), which denied the federal government the right to interfere. After 1890 Negro rights were further restricted by voting requirements that effectively denied them the franchise (see p. 54). Efforts to better conditions were made by such outstanding Negro leaders as _Booker T. Washington,_ who held that the ex-slaves must be educated before they could demand equality. Washington was responsible for founding the Normal and Industrial Institute at Tuskegee, Alabama (1881). Northern philanthropists also provided funds for Negro education; the Peabody Fund (1867) and the Slater Fund (1882) helped establish many schools.

2. The Immigrant Problem. Anti-immigrant sentiment was directed largely against the _new immigration_ (see p. 17) and Orientals. Organized labor was especially insistent that aliens be barred to protect jobs in America. This feeling led Congress to: 1) ban the entry of paupers, criminals, and the insane in 1882, and of any diseased person in

1891; 2) forbid Chinese immigration (1879) in a law that violated the Burlingame Treaty (1868) which had guaranteed a free movement of peoples between the two countries. President Hayes vetoed the bill but drafted a new treaty with China (1880) allowing the United States to restrict immigration. This was done in 1882 for a ten-year period; in 1902 the restriction was made permanent.

V. THE CITY AND CULTURAL PROGRESS. Urbanization stimulated cultural advance by: 1) allowing people of like interest to mingle for mutual stimulation; 2) providing such cultural facilities as libraries, schools, museums, orchestras, and theaters; 3) concentrating wealth which could then be used for cultural purposes.

A. The Educational Renaissance.

1. Spread of Public Schools. On the lowest school level was the _kindergarten,_ which was introduced into the St. Louis school system in 1873 and spread rapidly. _Grammar school_ education was made compulsory in state after state, although the rural South did not develop its educational system until after 1900. School enrollments more than doubled between 1870 and 1900, while illiteracy dropped from 20 per cent to 11 per cent. The increase in the number of _high schools_ was especially notable as states recognized their obligation to provide secondary education; the 500 high schools operating in 1870 had swelled to 6000 by 1900. On all these levels teaching was greatly improved by: 1) the recognition of teaching as a profession, made possible by the establishment of normal schools in all states; and 2) the popularization of a new philosophy of education propounded by _John Dewey._ Dewey held that the function of a teacher was to interest the pupil in learning rather than to force him to learn. He also taught the need of training for life in the classroom. The better instruction resulting kept many pupils in school.

2. College Education.

a. IMPROVEMENTS IN THE COLLEGES. The renaissance enjoyed by the colleges after the Civil War was due to: 1) the rise of educational leaders who had been well trained in German universities; 2) the _Morrill Act_ (1862) which offered federal land grants to states establishing agricultural and engineering schools, thus stimulating the growth of _state universities;_ and 3) the financial resources made available by industrialization. Wealthy philanthropists used their fortunes to found such schools as Vanderbilt, Johns Hopkins, Leland Stanford, and the University of Chicago.

b. CHANGES IN THE COLLEGES. The colleges were modernized and improved by: 1) broadening the curriculum to place greater emphasis on practical rather than classical subjects, an innovation that led to the development of the _"elective system"_ under Harvard's great president, _Charles W. Eliot;_ 2) emphasizing graduate instruction and research, with a corresponding growth of professional training in law, medicine, and other fields. _Daniel Coit Gilman,_ president of the _Johns Hopkins University,_ was a pioneer in this type of instruction.

3. Adult Education. The _Chautauqua Movement_ originated in 1874 when summer instruction was first offered on the banks of Lake Chautauqua in upstate New York. The meetings proved so popular that a four-year course of study and reading was worked out. By 1892 one hundred thousand people were enrolled. The movement soon spread over the United States, with a week of lectures during the summer and reading through the remainder of the year.

4. Public Libraries. All states after the Civil War authorized towns to use tax revenues for public libraries; by the close of the century these libraries existed everywhere. Their spread was stimulated by _Andrew Carnegie,_ who began founding town libraries in 1881. By 1900 he had given away $10,000,000 for this purpose. At the same time library methods were improved under the guidance of the _American Library Association_ (1876).

5. Newspapers. Daily newspapers increased from 700 in 1870 to 2500 in 1900, while circulation mounted from 2,500,000 to 15,000,000. This growth was partly the result of mechanical improvements, the most important being the invention of the _linotype_ by Otto Mergenthaler in 1886. Newspapers also underwent a twofold change: 1) mounting production costs brought increasing control of the press by large corporations, leading to growing editorial conservatism as the papers' viewpoint reflected the attitude of the business office rather than the editor; 2) the nervous tensions of urban life created a demand for colorful and terse news accounts, leading to the rise of *yellow journalism.* The pioneer was *Joseph Pulitzer,* who in 1883 purchased the *New York World.* Using flaming headlines, cartoons, and stories of crime and scandal, he soon made his paper the nation's most profitable. Of his many imitators the most successful was *William Randolph Hearst,* who acquired the *New York Morning Journal* in 1895. The circulation war betwen Pulitzer and Hearst set a new low in journalistic sensationalism.

6. Magazines. Monthly magazines increased from 280 in 1860 to 1800 in 1900. Some were excellent literary or critical journals, the most influential being *The Nation* under the able editorship of *Edwin L. Godkin* (1865-1899). *Harper's Weekly* was also a major political force, largely because of the cartoons of *Thomas Nast.* The modern magazine age, however, did not begin until 1883 when Cyrus H. K. Curtis founded the *Ladies' Home Journal.* Its editor, *Edward W. Bok,* realized that advertising rather than subscriptions could pay printing costs, thus producing an excellent magazine for ten cents. This was the origin of the popular magazine.

B. The Gilded Age. Critics have characterized the postwar era as "The Gilded Age," implying a crassness and lack of taste that was typical of most middle-class Americans. This judgment, however, ignores the remarkable progress made in literature, art, and architecture under the stimulus of industrialization and urbanization.

1. Progress in Literature. In the United States, as in all countries, the advent of the machine age was marked by a gradual shift from romanticism to *realism* as the grim realities of urban life influenced authors. This transformation proceeded in three stages:

a. THE LOCAL COLORISTS. In the 1870's and 1880's a school of writers described pre-Civil War America in faintly realistic terms, although their descriptions were highly romanticized. Each section of the nation had its chroniclers to record the changes wrought by industrialization or to dwell lovingly on the rural past. For the West the principal writers were *Mark Twain, Bret Harte,* and Joaquin Miller. Life in the Middle West was described by _Edward Eggleston_ and James Whitcomb Riley. Southern authors who glorified the plantation life of the prewar era were _Thomas Nelson Page_, F. Hopkinson Smith, George Washington Cable, and _Joel Chandler Harris_, author of the Uncle Remus stories. New England's golden days were recaptured by _Sarah Orne Jewett_ and Mary E. Wilkins Freeman.

    b. THE PSEUDO-REALISTS. Authors of the 1880's and 1890's wrote realistically of American society, but centered their attention on the upper middle class. _William Dean Howells_ and _Henry James_ were leaders of this school. Both presented accurate and merciless pictures of a society adjusting itself to a machine civilization.

    c. THE REALISTS. By the turn of the century, authors turned their attention to the sufferings of the lower class. Their pioneer was _Hamlin Garland_, whose _Main-Travelled Roads_ (1891) painted a savage picture of the drab life of a Middle-Western farmer. _Stephen Crane's Maggie, A Girl of the Streets_ (1892), which showed how society turned an innocent girl into a prostitute, was the first novel to picture the urban world realistically. Others who wrote in this tradition were _Frank Norris_ and _Jack London_.

    2. Progress in Painting and Sculpture. Scorning tradition, artists executed bold, realistic treatments of the American landscape and figure which bore little resemblance to the romanticized portraits of an earlier generation.

    a. PAINTING. American painters trained in France began returning to the United States in the 1870's. The _Society of American Artists_ (1877) which they organized to popularize their less conventional concepts included a number of excellent artists. _George Inness_ was a leading landscapist; _Winslow Homer_ was famed for his bold pictures of the sea; _James A. McNeill Whistler_ painted middle-class portraits realistically. The leading muralist was _John La Farge_.

    b. SCULPTURE. The foremost of many sculptors was _Augustus Saint-Gaudens_, whose statues did much to beautify the urban landscape. His figure on the tomb of Mrs. Henry Adams is considered by some to be the best in the history of

American sculpture. _Daniel Chester French,_ while less original, was also justly famed.

3. Progress in Architecture. The overornate homes and fantastic jigsaw ornamentation that made the hideous Victorian Gothic buildings of the period even more hideous helped characterize this as the "gilded age." Yet two important developments occurred:

a. RICHARDSON ROMANESQUE ARCHITECTURE was introduced by _Henry Hobson Richardson,_ whose first important building was the Trinity Church in Boston (1877). The comparative simplicity of this style, which was based on French Romanesque architecture, set a good example that others eventually imitated.

b. THE SKYSCRAPER was America's unique contribution to architectural beauty. Resulting from the necessity of space saving in urban centers, skyscrapers were first built in Chicago, where tradition was less strong than in the East. The Home Insurance Building (1885) set the pattern by towering ten stories high. The leading skyscraper architect was _Louis Sullivan,_ whose emphasis on functionalism as a basis for design has influenced building ever since.

4. Music. American contributions to music were few; only _Edward A. McDowell_ earned his reputation as a composer. More significant was the spread of musical appreciation among the people. The _New York Symphony Orchestra_ (1878) and the Boston Symphony Orchestra (1881) were followed by others in leading cities. The Metropolitan Opera House in New York was opened in 1883.

VI. THE RISE OF THE CITY: AN APPRAISAL. The city was the crowning monument to American industrialization. In it were focused the best and the worst innovations of the machine age:

A. Harmful Results of Urbanization. The slums, poverty, and class conflicts that centered in cities were the normal products of the transition taking place in American society. The humanitarians who expressed concern for the plight of the poor or who sought to improve the lot of workers did their best to convert the new social order to the uses of the many, but without success. Even today the United States is seeking a means of adjusting itself to a form of civilization not yet fully understood.

B. Beneficial Results of Urbanization. The rise of the city stimulated cultural progress as had nothing in America's past. The ease with which men of like interests could meet in cities, the wealth made available by a concentration of property, and the educational opportunities offered in thickly settled communities laid the basis for a cultural upsurge of lasting benefit. Even more significant was the gradual adjustment of the arts to the popular taste. The democratization of culture was an American contribution of the machine age.

ADDITIONAL READING

Standard histories of urbanization include Blake McKelvey, *The Urbanization of America* (1963), and Charles N. Glaab and A. Theodore Brown, *A History of Urban America* (1967). General interpretations of the impact of the city and industry on American culture are Gilman Ostrander, *American Civilization in the First Machine Age, 1890-1940* (1970), which argues that mechanization altered the whole nature of the nation's thought; and John Tomsich, *A Genteel Endeavor: American Culture and Politics in the Gilded Age* (1971), which studies a number of the leading writers, Daniel J. Boorstin, *The Americans: The Democratic Experience* (1973), brilliantly explains the democratization of American culture since 1865. Richard Hofstadter, *The Age of Reform* (1955), suggests challenging interpretations, while Chester McA. Destler, *American Radicalism, 1865-1901* (1946), deals with radical thinkers. The standard biographical treatments of two reformers are Charles A. Barker, *Henry George* (1955); and S. E. Bowman, *The Year 2000* (1958), on Edward Bellamy. S. R. Spencer, *Booker T. Washington* (1955), is also reliable, as is Ray Ginger, *The Bending Cross* (1949), on Eugene V. Debs. Readable studies of the influence of industrialism on religion are Aaron I. Abell, *The Urban Impact on American Protestantism* (1943); Henry May, *Protestant Churches and Industrial America* (1949); and Martin E. Marty, *Righteous Empire: The Protestant Experience in America* (1970). Progress in literature is described in Van Wyck Brooks, *The Confident Years, 1885-1915* (1952), and in art in Oliver W. Larkin, *Art and Life in America* (1949). Henry S. Commager, *The American Mind* (1950), is a cultural history of the period.

Chapter VII

The Populist Era
1890-1900

ℭ THE TRIUMPH OF CONSERVATISM

The conflicts of the industrial age reached a climax during the 1890's. On the one hand farmers and workers, better organized than ever before, demanded a greater share of the national wealth. On the other the masters of capital insisted on the right to operate as they pleased without interference from society or government. In this struggle the industrialists were victorious. By 1900 labor unions had been rendered powerless by the use of the injunction; the Sherman Antitrust Act and the Interstate Commerce Act reduced to uselessness by hostile courts; and the farmers so decisively beaten at the polls that they were ready to abandon their battle for economic equality. Yet the conservative triumph led to an inevitable reaction in the form of the Progressive Movement of the early twentieth century.

I. THE AGRARIAN CRUSADE. Farmer unrest, which had died down after the collapse of the Granger movement in the late 1870's (see pp. 57-60), revived in the 1880's.

A. Causes of the Agrarian Unrest.

1. The Social Factor. The rise of the city made the farmer aware of his own grim existence. As he read of gay times in lighted streets, or at theaters and parties, he grew more discontented with the monotonous drudgery of his own calling.

2. *Falling Prices.* The price of agricultural staples declined steadily through the 1880's and 1890's, until wheat sold at sixty-three cents a bushel, corn at thirty cents, and cotton at six cents a pound. The prices paid farmers were even lower. They insisted that they could not make money, but each year went further and further into debt.

3. *Inadequate Rainfall.* For a decade after 1887 rainfall in the West was below normal. On the semiarid plains the resulting droughts ruined thousands of farmers. Even in the Mississippi Valley yields were poor.

4. *Mounting Debts.* These were acquired during a brief boom period from 1880 to 1887. At this time eastern capitalists, seeking safe investments, sent agents through the West who literally pleaded with farmers to borrow money. The temptation was too strong to resist, especially as farmers reasoned that better machinery or more land would offset falling commodity prices. During the decade, as a result, farm mortgage indebtedness almost doubled. By 1890 there was one mortgage for every two persons in Kansas and North Dakota; one for every three in South Dakota, Minnesota, and Nebraska. In the South the situation was made worse by the *crop-lien system;* there a farmer mortgaged his growing crop at high interest rates to carry himself until harvest time. If the crop was not profitable, he lost his whole year's income.

5. *Growth of Farm Tenancy.* Mortgage foreclosures increased as low crop prices prevented farmers from paying their debts. By 1890 one-fourth of the farmers of Kansas were tenants or share croppers. In other western states the situation was nearly as bad. Apparently the United States was developing a peasant class.

B. **The Farmers' Solution.** Farmers reasoned that a more plentiful money supply would allow them to pay off their debts as well as increase the price of crops. Inflation was their principal demand through the 1880's and 1890's.

1. *The Monetary Problem.* Three types of money were in circulation in 1890: 1) *greenbacks* to the set sum of $346,681,012. 2) *National bank notes* issued by National banks on the basis of government bonds in their vaults. These decreased steadily as the retirement of the national

debt canceled bonds; the number in circulation declined from
$339,000,000 in 1873 to $168,000,000 in 1890. 3) _Gold
coins_ which increased in quantity only slowly; so little gold
was mined during this period that newly minted coins barely
replaced the National bank notes that were retired from
circulation.   Hence the nation's money supply, which
amounted to $2,000,000,000 in 1865, was no larger in 1890
despite a doubled population and a tripled business activity.
Farmers maintained that as debtors they suffered especially
from the declining purchasing power of the dollar. They
pointed out that a dollar that bought one bushel of wheat in
1865 paid for two bushels in 1890. Yet debts did not decline proportionately. This meant that a farm debtor had to
produce two bushels of wheat (at fifty cents a bushel) to pay
for a dollar he had borrowed when wheat was worth one
dollar a bushel.

2. The Answer to the Problem. The farmers' solution
was to increase the money supply either by printing more
greenbacks or by coining silver dollars.

a. THE GREENBACK INTERLUDE. Congressional enactment of the Resumption Act of 1875, which made greenbacks redeemable in gold, aroused protest in the form of the
Greenback Party (1878). This demanded the continued circulation of paper money and other reforms. Its nominee in
the election of 1880, _James B. Weaver_ of Iowa, polled only
300,000 votes, largely from among Mississippi Valley farmers. This meagre support doomed the party, although the
fourteen congressmen that it elected joined with Democrats
to prevent a further contraction of the number of greenbacks in circulation.

b. FREE SILVER. The farmer knew that large quantities
of silver were mined in the West. He also knew that through
most of the nation's history both gold and silver coins were
minted, a system known as _bimetallism_. This required that
the amount of precious metal in both types of coins be
exactly balanced: that the gold in a gold dollar be worth just
as much as the silver in a silver dollar. For some time this
ratio had been 16 to 1; there had been sixteen times as much
silver in a silver dollar as there was gold in a gold dollar.
This ratio had been upset by the gold discoveries after 1849.

So much was mined that it became less valuable, in relation to silver, than this ratio recognized. Hence silver dollars disappeared from circulation as they were melted down for the commercial sale of the precious metal. Congress recognized this situation in 1873 by ordering that no more silver dollars be coined, placing the country on a gold basis. No sooner was this done than new silver mines were opened. This metal became so plentiful that, if coined into dollars, the money supply would be greatly inflated. Farmers realized too late that the *Crime of 1873* (the Coinage Act mentioned above) had deprived them of a cheaper circulating medium. They demanded that the law be repealed and the *free and unlimited coinage of silver at the ratio of 16 to 1* be restored.

C. Stages of Organization. Once more, as in the Granger period, farmers organized to agitate for *"free silver."*

1. The Farmers' Alliances. Organization began in the South with the formation of the National Farmers' Alliance (1879) and the Agricultural Wheel (1882). These were combined in 1887 as the *Southern Farmers' Alliance,* with three million members. In the meantime the *Northern Farmers' Alliance,* formed in 1880, attracted two million members by 1890. Delegates from the northern and southern Alliances met in 1889 to agree upon a common program. This included support for free silver, a graduated income tax, government ownership of the railroads, and other reforms. Independent local parties based on this platform placed Alliance candidates in many offices in the *elections of 1890,* as well as sending fifty-three congressmen to Washington. Their success was due to the fanatical enthusiasm of the farmers. This was engendered by such inspirational speakers as *Pitchfork Ben Tillman* of South Carolina, *Sockless Jerry Simpson* of Kansas, *Ignatius Donnelly* of Minnesota, *James B. Weaver* of Iowa, and *Mary Lease* of Kansas, who won a place in every history textbook by urging farmers to "raise less corn and more Hell."

2. The Populist Party. Encouraged by their success in 1890, representatives of northern and southern Alliances met at Cincinnati in May, 1891, to form a new party. This they called the *People's Party,* or Populist Party. A second convention held at Omaha on July 4, 1892, nominated *James B. Weaver* as the party's presidential candidate and adopted the *Omaha Platform,* which promised a long list of progressive reforms: 1) free silver at the ratio of 16 to 1; 2) a circulating medium of $50 a person; 3) economy in government; 4) a graduated income tax; 5) postal savings banks; 6) government ownership of railroads and telegraph lines; 7) the direct election of senators; 8) the use of the initiative and referendum. This platform remained the ideal of progressives for a generation.

II. POLITICAL DEVELOPMENTS, 1892-1896.

A. The Election of 1892. The two principal issues were the Tariff (see pp. 51-54) and the money question. The Democrats nominated *Grover Cleveland,* whose support for a lower tariff was made clear during his first administration (1885-1889). *Benjamin Harrison* was renominated by the Republicans, despite his mediocre record between 1889 and 1892. Cleveland was elected by 277 electoral votes to 145 for Harrison. The remaining 22 electoral votes went to *James B. Weaver,* the *People's Party* candidate, who received a million popular votes. Cleveland's election was due primarily to hatred of the *McKinley Tariff* (see p. 54) and to his reputation for honesty.

B. The Second Cleveland Administration. The tariff and money issues that had so influenced the election remained the principal problems.

1. The Tariff Problem. Cleveland interpreted his election as a popular mandate for a lower tariff, especially as the McKinley Tariff had turned a $100,000,000 surplus in 1890 into a $70,000,000 deficit by 1894. Administration views were incorporated in the *Wilson Bill,* drafted by William L. Wilson, chairman of the House Ways and Means Committee. As adopted by the House in February, 1894, this was designed to increase the revenue while decreasing protection. Basic raw materials used in manufacturing—sugar, lumber, wool, iron ore, etc.—were admitted duty free while duties on manufactured goods were lowered. To offset the loss of revenue, higher taxes were levied on liquor, tobacco, and other luxuries. The bill also included the country's first *income tax:* a 2 per cent levy on incomes over $4000. The senate quickly ended Cleveland's hope of tariff reform. Under the influence of a swarm of lobbyists and such pro-tectionist Democrats as *A. P. Gorham* of Maryland, 634 amendments were added, most of them revising levels up-ward. The *Wilson-Gorham Tariff* (1894) lowered duties slightly, to about 40 per cent, but continued protection. Cleveland's hopes suffered another blow when the Supreme Court ruled in the case of *Pollock v. Farmers' Loan and Trust Company* (1895) that an income tax was unconsti-tutional.

2. The Money Problem.

a. BACKGROUND OF THE PROBLEM. Before Cleveland's election Congress had made two concessions to inflationists: 1) the *Bland-Allison Act* (1878) required the Secretary of the Treasury to purchase from $2,000,000 to $4,000,000 worth of silver bullion monthly for coinage into dollars; and 2) the *Sherman Silver Purchase Act* (1890) increased the amount of silver that the Treasury Department was forced to purchase to 4,500,000 ounces a month—about double the former quantity. This silver bullion was paid for in legal-tender treasury notes, redeemable in either gold or silver as the government decreed. The practice was always followed of redeeming the notes in gold, thus preserving the gold standard. Hence the measures did little to satisfy the sil-verites.

b. THE PANIC OF 1893. The money problem became acute after the *Panic of 1893*. This was caused by: 1) the decline of farmer purchasing power, which decreased the demand for manufactured goods; 2) a European depression which curtailed foreign markets; 3) speculative overinvest-ment in railroads and industrial plants; and 4) fears created among businessmen by the threat of free silver. This last was the immediate cause of the panic. For some time finan-ciers had agreed that the nation's finances would remain sound only so long as the gold reserve—set up in 1879 to redeem greenbacks—remained over $100,000,000. After the passage of the Sherman Silver Purchase Act this reserve was subjected to unusual pressure as both greenbacks and silver certificates were redeemed. Only a few weeks after

Cleveland's inauguration it dipped below $100,000,000. As fear spread, people rushed to obtain gold for their Greenbacks or treasury notes, further depleting the fund. In the resulting panic, business failures mounted, banks closed, 156 railroads went into receivership, and unemployment mounted until 4,000,000 men were out of work by the summer of 1894. So desperate was their plight that an army of unemployed from the Middle West, led by "General" Jacob Coxey, marched on Washington to demand a work-relief program financed by noninterest-paying bonds. *"Coxey's Army"* aroused more ridicule than sympathy.

c. CLEVELAND AND THE PANIC. Cleveland, a hard-money man, believed that the depression would end only when the public's confidence in the nation's currency was re-established by banishing the threat of inflation. Hence he took two steps:

I. *Repeal of Sherman Silver Purchase Act.* Congress was called into special session in August, 1893, to repeal the Sherman Silver Purchase Act (November, 1893), thus easing the strain on the gold reserve.

II. *Bond Issues.* Gold was borrowed from private interests to rebuild the gold reserve. The first bond issue of $50,000,000 (January, 1894) failed to accomplish this purpose, for the Wall Street syndicate making the loan simply drew gold from the treasury to pay for their bond purchases. A second issue (January, 1895) succeeded when the government stipulated that half the gold must be obtained from abroad. When a third issue of $100,000,000 was floated in January, 1896, public confidence returned and the depression ended. Cleveland's action, however, convinced farmers and workers that he had sold out to Wall Street, preparing the way for a revival of Populism.

III. THE ELECTION OF 1896.

A. Western Discontent. The agrarian revolt reached a climax between 1894 and 1896. This was due to:

1. Western Drought. Conditions were at their worst in 1894 and 1895.

2. Falling Farm Prices. Prices hit new lows as a result of the Panic of 1893, until wheat sold at forty-nine cents a bushel and cotton at six cents a pound.

3. Government Conservatism. Events of 1894-1895 seemed to indicate that both major parties were acting in the interests of Wall Street rather than those of the common people. These included: 1) passage of the Wilson-Gorham Tariff; 2) the smashing of the Pullman strike; 3) the outlawing of the income tax by the Supreme Court; 4) the judicial negation of the Sherman Antitrust Act in the Knight case; 5) the treatment suffered by Coxey's Army; and 6) Cleveland's repeal of the Sherman Silver Purchase Act and his reliance on Wall Street in ending the panic. Many ordinary people were convinced by these events that only the Populist Party had their interests at heart.

4. Effective Propaganda. In the West a small book by William H. Harvey, *Coin's Financial School* (1894), argued for free silver in a language that the common man could understand. It sold 100,000 copies monthly during this period. In the East Henry Demarest Lloyd's *Wealth Against Commonwealth* (1894) convinced thousands that the democratic process had broken down under pressure from Wall Street.

B. Growth of Populist Strength. Under the influence of these forces, enthusiasm for Populism took on some of the fervor of a holy crusade. In the West and South speakers such as *Tom Watson* of Georgia and *Ignatius Donnelly* of Minnesota were cheered by excited thousands. The Populist popular vote in the 1894 elections was half again as large as in 1892, and six Populist senators were sent to Washington. The real gainers, however, were the Republicans, who capitalized on lower-class dissatisfaction with Cleveland to win control of both House and Senate. The Populists, encouraged by their showing, looked forward to the election of 1896.

C. The Nominating Conventions. Populist leaders were aware that large "free-silver blocs" existed in both major parties. Hence they decided to let the Republicans and Democrats stage their nominating conventions first, confident that these silverites would bolt when the parties endorsed a gold standard. The People's Party would then gather in the malcontents, increasing its own strength.

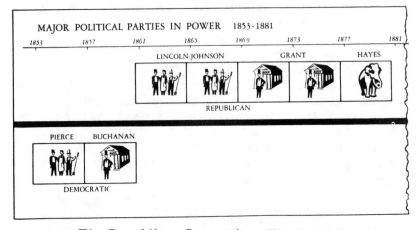

MAJOR POLITICAL PARTIES IN POWER   1853-1881

1. The Republican Convention. The Republicans, confident of victory over the depression-discredited Democrats, assembled in June. Their convention was dominated by *Marcus A. Hanna,* a wealthy Ohio industrialist who had entered politics to satisfy a lust for power. Under his tutelage they nominated *William McKinley* of Ohio, author of the McKinley Tariff and an unwavering conservative. The platform denounced Cleveland's record, praised protection, and advocated a gold currency. On its adoption thirty-four *Silver Republicans,* led by Senator *Henry M. Teller* of Colorado, walked out, announcing that they would support any party favoring free silver.

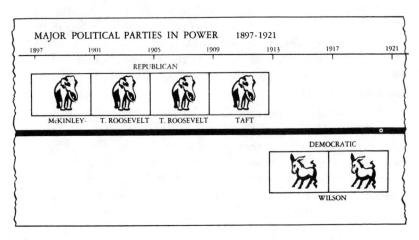

MAJOR POLITICAL PARTIES IN POWER   1897-1921

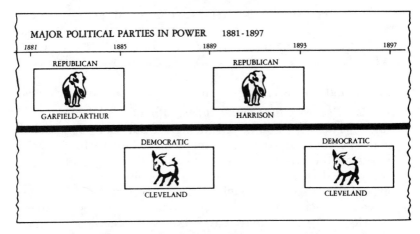

2. *The Democratic Convention.* The Democrats were divided when they met in Chicago on July 7, 1896. Southern and western delegates, led by *William Jennings Bryan* of Nebraska, had been agitating for free silver since 1894, while eastern representatives favored a sound money. The inflationists showed their strength when the platform committee proposed "the free and unlimited coinage of both gold and silver at the present legal ratio of sixteen to one." After supporting this proposition vigorously, they finally carried the day when Bryan delivered his *Cross of Gold speech,* in which he told the delegates: "You shall not press down upon the brow of labor this crown of thorns; you

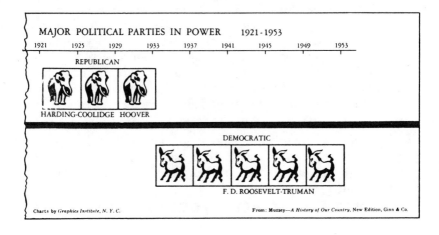

shall not crucify mankind upon a cross of gold." Swept away by this oratory, the convention endorsed free silver and nominated the thirty-six-year-old Bryan as its candidate. The platform was a progressive document that stole much Populist thunder by favoring reduced tariffs, antitrust legislation, and the outlawing of the injunction in labor disputes.

3. The Populist Convention. Populist leaders faced a dilemma: if they nominated their own candidate they would split the silverite vote and hand the election to the Republicans; if they endorsed Bryan's nomination they would submerge their own party. Believing that the nation's salvation depended on a more flexible currency, they did not hesitate. Bryan was selected as the party's nominee, but Tom Watson of Georgia was named vice-presidential candidate rather than the Maine banker, Arthur Sewall, selected by the Democrats. The platform not only advocated free silver but many of the liberal reforms contained in the Omaha Platform of 1892.

D. Campaign and Election.

1. The Campaigns. The *Battle of the Standards*—silver and gold—was bitterly fought. Party lines were ignored as silver Republicans supported Bryan and gold Democrats favored McKinley. Bryan gave thousands of speeches on an 18,000-mile tour, while the Republicans used a $4,000,000 fund to spread advertisements, tracts, and other propaganda everywhere. Newspapers reflected the conservatism of their owners by ridiculing Bryan; industrialists warned their workers that factories would be closed if the Democrats were successful. To make matters worse for Bryan, farm prices advanced sharply during the autumn of 1896, driven upward by grain failures in Russia and Argentina. This, combined with bountiful harvests in the United States, convinced many farmers that their fears were unjustified.

2. Results of the Election. The result was a decisive Republican victory. McKinley's popular vote was 600,000 greater than Bryan's, while the electoral vote was 271 to 176. Republicans carried the Northeast and Middle West; Democrats the South and West.

IV. THE McKINLEY ADMINISTRATION, 1897-

1901. Foreign affairs occupied most of McKinley's attention (see pp. 105-110), but two domestic issues were settled:

A. The Tariff Question. McKinley interpreted his victory as a mandate for protection. With both houses Republican, he called a special session of Congress immediately after his inauguration to enact the _Dingley Tariff_ (1897), which raised duties to a 57 per cent average—the highest in history. Returning prosperity after the Panic of 1893 allowed the Republicans to boast that the tariff was responsible, thus removing the issue from politics for a decade.

B. The Money Question. Prosperity also allowed the Republicans to deal firmly with the currency problem, especially as farm prices continued to rise through 1897 with crop failures in Europe. Sensing the decline of agrarian discontent, McKinley urged Congress to settle the currency issue forever. The result was the _Gold-Standard Act_ (1900) which made all forms of money redeemable in gold, at the same time increasing the gold reserve to $150,000,000.

V. AN APPRAISAL OF A DECADE OF CONSERVATISM.

A. The Triumph of Conservatism. The Populist era closed with conservatism completely triumphant. McKinley's election was only one part of a broad pattern of victory that included protective tariffs, the defeat of the income tax, judicial approval of the labor injunction, the negation of the Sherman Antitrust Act, and the imperialism of the Spanish-American War (see pp. 105-107). Farmers and workers had some reason to feel by 1900 that the cause of progressivism was permanently lost.

B. Nature of the Issues. Actually the battles of the 1890's were not fought between "conservatives" on the one hand and "radicals" on the other, nor was the progressive defeat more than temporary. Considered broadly, the farmers who supported Bryan were more conservative than the industrialists who espoused McKinley's cause. Their inspiration was not Karl Marx but Thomas Jefferson. They wanted a return to an earlier day when farmers shaped the nation's policies in the interest of agrarianism, when free competition rather than monopolistic greed regulated prices, when natural economic laws rather than a "money power" governed the flow of currency, and when the people rather than lobbyists for special interests controlled the government. In their insistence on a return to the practices of an earlier day the Populists were the true "conservatives."

C. Implications for the Future. Because the Populists' demands were in keeping with the American tradition, they could not be long denied. After the turn of the century, when the Progressive Period allowed the people to regain partial control of their nation's government and economy, the liberal program outlined in the Omaha Platform was gradually realized.

ADDITIONAL READING

Solon J. Buck, *The Agrarian Crusade* (1921), is brief but outdated; more satisfactory for the post-Granger era is John D. Hicks, *The Populist Revolt* (1931). Excellent for one agrarian protest is Irwin Unger, *The Greenback Era: A Social and Political History of American Finance, 1865-1879* (1964); discontent in the South is traced in Theodore Saloutos, *Farmer Movements in the South, 1865-1933* (1960). Nathan Fine, *Labor and Farmer Parties in the United States* (1929), stresses political developments. Sound biographies of Populist leaders include: C. Vann Woodward, *Tom Watson* (1938); Francis B. Simkins, *Pitchfork Ben Tillman* (1944); and Martin Ridge, *Ignatius Donnelly* (1962). Expert studies of the monetary question that exploded in Populism are Walter T. K. Nugent, *Money and American Society, 1865-1880* (1968), and Allen Weinstein, *Prelude to Populism: Origins of the Silver Issue, 1867-1878* (1970). Norman Pollock, *The Populist Response to Industrial America* (1962), stresses the impact of Populism on American reform. Recent biographies of the 1896 Populist candidate are Paolo E. Coletta, *William Jennings Bryan: Political Evangelist, 1860-1908* (1964); Charles M. Wilson, *The Commoner: William Jennings Bryan* (1970), which adds nothing to the story; and Louise W. Koenig, *Bryan: A Political Biography* (1971), a sound study. The election of 1896 is studied in Stanley L. Jones, *The Presidential Election of 1896* (1964), and Robert F. Durden, *The Climax of Populism: The Election of 1896* (1965).

CHAPTER VIII

America and the World

1877-1900

℃ THE END OF GEOGRAPHIC ISOLATION
Industrialization was responsible for a transformation in American foreign policy; each year after the Civil War the United States played a larger role in world affairs until by 1900 it had become an imperialistic nation, with colonies scattered over the globe and a prominent voice in international affairs. The overseas areas that interested the people, however, remained those of the prewar era. Americans were still indifferent to Europe and Africa, but increasingly concerned with Latin America and Asia. Interest in the southern hemisphere resulted from the application of the Monroe Doctrine to that region; interest in the Pacific area followed a pattern established by the China traders of the early Republic and implemented by such diplomatic steps as the commercial treaty with China of 1844 and Commodore Matthew Perry's opening of Japan to American trade in 1853.

I. THE ORIGINS OF AMERICAN IMPERIAL-ISM. America's new world role was forced on the nation by developments at home and abroad.

A. Causes for Growth of Imperialism.

1. The International Scene.

a. WORLD TRADE. Industrialization led to a demand for markets and raw materials. Hence the foreign trade of the United States increased from $400,000,000 in 1865 to $1,600,000,000 in 1890. More important than this expansion was the fact that more and more manufactured goods were exported. These could best be sold in the "underdeveloped" countries, whose primitive peoples were in constant danger of being engulfed by Europe's imperialistic powers unless the United States took them first. Diplomacy was needed to keep these markets open.

b. CAPITAL INVESTMENTS. Industrialization increased the amount of American capital available for investment. Financiers, seeking high interest returns, turned to underdeveloped areas where the risk was greatest and the rates correspondingly higher. Having made these investments they called on the government to protect their capital. Between 1870 and 1900 the sums invested abroad increased from nothing to $500,000,000.

c. THE EUROPEAN EXAMPLE. After the Franco-Prussian War (1871), newly united Germany and Italy entered the rush for colonial possessions, grabbing off such extensive territories in Africa and Asia that the other powers moved into action. In the scramble that followed, most of the primitive areas of the world were appropriated. The United States, increasingly aware of its physical pre-eminence among nations, hurried to get its share before everything was taken.

2. The Domestic Scene.

a. THE CLOSING OF THE FRONTIER. The gradual exhaustion of western lands, climaxed by the announcement in 1890 that the frontier no longer existed, bred expansionistic sentiment among the American people. With their own frontier closed they demanded lands elsewhere to which they could move.

b. IMPERIALISTIC PROPAGANDA. Numerous writers during the 1880's and 1890's urged overseas expansion. Typical was the Reverend Josiah Strong, whose book, *Our Country* (1885), proclaimed Anglo-Saxon superiority and stressed the nation's duty to extend its civilization over "backward" peoples everywhere. Equally important was Captain *Alfred T. Mahan,* a retired naval officer, whose numerous books glorified a large navy and preached the *Manifest Destiny* of the United States to rule "lesser" people.

c. MISSIONARY PRESSURE. Overseas missionaries had been active since the 1820's, particularly in the Pacific area. Now they demanded government aid, pointing out that the conversion of the "benighted heathen" would be easier under American rule. Their appeal was backed by many religious people.

d. NAVAL PRESSURE. America's modern navy originated in 1883 when Congress authorized the first steel cruisers. From that time on construction proceeded rapidly, until by 1893 the United States stood fifth in naval strength among the world's powers, and in 1900, third. Such a weapon tempted the people to test its strength.

B. Growth of Internationalism. The new global consciousness of the United States was shown by its willingness to enter into:

1. Collective Treaties. Between 1865 and 1900 fifteen treaties were signed dealing with such matters as cables, weights and measures, patents, etc.

2. International Agreements. Most famous of these was the *Geneva Convention* (1882) to establish the International Red Cross. This was largely the result of personal efforts by an American woman, *Clara Barton,* who was also responsible for the "American Amendment" (1884) allowing the Red Cross to undertake peacetime relief programs.

II. AMERICAN POLICY IN THE PACIFIC, 1877-1895.

A. The Hawaiian Islands.

1. Origins of Hawaiian Policy. American traders, whalers, and missionaries first interested the United States in the Hawaiian Islands during the early nineteenth century. In 1842 the State Department announced that the islands would not be open to colonization by any other nation, but a treaty of annexation was defeated by the Senate a few years later. The next important step was the *Reciprocity Treaty of 1875* which gave sugar and other native products the right to enter the United States duty free in return for a pledge by the Hawaiian king not to dispose of his territory to any other power. In 1884 the United States leased the excellent naval base at Pearl Harbor.

2. Steps Toward Annexation.

a. SUGAR AND THE TARIFF. The Reciprocity Treaty of 1875 stimulated sugar production. By 1890 sugar plantations owned by Americans were valued at $25,000,000 while the island's exports of $20,000,000 yearly all went to the United States. This thriving trade was upset by the _McKinley Tariff_ (1890), which placed all sugar on the free list and provided for bounties to American sugar growers. Moreover, a native ruler, Queen Liluokalani, or _Queen Lil_ as she was called, who had just ascended the Hawaiian throne, determined to confiscate all plantations and drive foreigners from the islands. Under these circumstances the sugar planters determined to seek American annexation; this would protect their estates from Queen Lil and also place their sugar within the tariff wall.

b. PROBLEM OF ANNEXATION. The planters, probably with the aid of the American minister, staged a revolution in January, 1893, then asked to be annexed. President _Benjamin Harrison_ was willing, but before a treaty could be negotiated _Grover Cleveland_ became President (March 4, 1893). A foe of imperialism, he withdrew the annexation treaty after investigation showed that the revolution did not represent native wishes. He did extend _recognition_ to the American-dominated government of the _Republic of Hawaii_.

B. The Samoan Islands.

1. Origins of American Interest.
The Samoan Islands of the South Pacific had been visited by sailors and missionaries since the 1830's. In 1872 a naval officer negotiated an agreement that gave the United States the fine harbor of _Pago Pago_ on the island of Tutuila; this arrangement was embodied in a formal treaty in 1878.

2. Efforts Toward Annexation.
The United States showed no desire to annex the islands until the 1880's when Germany and England also became interested in them. A musical-comedy war between adherents of these three powers reached a climax in 1889 when a German threat of annexation drew naval vessels of the three powers to the harbor at Pago Pago. The threat of conflict passed when a hurricane wrecked the fleets. Instead, the three nations entered into a _tripartite protectorate_ over the islands, the first "entangling

alliance" in the history of the United States. This was terminated in 1899 when the islands were divided between Germany and the United States, England receiving compensation elsewhere.

III. LATIN-AMERICAN POLICY, 1877-1895.

A. Pan-Americanism. Until the 1870's the United States interpreted the _Monroe Doctrine_ in a negative way: as an instrument to keep European nations from meddling in the western hemisphere. After that time the doctrine was transformed into a positive device to secure for the United States political primacy and economic favoritism among the American Republics.

1. International Arbitration. The United States first displayed its new aggressivism by offering to serve as mediator in disputes between Latin-American countries. Thus a boundary dispute between Argentina and Paraguay was settled in 1876, another between Mexico and Guatemala considered in 1881, and an attempt made to stop a war between Chile, Peru, and Bolivia over the nitrate districts of Tacna and Arica. England and the United States also arbitrated (1891) the _Bering Sea Controversy_ between Canadian and American seal fishermen.

2. Pan-American Congresses.

a. Origins of the Congresses. The originator was _James G. Blaine,_ Secretary of State under Garfield (1881) and Harrison (1889-1892). Knowing that the Latin-American countries sold most of their raw materials to the United States, yet purchased their manufactured goods in Europe, he proposed to secure a share of this market for American manufacturers by setting up a customs union. This would give Latin-American goods reciprocal preference in American ports in return for similar concessions by South American countries. His purpose in calling the first Pan-American Congress was to arrange this reciprocity.

b. The First Congress. Blaine called the first Congress in 1889 when delegates from eighteen countries met at Washington. His proposal of a customs union aroused no interest among the Latin Americans, who knew that 87 per cent of their goods entered the United States duty free.

Hence the sole result of the conference was the creation of the _Pan-American Union_ to serve as a clearing house for commercial information. Blaine obtained acceptance for his reciprocal trade plan when the McKinley Tariff (1890) included provisions for reciprocity with ten countries, but the policy was not generally adopted until the administration of Franklin D. Roosevelt.

B. Threats to Latin-American Friendship. Two incidents upset any international good will created by Blaine's Pan-Americanism:

1. The Chilean Episode. The United States minister to Chile, _Patrick Egan,_ adopted a hostile attitude toward a new government that took control of the country after a revolution in 1890-1891. The controversy reached a climax in October, 1891, when two American sailors were killed and eighteen wounded during a barroom brawl in Valparaiso. President Benjamin Harrison treated this fight as an international incident, demanding satisfaction which the Chilean government was unwilling to give. War was averted by the election of a new government in Chile, but the attitude of the United States left a bad impression throughout Latin America.

2. The Venezuelan Boundary Dispute. An ancient boundary dispute between Venezuela and British Guiana assumed new importance with the discovery of gold in the disputed area. Venezuela was willing to arbitrate, but England refused. Acting on the assumption that Britain's attitude violated the Monroe Doctrine by threatening the territory of a Latin-American power, President _Grover Cleveland_ through his Secretary of State, _Richard Olney,_ on July 20, 1895, warned that "grave consequences" would follow unless the British acceded. They answered in a blunt message (November 26, 1895) stating that the Monroe Doctrine was not involved and that the United States had no right to intervene. Cleveland then asked Congress to appoint a boundary commission whose findings the United States would enforce in any way necessary. Although Congress responded to this request, the President was condemned by newspapers and business leaders for creating a war scare. English opinion was also outspoken for peace.

This popular attitude, combined with the approach of the *Boer War* in Africa, forced England to back down and submit the dispute to arbitration. A tribunal eventually awarded most of the disputed area to British Guiana (1899). The incident not only strengthened the Monroe Doctrine but gave the United States new prestige in European eyes. The unexpected show of power, however, alarmed Latin Americans.

IV. THE SPANISH-AMERICAN WAR. The final break in cordial relations between the United States and Latin America came with the Spanish-American War.

A. The Cuban Question.

1. Background. The United States had been interested in Cuba for half a century. Its attitude was shown in the *Ten Years' War* (1868-1878) in which Cubans fought to free their island from Spain. During this struggle many filibustering expeditions from American ports aided the rebels. One vessel, the *Virginius*, was captured by Spain (1873) and eight Americans executed. War threatened until Spain apologized and paid an indemnity. The Ten Years' War ended with the Spanish victorious and the Cubans burdened with even heavier war taxes.

2. Changing American Attitude. Between the Ten Years' War and the 1890's the United States became much more interested in Cuba. This was due to:

a. ECONOMIC PENETRATION. American capital flowed into Cuba during the 1880's until investments there totaled $50,000,000 by 1893, while trade with the island amounted to $100,000,000 yearly. Moreover, the United States was dependent on Cuban sugar.

b. STRATEGIC INTERESTS. The growth of the navy made strategists aware of the need for Caribbean naval bases, especially as plans matured for a canal across Central America. Cuban bases would be necessary to protect this.

c. SPIRIT OF MANIFEST DESTINY. As Americans wakened to the fact that the United States was a major power, they paid increasing attention to the plight of "backward" people. The country's imperialistic destiny was the theme of Congressional orators such as *Albert J. Beveridge* and *Henry Cabot Lodge,* and of such scholars as Frank H. Giddings and John W. Burgess. Jingoistic newspapers also preached the need of expansion into "backward" areas. As a result the American people were far more ready to accept war with Spain in the 1890's than in the 1870's.

d. NEWSPAPER PROPAGANDA. Led by the *New York World* of *Joseph Pulitzer* and the *New York Journal* of *William Randolph Hearst,* the nation's "yellow press" was ready to use sensationalism as a circulation-builder, no matter what the cost. Warfare in Cuba allowed papers to print atrocity stories that aroused a demand for intervention.

3. The Cuban Revolution. A new revolt against Spain began in Cuba in February, 1895. This was caused by: 1) the continued autocratic rule of Spain; 2) the exploitation of Cuban peasants by Spanish landlords; and 3) the *tariff policy* of the United States. The latter was important. The McKinley Tariff (1890), which placed sugar on the free list, encouraged the expansion of sugar growing on the island. This was followed by the Wilson-Gorham Tariff (1894) which levied a 40 per cent duty on Cuban sugar, ruining the island's economy. The suffering that resulted drove the Cubans to revolt. In the fighting that followed, the insurgents adopted a policy of guerrilla warfare. The Spanish army, unable to capture the actual rebels, threw thousands of peasants into *Reconcentrados,* or concentration camps, where they died like flies. In one province alone, 50,000 perished.

4. American Interest in the Revolution.

a. SYMPATHY WITH THE CUBANS. This was fanned by newspaper accounts of suffering in the concentration camps. The *New York World* and the *New York Journal* particularly vied with each other in printing atrocity stories under blazing headlines. War was also demanded after a Spanish gunboat fired on an American ship, the *Alliance.*

b. POLICY OF GROVER CLEVELAND. Cleveland, who was President when the Cuban revolution began, did all in his power to preserve neutrality. Although recognizing a state of rebellion in Cuba, he refused to recognize the revolutionists as belligerents, despite a congressional resolution favoring such a step (1896).

c. Policy of William McKinley. McKinley was elected (1896) on a platform calling for Cuban independence.

i. _Events Leading to War._ McKinley's firm attitude toward Spain forced that country to modify its _reconcentración_ policy (1897) and to offer the Cubans a larger share of self-government. The Cubans refused, insisting on independence. At this point two events occurred that plunged the United States into war: 1) the publication of the _De Lome Letter_ (February, 1898), written by Dupuy de Lome, the Spanish minister to Washington. In this private letter, which was stolen from the Havana post office, he called McKinley a would-be politician interested only in the plaudits of the crowd. Spain's refusal to disavow the letter aroused great indignation. 2) The _sinking of the battleship Maine_ in Havana Harbor on February 15, 1898. The vessel was sunk by an external explosion with a loss of 260 men.

ii. _Preparation for War._ The sinking of the _Maine_ united American opinion behind war. Congress appropriated $50,000,000 for military purposes, but McKinley still sought to maintain the peace desired by financial and business interests. On March 27, 1898, he sent an ultimatum to Spain, asking an immediate armistice, the end of the _reconcentración_ policy, and American mediation of peace terms. The Spanish queen accepted the armistice proposal on April 9, apparently ending the threat of war.

iii. _Declaration of War._ Despite Spain's retreat, the popular clamor for war was so great that McKinley feared he would sacrifice the leadership of his party unless he acceded. Hence he sent a message to Congress on April 11 that ignored Spain's concessions and asked for a declaration of war. Congress responded on _April 17._ At the same time it adopted the _Teller Amendment_ which pledged the United States to acquire no Cuban territory and to turn the island over to its people as soon as their independence was won.

B. The Defeat of Spain. The war was so popular in the United States that a special bond issue of $200,000,000 was subscribed at once and additional taxes accepted without protest. These funds were used to raise the regular army from 28,000 to 62,000 men and to equip 200,000 volunteers.

Spain still enjoyed a military advantage, with an army of 200,000 men in Cuba and a navy that outranked that of the United States.

1. The War in Cuba. An expeditionary force of 15,000 Americans landed near Santiago, Cuba, between June 20 and June 25, 1898. The 1700 Spanish troops opposing them were defeated at the battles of El Caney and *San Juan Hill.* In the latter, volunteer cavalry recruited by Colonel *Theodore Roosevelt,* the "Rough Riders," gained the fame that helped make Roosevelt president. *Santiago* fell on July 13, 1898. The seven Spanish vessels in the harbor fled, but all were destroyed by a blockading American squadron. At the same time the bloodless conquest of Spanish Puerto Rico was begun by troops under General Nelson A. Miles.

2. The War in the Pacific. As soon as war was declared, Commodore *George Dewey,* with six cruisers, set out from Hong Kong for the Spanish-owned Philippines. On May 1, 1898, he ran the guns at *Manila Bay* and destroyed the entire Spanish fleet of seven vessels without losing an American life. The city of Manila was then besieged with the help of natives under *Emilio Aguinaldo* who were fighting for Filipino independence. Manila fell on August 13. In the meantime a lone cruiser captured *Guam* and other tiny islands scattered widely over the Pacific.

3. Cost of the War. Only 289 Americans were killed in battle, yet for every one of these, thirteen died of disease. At one time 75 per cent of the troops in Cuba were sick with yellow fever or malaria, despite the efficiency of the Red Cross. Improper clothing, inadequate health measures, and faulty medical knowledge were responsible. Public criticism led to an important discovery. In 1900 an army medical board under Major *Walter Reed* proved that yellow fever was transmitted by the bite of a species of mosquito. This knowledge allowed the subsequent American penetration of Central America with a minimum of risk from disease.

4. The Peace Terms.

a. THE TREATY OF PEACE. After three months of war, Spain began peace negotiations which ended in an armistice on August 12, 1898. The final peace treaty was signed at

Paris on December 10, 1898, after being dictated by the American commissioners. Cuba was handed over to the United States until it was ready for independence, while Puerto Rico and Guam were also annexed. The Philippines were taken but Spain was paid $20,000,000 in return.

b. THE PHILIPPINE QUESTION. The annexation of the Philippines marked a break with tradition. They were part of the Asiatic coast line, inhabited by an alien people, offered no room for American expansion, and could never expect statehood. McKinley apparently did not intend taking them when the war ended, but changed his mind between August and December, 1898, because: 1) the American people, who had been made imperialistically minded overnight by their military victories, demanded annexation; 2) businessmen awakened to the possibility of trade with millions of Orientals through the Philippine gateway; 3) missionaries who wanted the islands to safeguard their efforts emphasized the "white man's burden"; and 4) strategists insisted that if the United States did not take them, Germany or Japan would. The latter danger was made clear during the war when the presence of a German fleet near Manila precipitated a series of incidents that made scare headlines in the United States.

c. THE CONTEST OVER RATIFICATION. Anti-imperialistic sentiment was first shown when the treaty was placed before the Senate. The spokesman for this point of view was _George F. Hoar_ of Massachusetts, a Republican, who argued that annexation of the Philippines would submit the natives to rule without their own consent. Imperialists, led by _Albert J. Beveridge_ of Indiana, stressed the commercial and strategic advantages of ownership, and deplored _"hauling down the flag."_ Their arguments triumphed when the treaty was ratified (February 6, 1898) by a two-vote majority.

V. THE NEW PACIFIC POLICY, 1895-1900. Ownership of the Philippines committed the United States to a more aggressive policy on the Far East. That this met popular favor was shown in July, 1898, when the _Hawaiian Islands_ were annexed with scarcely a dissenting voice raised. The nation's destiny now required naval bases, no matter how acquired.

A. The Chinese Problem. The Sino-Japanese War (1894-1895), in which the Japanese wrested Formosa and other areas from China, demonstrated to European powers the weakness of the Chinese Empire. The result was a mad scramble for territorial concessions there; during the next five years England, France, Germany, and Russia obtained naval bases, ports, and spheres of influence. This alarmed the United States, where businessmen realized that the Philippines would be valueless if all China was closed to American trade. Missionaries also insisted that they could continue to operate in the Far East only with government protection.

B. The Open Door Policy. Great Britain was as concerned as the United States, for her trade with China was also threatened. In 1898 she proposed a joint alliance to protect trading rights, but this was rejected. Instead, *John Hay*, McKinley's able Secretary of State, in September, 1899, issued a series of notes to the powers, asking them to accept an *Open Door Policy* in China. This meant that all nations controlling portions of China would grant free trading opportunities—including equal tariffs, railroad rates, and harbor duties—to all nations. When all but Russia agreed, Hay announced the Open Door Policy to be in operation.

C. The Boxer Rebellion. Aroused by the plunder of their nation, some of the more nationalistic Chinese formed a secret society, the *Boxers,* to drive out the "foreign devils." In June, 1900, the members laid siege to the foreign legations of Peiping and massacred three hundred people. A joint expeditionary force, including 2500 Americans, was sent to the aid of the beleagured residents. At the same time Secretary of State Hay announced that the United States would oppose any attack on the territorial integrity of China. Hay carried out this policy with great difficulty after the rebellion was crushed, but in October, 1900, England and Germany agreed to the Open Door and the preservation of Chinese independence. He could not, however, prevent the powers from laying heavy indemnities on China. Of the $25,000,000 awarded the United States, the government returned $17,000,000. The Chinese showed their gratitude by setting aside money to send their students to American colleges.

VI. IMPERIALISM: GOOD OR EVIL? Did the nation—and the world—benefit from the altered foreign policy of the United States? What were the results of the new imperialism?

A. The Myth of Isolationism Was Shattered. Although never actually isolated from Europe or Asia, the American people had clung to the belief that they could remain aloof from world affairs. This feeling took root between 1815 and 1898 only because no major war was fought during that time; had such a struggle occurred, the Americans would have been involved as they were in the Napoleonic Wars or in World Wars I and II. With the Spanish-American War this myth was discredited, allowing the country to play a larger world role than in the past.

B. The Democratic Principle Was Threatened. Government by consent of the governed had been a fundamental axiom of the American people for a century. Yet in annexing the Philippines, Hawaii, Guam, and Puerto Rico the United States ignored that basic concept. The cause of democracy suffered as a result.

C. American Nationalism Was Intensified. One tragedy of the shrinking world was that the machines which brought men closer physically also created the differences that drove them apart. Antagonisms resulting from friction between nations as they struggled for world possessions laid the basis for the wars of the twentieth century.

D. America's New-World Supremacy Was Confirmed. The expulsion of Spain from Cuba ended a period of history that began with Columbus' voyage. From 1899 on, the United States dominated the western hemisphere.

ADDITIONAL READING

Milton Plesur, *America's Outward Thrust: Approaches to Foreign Affairs, 1865-1890* (1971), clearly surveys foreign policy during the Gilded Age. Brief factual accounts are in general histories of American policy such as Richard W. Leopold, *The Growth of American Foreign Policy* (1962). The emergence of the United States as a world power is the theme of Ernest May, *Imperial Democracy* (1961), while Walter LaFeber, *The New Empire* (1963), is an interpretation of American expansion for the period 1860-1898. Dexter Perkins, *A History of the Monroe Doctrine* (1950), relates expansion to the American national ideal, as does A. K. Weinberg, *Manifest Destiny* (1935). Relations with Samoa and Hawaii are described in G. H. Ryden, *Foreign Policy of the United States in Relation to Samoa* (1933), W. A. Russ, *The Hawaiian Revolution* (1959), and Merze Tate, *Hawaii: Reciprocity or Annexation* (1968. The story of the Spanish-American War is told in Walter Millis, *The Martial Spirit* (1931), and Frank Freidel, *The Splendid Little War* (1958). Military events are discussed in Graham A. Cosmas, *An Army for Empire: The United States Army in the Spanish-American War* (1971). Ernest R. May, *American Imperialism: A Speculative Essay* (1968), examines the forces that converted the United States to imperialism during the war.

CHAPTER IX

The Progressive Period
1900-1917

ℭ THE PROMISE OF PROGRESSIVISM

The triumph of conservatism and imperialism in the 1890's forced middle-class Americans to ask an important question. Should the results of industrialization be farm peasantry, worker poverty, and the exploitation of colonial peoples? And how could these evils be remedied? The answer, they believed, was two-fold; they must: 1) restore the government to the hands of the people, and 2) use that popularly controlled government to regulate industry, finance, transportation, agriculture, and foreign policy in the interest of the many rather than the few. As they carried out that program in the early twentieth century, the United States entered on that phase of its history known as the Progressive Period.

I. THE ORIGINS OF PROGRESSIVISM.

A. European Background. In Europe, where the impact of industrialism was felt earlier than in the United States, the need for government control of business was recognized by the middle of the nineteenth century. Particularly rapid strides were made in the 1880's when _Germany_ under Prince Bismarck adopted a national program of social security—workingmen's compensation, old-age pensions, government care of the sick, etc.—as an answer to the radical Marxian socialists. _England_ followed in the early twentieth century with a New Liberalism responsible for health acts, national housing legislation, social security, accident compensation, minimum-wage laws, old-age pensions, and the like. Similar measures in France and Italy provided an example that the United States could not ignore.

B. American Background.

1. Conditions Demanding Reform.

a. BREAKDOWN OF THE MORAL CODE. As soulless corporations assumed control of American enterprise, the moral code that had assured decency in the individualistic society of the past no longer sufficed. Corporate directors, shifting responsibility for sin from themselves to their companies, engaged in practices they would not have condoned as individuals: the sale of impure food or drugs, use of inferior materials, corrupt weighing of merchandise, fraudulent advertising of stocks, employment of children, and other things harmful to society. Government action was needed to protect the people from exploitation.

b. GROWTH OF MONOPOLIES. The trend toward monopoly continued into the twentieth century, despite the Sherman Antitrust Act (1890). By 1903, 185 monopolies, capitalized at $3,000,000,000, controlled much of the nation's production. These stifled competition from small businesses, charged exhorbitant prices, and exploited workers.

c. CONCENTRATION OF WEALTH. By 1900, as a result of the continued growth of industrial fortunes, 1 per cent of the people owned 50 per cent of the nation's wealth, while the top 12 per cent controlled 90 per cent. The growth of a wealthy class threatened political democracy, for rich industrialists could buy up legislatures or subsidize candidates to protect their interests. Reformers believed that a redistribution of wealth was necessary to restore true democracy.

d. CORRUPTION OF POLITICS. Progressives soon found that before they could work through government to reform business they must reform government itself. This was partly because institutions adopted by an earlier agrarian society proved incapable of functioning in an industrialized civilization, and partly because the mediocre politicians who held office could be bribed or otherwise controlled by industry. Reform of government was as much a part of Progressivism as was the attack on monopoly.

2. Propaganda for Reform.

a. PROTEST OF THE INTELLECTUALS. Intellectuals who diagnosed the ills of society laid the basis for Progressivism. Their pioneer was *Lester F. Ward*, the father of American sociology, whose *Dynamic Sociology* (1883) urged social planning to equalize opportunity for mankind. Equally important was *Thorstein Veblen*, author of *The Theory of the Leisure Class* (1899) and other economic classics, who exposed the inefficiencies of laissez-faire capitalism that retarded the maximum employment of men and machines. Even more influential was *John Dewey*, academic philosopher and educator, who taught that educational, economic, and governmental institutions should be used to change man's environment and thus improve his behavior. Herbert Croly, *The Promise of American Life* (1909), decried "chaotic individualism" and pleaded for government regulation through democratic processes. All these intellectuals, and others like them, had in common their rejection of laissez faire and their belief in *progress through social planning*. This was the theory that underlay Progressivism.

b. THE MUCKRAKERS. Between 1902 and 1908 a group of writers exposed the evils of business monopoly and government corruption in terms understandable to laymen. First of the muckrakers was *Ida M. Tarbell*, whose *History of the Standard Oil Company* appeared in *McClure's Magazine* during 1902-1903. This work set the pattern by describing the way in which Standard Oil fleeced consumers and ruined competitors. It was followed by numerous exposés of other corporations in magazine and book form. Most important among these were: Thomas W. Lawson, *Frenzied Finance*, which exposed the business methods of Amalgamated Copper; *Lincoln Steffens*, *The Shame of the Cities*, which dealt with corruption in city governments; David Graham Phillips, *The Treason of the Senate*, which revealed corruption in that body; Burton J. Henrick, *The Story of Life Insurance*; and *Upton Sinclair*, *The Jungle* which laid bare conditions in the meat-packing industry with such realism that half the nation ate vegetables for months.

c. ORGANIZED LABOR. The American Federation of Labor, which grew from 550,000 to 2,400,000 members during this period, threw its weight behind Progressive reform. In 1906 it departed from precedent by endorsing political candidates favorable to labor, thus increasing its national influence. Less important, but more in the public eye, were the *Industrial Workers of the World,* a militant union formed in 1905 by *"Big Bill" Haywood* to unite unskilled workers. Its object was to abolish capitalism by the strike, boycott, and sabotage. Although never boasting more than 60,000 members, the I.W.W. kept the West in turmoil for a decade, and in 1912-1913 staged strikes in eastern textile mills. It lost influence rapidly after 1917 when it opposed American participation in World War I.

d. RADICAL THINKERS. Criticism of the established order was effectively voiced by the *Socialist Party* under *Eugene V. Debs.* While demanding public ownership of facilities for production and distribution, the Socialists exposed the evils of American capitalism so persuasively that they polled nearly a million votes in 1912. One Socialist, *Victor L. Berger,* was elected mayor of Milwaukee in 1910. The support for this party convinced many politicians that reform was needed to prevent the further spread of radical theories.

II. PROGRESSIVISM IN CITIES AND STATES.

Reform began in local governments, which were closest to the people. It was directed toward: 1) restoring popular rule, and 2) obtaining social legislation to benefit the masses.

A. The Striving for Democracy. The problem of giving the people a more direct voice in their government was attacked on two levels:

1. City Government. Reformers directed their attention to wiping out corruption and scrapping archaic political institutions.

a. THE ATTACK ON CORRUPTION. The attack on *bossism* was led by civic-minded mayors who gained control in city after city. Most famous among them were *"Golden Rule" Jones* of Toledo and *Tom Johnson* of Cleveland, who fought for the public control of utilities, abolished corruption, and made their cities models for reformers.

b. POLITICAL REFORM. Reformers realized that efficient city administration could be secured only by substituting a managerial type of government for the archaic system of mayors and councils. This was achieved by: 1) *Municipal Home Rule,* which was adopted in fifteen states by 1915, allowing cities to frame their own charters without state interference; 2) the *commission plan,* first used in Galveston in 1900, which placed city government in the hands of a commission of experts; 3) the *city manager plan,* inaugurated by Dayton, Ohio, in 1913, which employed a specially trained city manager.

2. State Government. Corruption was attacked by such reforming governors as *Charles Evans Hughes* of New York, *Robert M. LaFollette* of Wisconsin, *Woodrow Wilson* of New Jersey, and *Hiram Johnson* of California, all of whom later became national progressive leaders. Their reforms, most of which originated in the western states, included:

a. DIRECT PRIMARIES. These allowed party members to name candidates rather than simply to choose between those selected by bosses. Two-thirds of the states followed Wisconsin's example by adopting direct primaries after 1903.

b. INITIATIVE, REFERENDUM, AND RECALL. The *initiative* allowed voters to propose laws directly, either for legislative action or for submission to the electorate. The *referendum* was a device to let the people approve or reject, by popular vote, laws passed by the legislature. The *recall* permitted voters to remove an elected official before his term expired.

c. DIRECT ELECTION OF SENATORS. By allowing state legislators to elect Senators, as the Constitution provided, wealthy men were able to bribe their way into that national body. To offset this, the states, beginning with Nevada in 1899, required candidates for the state legislatures to endorse a Senatorial candidate chosen in a state-wide primary election. By 1912 thirty states had such laws. The *Seventeenth Amendment* (1913), which provided for the direct election of Senators by popular vote, simply recognized a democratic change already completed.

d. WOMEN'S SUFFRAGE. A movement to enfranchise

the feminine half of the population was already under way before 1900 (see pp. 77-78). During the progressive period additional political rights were extended to them, until by 1914 they enjoyed full equality in eleven states, all in the West. National women's suffrage, however, had to wait until 1920 when the _Nineteenth Amendment_ was ratified in grateful recognition of women's work in World War I.

B. Social Legislation.

1. Protection of Workers. _Child-labor_ laws were passed in thirty-eight states by 1912, limiting the hours of work for children, raising the age limit for employment, and forbidding night work. Twenty-eight states set _maximum working hours_ for women, while twenty-four established the _eight-hour day_ for men laborers on public works. Many also limited the working day for men in mining, transportation, and other hazardous employments. Maryland (1902) pioneered in a _workingmen's compensation law_, making the employer liable for injuries suffered by employees; by 1917 all but ten states had such laws.

2. Regulation of Business. Laws setting railroad rates were passed by many states in 1906 and 1907. Other measures used the states' taxing power to limit profits of corporations and to redistribute wealth through income and inheritance levies.

3. Social Legislation and the Courts.

a. EARLY CONSERVATIVE DECISIONS. At first, courts invalidated most of the state progressive laws. This was done under the _Fourteenth Amendment,_ which forbade any state to deprive a person of life, liberty, or property without due process of law. The courts held that laws setting minimum wages or maximum hours, forbidding child labor, and providing for workingmen's compensation either deprived the employer of his property or the employee of his liberty. Thus in _Lochner v. New York_ (1905) the Supreme Court outlawed a New York statute limiting bakers to a ten-hour day on the grounds that the measure was not essential to the health of either the baker or the community.

b. JUDICIAL APPROVAL. Under the influence of progressivism the Supreme Court gradually liberalized its views. In _Muller v. Oregon_ (1908) it approved an Oregon law setting a ten-hour day for women workers. The Court's decision departed from precedent by showing the harmful social results of excessive labor for women. In *Bunting v. Oregon* (1917) the principle was extended to a ten-hour law for all factory workers.

III. THEODORE ROOSEVELT AND PROGRESSIVISM.

A. Roosevelt as President. In the *Election of 1900* McKinley was re-elected over William Jennings Bryan in a contest that hinged largely on Republican imperialism. Scarcely had he taken office when he was assassinated by a crazed anarchist, elevating to the presidency *Theodore Roosevelt,* who launched national progressivism.

1. Character of Roosevelt. Although honest and efficient, Roosevelt was not a real progressive. He was so aristocratic in background that his faith in democracy was intellectual rather than instinctive, so unschooled in economics that he often failed to understand important issues, so thoroughly a politician that he was willing to compromise rather than fight for reform. His contribution to progressivism was his ability to dramatize issues and lead men. Like Jackson or Lincoln before him, or Wilson or F. D. Roosevelt after him, he provided the executive leadership necessary for progress. This was shown in his dealings with Congress.

2. Roosevelt and Congress.

a. THE INAUGURAL MESSAGE. Roosevelt's first message to Congress horrified Republican conservatives. In it he asked for: 1) an attack on the "serious social problems" facing the nation; 2) legislation to allow the regulation, rather than the prohibition, of business combinations; 3) broader power over the railroads; and 4) the conservation of natural resources. Congress, dominated by such conservatives as Speaker *Joseph Cannon* in the House and *Mark Hanna* in the Senate, refused to respond to this plea. Roosevelt then carried his case to the people in a speaking tour in behalf of his *Square Deal.* Although arousing popular support in this way, Roosevelt would not have stirred Congress into action except for a fortunate incident: the coal strike of 1902.

b. The Anthracite Coal Strike of 1902. This began in May, 1902, when the *United Mine Workers* walked out to obtain a shorter day, better wages, and union recognition. The mine owners refused to negotiate or to submit the issues to arbitration, despite the threat to public welfare as winter approached. In October, Roosevelt offered to serve as peacemaker, but while the union was willing to submit its case to arbitration, the owners denied his right to interfere in any way. Not until the President threatened to call out troops to operate the mines did the owners submit. The strike was settled on October 23, 1902, when a presidential arbitration board granted the miners a nine-hour day and a 10 per cent pay increase, but not recognition of their union as a bargaining agency. The indifference of the mine owners to public welfare greatly influenced public opinion. Hence Congress was forced to make grudging concessions to Roosevelt's demands.

3. The Election of 1904. Roosevelt did not really control Congress, however, until after he was elected in his own right. His popularity forced the *Republicans* to renominate him in 1904, although the platform contained few references to his progressive program. The *Democrats,* having lost faith in Bryan's liberalism, nominated Judge *Alton B. Parker,* a conservative New York lawyer. The voters had their choice between a conservative party with a liberal candidate and a liberal party with a conservative candidate. In this situation Roosevelt's personal magnetism proved decisive. His electoral-college majority was 336 to 140 and his popular vote even greater than that achieved by McKinley over Bryan. With this mandate Roosevelt was able to launch his progressive program.

B. Roosevelt and the Trusts.

1. The Roosevelt Trust Program. Roosevelt knew that the election of 1900 was a decision against trust regulation, but he was also aware of the popular clamor against monopoly. Hence his "trust busting" was more verbal than real. His actual purpose was not to dissolve monopolies but to do away with their evils. To this end he asked Congress to create a *Department of Commerce and Labor* (1903) and a *Bureau of Corporations* (1903), both authorized to investigate business combinations and to warn them against harmful practices.

2. Enforcement of the Sherman Act. Roosevelt won his first victory as a "trust buster" when his Attorney General brought suit against the Northern Securities Company, a holding company controlling the Northern Pacific, Great Northern, and Chicago Burlington and Quincy railroads. In *Northern Securities Company v. United States* (1904) the Supreme Court held this to be a combination in restraint of trade, reversing its decision in the *Knight Case* (see p. 68). Thus encouraged, Roosevelt pushed other prosecutions, obtaining twenty-five indictments during his administrations.

C. Railroad Regulation. Despite the Interstate Commerce Act (see p. 61), railroad consolidation had gone on so rapidly that by 1904 six systems controlled three-fourths of the nation's mileage. Roosevelt attacked railroad monopoly in two acts passed by Congress:

1. The Elkins Act (1903). This made illegal the granting or accepting of secret *rebates,* and provided that both the road granting the rebate and the shipper accepting the lower rate could be punished. Under the law the Standard Oil Company was fined $29,000,000 in 1907, although the sentence was set aside by a higher court.

2. The Hepburn Act (1906). This measure was accepted by the roads as a means of checking progressive demands for rate-fixing powers for the Interstate Commerce Commission. It: 1) gave the I.C.C. power to reduce unreasonable or discriminatory rates subject to review by the courts; 2) increased the size of the I.C.C. from five to seven members and extended its jurisdiction over pipe lines, terminals, ferries, and express companies; 3) placed on the railroads the burden of showing that a rate was not unreasonable; 4) forbade free passes to all but employees; and 5) forbade the roads to carry commodities in the production of which they were interested. The Hepburn Act gave the I.C.C. real power for the first time since it was created in 1887. Yet it did not satisfy such reformers as *Robert M. LaFollette,* who wished it to have power to evaluate railroad property as a preliminary to setting rates that would give roads a fair return on their investment.

D. The Conservation Movement. By 1900 the United States faced the exhaustion of its mineral and timber lands. Roosevelt's interest in the West allowed him to make his greatest contribution by protecting these natural resources.

1. Timber Conservation. Acting under a *Forest Reserve Act* that had been passed in 1891, Roosevelt withdrew 150,000,000 acres of timber land from sale, in addition to 85,000,000 acres in Alaska. This land was transformed into national forests under the able administration of *Gifford Pinchot.* In addition, a national conference on conservation (1908) inspired forty-one states to create conservation commissions. A National Conservation Commission (1909) also stressed the preservation of resources.

2. Land Reclamation. The *Newlands Reclamation Act* (1902) authorized the use for irrigation purposes of money obtained from land sales in sixteen semiarid states. Under this law dams were built and the task of reclaiming the area begun.

E. Public Health Measures. In 1906 Roosevelt secured from Congress a *Pure Food and Drugs Act,* which banned the use of harmful drugs, chemicals, or preservatives in food or medicine shipped in interstate commerce. The measure was passed partly because of Upton Sinclair's revelations of meat-packing plants in his novel, *The Jungle,* and partly because of the muckrakers' crusade against adulterated foods and drugs.

IV. THE TAFT ADMINISTRATION.

A. The Election of 1908. *William Howard Taft* of Ohio was Roosevelt's choice as successor. He was nominated by the *Republicans* on a platform calling for trust regulation and a tariff that would recognize the difference between the cost of production at home and abroad. The *Democrats,* returning to the progressive camp, selected *William Jennings Bryan* once more. Their platform stressed the tariff question and the autocratic powers of the speaker of the House. Taft was chosen with 321 electoral votes to 162 for Bryan, but Bryan's popular vote was a million greater than Parker's in 1904.

B. Taft as President. Fundamentally conservative, Taft lacked Roosevelt's power to dramatize issues or lead Congress.

1. The Tariff Question. Bryan's emphasis on the tariff during the campaign forced Taft to endorse lowered duties. The House responded with the Payne Bill which followed the President's suggestions, but the Senate made 847 amendments, most of them upward. The *Payne-Aldrich Tariff* (1909) was bitterly opposed by progressive Republicans like *LaFollette* and *Beveridge*. Taft, however, not only signed the measure but in his *Winona Speech* declared it "the best the Republican Party ever passed." His popularity declined rapidly as a result.

2. The Ballinger-Pinchot Controversy. Gifford Pinchot, chief forester, in 1909 accused Richard A. Ballinger, Secretary of the Interior, of a lack of zeal in protecting natural resources from private exploitation. When Taft decided that the charges were unjust, he dismissed Pinchot, giving rise to the impression that he was undermining Roosevelt's conservation program.

3. Contest Over the Speakership. Democrats and Progressive Republicans alike objected to the autocratic powers of *Joseph Cannon,* Speaker of the House. Through his power to appoint committees and to dominate the rules committee he prevented progressive measures from reaching the floor of the House. In 1910 Republican insurgents under *George W. Norris* of Nebraska joined with Democrats to deprive Cannon of his power to appoint the rules committee or serve as a member. A year later, all committees were made elective. Taft's refusal to support the progressives in this controversy contributed to his unpopularity.

4. Canadian Reciprocity. Taft's inept handling of these problems led to a Democratic victory in the *Congressional elections of 1910.* To regain lost strength, the President drafted a reciprocity treaty with Canada which lowered the American duty on foodstuffs in return for similar Canadian reductions on manufactured goods. The measure passed Congress in 1911 with Democratic help. This not only cost Taft farmer support, but when Canada rejected the agreement he lost face.

C. Taft and Progressivism. Taft's political blunders concealed the fact that his record as a progressive was as outstanding as Roosevelt's. He sponsored:

1. Railroad Legislation. The *Mann-Elkins Act* (1910) remedied defects in the Hepburn Act. It: 1) gave the I.C.C. jurisdiction over telephone and telegraph lines; 2) authorized the I.C.C. to suspend rate increases until satisfied that they were reasonable; and 3) created a Commerce Court to hear appeals from the I.C.C.

2. Trust Busting. Under Taft twice as many suits were brought against trusts as under Roosevelt. Most important were those against the *Standard Oil Company* of New Jersey and the *American Tobacco Company,* both decided in 1911. In these the Supreme Court redefined the Sherman Act by deciding that it did not forbid all combinations, but only those that unduly or unreasonably restrained trade. This doctrine was called the *rule of reason.*

3. Minor Progressive Laws. These included: 1) a measure creating a *postal savings bank* and a *parcel post service;* 2) the division of the Department of Commerce and Labor into two departments; 3) laws limiting the amounts that could be spent on political campaigns and requiring the publication of all contributions; and 4) the *Sixteenth Amendment* (1913) which authorized income taxes. Taft also showed his support of *conservation* by withdrawing oil lands from sale, creating new national forests, and setting up the *Bureau of Mines.*

V. THE ELECTION OF 1912.

A. The Revolt of the Insurgents. The split between Republican Progressives (or Insurgents) and conservatives decided the election of 1912. Organized as the *Progressive Republican League* (1911) under Senator *Robert M. LaFollette* of Wisconsin, the Insurgents cast about for a standard bearer who could unseat Taft in the Republican convention. After a period of indecision, *Theodore Roosevelt,* in February, 1912, announced that he would be their candidate. He laid down the principles of his *New Nationalism* in a series of speeches: honesty in government, the regulation of business, conservation of natural resources, and the reconstruction of society by political action. _LaFollette_ also announced his own candidacy.

B. The Nominating Conventions.

1. The Republican Convention. The contest between Taft, Roosevelt, and LaFollette was bitter. _Taft,_ however, controlled the machines so completely that all disputed delegates were awarded to the President, who was renominated on the first ballot. The platform avoided a stand on all vital issues.

2. The Progressive Convention. Roosevelt and his followers, reassembling at Chicago as the Progressive Party, chose the ex-president as their candidate on a platform embodying the New Nationalism. They adopted the _bull moose_ as their symbol to match the elephant and donkey of the other parties.

3. The Democratic Convention. The jubilant Democrats recognized the chance of victory over a divided opposition. After a spirited contest between liberal and conservative factions, the liberals triumphed with the nomination of _Woodrow Wilson,_ a scholar and college president who had gained fame as the progressive governor of New Jersey. The platform pledged tariff reform, enforcement of the Sherman Act, outlawing of the labor injunction, and better banking and currency laws.

C. Outcome of the Election.
Wilson was elected with 435 electoral votes to 88 for Roosevelt and 8 for Taft. His popular vote was only 42 per cent of the total. This did not mean that Wilson's principles were endorsed by a minority of the people. Instead, the progressive measures supported by Wilson, Roosevelt, and Eugene V. Debs (who polled nearly a million votes on the Socialist ticket) commanded the support of three-fourths of the voters.

VI. THE WILSON ADMINISTRATION. Under Wilson, Progressivism reached a climax. A trained political scientist and author of a monumental work on _Congressional Government_ (1885), the President realized that strong executive leadership was necessary for progress. Hence he went beyond Roosevelt in imposing his will on Congress, even abandoning a practice used since the days of Jefferson when he read his own messages to that body. The result was a mass of legislation unequalled in any administration to that time.

A. Tariff Reform. When lobbyists descended on the special session of Congress that Wilson called to revise the tariff downward, he exposed their tactics to the newspapers. The resulting _Underwood Tariff_ (1913), while retaining certain protective features, lowered duties on more than one hundred items, including food, textiles, iron, and steel. To offset the loss in revenue a graduated _income tax_ (authorized by the _Sixteenth Amendment_) was adopted.

B. Currency Reform.

1. Background of Reform. Progressives had demanded modernization of the archaic currency system ever since the Populist era. Their demands were given weight by the Panic of 1907 and by disclosures of a "money trust":

a. PANIC OF 1907. This "Bankers' Panic" occurred while the national economy was sound, and resulted from overspeculation in securities by a few financiers. The business failures and unemployment that followed called attention to: 1) the unreasonable control over the country's money supply exercised by private banks; and 2) the inelasticity of the currency. Many business failures occurred because national banks, unable to enlarge the volume of national bank notes they issued, could not supply tottering firms with loans. The _Aldrich-Vreeland Act_ (1908) attempted to meet this situation by allowing national banks to issue additional notes in periods of emergency, but this was only a stopgap.

b. THE "MONEY TRUST." Two congressional investigations disclosed the need for reform: 1) the _National Monetary Commission_ (1908-1912) listed seventeen defects in the banking and currency system, including such a concentration of funds in New York City that business elsewhere was handicapped. It recommended a complete revision of the banking laws and the establishment of a central reserve bank. 2) _The Pujo Committee_ (1911), a special committee of the House, disclosed that a few financiers controlled not only the finances but much of the business of the United States, through a series of interlocking directorates.

2. The Federal Reserve Act (1913). Wilson's financial program aimed at three objectives: 1) a more elastic currency; 2) greater cooperation among banks in times of crisis; and 3) less concentration of money power in the hands of a few bankers. His recommendations were embodied in the *Federal Reserve Act* (1913), which was drafted by Senator *Carter Glass* of Virginia and other congressmen. Its provisions were these: 1) The country was divided into twelve districts with a *Federal Reserve bank* in each. 2) These banks were to serve as depositories for the cash reserves of national banks in their districts and such state banks as cared to join the system. They carried on no private business, serving instead as banks for banks. 3) The Federal Reserve banks were authorized to issue *Federal Reserve notes* on the basis of securities deposited with them by member banks. 4) The Federal Reserve banks could loan money to member banks when needed to prevent a crisis. 5) The system was administered by a *Federal Reserve Board*.

3. Other Financial Reforms. Easier credit for farmers was obtained by the *Federal Farm Loan Act* (1916), which created twelve Farm Loan banks similar to the Federal Re-

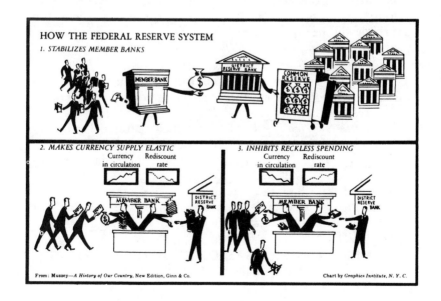

HOW THE FEDERAL RESERVE SYSTEM

1. STABILIZES MEMBER BANKS

2. MAKES CURRENCY SUPPLY ELASTIC

Currency in circulation / Rediscount rate

3. INHIBITS RECKLESS SPENDING

Currency in circulation / Rediscount rate

From: Muzzey—*A History of Our Country*, New Edition, Ginn & Co.   Chart by *Graphics Institute, N. Y. C.*

serve banks. These were authorized to loan money on farms, buildings, and improvements up to 70 per cent of their value at interest rates not over 6 per cent.

C. The Regulation of Business. In a special congressional message (January, 1914) Wilson called for five measures to break up monopolies: 1) a law prohibiting interlocking directorates; 2) authority for the I.C.C. to regulate railroad rates; 3) an exact definition of "combinations in restraint of trade"; 4) a federal trade commission to correct harmful business practices; and 5) penalties for individuals as well as firms that violated the antitrust acts. Congress responded with:

1. The Federal Trade Commission Act (1914). This created a _Federal Trade Commission_ empowered to issue "cease and desist" orders to any firm found guilty of unfair methods of competition.

2. The Clayton Act (1914). This: 1) defined the "unfair methods of competition" that the Federal Trade Commission was empowered to forbid; these included interlocking directorates, acquisition of a corporation's stock by a competing concern, price discrimination tending to create a monopoly, tying agreements, and the like; 2) made officers of corporations liable for illegal acts of those corporations; 3) exempted labor unions from the antitrust acts and forbade the use of the labor injunction except where necessary to protect property. Workers hailed this provision as the _Magna Charta of Labor._

D. Further Social Legislation. A number of measures were adopted after the Democrats regained control of Congress in the _Elections of 1914._ These included: 1) the _LaFollette Seamen's Bill_ (1915) which required better living and working conditions for ocean and lake sailors; 2) the _Adamson Act_ (1916) setting an eight-hour day for railroad workers; and 3) the _Keating-Owen Act_ (1916) excluding from interstate commerce the products of firms employing children under fourteen. This last measure was declared unconstitutional in the case of _Hammer v. Dagenhart_ (1918).

VII. AN APPRAISAL OF PROGRESSIVISM. The progressive period demonstrated:

A. The Need for Executive Leadership. The progressive period showed that party responsibility was so lax that progress was possible only with strong executive leadership. This was the case because congressmen, once they were elected, succumbed to the lure of lobbyists or reverted to the conservatism of their class. This left the parties, which were essentially combinations of local machines without strong national cohesion, powerless to carry out programs promised in presidential platforms. Realizing this, Wilson made himself virtually a prime minister by combining the functions of executive and party leader. The impressive legislative record of his administration was the result.

B. The Persistence of Liberalism. The achievements of the progressives were virtually those demanded by Populists a generation before. They had asked for a more flexible currency, the direct election of senators, a parcel post service, postal savings banks, a graduated income tax, the initiative and referendum, outlawing of the labor injunction, and other reforms, all of which were secured by 1916. Especially significant was the fact that these Populist planks were adopted by both Democrats and Republicans, indicating the basic unity of liberal platforms, which had little to do with party labels.

C. The Need for Continued Liberal Action. Within a few years after 1916 the Clayton Act was virtually a dead letter, with business again endulging in "unfair" practices and labor restricted by injunctions. The same fate waited most of the measures of the progressive period. This was largely the result of the American tendency toward inertia; mistaking success in battle for victory in the war, liberals relaxed their vigilance, only to lose much that they had gained.

ADDITIONAL READING

George E. Mowry, *The Era of Theodore Roosevelt, 1900-1912* (1958), is the best general survey, although there is additional information in such biographies as George E. Mowry, *Roosevelt and the Progressive Movement* (1946), and William H. Harbaugh, *Power and Responsibility: The Life and Times of Theodore Roosevelt* (1961). John M. Blum, *The Republican Roosevelt* (1954), expertly discusses political activities. Economic aspects are described in Harold U. Faulkner, *The Decline of Laissez Faire* (1951), while the emergence of a reform spirit is the theme of C. C. Regier, *The Era of the Muckrakers* (1932), and Louis Filler, *Crusaders for American Liberalism* (1939). Two biographies deal with a leading reformer: Robert C. Bannister, Jr., *Ray Stannard Baker* (1966); and John E. Semonche, *Ray Stannard Baker* (1969). Standard on the Ballinger-Pinchot controversy is James Penick, Jr., *Progressive Politics and Conservation* (1968). Henry F. Pringle, *The Life and Times of William Howard Taft* (1939), deals solidly with that administration. The best account of the first Wilson administration is Arthur S. Link, *Woodrow Wilson and the Progressive Era* (1954); the same author's multi-volume biography is fuller. A brief summary is John A. Garraty, *Woodrow Wilson* (1956). William E. Leuchtenburg. *The Perils of Prosperity, 1914-1932* (1958), is an excellent survey, while the social scene is described in Henry F. May, *The End of American Innocence* (1959).

CHAPTER X

Foreign Policy
of the Progressive Period
1900-1917

⟨THE NATIONALISTIC SPIRIT

The liberal domestic program of the Progressive presidents contrasted strongly with their foreign policy. Between 1900 and 1917 the United States warred ruthlessly on subject peoples, dominated weaker neighbors, and exerted its power over much of the world. This nationalistic spirit could be traced to: 1) the sense of national superiority that followed the easy victory in the Spanish-American War; and 2) the situation in Europe. There the major powers were guilty of the same integral nationalism; they built large navies, launched armament programs, engaged in power politics, and expanded their colonial empires. Their clashing interests bred the tensions that finally resulted in World War I.

I. SHAPING A COLONIAL POLICY. The United States emerged from the Spanish-American War with outright possession of the Philippines, Puerto Rico, and the Hawaiian Islands, as well as responsibilities toward Cuba. How should these dependencies be governed? Should their people be prepared for self-rule? Should they be allowed to govern themselves as states? The Courts and Congress tried to answer these questions.

A. The Courts and Colonial Policy. During 1900 and 1901 the Supreme Court was asked to decide whether the Constitution followed the flag—that is, whether America's colonial peoples had the same Constitutional rights as native Americans. Its answer was given in the _Insular Cases_, of which the most important were _Downes v. Bidwell_ (1900) and _De Lima v. Bidwell_ (1901). The Court held that certain _fundamental rights_ were common to all people under American jurisdiction, but that _formal rights_ (such as trial by jury) could be extended to colonials by act of Congress only. In effect this ruling stated that colonial peoples were not citizens of the United States until citizenship was conferred upon them, thus giving Congress a free hand to administer the colonies as it chose.

B. Congressional Policy.

1. The Hawaiian Islands and Alaska. An _Organic Act_ (1900) incorporated _Hawaii_ as a territory of the United States, granted citizenship to its inhabitants, and authorized an elective legislature and a governor appointed by the President. _Alaska_, which had been neglected since its purchase in 1867, attracted attention when the Klondike Gold Rush (1896) increased its population. Territorial status, with the usual elected assembly and appointed governor, was granted in 1912. In 1958, Alaska became the 49th state and in 1959, Hawaii became the 50th state.

2. Puerto Rico. By the _Foraker Act_ (1900) Congress made the people citizens of Puerto Rico but not of the United States, and provided for a legislature with an elected lower house and an appointed upper house. The governor was also appointed in Washington. In 1917 the _Jones Act_ conferred citizenship on Puerto Ricans as well as making the upper house elective. Puerto Rican demands for home rule continued, largely because of the poverty of the island.

3. The Philippines.

a. THE INSURRECTION. When the Philippines were annexed, the Senate adopted the _McEnery Resolution_ (1899) declaring that the islands would not be kept permanently. The natives, however, were so desirous of independence that when a commission (1899) reported that they were not ready for self-government a revolt began. With _Emilio_

Aguinaldo as their leader they fought bitterly until 1902, when the insurrection was crushed by methods that aroused criticism from anti-imperialists in the United States.

b. GOVERNMENTAL BEGINNINGS. A _Philippine Commission_ (1901) of three Filipinos and five Americans under _William Howard Taft_ was appointed to devise a government for the islands. Its recommendations were embodied in the _Organic Act of 1902_ This: 1) granted the suffrage to literate males over twenty-three, 2) made the Filipinos citizens of the Philippines but not of the United States, and 3) extended to them most of the constitutional guarantees enjoyed by Americans. _Taft_ was made governor-general, and ruled with the Commission. In 1907 an elected legislature was added, with the appointed Commission serving as the upper house.

c. ECONOMIC DEVELOPMENT. Taft and his successors improved the lot of the Filipinos. Extensive holdings were purchased from three Catholic orders and the land sold on easy terms to small farmers. Public works were built, a currency system installed, and health improved. Spectacular gains in educational facilities increased the number of pupils from 5000 in 1898 to 1,000,000 in 1920, while the University of the Philippines (1909) provided for higher education. This benevolent system was responsible for a population gain of three million between 1900 and 1917.

d. MOVEMENT FOR INDEPENDENCE. The Filipinos still wanted independence, and their cause was sponsored by the Democratic Party. When Woodrow Wilson was elected President he urged Congress to allow them more self-rule as a step toward freedom. The resulting _Jones Act_ (1916) made both houses of the legislature elective, extended the franchise to all men over twenty-one, and promised independence as soon as the Filipinos were capable of caring for themselves. The Republican victory in 1920 ended their hopes until the administration of F. D. Roosevelt.

4. Minor Possessions. Guam, Samoa, and other Pacific islands were ruled by governors appointed by the Navy Department. The _Danish West Indies_ or _Virgin Islands,_ which were purchased from Denmark in 1917, were also placed under an appointed governor. Local self-rule was gradually extended there until 1927, when the people were made citizens of the United States.

II. FOREIGN POLICY OF THEODORE ROOSEVELT, 1901-1909.

A. Building the Panama Canal.

1. Background of the Canal Project. As early as 1850 the *Clayton-Bulwer Treaty* between the United States and England provided that any canal across Central America should be jointly built and not fortified. Although a triumph at the time, this treaty later lessened American interest in a waterway, for by the late nineteenth century the United States was determined to build and fortify its own canal. Hence the first efforts were made by a French company headed by *Ferdinand De Lesseps,* builder of the Suez Canal, which obtained a franchise from Panama in 1879. After sinking $26,000,000 the company failed, transferring its franchise to the *Panama Canal Company.* An American company, the Maritime Canal Company, also went bankrupt in 1893 while trying to dig a canal across Nicaragua. The United States was unwilling to aid either so long as international control was necessary. In 1901, however, Roosevelt's Secretary of State, *John Hay,* negotiated with England the *Hay-Pauncefote Treaty* which granted the United States exclusive control.

2. Selection of a Route. Two routes were possible, one across the Isthmus of Panama, which was owned by Colombia, the other across Nicaragua. A congressional commission named to choose a site preferred the Panama route, but recommended the route across Nicaragua as the price asked by the French Panama Canal Company for its franchise was too high. When the French company cut its price in half, the *Spooner Act* (1902) was passed, authorizing Roosevelt to proceed with the Panama route.

3. Canal Diplomacy.

a. NEGOTIATIONS WITH COLOMBIA. In January, 1903, the Colombian minister in Washington signed the *Hay-Herran Treaty* which leased a ten-mile strip across Panama to the United States in return for $10,000,000 and an annual rental of $250,000. In August the Colombian senate rejected the treaty, feeling 1) that it surrendered too much power to the United States, and 2) that the compensation was inadequate. Roosevelt was outraged and made his feelings clear.

b. THE PANAMA REVOLUTION. Especially alarmed by Colombia's action were members of the French Panama Canal Company, who would lose $40,000,000 if they did not sell their rights to the United States before their franchise expired in 1904. Using as their agent a Panamanian revolutionist, _Philippe Bunau-Varilla,_ they planned a revolution to free Panama from Colombia. Roosevelt was probably informed of their plans; in October, 1903, he ordered a naval vessel to Panama with orders to keep the railroad across the isthmus open. The planned rebellion broke out on November 3, 1903, in the city of Panama. A day later United States troops were landed to keep Colombian soldiers from reaching the scene, and on November 6 Secretary of State Hay formally recognized the _Republic of Panama._ On November 18 a treaty with the new republic gave the United States perpetual control of a ten-mile zone across the isthmus. Roosevelt's conduct was virtually without precedent as an example of international bad taste. Not until 1921 were Colombia's ruffled feelings soothed by a grant of $21,000,000.

4. Constructing the Canal. Work began in 1906 under the direction of Colonel _G. W. Goethals_ of the army, and was completed in 1914. Equally important was the sanitary work of Colonel _W. C. Gorgas,_ who reduced tropical diseases among workers to a minimum.

B. Roosevelt's Caribbean Policy. Once the Panama Canal was built, American naval strategy depended on shuttling the fleet between the Atlantic and Pacific oceans. As the canal was vital to national defense, no European nation could be allowed a foothold in the Caribbean. Hence the United States adopted a new aggressive policy toward the Caribbean, designed to prevent any nation from gaining an excuse to intervene in the region.

1. Policy Toward Cuba. Mounting imperialistic sentiment soon caused the United States to regret the _Teller Amendment_ (see p. 107), in which it had promised freedom for the Cubans as soon as they could care for themselves. Instead, its policy was directed toward keeping Cuba under its own thumb.

a. GOVERNMENTAL BEGINNINGS. A military commission under Major General *Leonard Wood* (1899) brought order to the chaotic island preliminary to the calling of a constitutional convention (1900) which drafted a constitution modeled on that of the United States. This document, however, made no mention of Cuban-American relations. Angry at this slight, Congress responded by adopting the *Platt Amendment* (1901) and instructing the President to prolong military occupation until its provisions were inserted in the Cuban constitution. These provided that: 1) Cuba could make no international commitments impairing its sovereignty without the consent of the United States; 2) Cuba could contract no debts that could not be paid from its ordinary revenues; 3) the United States could intervene whenever necessary to preserve Cuban freedom or orderly government; and 4) two naval bases were granted the American navy. These provisions were reluctantly accepted and in 1902 independent Cuba installed its government.

b. APPLICATION OF THE PLATT AMENDMENT. The Cubans, untrained in self-government, were guilty of political misconduct that gave the United States several excuses to intervene. In 1906 civil disorders following an election led to a three-year occupation. Marines were landed in 1912 to protect American interests, and in 1917 more troops were sent to quell election disorders.

c. ECONOMIC PENETRATION OF CUBA. American investments in Cuba increased from $80,000,000 in 1901 to $1,500,000,000 thirty years later. Most of this went into sugar plantations which were controlled by a few banking houses, the National City Bank of New York being most important. This economic vassalage proved as objectionable to most Cubans as the Platt Amendment, and helped account for the rise of a spirit of Cuban nationalism that complicated relations between the two governments. On the other hand, the American policy resulted in political stability and a measure of economic prosperity.

2. The Venezuelan Crisis.

a. ORIGINS OF THE VENEZUELAN INCIDENT. In 1902 England, Germany, and Italy blockaded Venezuela to force that country to pay its long-standing debts. President Roosevelt, alarmed by the presence of European fleets in the Caribbean, brought secret pressure on Germany to withdraw and accept arbitration. His efforts succeeded when Germany agreed to submit its claims to the Hague Tribunal.

b. THE DRAGO DOCTRINE. The incident served as an excuse for Luis Drago, Argentina's minister of foreign affairs, to announce that no nation had the right to intervene in the affairs of another nation to collect debts due its citizens. The *Drago Doctrine* was accepted by the American State department, and in modified form by the Second Hague Conference (1907).

3. The Roosevelt Corollary.

In his annual message of 1904, Roosevelt announced that chronic wrongdoing by any American republic might compel the United States to exercise an international police power to restore order. This meant that if any weak Caribbean or Central American nation was unable to meet its financial obligations, or to protect the lives and property of European nationals, the United States would intervene to forestall intervention by other powers. This was known as the *Roosevelt Corollary to the Monroe Doctrine*. It was applied in 1905 when Santo Domingo was unable to pay its European debts. Roosevelt placed an American financial expert in charge of the Dominican treasury until the debts were paid.

C. Roosevelt and World Politics. The new international role of the United States became clear as Roosevelt led the country into world affairs, largely in the interest of global peace.

1. The Hague Conferences.

The world-wide democratic surge, of which American progressivism was a part, inspired an attack on the use of war as a means of settling international grievances. The *First Hague Conference* (1899) was designed to set up machinery for the arbitration of conflicts among the twenty-six participating nations. The result was the establishment of the *Permanent Court of Arbitration* to hear disputes and recommend settlements.

President Roosevelt was largely responsible for calling the *Second Hague Conference* (1907), where representatives from forty-four countries adopted additional rules governing arbitration as well as sanctioning the Drago Doctrine. Of the seventeen disputes settled by the Hague Tribunal between 1902 and 1917, four involved the United States. The most important concerned the rights of American fishermen in Canadian waters (1910) and was settled in America's favor.

2. Arbitration Treaties. In 1904 Roosevelt laid before the Senate treaties with twenty-two powers which bound the signers to submit all disputes to the Hague Tribunal save those involving vital interests, independence, or national honor. These were ratified in 1908-1909, extending the principle of arbitration.

3. Relations with Japan.

a. THE TREATY OF PORTSMOUTH. A *Russo-Japanese War* (1904-1905) threatened the *Open Door* in China by making Japan the dominant power in the Far East. Although sympathetic to Japan, Roosevelt persuaded both warring powers to recognize the neutrality of all Chinese territory outside of Manchuria. He also used the threat of American intervention on Japan's side to prevent France and Germany from aiding Russia. As the war drew to a close, he persuaded the belligerents to meet at Portsmouth, New Hampshire (September, 1905), to draft a peace treaty. His good offices brought the United States little advantage, for while Japan obtained many territorial concessions from beaten Russia, Roosevelt was blamed for blocking still more generous terms.

b. JAPAN AND THE OPEN DOOR. Japan's new strength continued to threaten the Open Door policy after 1905. To protect the American position, Roosevelt's Secretary of State, Elihu Root, negotiated the *Root-Takahira Agreement* (1908), in which the two nations agreed to respect each other's territorial possessions in the Pacific, and to support Chinese independence and the Open Door.

4. The Algeciras Conference. When war threatened between France and Germany over territorial claims in Morocco (1905-1906), Roosevelt urged France to agree to a conference on the question. The resulting Algeciras Conference (1906) temporarily settled the difference.

III. WOODROW WILSON'S FOREIGN POLICY, 1913-1917.

A. The Japanese Problem. Growing tension that resulted from American efforts to restrict Japanese expansion in the Far East was increased by a controversy over immigration. Since the 1890's, Californians had resented the influx of immigrants from Japan. They acted first in 1906 when San Francisco relegated Japanese children to separate schools. When Japan protested, President Roosevelt persuaded San Francisco to rescind its order, at the same time obtaining from the Emperor a *Gentleman's Agreement* (1907) to prevent the further immigration of coolie laborers. Although this was lived up to, continued nativistic sentiment in California led to the *Webb Act* (1913), which forbade Japanese to own land in the state. When this law was evaded by transferring land titles to American-born children (who were citizens under the Fourteenth Amendment), California adopted the *Asiatic Land Law* (1920) forbidding the practice. Each of these steps, which were taken over Wilson's protests, created friction between the two nations.

B. Panama Canal Controversy. As the Panama Canal neared completion, Congress passed the *Tolls Act* (1912) which provided that foreign vessels using the canal must pay larger fees than American vessels. *England* protested that this violated the "equality of treatment" guaranteed in the Hay-Pauncefote Treaty. Wilson supported England in this controversy, believing that friendship with that nation was essential in the troubled world situation. His pressure forced Congress to repeal the Tolls Act in 1914.

C. Wilson's Caribbean Policy.

1. "Dollar Diplomacy." As American investments in the Caribbean increased (see p. 136), a new element was introduced into American Caribbean diplomacy. Instead of directing its policy solely toward guarding approaches to the Panama Canal, the United States interested itself in protecting American investments which were threatened by internal revolutions. Although Wilson openly repudiated this "dollar diplomacy" he was responsible for repeated intervention in the Caribbean and Central American areas.

2. Intervention in Santo Domingo. When in 1916 a revolution threatened the local government, marines were sent to the island, where they remained for a decade. The occupation restored financial solvency and political tranquility to Santo Domingo, but was greatly resented by the natives. Troops were not withdrawn until 1924, and then American control of the customs service continued.

3. Intervention in Nicaragua. Marines who were landed in Nicaragua to prevent a revolution and protect American loans stayed on until 1925. The Republic's sovereignty was further invaded in 1914 when a treaty granted the United States the right to build a Nicaraguan canal and certain naval bases in return for a $3,000,000 payment. When the marines were withdrawn in 1925 such violent disorders broke out that they were returned in 1926. Nicaragua was actually an American protectorate, although the United States had no treaty rights to exercise such a power.

4. Intervention in Haiti. Financial anarchy in Haiti, with a threat of European intervention, led to the sending of troops to that Republic in 1915. A treaty that year also gave the United States control of the Haitian customs service, finances, and police force. Although the American administration was marked by efficiency, it was greatly resented.

D. Relations with Mexico.

1. Overthrow of Diaz. For thirty-five years Mexico was ruled by *Porfirio Diaz*, a dictator who ended popular government and awarded Mexico's lands to great estate holders. A revolution (1910-1911) that toppled Diaz from power was short-lived; a counterrevolution engineered by the landholders in 1913 restored a conservative government under General *Victoriano Huerta.* The internal situation in Mexico was now clear. On one side were the large landholders backed by foreign capital and with Huerta as their leader; on the other, the bulk of the middle class and peons who were led by *Venustiano Carranza.*

2. Wilson and Huerta. Most European powers recognized the Huerta regime but Wilson refused, despite pressure from American business interests whose $1,500,000,000 investment in Mexico gave them control of two-thirds of the nation's mines, oil fields, rubber plantations, and railroads. Wilson's refusal was based on the fact that Huerta's government rested on force. This represented a departure from traditional American policy, which had been to recognize any stable government, no matter how installed. The controversy over recognition was brought to a head in 1914 when Mexican police arrested several American sailors. When Huerta refused to apologize, the Mexican port of Vera Cruz was captured. War seemed certain until the *A.B.C. Powers* (Argentina, Brazil, and Chile) offered to mediate. When the United States accepted and Huerta refused, he lost support so rapidly that in July, 1914, he fled from Mexico.

3. Wilson and Carranza. The leader of the popular party, Carranza, became Mexican president in August, 1914. Two months later troops were withdrawn from Vera Cruz and the government given *de facto* recognition. Mexico remained chaotic for several years, however, largely because of the government's failure to satisfy the peasants' land hunger. In the resulting disorders 400 Americans were killed, while property losses reached $200,000,000. The principal troublemaker was *Francisco Villa,* a former bandit who led constant attacks on the Carranza government. To stop these, Wilson persuaded the A.B.C. powers to join the United States in affording full recognition to Carranza (1915). In retaliation Villa raided Columbus, New Mexico (March, 1916), killing seventeen Americans. With Carranza's permission the United States sent a military expedition under General *John J. Pershing* into Mexico on Villa's trail, but failed to capture the bandit. The troops were withdrawn in January, 1917, as America prepared to enter World War I.

4. The Mexican Constitution of 1917. A constitution adopted in 1917 not only contained provisions to aid workers and peasants but also proclaimed the national ownership of all oil and mineral resources. This threatened many American investors. In the resulting disorders Carranza was assassinated, and *Alvaro Obregon* became president (1920). He agreed (1923) that American mineral and oil rights obtained before 1917 would not be threatened, and that foreigners would be compensated for expropriated lands.

IV. AN APPRAISAL OF AMERICAN FOREIGN POLICY, 1900-1917.

A. World Role of the United States. During this period the United States had its first chance to practice the new role that it would play in the world. Its policy was directed to two ends: 1) *To maintain peace.* This was shown by its support of the Hague Conferences, international arbitration, the mediation of disputes, and other attempts to settle conflicts by means short of war. 2) *To protect downtrodden people.* This purpose underlay Wilson's Mexican policy with its refusal to recognize an unpopular government that had obtained power by force. In both of these objectives the United States assumed a positive world role to better the lot of men, just as its domestic legislation was directed to the same end.

B. The Role of the United States in Hemispheric Affairs. The high idealism displayed in world politics was in marked contrast to the imperialistic Caribbean policy of these years.

1. Reasons for Caribbean Policy. Three factors combined to force this policy on the United States: 1) *Dollar diplomacy* played a part as investments increased and investors brought pressure on the government to protect their loans. Yet they had little influence on Roosevelt or Wilson. 2) *Canal policy* was more important. Having based its whole defensive strategy on the Panama Canal, the United States could not afford to allow any European power to secure a foothold in the Caribbean. This explained intervention in many cases, as well as the Roosevelt Corollary to prevent European powers from using force to collect debts. 3) *Idealism* doubtless convinced Roosevelt and Wilson that they could better the lot of the common people by intervening. The health programs, educational innovations, and public works construction did benefit the areas materially.

2. Results of Caribbean Policy.

a. BENEFICIAL RESULTS. The United States did accomplish its purpose of protecting the entrance to the Panama Canal.

b. HARMFUL RESULTS. Latin Americans were left fearful and distrustful of the "Colossus of the North." This was especially the case with the A.B.C. powers, which felt that their stability and advanced civilization entitled them to be treated as equals. Not until the Good Neighbor policy of F. D. Roosevelt were more cordial relations restored.

ADDITIONAL READING

A useful brief survey is in Richard W. Leopold, *The Growth of American Foreign Policy* (1962); Foster R. Dulles, *America's Rise to World Power, 1898-1954* (1955), is fuller but less interpretative. Raymond A. Esthus, *Theodore Roosevelt and the International Rivalries* (1970), is excellent on Roosevelt's policies but neglects the Caribbean; this is studied in Edward Wagenknecht, *The Seven Worlds of Theodore Roosevelt* (1958). Panama Canal diplomacy is analyzed in Lawrence O. Ealy, *Yanqui Politics and the Isthmian Canal* (1971); and intervention in Cuba in Allan R. Millett, *The Politics of Intervention: The Military Occupation of Cuba, 1906-1909* (1968). Walter V. and Marie V. Scholes, *The Foreign Policies of the Taft Administration* (1970), is standard. Bradford Perkins, *The Great Rapprochement: England and the United States, 1895-1914* (1968), is a brilliant interpretation. Relations with the Far East are the theme of Paul A. Varg, *The Making of a Myth: The United States and China, 1897-1912* (1968), an extended essay; Jerry Israel, *Progressivism and the Open Door: America and China, 1905-1921* (1971); Raymond A. Esthus, *The United States and Japan* (1966); and A. W. Griswold, *The Far Eastern Policy of the United States* (1938). Arthur S. Link, *Wilson the Diplomatist* (1956), is standard; the best discussions of his Mexican policies are in Kenneth J. Grieb, *The United States and Huerta* (1969), which deals with the 1913-1914 period, and Robert F. Smith, *The United States and Revolutionary Nationalism in Mexico* (1972), which carries the story to 1932.

~~~~~~~~~~~~~~~~~~~~~~~~~~~~~~~

CHAPTER XI

The United States
and World War I
1917-1920

~~~~~~~~~~~~~~~~~~~~~~~~~~~~~~~

₡ PROGRESSIVISM AND WAR

Throughout American history each period of rapid progress toward economic, social, and political democracy has been brought to a close by a major war. This is because such periods infect the people with a crusading zeal that makes them willing to fight for their ideals. Thus the abolitionism that precipitated the Civil War was rooted in Jacksonian Democracy, while the idealism of the New Deal prepared the people to battle dictatorship in World War II. Similarly the progressive period inspired Americans to look upon World War I as a holy crusade in behalf of justice, democracy, and equality for all peoples.

I. THE ROAD TO WAR.

A. European Background. Between 1900 and 1914 Europe divided into two armed camps, with the *Central Powers* (Germany and Austria-Hungary) on one side and the *Triple Entente* (England, France, and Russia) on the other. The crisis that touched off the conflict between them came on June 28, 1914, when a Serbian patriot assassinated the heir to the Austro-Hungarian throne. When Austria declared war on Serbia, Russia came to the aid of her Slavic neighbor, and Germany joined the Austrians. One by one

144

the other European nations were drawn into the conflict by the alliances that held them together, until the middle of 1915 when all the continent was at war.

B. The Problem of Neutrality. Although Wilson pleaded with the American people to remain neutral in thought and action (August 4, 1914), both their basic sympathies and the events of the war inclined them from the beginning to favor the Allies rather than the Central Powers.

1. Basic Factors Influencing Opinion.

a. CULTURAL TIES. Most Americans were conscious of their cultural affinity with England, based on a common background, language, and traditions. About one-half the people were of English or Canadian descent, and only one-fifth of German or Austrian background.

b. PSYCHOLOGICAL FACTORS. German militarism offended the sense of democracy engrained in the American people, while that country's ruthless invasion of Belgium aroused deep resentment. As the war progressed, an efficient British propaganda, which emphasized imaginary German atrocities, intensified the conviction that England was fighting for human decency. The Allies' cause was strengthened by the fact that they controlled most of the avenues of communication between Europe and the United States, excluding only the wireless and special correspondence.

c. ECONOMIC FACTORS. England's navy blockaded the Central Powers, confining all American trade to the Allied countries. This trade grew rapidly as American factories and farms assumed the task of sustaining the armies and civilian populations of the Allies. Munitions exports alone increased from $40,000,000 in 1914 to $1,300,000,000 in 1916. These purchases were financed by floating loans in the United States; by 1917 the Allied governments had borrowed $2,300,000,000 from Americans while loans to the Central Powers totaled only $27,000,000. This economic stake in an Allied victory probably influenced few people, for the businessmen who had purchased most of the bonds favored neutrality as the best means of obtaining additional profits.

2. The Conflict Over Neutral Rights. The efforts of

both warring groups to control the seas proved the decisive factor in forcing the United States into the conflict.

a. THE CASE AGAINST ENGLAND. Britain's attempt to starve the Central Powers into submission led her to violate all rules of international law as codified in the *Declaration of London* (1909), which England had not signed. Among her questionable acts were: 1) extension of the *contraband* list to include food and other items not previously considered articles of war; 2) expansion of the *doctrine of continuous voyage* to allow the confiscation of goods in neutral vessels bound for neutral ports; 3) rationing goods sent to European neutrals by the United States to prevent them from sending their own produce to the Central Powers; and 4) blacklisting firms suspected of trading with Germany. Each of these steps was protested by the Wilson government, but England always replied that she had not signed the Declaration of London and was not bound to obey its provisions. Pro-Allied sentiment prevented Wilson from forcing Britain's hand with an arms embargo.

b. THE CASE AGAINST GERMANY. Faced with economic

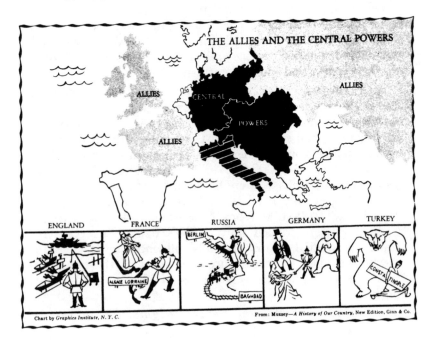

THE ALLIES AND THE CENTRAL POWERS

ALLIES
CENTRAL POWERS
ALLIES
ALLIES

ENGLAND FRANCE RUSSIA GERMANY TURKEY

ALSACE LORRAINE
BERLIN
BAGHDAD
CONSTANTINOPLE

Chart by *Graphics Institute, N. Y. C.*   From: Muzzey—*A History of Our Country*, New Edition, Ginn & Co.

strangulation unless the Allied blockade was broken, Germany resorted to the submarine warfare that finally brought the United States into the war.

I. *Beginning of Submarine Warfare.* In February, 1915, Germany announced that all enemy ships would be sunk on sight in the waters surrounding the British Isles, and that neutral ships should avoid the area to prevent "unfortunate mistakes." Wilson warned the Germans that they would be held "strictly accountable" for the loss of American lives or property. Despite this warning, a submarine on March 28, 1915, sank the British ship *Falaba,* and on May 1 the American tanker *Gulflight.* Germany apologized for the latter sinking, but refused to abandon submarine warfare.

II. *Sinking of the Lusitania.* On May 7, 1915, the crack Cunard liner, the *Lusitania,* was torpedoed off the Irish coast with a loss of 1200 lives including 128 Americans. Popular resentment in the United States was so great that war seemed certain. Wilson sent a series of notes demanding that Germany make reparation for damages and abandon her lawless practices; his second note was so warlike that his Secretary of State, *William Jennings Bryan,* resigned in protest, holding that Americans should not travel on belligerent ships. He was replaced by *Robert Lansing,* who was more sympathetic to England. Meanwhile a second British liner, the *Arabic,* was torpedoed on August 19, 1915. The protest was so violent that on September 1, 1915, Germany promised to sink no more passenger ships without provision for the safety of the passengers.

III. *The Sussex Pledge.* On March 24, 1916, the French liner, *Sussex,* was sunk, injuring several Americans. As this violated the *Arabic Pledge,* Wilson delivered an ultimatum in which he threatened to sever diplomatic relations unless unrestricted submarine warfare was abandoned. Convinced that war was certain unless she backed down, Germany issued the *Sussex Pledge* (May, 1916), agreeing not to sink merchant ships "without warning and without saving human lives." This ended the submarine controversy for nine months.

C. Preparedness for War. By 1916 the "rape of Belgium," the submarine warfare, and atrocity propaganda had convinced many Americans that only the defeat of the Central Powers would save the United States from eventual attack. As interventionist sentiment grew, Wilson made a vain effort to bring peace to Europe, at the same time preparing for war.

1. Wilson's Early Peace Efforts. The President was convinced that American participation could only be avoided by ending the war. In February, 1916, when the contestants were deadlocked on the western front, he sent his confidential agent, Colonel *Edward M. House,* to Europe with proposals for a peace conference. Both England and Germany rejected the proposal.

2. Military Preparedness. Pressure for an American armament program was exerted by the *National Security League,* which was financed by munitions and industrial interests, and by such influential spokesmen as *Theodore Roosevelt* and General Leonard Wood. Fearing that rearmament would increase the demand for war, Wilson resisted as long as possible, but backed down as the election of 1916 approached. Under his prodding Congress passed: 1) the *National Defense Act* (June, 1916) which increased the size of the army, placed the state militia under federal control, and inaugurated military training in schools and colleges; 2) the *Naval Appropriation Bill* (August, 1916) which authorized the construction of many new warships; and 3) the *United States Shipping Board Act* (September, 1916) which appropriated $50,000,000 to buy or build merchant vessels. At the same time Wilson created a *Council of National Defense* to mobilize industry if war came.

D. The Election of 1916.

1. The Nominating Conventions. The Democrats renominated Wilson on a platform boasting of his domestic reforms, tariff policy, and efforts to keep the peace. When the Republicans, refusing to heed the pleading of Progressives, chose as their candidate *Charles Evans Hughes,* the New York Supreme Court Justice, the Progressive Party retaliated by nominating Theodore Roosevelt once more. Roosevelt refused to run, asking Progressives to follow him back into the Republican camp. Most refused to do so, supporting Wilson instead.

2. The Election. Wilson's domestic program and the Democratic slogan *"He Kept Us Out Of War"* proved more effective than the Republican attacks on the President's diplomacy and pacifism. He was re-elected by a very close vote, having a popular majority of 600,000 and 277 electoral votes to 254 for Hughes. The South and Far West favored Wilson; the East and Middle West supported Hughes.

E. American Entry in World War I.

1. Wilson's Final Peace Efforts. Viewing the election as a mandate for his program, Wilson decided on a final attempt to end the European war by a negotiated peace. In December, 1916, he asked the belligerents to state the terms on which they would cease hostilities. He reported the results in a memorable address to Congress on January 22, 1917. The Central Powers, he said, demanded impossible territorial claims and reparations; the Allies also asked full reparations and guarantees for the future. As these terms were irreconcilable, Wilson laid down his own terms for a just peace : 1) it must be a "peace without victory"; 2) the right of self-determination and the equality of all nations must be recognized; 3) military and naval armaments must be limited; 4) the freedom of the seas must be guaranteed; 5) secret alliances must be abandoned; and 6) a league to enforce peace must be formed. These proposals aroused little enthusiasm in the United States and none at all among the belligerents.

2. Causes for American Entry.

a. RENEWAL OF SUBMARINE WARFARE. On January 31, 1917, Germany informed the United States that after February 1 all merchant ships bound for the British Isles or the Mediterranean, whether belligerent or neutral, would be sunk on sight. The Central Powers knew that this meant American entry, but believed their submarines could starve England into submission before aid became effective. Wilson severed diplomatic relations at once, then asked Congress for authority to arm merchant ships to run the submarine blockade. When a bill for this purpose was defeated by a filibuster of southern and western Progressives under *Robert LaFollette,* the President found authority for the step in an ancient statute. Between February 3 and April 1 eight American ships were sunk.

b. THE ZIMMERMANN NOTE. In February, 1917, the United States obtained a copy of a note from Germany to Mexico, promising that country Texas and the Southwest if it entered the war. When this was published on March 1 it aroused great resentment.

c. THE RUSSIAN REVOLUTION. In March, 1917, the Tsar of Russia was overthrown and a republican government established. Now all the Allies were democracies, all the Central Powers autocracies.

3. The United States Enters the War. On April 2, 1917, Wilson asked Congress for a declaration of war. On April 6 a war resolution was passed by overwhelming majorities that reflected the popular will.

II. THE UNITED STATES IN WORLD WAR I.

A. The Home Front. The Allies' supplies of food, munitions, and industrial goods were so nearly exhausted that November 1 had been set as the day they must sue for peace unless they received American aid. Hence the task of the United States was to mobilize not only manpower but factories and farms. This was entrusted to the *Council of National Defense,* which assumed dictatorial powers over the nation's economy.

1. Mobilizing Manpower. A *Selective Service Act* (May, 1917) required all men to register for a draft. Under this law 2,200,000 men were inducted into the army. With the regular army, national guard, and smaller branches of the service, this raised the armed force of the United States to 4,000,000. All were given six months' basic training in one of thirty-two camps, while officers were trained in other camps or in colleges. Eventually 2,000,000 men were sent overseas.

2. Mobilizing Industry. To consolidate factory production, the Council of National Defense in July, 1917, created a *War Industries Board* under *Bernard M. Baruch.* This was given dictatorial powers over manufacturing. It standardized products to cut costs, told factories what they could or could not manufacture, developed new industries, fixed prices, and in various ways increased the nation's production 20 per cent before the war's end.

3. Mobilizing Transportation.

a. OVERSEAS SHIPPING. An *Emergency Fleet Corporation* (April, 1917) was authorized to purchase, build, or requisition enough ships to bridge the Atlantic despite submarine attacks. This organization, which worked under the direction of the *War Shipping Board*, appropriated German ships that were in American ports, bought neutral ships, and built so many vessels that the tonnage of the merchant marine increased from one million to ten million. Within a year it was building two ships for every one sunk by submarines.

b. DOMESTIC TRANSPORTATION. The railroads soon bogged down under the heavy strain of moving goods to the east coast. In December, 1917, they were taken over by the government, which operated them henceforth as one system. This proved highly efficient, but the high rental costs and low rates charged shippers cost the government $700,000,000.

4. Mobilizing the Farmers.

To assure adequate food for the United States and its allies, a *Food Administration* was created (August, 1917) with *Herbert Hoover* in charge. This stimulated grain production by promising to buy all wheat at $2 a bushel, while the production of other crops was encouraged in the same way. At the same time consumption was curtailed by campaigns urging the people to "hooverize" or find substitutes for meat and cereals. Food exports in 1918 were twice those of any prewar year.

5. Mobilizing the Natural Resources.

A *Fuel Administration* under Harry A. Garfield was created to stimulate production, and cut down consumption, of coal and oil. This not only spurred miners to greater efforts, but instituted "fuelless Mondays" and "gasless Sundays" as well as inaugurating daylight-saving time to conserve coal.

6. Mobilizing Finance.

The United States not only paid its own wartime expenses of $22,000,000,000 but loaned $9,000,000,000 to the Allies to purchase goods in this country. These sums were raised by: 1) taxes, which were increased in volume and variety; and 2) loans in the form of *"Liberty" bonds* sold to the American people. In all, five issues were floated, of from $2,000,000,000 to $6,000,000,000, and all were oversubscribed.

7. *Mobilizing Public Opinion.*

a. DOMESTIC PROPAGANDA. Congress established the *Committee on Public Information* (April, 1917) under a liberal journalist, *George Creel,* to mobilize American thought. This committee inundated the nation with a flood of propaganda in newspaper advertisements, posters, motion pictures, books, pamphlets, and speeches. Every individual was made aware of the lofty war aims of the United States and its Allies.

b. FOREIGN PROPAGANDA. This was designed to break down the will to fight among enemy peoples. Wilson from the first held that the war was with the governments of the Central Powers, not with the people. This point he emphasized in a series of lofty messages, hoping to weaken enemy resistance and lay a moral basis for the peace negotiations. His program was climaxed on January 22, 1918, when he outlined to Congress the *Fourteen Points* that he deemed essential to a just peace. In addition to suggestions for territorial changes in Europe he proposed: 1) open diplomacy to replace secret treaties; 2) freedom of the seas; 3) removal of economic barriers between nations; 4) armament reduction; 5) readjustment of colonial claims with the people concerned having an equal voice in the settlement; 6) the redrawing of European boundaries along national lines; and 7) the formation of an association of nations.

c. TREATMENT OF DISLOYALTY. Although most Americans, including those of German descent, were completely loyal, a handful of Socialists branded the war as a capitalistic crime. Their utterances aroused a hysterical attack on disloyalty. Three measures were adopted: 1) an *Espionage Act* (June, 1917) provided heavy penalties for attempts to obstruct recruiting or spread treason among troops; 2) a *Sedition Act* (May, 1918) extended the penalties to those who obstructed the sale of bonds, discouraged recruiting, or uttered language abusive of the government, the Constitution, or the flag; 3) a statute of October, 1918, authorized the deportation without jury trial of aliens who advocated the overthrow of the government. Under these laws about 190 persons were tried (including Eugene V. Debs), almost half of whom were convicted. In addition, loyal German-

Americans were abused, the German language banned from schools, and persons with German names subjected to indignities.

B. The European Front.

1. Naval Operations. The navy's task was: 1) to sink submarines, and 2) to convoy troop ships. Under *Admiral William S. Sims* a mine barrage was laid along the coast of Europe to keep U-boats in port. In addition a device was perfected to detect submarines, thus making their destruction easier. About half the German undersea fleet was destroyed during the last year of the war. Ships were also convoyed successfully; only six transports were torpedoed and of these, two made port.

2. The Army in France.

a. TRANSPORTING THE ARMY. An *American Expeditionary Force* (A.E.F.) was sent abroad as soon as troops could be trained, although only 200,000 reached France during 1917. In 1918, however, nearly 2,000,000 reached the front. Secretary of War *Newton D. Baker* placed the A.E.F. under *General John J. Pershing,* while the task of shipping supplies was entrusted to the Services of Supply. This efficient organization built docks, erected warehouses, laid miles of railroad and telegraph lines, and distributed seven million tons of supplies.

b. THE MILITARY SITUATION. Germany's drive to end the war before American aid became effective almost succeeded. In October, 1917, Italy was demoralized by defeat at *Caporetto,* while in March, 1918, the Russian communists withdrew that country from the war with the *Treaty of Brest-Litovsk.* This allowed Germany to concentrate all her troops on the western front, where she enjoyed numerical superiority. Between March and June, 1918, she launched three offensives against the British and French troops who had held her at bay in northwestern France. By June 15 the Kaiser's armies reached the right bank of the Marne, threatening Paris. To check this drive, Marshall *Ferdinand Foch* of France was made supreme commander of all Allied forces, while American troops were rushed overseas so rapidly that between March and October, 1918, 1,750,000 reached France.

c. AMERICAN MILITARY OPERATIONS. American troops saw their first serious fighting after July 15, 1918, when the Germans began the _Second Battle of the Marne_. With the French they stemmed the advance on _Chateau-Thierry_, then led a counterattack on the German lines at Soissons. Again in September Americans won back the _St. Mihiel_ salient, a triangle jutting into Allied territory. More important was the forty-seven-day battle, beginning in September, that captured the _Meuse-Argonne_ area and cut a railroad that supplied much of the German front. More than 1,200,000 Americans fought in this battle. As similar defeats were suffered all along the Hindenburg Line, the Germans hastily installed a parliamentary government (October 3, 1918), and informed Wilson that they would consider peace on the basis of the Fourteen Points. After a month of negotiations General Foch was instructed to negotiate an armistice. This was signed on November 11, 1918, two days after the Kaiser fled to Holland. About 5000 American soldiers, however, co-operated with other Allied troops in fighting minor engagements against the Russian communists at Archangel and Murmansk (September, 1918-May, 1919). Another expeditionary force remained in eastern Siberia until January, 1920.

III. WILSON AND THE PEACE CONFERENCE.

A. Obstacles to a Just Peace.

1. The American Situation. Just before the armistice, sweeping victories in the _elections of 1918_ gave the Republicans control of both houses of Congress. This repudiation of Wilson was due to dislike of his dictatorial methods and to normal dissatisfaction with wartime controls. The President was no longer able to speak for American opinion.

2. French and British Attitudes. Both were determined to punish Germany for causing the war. France especially wanted territorial concessions and reparations, as well as a permanently weakened Germany.

3. The Secret Treaties. Before and during the war the Allies negotiated numerous secret treaties providing for a division of spoils. Wilson knew of their existence but felt that his financial whip hand over the Allies would force them to abandon their selfish ambitions.

4. The Communist Menace. Communism threatened to spread over Europe amidst the chaos and poverty that followed the war. In the face of this danger Wilson was forced to accept any terms that would bring peace, rather than prolonging discussion while communism spread. All of these things doomed his hope for a just peace based on the Fourteen Points.

B. The Peace Negotiations.

1. The American Delegation. Breaking all precedent, Wilson led the American delegation to Paris. With him were Colonel House, Secretary of State Lansing, General Tasker H. Bliss, and Henry White, a career diplomat. Only White was a Republican, while no member of the House or Senate was included. Wilson deliberately chose a weak delegation as he expected to write the treaty himself.

2. The Negotiations. The Peace Conference opened at Versailles on January 18, 1919. All important decisions were made by the _Big Four: Wilson_ for the United States, Georges _Clemenceau_ for France, David _Lloyd George_ for England, and Vittorio _Orlando_ for Italy. Wilson was forced to back down repeatedly before these skilled diplomats, until little remained of the idealistic peace he had planned. Unsatisfactory as was the treaty, however, it was less selfish than if Wilson had not been there.

3. Terms of the Treaty of Versailles (June 28, 1919). The final treaty: 1) forced Germany to admit her guilt for the war; 2) stripped her of her colonies; 3) took from her Alsace-Lorraine, Posen, the Saar Basin, parts of Schleswig and Silesia, and other territories; 4) forced her to pay reparations (later fixed at $56,500,000,000) for the cost of the war; and 5) stripped away her entire military and naval establishment.

4. The League of Nations.

a. WILSON AND THE LEAGUE. On Wilson's insistence, the conference on January 25, 1919, authorized a special committee to draw up a constitution for a League of Nations. When adopted in February this was made an integral part of the treaty. Wilson later obtained amendments to the covenant (constitution) after consulting leaders at home, hoping to make the League acceptable to Americans.

b. ORGANIZATION OF THE LEAGUE. The Covenant of the League provided for: 1) an _Assembly_ in which all member nations had an equal voice; 2) a _Council_ made up of representatives from the United States, England, France, Italy, Japan, and four other nations elected by the Assembly; 3) a _Secretariat_, permanently located at Geneva, to handle routine work of the League.

c. PURPOSES OF THE LEAGUE. Member nations pledged themselves in the Covenant to: 1) respect and preserve against external aggression the territorial integrity and political independence of all member nations _(Article X)_; 2) submit to the League all disputes threatening war; 3) employ military and economic sanctions against nations resorting to war; 4) reduce armaments; and 5) cooperate in setting up a _Permanent Court of International Justice_ to settle disputes.

C. American Rejection of the Treaty.

1. Objections to the Treaty. Opposition to the Versailles Treaty was voiced as soon as it was submitted to the

THE LEAGUE of NATIONS

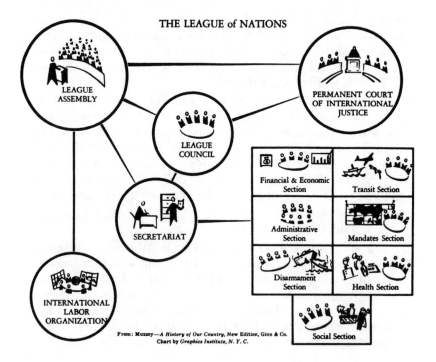

From: Muzzey—*A History of Our Country*, New Edition, Ginn & Co.
Chart by *Graphics Institute, N. Y. C.*

Senate for ratification on July 10, 1919. This was based on:
1) political jealousy aroused by Wilson's refusal to consult
Republican senators in drafting the treaty; 2) liberals' dislike of the treaty's realistic features; 3) the opposition of
such racial groups as German-Americans, Irish-Americans,
and Italian-Americans, who resented the way their countries
had been treated; 4) fear that participation in the League
would involve the United States in European troubles. In
addition, Republicans attacked the treaty as a means of dis-
crediting the Democrats politically.

2. Division of the Senate. The Senate divided into
three groups: 1) Democratic followers of Wilson who favored ratification at once; 2) *"Irreconcilables"* under *Hiram
Johnson* of California, *William E. Borah* of Idaho, and
Robert LaFollette of Wisconsin, who advocated isolation
from Europe and the complete rejection of the League; 3)
moderates who favored participation in the League only if
certain *reservations* were added to the Covenant to protect
American interests.

3. Action by the Senate. The leader of the *reservationists, Henry Cabot Lodge* of Massachusetts, proposed
fourteen amendments to the League Covenant, the most
important exempting the United States from sending troops
under Article X without congressional approval. Wilson refused to accept this formula, carrying his case instead to the
people with a speaking tour through the Middle West.
There he suffered a paralytic stroke which permanently in-
capacitated him. On November 19, 1919, the League was
defeated by the Senate, both with and without reservations.
Again in March, 1920, it failed to receive the necessary two-
thirds majority, although the vote was 49 to 35 in favor.
When the Democrats were defeated in the election of 1920,
the Republicans accepted the vote as a mandate against the
League. On August 25, 1921, Congress adopted a *joint
resolution* declaring the war at an end.

IV. MODERN IMPLICATIONS OF WORLD WAR I.

A. Why the United States Fought. World War I
demonstrated that the United States could not stay isolated
from any major European war. Historians have quarreled

since 1917 as to the exact causes for American entry, but they agree that participation was inevitable. Their conclusions may be summarized in this way:

1. Cultural Ties. The American people were unneutral from the beginning, favoring an Allied victory. This was because: 1) a majority traced their ancestry to England or Canada; 2) they remembered French aid during the American Revolution and continued friendship with France since that time; 3) they were convinced that the struggle was between democratic and despotic nations. With the people unneutral, neutrality was impossible.

2. Influence of Allied Propaganda. The effectiveness of Allied propaganda was shown by the hysterical hatred of German-Americans and others suspected of disloyalty. Yet the propaganda was effective only because Americans wanted to believe. This was shown by the complete failure of German propaganda.

3. Economic Factors. During the 1930's many historians and politicians tried to prove that America's economic stake in an Allied victory forced American entry; participation, they said, resulted from pressure from munitions makers, international bankers, and other "merchants of death." Yet no shred of evidence can be found to show that bankers or munitions makers had any influence on the President or members of Congress who voted for war.

4. Idealistic Factors. More important than propaganda or economic factors were the ideals of the people and their President. The majority believed that the German "Rape of Belgium," Junker militarism, and the submarine campaign all showed that the Central Powers menaced civilization. President Wilson, moreover, felt that the United States would be in a stronger position to dictate a just peace as a participant than as a spectator.

5. National Interest. The principal cause for American participation was the same as in all wars: to protect the national interest. By the spring of 1917 Russia had withdrawn from the war and Italy was beaten. France was stalemated on the Hindenburg line while its resources dwindled; England was only months away from capitulating before the submarine blockade. American entry alone would prevent

Germany from reigning supreme over Europe. In such a situation the safety of the United States would have been threatened. The nation went to war to preserve its sovereignty and institutions.

B. Why the United States Rejected the League. Not one individual, but three groups, were to blame for the recurrence of isolationism that prevented the United States from joining the League of Nations:

1. The Democratic Irreconcilables. Wilson's failure to consult the opposition party in drafting the treaty, his unwillingness to take Senate leaders into his confidence, his dictatorial methods of dealing with Congress, and his refusal to compromise with the reservationists, all contributed to the rejection.

2. The Republican Irreconcilables. Equally to blame were the Republicans under Henry Cabot Lodge who used the treaty to discredit the Democrats. Lodge's reservations were actually designed to defeat the treaty, rather than make it acceptable. He hoped in his way to create an issue for the election of 1920.

3. The American People. At the beginning of the battle over ratification the majority of Americans favored the League. Yet they were so indifferent to world affairs that they allowed politicians of both parties to reject the instrument that might have prevented World War II. That second conflict was needed to teach them that the United States could only stay out of war by helping keep the world at peace.

ADDITIONAL READING

Ross Gregory, *The Origins of American Intervention in the First World War* (1971), is a capable brief analysis, but a more thorough study is Ernest R. May, *The World War and American Isolation, 1914-1917* (1959). H. C. Peterson and Gilbert C. Fite, *Propaganda for War* (1939), analyzes the effect of Allied and German propaganda on the American decision. Good general accounts are also in Arthur S. Link, *Wilson: The Struggle for Neutrality, 1914-1915* (1960), and D. M. Smith, *Robert Lansing and American*

Neutrality (1958). The third volume of Paolo E. Coletta, *William Jennings Bryan* (1969), is a thorough treatment of some diplomatic problems. A popular but sound summary of the military experience is Edward M. Coffman, *The War to End All Wars: The American Military Experience in World War I* (1968). Life on the home front during the war is described in Preston W. Slosson, *The Great Crusade and After* (1937), and H. N. Scheiber, *The Wilson Administration and Civil Liberties* (1960). Thomas A. Bailey, *Wilson and the Peacemakers* (1947), is anti-Wilson in tone. The opposite viewpoint is presented in D. L. Fleming, *The United States and the League of Nations* (1932). Ralph Stone, *The Irreconcilable: The Fight Against the League of Nations* (1970), is excellent on this topic.

CHAPTER XII

The Era of "Normalcy"
1920-1932

⟪NATIONALISM AND CONSERVATISM

During the decade following World War I a war-weary people, disillusioned by the realities of the peace and rendered indifferent to society by prosperity, reverted to the conservatism and nationalism that was typical of all postwar eras. Yet the persuasive influences of progressivism and internationalism could not be completely rejected. On the domestic front the Republican presidents of the period praised laissez faire, yet adopted many of the regulatory measures that had proven efficient during wartime. In foreign policy they rejected the League and world cooperation, yet carried the nation into the world arena to a degree that would have scandalized isolationists a generation before.

I. READJUSTMENT TO A PEACETIME ECONOMY.

A. Economic Demobilization.

1. The Railroads. Wilson wished to return the railroads to private ownership but to retain the more desirable features of unified operation. The result was the _Esch-Cummins Transportation Act_ (1920) which provided: 1) the Interstate Commerce Commission was authorized to evaluate railroad property and fix rates that would allow a fair return on the investment; 2) a _recapture clause_ ruled that all returns over 6 per cent would be divided between the road and the government; 3) railroad combinations were encouraged in the interest of efficiency; and 4) a *Railway Labor Board* was created to mediate labor disputes on interstate carriers. The act's failure to operate satisfactorily was due largely to a dispute between the I.C.C. and the roads on the means of evaluating railroad property for rate-fixing purposes. The I.C.C. wished evaluation to rest on reproduction cost in 1914; the roads, on reproduction cost in the 1920's, which would be far higher. The Supreme Court in *St. Louis and O'Fallon Railway Co. v. United States* (1929) eventually accepted the railroads' contention, defeating the purposes of the act.

2. The Merchant Marine. The *Merchant Marine Act* (1920) authorized the United States Shipping Board to dispose of the 1500 ships that it owned at the end of the war, and to loan the resulting proceeds to ship builders. When this failed to stimulate the construction of a sizeable merchant marine, the Jones-White Act (1928) increased the amount that could be loaned for ship construction and granted generous mail contracts to American vessels.

B. Veterans' Legislation.

1. Disability Compensation. A *Veterans' Bureau* (1921) was authorized to administer pensions and hospitalization for the benefit of veterans disabled during the war.

2. Adjusted Compensation for War Service. A *Bonus* for all soldiers, varying with the term of service, was advocated by the *American Legion* (1919) and other veterans' organizations. An *Adjusted Compensation Act* (1924) granted each veteran a twenty-year endowment policy based on the length of time he had served overseas. Owners could borrow against these from the government at 6 per cent interest. Pressure from a depression-ridden "Bonus Army" forced Congress in 1936 to authorize payment of the veterans' certificates in 3 per cent bonds that could be redeemed at once.

C. Social Readjustments.

1. Prohibition. The war allowed prohibitionists to argue that cereals should be used for food rather than for beer or whiskey. Their pressure led Congress to adopt the

Eighteenth Amendment (December, 1917), which was ratified by January, 1920. This forbade the manufacture and sale of all intoxicating beverages, which were defined by the *Volstead Act* (1919) as those containing more than one-half of 1 per cent of alcohol. Despite federal efforts to enforce the measure, drinking not only increased but became more fashionable during the next decade.

2. Women's Suffrage. The wartime efforts of women in jobs that ranged from Red Cross nursing to serving as "farmerettes" won support for women's suffrage. The *Nineteenth Amendment,* granting women the vote, was adopted by Congress in 1919 and ratified in 1920.

II. POLITICS OF THE 1920's.

A. The Harding Administration.

1. The Election of 1920. The Republicans nominated *Warren G. Harding,* a small-town Ohio politician whose party regularity and support of the Lodge reservationists appealed to standpatters. The platform attacked Wilson's "autocracy" and hedged on the League issue. *Calvin Coolidge,* governor of Massachusetts, was selected as Harding's running mate. The Democrats named *James M. Cox* of Ohio, a mild liberal, with *Franklin D. Roosevelt* as vice-presidential candidate. Their platform praised Wilson's record, and endorsed the League. The voters, reacting against wartime controls, gave Harding an overwhelming majority.

2. The Harding Scandals. Harding surrounded himself with mediocre politicians, many of whom were members of his "Ohio Gang." The result was a series of scandals that rivaled those of Grant's administration.

a. THE BUREAU SCANDALS. The director of the Veterans' Bureau, *Charles R. Forbes,* was found guilty of squandering $200,000,000 in his two years in office, much of it in fraudulent hospital contracts, and was sentenced to prison. The alien property custodian was disclosed to have fraudulently disposed of German chemical patents and other valuable property. Harding's Attorney General, *Harry M. Daugherty,* was dismissed from office as the result of the illegal sale of liquor permits.

b. THE TEAPOT DOME SCANDALS. In 1921 the administration of naval oil reserves was transferred from the Navy Department to Secretary of the Interior _Albert B. Fall._ Fall in 1922 secretly leased the _Teapot Dome Oil Reserve_ in Wyoming to a prominent oil man, _Harry F. Sinclair,_ and the _Elks Hills Reserve_ in California to _Edward L. Doheny._ When a Senate investigating committee under _Thomas J. Walsh_ of Montana disclosed that Sinclair had "lent" Fall $100,000, both Sinclair and Fall were imprisoned and the leases canceled.

3. Death of Harding. Although personally innocent, Harding was so demoralized by these revelations that he died on August 2, 1923.

B. The Coolidge Administration.

1. Coolidge as President. Coolidge became President on the death of Harding. A taciturn man with a reputation for honesty, he quickly won the confidence of his country. His well-publicized statement: "The business of America is business," summed up the laissez-faire philosophy that governed his administration.

2. The Election of 1924.

a. THE NOMINATING CONVENTIONS. Coolidge was nominated unanimously by the _Republicans._ The _Democrats,_ on the other hand, were divided into an immigrant-labor-city faction led by Alfred E. Smith of New York, and a rural-southern-western faction under William G. McAdoo of California. When these two candidates remained deadlocked for ballot after ballot during the convention, the nomination was finally given to a conservative dark horse, _John W. Davis_ of New York. Liberals, who could see no difference between Coolidge and Davis, joined with Socialists to form the _Progressive Party_ which nominated _Robert M. LaFollette_ of Wisconsin. Their platform called for tariff revision, public ownership of waterpower, farm relief, outlawing the labor injunction, and other progressive measures.

b. RESULTS OF THE ELECTION. Coolidge won a decisive victory, with an electoral vote of 328 to 136 for Davis and 13 for LaFollette. The Republicans also won control of both houses of Congress.

C. The Election of Herbert Hoover.

1. The Nominating Conventions. Coolidge declined to be a candidate in 1928, although his cryptic "I do not choose to run" allowed supporters to hope that he could be drafted. The *Republicans* nominated *Herbert Hoover,* an engineering-trained businessman whose administration of Belgian relief during the war pleased humanitarians and whose record as Secretary of Commerce under Coolidge won the confidence of businessmen. *Alfred E. Smith's* popularity had grown so rapidly that he was nominated without difficulty by the *Democrats.*

2. The Campaign and Election. Although the platforms of the two parties were almost identical, the contest gained color through the personalities of the candidates. Smith departed from the Democratic platform to denounce prohibition and the partnership between Republican politicians and industrialists. Hoover retaliated by branding Smith's program as state socialism. Smith was handicapped, particularly in rural areas, by his Catholic religion, his opposition to prohibition, and his Tammany background. Hence he won only 87 electoral votes to 444 for Hoover. Even the Solid South went Republican, with the exception of the Gulf States, South Carolina, and Arkansas.

III. THE DOMESTIC SCENE UNDER REPUBLICAN CONTROL, 1920-1932.

A. Social Conflicts. The conservatism and nationalism of the era were shown in the wave of bigotry that swept the United States.

1. The Great Red Scare.

a. CAUSES FOR UNREST. The hysterical fear of anything that threatened the status quo was occasioned by: 1) The *spread of communism* in Europe after the Russian Revolution. 2) *Labor disputes* that multiplied when employers, freed of wartime controls, tried to offset gains made by organized labor during the war. Labor responded with strikes that involved 4,000,000 workers during 1919. Most famous were the *Boston Police Strike,* which was broken up by Governor Calvin Coolidge, and the coal strike of the United Mine Workers, which was defeated by the use of the federal injunction. 3) *The Recession of 1920.* Wartime prosperity broke sharply in 1920 with the falling off of the foreign demand for American goods. During 1921 business failures left 5,000,000 men unemployed. Industry quickly recovered, but agriculture remained depressed for a decade.

b. THE ATTACK ON MINORITY GROUPS.

I. *The Palmer Raids.* Sensing the popular hatred of communism, Wilson's Attorney General, *A. Mitchell Palmer,* during 1919-1920 deported suspected radicals, raided the homes and offices of socialists and communists, and arrested hundreds whose economic views were unorthodox. In the end nearly all were released.

II. *The Sacco-Vanzetti Case.* In 1920 two Italian immigrants, *Nicola Sacco* and *Bartolomeo Vanzetti,* were arrested on a murder charge near Boston. Despite contradictory evidence, they were sentenced to hang when the trial revealed that they were atheists and anarchists. They were executed in 1927 after a period of controversy that attracted world attention.

III. *Suppression of Socialists.* In 1920 the New York legislature expelled five socialists for no other crime than party membership. In twenty-four states criminal-syndicalism laws made membership in the Socialist or Communist parties a criminal offense. This attack on civil liberties was upheld by the Supreme Court in *Schenck v. United States* (1919), which sanctioned the conviction of a man who had criticized conscription, and *Abrams v. United States* (1919), which imposed a twenty-year sentence on Jacob Abrams for distributing a pamphlet asking workers to rise against American military intervention in Russia. Both cases were notable for the ringing dissenting opinions of the great liberal justice, *Oliver Wendell Holmes.*

2. The Ku Klux Klan. The modern Klan originated in Georgia in 1915 but gained strength only in the 1920's. Dedicated to an attack on Negroes, Jews, Catholics, aliens, religious modernists, pacifists, and internationalists, it grew so rapidly that it boasted five million members by 1924, largely in the West and South. Its program of terrorism not only spread fear among minorities, but also allowed the Klan to gain political control in several states, notably Indiana. This eventually aroused resentment, but the Klan's decline after 1925 was due largely to internal corruption.

3. Immigration Restriction. Nativistic sentiment, together with fear of an alien flood from war-devastated Europe, was responsible for the *Immigration Act of 1921* which limited immigration from any country to 3 per cent of that nation's nationals residing in the United States in 1910. This *Quota System* not only reduced migration to a trickle, but also discriminated against aliens from southern and eastern Europe. The *Johnson Act* (1924) : 1) lowered the quota from each country to 2 per cent of that nation's nationals in the United States in 1890, further discriminating against the New Immigration; 2) allowed the unrestricted migration of native-born Canadians and Latin Americans; and 3) barred Oriental immigration entirely. This provision greatly offended Japan, which had already stopped migration to the United States under the Gentleman's Agreement (see p. 139).

4. Protests of the Intellectuals. The intolerance and nationalism of the 1920's aroused intellectuals not to protest but to ridicule. Some fled to Paris to escape a country so sunk in materialism that aesthetic values were forgotten. Others subjected their native land to tirades of abuse and criticism. Their leader was *Henry L. Mencken*, who turned his magazine, *The American Mercury*, into the bible of the intellectuals. Novelists reflected the same critical spirit, as attested by Sinclair Lewis' *Main Street* (1920) and *Babbitt* (1922), Sherwood Anderson's *Winesburg, Ohio* (1919), and Theodore Dreiser's *An American Tragedy* (1925).

B. Government and Industry, 1920-1932. The Republican legislative program was designed to aid business through budgetary reforms, tariff policy, and the sanction of industrial consolidation.

1. Budgetary Reforms. The Republican program of economy and tax reduction was aided by a congressional measure creating the *Budget Bureau* (1921) to prepare estimates of federal revenue and recommend expenditures. Neither this nor the business-minded Secretary of the Treasury who served under Harding and Coolidge, *Andrew Mellon*, could affect many economies in government. Instead, tax reductions in the higher income brackets and on certain businesses were made possible only by the prosperity of the decade. This helped reduce the national debt from $24,000,-000,000 in 1920 to $16,000,000,000 in 1930.

2. Tariff Legislation.

a. THE FORDNEY-McCUMBER TARIFF (1922). This raised tariffs to the highest level in American history. To temper criticism Congress authorized the Tariff Commission to recommend changes that would equalize production costs at home and abroad, and gave the President power to raise or lower duties as much as 50 per cent. This flexible clause was used thirty-seven times, thirty-two to raise duties.

b. THE HAWLEY-SMOOT TARIFF (1930). Hoover was apparently interested in genuine tariff reform, but lobbyist pressure on the Republican majority in Congress resulted instead in the *Hawley-Smoot Bill*, which raised duties another 20 per cent. Hoover signed the measure despite protests from many manufacturers and all economists. Within two years twenty-five nations passed retaliatory tariffs raising duties on American goods. This: 1) injured the foreign trade of the United States; 2) forced many manufacturers to move their plants abroad; and 3) fostered the spirit of economic nationalism that helped precipitate World War II.

3. Business Consolidation.
Holding companies and trade associations were used to create industrial monopolies with Republican approval.

a. HOLDING COMPANIES. These were corporations that owned the stock of several producing companies; in the field of hydroelectric power especially, holding companies were pyramided on holding companies for several layers above the actual producers of electricity. The resulting division of profits raised electrical rates. Nor did the *Federal Power Commission* (1920) prevent this consolidation, as its sympathies were with the power interests. Liberal protests were led by Senator *George W. Norris* of Nebraska, who campaigned for the government operation of a war-built power and fertilizer plant at *Muscle Shoals* on the Tennessee River. This was branded as socialism by the Republican presidents, who twice vetoed Muscle Shoals bills.

b. TRADE ASSOCIATIONS. More than four hundred combinations of manufacturers were formed under Herbert Hoover as Secretary of Commerce. Through these, producers of particular commodities (hardware, textiles, etc.) united to pool information, fix prices, cooperate in advertising, standardize wages, share purchases, and in other ways eliminate competition.

c. RESULTS OF REPUBLICAN POLICY. By the end of the Hoover administration monopoly was more widespread than in 1900. Fifty-three per cent of the corporate wealth was owned by 594 corporations, while the largest twenty banks controlled 27 per cent of the nation's banking deposits. In the extractive industries one corporation owned all the aluminum deposits, another more than half the iron ore, and eight others three-fourths of the anthracite coal.

C. Government and Agriculture, 1920-1932.

1. Agricultural Depression. Agriculture never recovered from the Recession of 1920. As prices slid downward almost 75 per cent between 1920 and 1932, farm income declined from $15,000,000,000 to $5,000,000,000. This slump was caused by the contraction of European markets and world overproduction. At the same time higher taxes and mounting prices for manufactured goods further reduced the farmers' income, while the burden of debt contracted during the prosperous wartime period hung over their heads.

2. Republican Efforts at Reform.

a. EXPANDED CREDIT FACILITIES. In 1921 Congress revived the *War Finance Corporation* as a lending agency to finance the export of farm surpluses. The credit facilities of the *Farm Loan Banks* (see pp. 127-128) were also broadened, while the *Intermediate-Credits Act* (1923) authorized loans on livestock and crops bound for market.

3. Farmers' Demands. Acting through a bipartisan *Farm Bloc* in Congress, the farmers sought relief through two devices:

a. THE EQUALIZATION FEE. This was embodied in the *McNary-Haugen Act* which was debated in several congresses and passed in 1927 and 1928, only to be vetoed by President Coolidge. It provided that the government should purchase all surplus crops not needed to supply the domestic market. These would then be sold abroad at the world price. The loss suffered from any unfavorable difference between the world price and the tariff-protected domestic price would be met by an *Equalization Fee* collected from the growers.

b. THE EXPORT DEBENTURE PLAN. This proposed payment of government bounties for agricultural exports. These bounties would be paid in the form of *Debentures* which would be interchangeable with import duties. Such a bill was vetoed by President Hoover.

4. The Hoover Farm Program. To offset farmer agitation for the McNary-Haugen Act, Hoover urged on Congress the *Agricultural Marketing Act* (1929). This created a *Federal Farm Board* which was authorized to stimulate cooperatives, encourage crop limitation, and peg the price of crops by purchasing surpluses to withhold them from the market. The Board bought large quantities of wheat and cotton, only to see the price of those commodities decline still more, leaving the government with a heavy loss. The farm problem remained pressing at the close of the Hoover administration.

IV. FOREIGN POLICY OF THE REPUBLICANS, 1920-1932. The end of isolationism was shown by the way in which the Republican presidents, although professedly rejecting an international role for the United States, cooperated with other nations in seeking world collective security.

A. The Search for Collective Security.

1. Relations with the League and World Court.

a. PARTICIPATION IN THE LEAGUE OF NATIONS. The fifty-four nations that joined the League made it an instrument for world peace that the United States could not ignore. In 1922 Secretary of State *Charles Evans Hughes* began sending "unofficial observers" to sessions that involved American interests; after 1924 official delegates were sent. By 1932 the United States had adhered to thirteen international agreements arranged by the League.

b. STRUGGLE OVER THE WORLD COURT. The Permanent Court of International Justice was established at the Hague in 1922. Its organization was planned by an American jurist,

Elihu Root, and Americans were also included on its panel of eleven justices. President Harding in 1923 recommended adherence to the World Court, but the move was defeated by Senate isolationists. In 1926 the Senate finally voted to join if the Court would accept five reservations, the most important prohibiting the judges from handing down advisory opinions that involved American interest without American consent. Although these were accepted, the Senate took no further action. American adherence was finally rejected in 1935 by a Senate vote of 52 to 36—seven less than the needed two-thirds.

2. Naval Disarmament.

a. THE WASHINGTON CONFERENCE (1921). Nine nations, meeting at the invitation of the United States, heard Secretary of State Hughes propose a drastic cut in naval armament. The _Five-Power Treaty_ that resulted (1922) set the naval ratio in capital ships for the United States, Great Britain, and Japan at 5-5-3, with 1.75 for Italy and France.

b. THE GENEVA CONFERENCE (1927). The Five-Power Treaty did not outlaw competitive building of cruisers, destroyers, and submarines. To check this, President Coolidge called a five-power conference at Geneva in 1927. As France and Italy refused to attend, the conference accomplished nothing.

c. THE LONDON CONFERENCE (1930). A five-power conference called by President Hoover extended the capital-ship ratio to auxiliary ships, although allowing Japan somewhat greater strength. France and Italy refused to ratify the treaty, which was also abrogated by Japan in 1934.

3. Efforts to Outlaw War. In 1927 the French Premier Aristide Briand suggested to Coolidge's Secretary of State. Frank B. Kellogg, a nonaggression treaty with the United States. Kellogg expanded this into an international document, known as the _Pact of Paris_, or the _Kellogg-Briand Pact_ (1927), whose signers renounced war as an instrument of national policy. Although eventually agreed to by sixty-two nations, the Pact was ineffective as it lacked means of enforcement.

B. The Problem of War Debts. The United States loaned $10,000,000,000 to its Allies for war and reconstruction purposes. These were the _war debts._

1. Difficulty of Repayment. Repayment was difficult because: 1) High American tariffs prevented repayment in goods, while the United States already owned most of the world's gold supply; 2) The debtor nations had loaned money to other allied powers, and felt that these debts must be paid before they paid the United States; 3) The debtor nations hoped to make repayment by using German _reparations,_ but Germany had no means of paying the $33,000,000,000 demanded of it, and defaulted within a year; 4) The Allies felt that their sacrifices in men and money during the early years of the war could only be compensated if the United States canceled the war debts. Americans, on the other hand, looked on the loans as investments that must be returned.

2. Financial Negotiations.

a. REFUNDING THE WAR DEBTS. Between 1923 and 1930 treaties were drafted with seventeen of the debtor nations to extend the period of payment and reduce the original 5 per cent interest charges by about one-half.

b. SCALING DOWN REPARATIONS. To facilitate German reparation payments that would allow the Allies to pay their war debts, the original excessive sum was gradually reduced. In 1924 the _Dawes Plan_ lowered the amounts due, worked out a schedule of payments, and arranged for loans from the United States to speed German economic recovery. By borrowing in the United States Germany met her payments under this plan until 1929, when she again defaulted. The _Young Plan_ (1929) further reduced the amount due to $27,000,000,000, spread payments over fifty-nine years, and provided for a further reduction should the United States consent to scaling down the war debts.

3. End of the Controversy. The great depression made payment of either reparations or war debts impossible. In 1931 President Hoover announced a one-year _moratorium_ on both. A year later the _Lausanne Conference_ (1932) reduced German reparations to $714,000,000 under the assumption that the United States would also cancel its war debts. When Congress refused, all European nations save Finland defaulted on their payments. By the end of 1933 the controversy was over, leaving a residue of irritation behind.

C. Relations with the Far East.

1. The Rise of Japan. American interest in the Far East declined as the Open Door policy and the acquisition of the Philippines did not result in the expected economic benefits. Japan took advantage of this and of Europe's preoccupation in World War I to assert her own supremacy. In 1915 she forced China to accept her *Twenty-One Demands* and thus become virtually a protectorate of Japan, which also secured special concessions in Manchuria, Mongolia, and the Shantung Peninsula. To placate the United States, the *Lansing-Ishii Agreement* (1917) was negotiated, in which both nations affirmed the Open Door and pledged themselves to respect the territorial integrity of China. Japan's propinquity, however, was recognized as giving her a paramount interest in the Far East.

2. The Washington Conference (1921). This conference not only considered naval disarmament (see p. 171) but the Far Eastern situation. Two treaties resulted:

a. THE FOUR-POWER TREATY (December, 1921). The United States, England, France, and Japan pledged themselves to respect each other's rights in the Pacific area and to settle all conflicts by joint conference.

b. THE NINE-POWER TREATY (February, 1922). The signers bound themselves to safeguard China's rights and interests, to respect its territorial integrity, to maintain the Open Door, and to refrain from seeking special concessions or spheres of influence. Although containing no provisions for enforcement, these two treaties shifted the burden of maintaining China's independence from the United States and England to all the great powers.

3. Japanese Aggression. In 1931 Japan invaded Manchuria, violating the Washington treaties, the Kellogg-Briand Pact, and the League Covenant. The United States sent an official representative to sit with the League Council in this emergency, but England's refusal to cooperate doomed chances of positive action. Hoover's Secretary of State, Henry L. Stimson, announced that his government would refuse to recognise conquests made in violation of the Kellogg-Briand Pact—a declaration known as the *Stimson Doctrine* (1932). Despite this rebuff, Japan set up in Manchuria the puppet state of *Manchukuo*, then extended its military conquests into northern China. Continued protests led Japan to withdraw from the League in 1933. The chain of events leading to World War II had begun.

D. Relations with Latin America.

1. The Mexican Problem. The Mexican Constitution of 1917 gave the government ownership of all mineral and oil resources. If interpreted retroactively, this threatened to wipe out American investments of $300,000,000. The Harding government not only refused to recognize the Mexican government but threatened war until 1923, when the Mexican courts held that the provision was not retroactive. The controversy continued, however, as nationalization of resources went on. Not until 1927 was it brought to a close by a new ambassador, *Dwight L. Morrow,* an able lawyer opposed to dollar diplomacy. His diplomacy persuaded Mexico to modify its oil and mineral laws, as well as to adopt a church policy less offensive to American Catholics.

2. The Caribbean Policy.

a. WITHDRAWAL FROM THE CARIBBEAN. Increasing governmental stability in the Caribbean and Central America, combined with growing public sentiment against dollar diplomacy, led to a gradual withdrawal of American marines from that area. They were removed from Santo Domingo in 1922 and from Nicaragua in 1925.

b. REDEFINING THE MONROE DOCTRINE. The Clark Memorandum, drafted by the State Department in 1928, stated that the Monroe Doctrine was directed toward Europe rather than Latin America, thus giving the United States no superior position over the other Republics in the hemisphere. This was a step toward interpreting the Doctrine as the joint concern of all the Americas rather than of the United States alone.

V. PANIC AND DEPRESSION, 1929-1932.

A. Prosperity in the 1920's.

1. Business Prosperity. After the recession of 1920

business enjoyed unparalleled prosperity, as the expansion of new industries (automobiles, radio, motion pictures, electrical appliances, and chemicals) lifted production to new heights. Prophets told the people that prosperity was a permanent feature of the "new economic era," and that both wages and output would spiral upward for all time.

2. The Speculative Boom. With security assured by the "new economy" Americans felt free to invest their savings in stocks. Speculative buying by all classes drove common stocks from 117 to 225 between December, 1928, and September, 1929. This rise encouraged people to buy widely on credit, confident that their investments would pay all debts. This, in turn, stimulated greater production. "Two cars in every garage" seemed within the reach of all.

3. Unsound Features of the Economy. Despite prosperity, the economy contained many weak spots: 1) Technological unemployment mounted steadily as machines took over the work of men. Between two and four million men were constantly out of work, decreasing buying power. 2) The agricultural depression after 1920 lowered the purchasing power of farmers. 3) Overseas trade steadily declined as a result of the Republican tariff policy and the disturbing influence of the war-debt and reparation controversies. 4) The new wealth was largely in the hands of the few, while the wages of the principal consumers—the workers—did not keep pace with prices. 5) Credit buying meant that many Americans were poor even though spending lavishly; once their confidence in the future was shaken, they would stop buying. 6) Production in basic industries began to slip in the late 1920's, as the demand declined for coal, textiles, new homes, steel, and automobiles.

B. The Crash of 1929.

1. The Collapse of the Stock Market. Stock prices began to decline on October 21, 1929. As panic selling spread, they plunged rapidly lower, losing 40 per cent in a month. For the next three years they slid downward at a slower rate; during the period the average of leading stocks fell from 252 to 61. Millions were ruined by the crash, while others who had thought themselves secure stopped buying luxuries in an effort to conserve their savings.

2. The Coming of the Great Depression. The collapse of public confidence slowed purchases of industrial and farm produce. Prices fell, business failures mounted, factories closed, the number of unemployed rose to 15,000,000 persons by 1932, and drastic wage cuts curtailed the purchasing power of those still working. Within three years 5000 banks closed their doors. Farmers were further hit by a severe drought in 1930 and subsequent years.

C. Hoover and the Depression. Hoover maintained that the panic was psychological, and that prosperity would return if manufacturers kept wages and prices up. When this plea failed he was forced to act.

1. The Unemployment Problem. Hoover insisted that the burden of relief should be borne by private philanthropy and local governments. He refused to sanction a dole or government-supported public works.

2. The Reconstruction Finance Corporation (1932). Democrats and progressive Republicans created the R.F.C. to loan money to banks and railroads on the theory that stability at the top of the business structure would eventually benefit all the people. In all the R.F.C. loaned $11,000,-000,000 without appreciably halting the depression. Its aid, however, doubtless saved many enterprises that would otherwise have failed.

3. The Norris-LaGuardia Act (1932). The product of efforts by Democrats and Republican insurgents, this measure outlawed the injunction in labor disputes.

VI. THE ERA OF "NORMALCY": AN APPRAISAL.

A. The Spirit of the 1920's. During the 1920's the American people were indifferent to domestic society and to the world. This was due to:

1. Disillusionment. Americans had sacrificed much during the progressive era and World War I to secure social justice for all, adjust economic inequalities, "make the world safe for democracy," end war, and check the persecution of minorities. Having pitched their hopes too high, they were utterly disillusioned by the realities of the postwar world. When autocracy, oppression, and war still continued, Americans came to the conclusion that the world was not worth saving.

2. Prosperity. With insecurity relegated to the past by technological changes, Americans could afford to think of themselves as independent of both society and government. Seldom have a people been so individualistic and materialistic as in the era of "normalcy."

B. Impact of American Disillusionment.

1. On Domestic Policy. Indifference to social problems was shown by the failure of Americans to punish the Republicans for the Harding scandals; almost half the voters stayed home at each election during the 1920's. Left free to follow their own policies without fear of public censure, politicians could openly support the upper class to which they belonged (by tariffs, tax reduction, aid to business consolidation, etc.) while ignoring the lower class (as indicated by their failure to enact farm or labor legislation). As a result, the economic order was thrown out of balance, with too large a share of the national wealth going to business leaders, too little to farmers and workers. The resulting decline in purchasing power was a fundamental cause of the great depression.

2. On Foreign Policy. Popular indifference to the actions of government officials was probably responsible for the enlightened American foreign policy of the era. These officials were less influenced by outworn traditions than the masses, and hence better able to see that the day of isolationism was gone. Their efforts toward world security, although fruitless, prepared the way for the important changes inaugurated by Franklin D. Roosevelt.

ADDITIONAL READING

Two excellent surveys of the era are John D. Hicks, *Republican Ascendancy, 1921-1933* (1969), and William E. Leuchtenburg, *The Perils of Prosperity, 1914-1932* (1958). Frederic L. Paxson, *Postwar Years: Normalcy* (1948), and Karl Schriftgiesser, *This Was Normalcy* (1948), are in greater detail but less interpretative. The period may also be studied in two thorough biographies: Donald R. McCoy, *Calvin Coolidge: The Quiet President* (1967), and Robert K. Murray, *The Harding Era: Warren G. Harding and His*

Administration (1969). Other biographical studies of importance include Dexter Perkins, *Charles Evans Hughes* (1956) ; Oscar Handlin, *Al Smith and His America* (1958) ; and Arthur M. Schlesinger, Jr., *The Age of Roosevelt: The Crisis of the Old Order, 1919-1933* (1955), the latter largely on the Hoover Era. Intellectual and social developments are described in Robert M. Crunden, *From Self to Society, 1919-1941* (1972), which surveys thought patterns; and George N. Knoles, *The Jazz Age Revisited* (1955), which is excellent on the social scene. Frederick L. Allen, *Only Yesterday* (1931), is a popular re-creation of the atmosphere of the day. L. Erhan Ellis, *Republican Foreign Policy, 1921-1933* (1968), is a thorough survey; aspects of the subject are expertly considered in Selig Adler, *The Isolationist Impulse* (1957), Robert H. Ferrell, *Peace in Their Time* (1952), and Alexander de Conde, *Herbert Hoover's Latin American Policy* (1951). The standard study of the coming of the depression is John K. Galbraith, *The Great Crash* (1955).

~~~~~~~~~~~~~~~~~~~~~~~~

CHAPTER XIII

The New Deal
1933-1941

~~~~~~~~~~~~~~~~~~~~~~~~

❡THE PHILOSOPHY OF THE NEW DEAL

The domestic program of Franklin D. Roosevelt was not a "revolution." Since the 1880's the American government had assumed an increasingly positive role in safeguarding human welfare; in both the states and nation an impressive body of laws regulated business enterprise or sought to guard the common man from the buffeting of economic storms. This progressive tradition was forgotten during World War I and the reactionary period that followed. Hence Roosevelt's task was to bring government and the economy abreast again after a twenty-year lag. This necessity, combined with the need for hurried action in the midst of the great depression, created the impression that the New Deal was revolutionary rather than evolutionary.

I. INAUGURATING THE NEW DEAL.

A. The Election of 1932.

1. The Republican Campaign. Recognizing the inevitability of their defeat as the depression party, the Republicans nominated *Hoover* without enthusiasm. Their platform praised his handling of the depression, which was blamed on the European situation.

2. The Democratic Campaign. Roosevelt's popularity as governor of New York (1928-1932) elevated him to the leadership of his party, displacing Al Smith, who vainly led a "stop Roosevelt" movement during the convention. When this failed, Roosevelt was nominated without serious opposition. The platform promised: 1) unemployment relief and social security; 2) legislation favorable to labor; 3) the "restoration of agriculture"; 4) federal regulation of security exchanges, utility rates, and holding companies; 5) the development of publicly owned electric power; 6) reciprocal trade agreements with other nations; 7) repeal of the Eighteenth Amendment; and 8) "a continuous responsibility of government for human welfare."

3. Results of the Election. Hoover campaigned on the theme: "It might have been worse." Roosevelt, on the other hand, stressed the plight of the "forgotten man" and promised a "new deal" for the people. This won him an unprecedented popular vote of 23,000,000 to 16,000,000 for Hoover, while the electoral vote was 472 to 59. Only two states outside of New England gave their votes to Hoover.

4. The Twentieth Amendment. This _Lame Duck Amendment,_ which went into effect just as Roosevelt took office, provided that Congressmen should be seated on January 3 following each election, and the President inaugurated on January 20. It also gave Congress power to act should the President and Vice-President die in office.

B. The First Recovery Measures.

1. Inauguration of Roosevelt. By March 4, 1933, when Roosevelt was inaugurated, 15,000,000 people were out of work, while runs had closed virtually every bank in the country. Rather than minimizing the disaster as had Hoover, Roosevelt's inaugural address admitted the "dark realities of the moment" but called on the people not to lose hope. "The only thing we have to fear," he said, "is fear itself." Outlining a program for recovery, he warned that he would ask for broad executive powers to wage war on the depression if Congress did not act.

2. The Financial Crisis.

a. THE BANK HOLIDAY. With nearly all banks closed by runs and confidence at a low ebb, Roosevelt immediately declared an official _bank holiday_ which closed all banks. At the same time he called Congress into special session to meet on March 9, 1933.

b. Early Banking Legislation. An *Emergency Banking Law* was passed only a few hours after Congress met. This provided for the early reopening of all sound banks, and named a Bank Conservator to aid those not in liquid condition. Most of the banks soon were functioning under this measure. An Economy Act (March 10, 1933) authorized the President to reduce government salaries, pensions, and veterans' benefits, affecting a saving of $500,000,-000 yearly. At the same time taxes were raised slightly in an effort to balance the budget.

II. **THE NEW DEAL DOMESTIC PROGRAM, 1933-1936.** The New Deal program aimed at three objectives: *relief* for workers, farmers, and the unemployed; *recovery* for the nation's economy; and *reform* to prevent economic maladjustments in the future.

A. **Relief Measures, 1933-1936.** Rejecting the dole as used in England, Roosevelt shaped a program of *work relief* that took many forms.

1. *Emergency Relief Projects.*

a. The Civilian Conservation Corps (April, 1933) was created to employ young men from destitute families. Scattered in 2600 camps, the 1,600,000 youths who received C.C.C. training performed an invaluable service in protecting natural resources, building parks, and the like.

b. The Federal Emergency Relief Administration (May, 1933). The *F.E.R.A.* was designed to provide the states with relief funds until federal relief could begin functioning. Between 1933 and 1935 it distributed $3,000,-000,000 to the states for the unemployed.

c. The Civil Works Administration (1933). The *C.W.A.* gave temporary work relief through the winter (November, 1933-May, 1934) to 4,000,000 jobless.

d. The United States Employment Service (1933) was designed to link state and local employment exchanges into a nation-wide organization that would find jobs for the unemployed.

2. *Long-Range Relief Projects.*

a. The Public Works Administration (June, 1933). Under Secretary of the Interior *Harold Ickes* the

P.W.A. was assigned numerous heavy construction projects —waterworks, schools, bridges, and the like. Operating through private construction firms, the P.W.A. eventually did much to relieve unemployment.

b. THE WORKS PROGRESS ADMINISTRATION (April, 1935). When early relief measures failed to ease pressure on the government, the President proposed that unemployables be returned to the states for direct relief, and that employables be assigned to socially valuable undertakings rather than trivial tasks. Congress responded by creating the *W.P.A.* under *Harry Hopkins,* with an initial appropriation of $5,000,000,000. By March, 1936, 4,000,000 persons were employed on the W.P.A., building schools, parks, roads, irrigation dams, and other civic improvements. Important branches of the bureau included the *Federal Arts Project,* which employed actors, painters, writers, and other white-collar workers in jobs suited to their skills, and the *National Youth Administration* (N.Y.A.) which helped 400,000 youths continue their education.

B. Recovery Measures, 1933-1936.

1. Monetary Reform. The New Deal financial program was based on the theory that the dollar, deflated by the depression, must be inflated to raise prices.

a. REPUDIATION OF THE GOLD STANDARD. In April, 1933, the United States went off the gold standard, while a month later the President was authorized to inflate the currency by adding $3,000,000,000 in new treasury notes, or by reducing the gold content of the dollar up to 50 per cent. At the same time the government began purchasing gold at home and abroad at high prices, thus seeking to devaluate the dollar still further.

b. RETURN TO A PARTIAL GOLD STANDARD. Congressional and business criticism of "currency tinkering" forced Roosevelt to renew partial currency controls. In February, 1934, he reduced the gold content of the dollar to 59.06 cents, while Congress set up a $2,000,000,000 stabilization fund to regulate the devaluated dollar in relation to other forms of currency.

c. RESULTS OF MONETARY REFORM. The financial measures did not succeed in raising prices, while security holders lost heavily. On the other hand, foreign trade was stimulated by dollar devaluation, which lowered the price of American goods abroad.

2. Pump-Priming Measures. The New Deal attempted to stimulate industrial recovery by several measures designed to encourage private enterprise.

a. RECONSTRUCTION FINANCE CORPORATION. Although created by the Hoover administration, the R.F.C. was given new powers in 1934, when it was authorized to grant loans to industries as well as to railroads and banks. In all, $11,-000,000,000 was loaned before 1936, most of the money being returned shortly afterward.

b. RESIDENTIAL CONSTRUCTION. Home building had shrunk to a negligible point by 1933, while many home owners were unable to keep up their mortgage payments. To remedy this situation three measures were passed: 1) The *Home Owners Loan Corporation* (1933) was authorized to loan money to mortgage holders faced with the loss of their property. The H.O.L.C. saved the homes of more than 1,000,000 persons. 2) *The Federal Housing Administration* (1934) was empowered to insure mortgages issued by private concerns for construction purposes. 3) *The United States Housing Authority* (1937) assisted local governments in slum-clearance projects and the building of low-cost housing.

3. Agricultural Recovery. Between 1920 and 1933 the value of farm holdings had declined $42,000,000,000, while by 1933 two of every five farms were mortgaged. The New Deal attempted to stimulate agriculture and thus restore farm purchasing power.

a. THE PROBLEM OF FARM DEBTS. Mortgage foreclosure proceedings threatened to reduce the nation to a system of tenant farming. To combat this several laws were passed:

i. *Federal Farm Loan Act* (May, 1933). This created a Farm Credit Administration (F.C.A.) to refinance agricultural mortgages at 4 per cent (later 3 per cent), and to loan money to farmers who had already lost their lands by foreclosure.

II. *Frazier-Lemke Act* (1934). This law, which postponed mortgage foreclosure for six years if the farmer paid adequate rent during that period, was declared unconstitutional in the case of *Louisville Joint Stock Co. v. Radford* (1935). A second Frazier-Lemke Act (1935) accomplished the same purpose for a three-year period.

III. *The Resettlement Administration* (1935), which after 1937 was known as the *Farm Security Administration* (F.S.A.) purchased 17,000 farms on submarginal lands, allowing their owners to move to better sites.

b. THE FARM CROP PROBLEM. Recognizing that foreign markets were closed to American agricultural produce, and that farmers produced more than the nation could consume, Roosevelt's agricultural program was designed to reduce the acreage devoted to basic crops, and eventually the number of farmers.

I. *Agricultural Adjustment Act* (May, 1933). This created an *Agricultural Adjustment Administration* (A.A.A.) authorized to enter into agreements with farmers willing to reduce the acreage of such basic crops as cotton, wheat, corn, and tobacco. Farmers accepting these agreements would be paid subsidies, the money to be raised by taxing processers of farm goods (flour millers, meat packers, etc.).

II. *Operation of Agricultural Adjustment Act.* During 1934 cotton growers withdrew 10,000,000 acres from production, wheat growers 8,000,000 acres, and other producers comparable amounts. The resulting increase in prices, combined with the shortages following a severe drought and the payment of government subsidies, raised farm income from $5,150,000,000 in 1932 to $8,700,000,000 in 1935.

III. *Overthrow of the A.A.A.* Opposition to the A.A.A. was voiced by consumers who resented increased prices, processers who objected to the tax on their services, and theorists who felt that an "economy of scarcity" was ill suited to a land where millions were underfed. An additional constitutional objection was raised by the Supreme Court in *United States v. Butler* (1936). The Act was held unconstitutional as an invasion of the rights of the states, and an improper exercise of the congressional taxing power.

IV. *Soil Conservation and Domestic Allotment Act* (1936). This was the administration's attempt to salvage something from its farm program. Benefit payments were authorized for farmers who gave up the use of worn-out land or shifted crops in the interest of soil conservation. They were to be administered by the states under federal standards. The measure was largely ineffective.

4. Industrial Recovery Measures.

a. NATIONAL INDUSTRIAL RECOVERY ACT (1933). The *National Recovery Administration* (N.R.A.), under *Hugh S. Johnson,* was authorized to draw up a "code of fair competition" for each major industry. A "blanket code" promulgated by the President as a model for others prohibited child labor, set a thirty-six hour week for workers and a forty-hour week for clerks, and established a minimum wage of forty cents an hour. The act also included a section (*Section 7a*) requiring the codes to grant workers "the right to organize and bargain collectively through representatives of their own choosing." This was enforced by a *National Labor Board* (N.L.B.) under Senator *Robert F. Wagner* of New York.

b. OPERATION OF THE N.R.A. Within two years 750 codes were drawn up, largely by representatives of big business. These set minimum wages and maximum working hours, abolished child labor, established prices, limited production, and assigned quotas for particular plants. Small businessmen soon complained that the codes discriminated against them, while liberals charged that the N.R.A. was creating giant monopolies. Conservatives were equally exercised over the rights given labor in Section 7a, especially when workers staged a series of strikes during 1934 and 1935.

c. OVERTHROW OF THE N.R.A. The Supreme Court, in *Schechter Poultry Corp. v. United States* (1935), declared the National Industrial Recovery Act unconstitutional on three grounds: 1) the measure illegally delegated congressional power to the President; 2) it violated the commerce power by assuming that Congress had authority over production; and 3) it sanctioned the illegal invasion of state authority by the national government.

d. LATER INDUSTRIAL MEASURES. Two laws salvaged something from the wreckage of the N.R.A.: 1) The *Wagner-Connery Act* (1935) created a *National Labor Relations Board* (N.L.R.B.) to prevent unfair practices in labor relations affecting interstate commerce. These included the coercion of employees, company domination of unions, discrimination against union members in employment or tenure, and the refusal to bargain collectively with workers. 2) The Guffey Coal Act (1935) applied a form of code control to the coal industry. This measure was declared unconstitutional in *Carter v. Carter Coal Company* (1936).

C. Reform Measures, 1933-1936.

1. Reform in Banking and Finance.

a. GLASS-STEAGALL BANKING ACT (1933). Designed to prevent future collapses of the private banking system, this forbade banks to engage in the investment business, restricted the speculative use of bank credits, and expanded the Federal Reserve system to banks previously excluded. Its most popular provision created the *Federal Deposit Insurance Corporation* (F.D.I.C.) to insure all deposits up to $5000.

b. THE REGULATION OF SECURITIES.

I. *Truth in Securities Act* (1933). This required: 1) all securities offered for sale in interstate commerce to be registered with the Federal Trade Commission; 2) that each issue contain accurate information allowing the buyer to judge the soundness of the corporation; and 3) that the directors be held criminally liable for any false information.

II. *The Securities Exchange Act* (1934). All stock exchanges were required to obtain licenses from the *Securities and Exchange Commission* (S.E.C.) which was given broad powers to regulate their activities. The power of registering securities was also transferred from the Federal Trade Commission to the S.E.C.

2. Hydroelectric Power.

a. TENNESSEE VALLEY AUTHORITY (1933). The *T.V.A.* was created by the Muscle Shoals Act with power to build and operate power-producing dams in the Tennessee River Valley, to manufacture nitrates, to sell electric power, and to rehabilitate the seven-state area through which the river ran. This launched an important experiment in government ownership. By 1938 the T.V.A. was distributing electric power to 40,000 homes and farms; by 1941 it served 400,000 customers. Moreover, the lowered cost of electricity served as a "yardstick" for private companies in the area, forcing them to lower their rates enough to save $50,000,000 yearly for users. A similar program was begun in the _Columbia River Basin_ with the building of Grand Coulee Dam (1933) and Bonneville Dam (1937). These not only provided cheaper electricity for the Northwest but allowed a million acres of arid land to be reclaimed.

b. RURAL ELECTRIFICATION ADMINISTRATION (1935). The R.E.A. was authorized to build power plants and high tension lines in rural areas. Within five years it brought electricity to farmers in forty-three states.

c. WHEELER-RAYBURN ACT (1935). This authorized the S.E.C. to confine holding companies to natural regions, and to eliminate holding companies that had more than one intervening company between them and the operating company.

3. Social Security.

a. PRESSURE FOR SOCIAL SECURITY. In 1932 only twenty-eight states provided old-age assistance, and only two unemployment insurance, although both were common in European countries. Unemployment and the growing tendency of employers to hire only young workers created a popular demand for relief that took such dangerous forms as the _Townsend Plan._ This promised pensions of $200 monthly to all over the age of sixty, providing they spent all their money each month. To check the demand of millions for such unworkable schemes as this, a social security act was called for.

b. THE SOCIAL SECURITY ACT (1935). This provided: 1) old-age insurance, beginning at the age of sixty-five, and financed by an equal tax on the worker and employer; 2) unemployment compensation, administered by the states, but financed by a federal tax on payrolls; 3) federal aid to the states for destitute persons, child health, maternity care, crippled children, the aged, and the blind; 4) administration of the measure by a Social Security Board.

c. OPERATION OF THE SOCIAL SECURITY ACT. Within two years old-age pensions and unemployment-insurance schemes in all states insured 21,000,000 people against unemployment and 36,000,000 against a penniless old age. Although attacked by conservatives as inflicting new burdens on industry, and by liberals as providing insufficient benefits, the measure was welcomed by a majority of the people and upheld as constitutional by the Supreme Court.

III. THE CLIMAX OF THE NEW DEAL, 1936-1941.

A. The Election of 1936.

1. Opposition to the New Deal. Although popular with a majority of the people, the New Deal was attacked from both right and left:

a. CONSERVATIVE OPPOSITION. Conservatives complained that the New Deal: 1) was fastening an unmanageable debt on the country ($34,000,000,000 by 1936) through its deficit financing; 2) unreasonably interfered with business; 3) gave too much power to the President and thus weakened democracy; 4) encouraged labor organization; and 5) constantly violated the Constitution. These objections were voiced both by Republicans and by conservative Democrats under Alfred E. Smith, who in 1934 formed the *Liberty League* to combat Roosevelt.

b. RADICAL OPPOSITION. The masses were organized by such rabble-rousers as Senator Huey P. Long of Louisiana, whose Share-Our-Wealth Society promised to divide all wealth among the poor; Dr. Francis E. Townsend, who promised pensions of $200 monthly to all over sixty; and the Reverend Charles E. Coughlin, Detroit's radio priest, who demanded a nationally controlled currency system. In all, several millions followed these prophets, all of whom were pledged to defeat Roosevelt in 1936.

2. The Candidates. The *Republicans* nominated *Alfred M. Landon* of Kansas, who reminded his followers of a middle-western Calvin Coolidge. The platform promised to continue all New Deal measures, but without extra cost and with no danger to the Constitution or the "American system of free enterprise." The _Democrats_ renominated _Roosevelt_ by acclamation and adopted a platform that eulogized the New Deal. Disgruntled supporters of Coughlin, Long, and Townsend banded together as the _Union Party_ to nominate Congressman _William Lemke_ of North Dakota. Their platform was a hodgepodge of promises to all groups represented in the party.

3. Results of the Election. Despite the almost solid opposition of the press, Roosevelt carried every state but Maine and Vermont ("As Maine goes so goes Vermont" became a popular Democratic jibe), with 523 electoral votes to 8 for Landon. Democrats also swept both houses of Congress. The Union Party polled only 900,000 votes, while the combined vote of Socialists and Communists was less than 300,000.

B. The Battle over Court Reorganization.

1. Origins of the Conflict. Between 1935 and 1937 the Supreme Court held seven basic New Deal laws unconstitutional, usually by a narrow majority. In all, the four conservative judges used such intemperate language that they were suspected of allowing prejudice rather than reason to dictate their decisions. Even Republicans were aroused when the majority held in _Morehead v. New York ex rel. Tilaldo_ (1936) that state minimum-wage laws for women and children were unconstitutional. Democrats explained the Court's conservatism by pointing out that seven of the nine justices had been appointed by Republican presidents, while six were over seventy years of age.

2. The Court Reorganization Bill. In February, 1937, Roosevelt asked Congress to enlarge the Supreme Court from nine to fifteen members, if judges declined to retire at the age of seventy. The measure also proposed less controversial changes in the lower courts.

3. The Battle over Reorganization. The controversy over the court bill was occasioned by the fact that Congress was already beginning to strain against presidential control and welcomed a chance to assert itself. This was because: 1) the improved economic situation encouraged legislators to act on their own; 2) many Democrats viewed the President's dominance over Congress as an unwarranted extension of the executive power; 3) southern conservatives sought a chance to assert themselves without party censure; and 4) the overwhelming Democratic majorities in the 1936 election stimulated Democratic divisions by convincing many that the opposition was ineffective. Hence Republicans and Democrats alike denounced the "Court-packing" bill in a bitter debate that lasted through the spring and summer of 1937.

4. Reversal by the Supreme Court. While the debate raged, the Court suddenly reversed itself and handed down favorable decisions on several New Deal measures. The most important of these, *National Labor Relations Board v. Jones and Laughlin Steel Corporation* (1937), upheld the National Labor Relations Act by ruling that labor relations in factories producing for interstate commerce were subject to congressional control. Other measures validated by the Court included the Social Securities Act, the second Frazier-Lemke Mortgage Law, a Railway Labor Act, and a Washington state minimum-wage law identical with the one held unconstitutional nine months before. A popular witticism of the day was "A switch in time saves nine."

5. Defeat of Court Reorganization. Congress defeated the Court Reorganization Bill in August, 1937. During the next few years Roosevelt achieved his end when the death or retirement of older justices allowed him to place younger and more liberal judges on the bench. The result was a series of progressive decisions for the first time since World War I.

C. Labor Legislation, 1936-1941.

1. Origin of the C.I.O. Economic recovery, and the growing strength of unions under the stimulus of New Deal laws, encouraged a division in the ranks of labor. This began when unskilled workers, long excluded from the American Federation of Labor, found a leader in *John L. Lewis,* president of the A.F. of L. United Mine Workers, who maintained that unions should be organized along industrial rather than craft lines—that is, that all steel workers, or mine workers, or automobile workers, should be in one union regardless of crafts or skills. When the A.F. of L. refused to back him, Lewis formed the *Committee for Industrial Organization* (C.I.O.) to organize the steel and automobile industries. His first victory was won when the _United Automobile Workers_, a C.I.O. union, used the _sit-down_ strike to force recognition from General Motors Corporation (November, 1936). The _steel industry_ also came to terms in March, 1937, when the United States Steel Corporation accepted the C.I.O. as a bargaining agent for its employees. Violent strikes at plants of the Republic Steel Company and other smaller producers later won recognition there.

2. Division of the A.F. of L. By the fall of 1937 the C.I.O. had 3,700,000 members and the A.F. of L. 3,600,000. This led to such internal conflicts that in November, 1938, the two split, the Committee for Industrial Organization changing its name to the Congress for Industrial Organization.

3. Fair Labor Standards Act (1938). The C.I.O.-A.F. of L. conflict called attention to the need for additional labor legislation. The _Fair Labor Standards Act_ (1938) provided for an eventual forty-hour week and a forty-cent-an-hour minimum wage for all workers in firms producing for interstate commerce. This was to be approached gradually until the full objective was reached by 1945. The measure was popularly known as the _Wages and Hours Law_.

D. Farm Legislation, 1936-1941.

1. Plight of the Farm Worker. The agricultural measures of Roosevelt's first term failed to solve the problem of _southern tenancy_. Almost half the southern farms were operated by _share croppers_ who benefited little from the crop-restriction program of the A.A.A. In desperation they formed the Southern Tenant Farmers' Union (1934) to press for relief. Equally alarming was the plight of those driven from their farms by the drought of 1934-1935 that turned much of the Southwest into a _dust bowl_. Many made their way into California, where they competed for the few jobs available. Their hardships were popularized by John Steinbeck's novel, _The Grapes of Wrath_ (1939).

2. Legislative Remedies.

a. THE BANKHEAD-JONES ACT (1937). The Farm Security Administration (F.S.A.) was authorized to make long-term, low-interest loans to share croppers who wished to purchase their lands. The F.S.A. also made subsistent grants to migratory workers in California.

b. THE AGRICULTURAL ADJUSTMENT ACT (1938). Replacing the law of 1933 that had been declared unconstitutional, this provided: 1) that the Secretary of Agriculture could fix the acreage for basic crops each year and establish "marketing quotas" to restrict the sale of surpluses; 2) that in bad crop years the A.A.A. would grant farmers "parity payments" sufficient to offset the difference between the low price and the price their produce would have commanded before World War I; 3) that farmers who adopted anti-erosion practices should be given conservation payments; and 4) that the government provide storage space and loans for surplus crops to assure an "ever normal granary." The measure failed to reduce the 1939 crop, while in subsequent years demands from war-torn Europe outbalanced supply.

E. Congressional Elections of 1938.

1. The Recession of 1937-1938. A sharp business recession, caused by the curtailment of government relief spending in 1936-1937, brought a return of hard times between August, 1937, and June, 1938. Revived federal spending restored comparative prosperity during the fall of 1938. The recession, however, was one factor influencing the election. The other was Roosevelt's attempt to *"purge"* anti-New Deal Democrats from Congress by appealing to the people for their defeat. This "interference" with legislative independence cost him some votes.

2. Outcome of the Elections. Although Democrats retained control of both houses of Congress, their majorities were so reduced that for the first time since 1933 the Republicans could operate as an effective minority.

3. Governmental Reorganization. Roosevelt seized the period of calm after the election to press for a reorganization of the executive departments of the federal government. This was designed to abolish overlapping bureaus, eliminate waste, and increase efficiency. Congressional authorization to carry out this reform (1939) resulted in elimination of twenty-three bureaus. Closely related was the *Hatch Act* (1939), which forbade employees below policy-making positions to engage in political activities.

IV. AN EVALUATION OF THE NEW DEAL.

A. End of the New Deal. For all effective purposes the New Deal came to an end after the Congressional elections of 1938. Roosevelt continued in office until his death in 1945, but during the remaining years, an effective Republican opposition and the preoccupation of the President with foreign affairs brought a virtual end to domestic reform.

B. Results of the New Deal.

1. Harmful Results. On the debit side, the New Deal: 1) vastly increased the federal debt; 2) stimulated the growth of class consciousness among farmers and workers; 3) fostered bureaucracy and administrative inefficiency; 4) slowed the growth of civil service reform by multiplying offices outside the merit system; 5) infringed upon free business enterprise; and 6) brought the nation face to face with its most serious future problem: How far could economic regulation be extended without sacrificing the liberties of the people? Although democracy was not threatened by any New Deal measures, the question remained one of the most troublesome confronting the United States during and after World War II.

2. Beneficial Results. On the credit side of the ledger, the New Deal: 1) allowed the nation to weather its most serious depression without upsetting the capitalistic economy; 2) brought labor and agriculture on the one hand, and industry on the other, into better balance; 3) fostered a more equitable distribution of the national wealth; 4) conserved many of the country's resources; and 6) established for all time the principle of positive government action to rehabilitate and preserve the human resources of the nation.

ADDITIONAL READING

The best brief survey is William E. Leuchtenburg, *Franklin D. Roosevelt and the New Deal* (1963); fuller are the still unfinished multi-volume biographies by Arthur M. Schlesinger, Jr., *The Age of Roosevelt* (1957-), and Frank Friedel, *Franklin Delano Roosevelt* (1952-). An excellent single-volume biography is James M. Burns, *Roosevelt: The Lion and the Fox* (1956). The criticism bred of New Deal policies is studied in George Wolfskill and John A. Hudson, *All But the People: Franklin D. Roosevelt and His Critics* (1969). The social history of the New Deal era is told in Dixon Wecter, *The Age of the Great Depression* (1948), the economic history in Broadus Mitchell, *Depression Decade* (1948), the labor history in Irving Bernstein, *The Turbulent Years: A History of the American Worker, 1933-1941* (1970), and the intellectual history in Arthur A. Ekirch, Jr., *Ideologies and Utopias: The Impact of the New Deal on American Thought* (1969). William F. McDonald, *Federal Relief Administration and the Arts* (1969), surveys the impact of the four arts projects on the nation's culture. A convenient and authentic discussion of legal aspects is in Paul L. Murphy, *The Constitution in Crisis Times, 1918-1969* (1972). George B. Tindall, *The Emergence of the New South* (1967) describes the impact of Roosevelt's policies on that area; important for one major development is William H. Droze, *High Dams and Slack Waters: TVA Rebuilds a River* (1965). Harry T. Williams, *Huey Long* (1969), is a prize-winning biography of a leading southern opponent. Among the treatments of Roosevelt critical of the New Deal, the best is Edgar E. Robinson, *The Roosevelt Leadership, 1933-1945* (1955), which focuses on political history.

~~~~~~~~~~~~~~~~~~~~~~

Chapter XIV

Foreign Policy of the New Deal

1933-1941

~~~~~~~~~~~~~~~~~~~~~~

ℭ THE ROAD TO WORLD WAR II

World developments between World War I and World War II were shaped largely by the breakdown of collective security. For this the United States was partially responsible. Rejecting global responsibility, the American people revived faith in isolationism, believing that they could stay aloof from the troubles of Europe and Asia. By declining to join the League of Nations and the World Court, by withdrawing from the Far East, and by erecting tariff barriers around their country, they contributed to the rise of nationalism, at the same time undermining the little faith left anywhere in collective efforts to preserve the peace. Their selfishness left the world prey to avaricious dictators whose totalitarian states could only endure by expanding. This expansion plunged the world—and the United States—into World War II.

I. THE GOOD NEIGHBOR POLICY. In his inaugural address President Roosevelt dedicated the United States "to the policy of the good neighbor—the neighbor who resolutely respects himself and, because he does so, respects the rights of others." This policy was effectively applied toward certain Pacific areas and Latin America.

A. Philippine Independence.

1. Origins of Independence Movement. Although the United States promised the Filipinos their independence in 1916 (see p. 133), Republican presidents took no steps to carry out the pledge. The Democratic victory of 1932, and a depression-born desire to be rid of the "white man's burden," revived interest in separation. Four groups especially pressed for independence; 1) sugar growers who disliked competition from the islands; 2) organized labor resentful of Filipino immigration; 3) dairy interests seeking to exclude Philippine coconut oil; and 4) anti-imperialists who had long campaigned against domination of colonial peoples.

2. Achievement of Independence. The _Hawes-Cutting Act_ (1933), passed by a Democratic Congress in the last days of the Hoover administration, provided for freedom after ten years but gave the United States the right to retain military and naval bases on the islands. When this offer was rejected by the Filipinos, the _Tydings-McDuffie Act_ (1934) was passed. This gave up all claim to military bases, and left the problem of naval bases to future negotiations. Under this measure the _Philippine Commonwealth_ inaugurated its first president, Manuel _Quezon,_ in November, 1935. After the proscribed probationary period the Philippines attained their freedom on July 4, 1946.

B. Withdrawal from the Caribbean.

1. Change in American Policy.

a. DECLINE OF DOLLAR DIPLOMACY. Dollar diplomacy lost popularity during the great depression. This was because Americans believed: 1) that intervention in Latin America meant higher taxes for the benefit of a few business concerns; 2) that the ill will created by intervention handicapped trade relations; 3) that hemispheric solidarity was needed to combat European fascism; and 4) that they should set their own economic house in order before meddling with other nations.

b. STATEMENT OF AMERICAN POLICY. At a Pan-American Conference at _Montevideo_ (1933) Secretary of State _Cordell Hull_ joined with other American nations in accepting a pact that denied the right of any country to intervene in the affairs of other countries. Roosevelt also declared that the administration's policy was "opposed to armed intervention."

2. Application of the Policy.

a. ABROGATION OF THE PLATT AMENDMENT. When disorder broke out in depression-ridden Cuba, the United States not only refrained from sending troops but in May, 1934, signed a treaty abrogating the Platt Amendment (see p. 106).

b. WITHDRAWAL OF AMERICAN TROOPS. In 1930 President Hoover recalled marines from Haiti, and in 1933 from Nicaragua (see p. 174). Roosevelt continued this policy withdrawing the last troops from Haiti in 1934, and in 1940 ending the American customs receivership over the Dominican Republic. In 1936 a treaty with Panama relinquished all rights to intervene in that country.

C. The Mexican Expropriation Controversy. Acting under the Constitution of 1917 (see p. 174) Mexico in 1938 expropriated foreign oil properties valued at $400,-000,000. Instead of intervening to protect American capital, the United States admitted Mexico's rights to take over these properties, but insisted that the owners be compensated. A joint commission agreed upon the sums due, and in 1939 the Mexican government began payment.

D. Reciprocal Trade Agreements. In June, 1934, Congress authorized the President to raise or lower tariff duties up to 50 per cent in return for reciprocal concessions from other nations. Within five years treaties were negotiated with twenty-one countries, including more than half the Latin-American republics. These treaties not only stimulated foreign trade, but helped undermine economic nationalism.

E. Achievement of Hemispheric Solidarity. The rise of dictators in Europe emphasized the need for unity in the Americas. This was achieved through a series of conferences: 1) The _Rio de Janeiro Conference_ (1933) condemned wars of aggression and bound the signers not to recognize territory acquired by force; 2) The _Buenos Aires Conference_ (1936), which was attended by Roosevelt, reaffirmed earlier pledges of collective security and pledged the American nations to consult together on peace measures whenever war threatened any one of them; 3) The _Lima Conference_ (1938) adopted resolutions condemning racial or religious persecution and declared against the activity of aliens who remained loyal to their native land—two measures aimed particularly at Nazi Germany.

F. Significance of the Good Neighbor Policy. In effect the United States used the good neighbor policy to declare that it was no longer the sole interpreter of the Monroe Doctrine. Instead, the nations of the western hemisphere would act together as equals in the quest for collective security.

II. THE PROBLEM OF NEUTRALITY, 1933-1939.

A. Rise of Totalitarianism. During the 1920's and 1930's four dictatorial powers rose to challenge the democratic nations:

1. The Union of Socialist Soviet Republics. Established by revolution in 1917, the U.S.S.R. based its economy on a Marxian system of government-owned land and industry. Power was centered in a restricted Communist Party, which after 1924 was dominated by _Josef Stalin._ He subordinated the plan for a world communist revolution that had been developed by Trotsky and earlier revolutionists, concentrating instead on the internal development of Russia through a succession of "five-year plans."

2. Italy. Following a march on Rome in 1922, _Benito Mussolini_ became dictator of Europe's first fascist nation. He preached the doctrine of state supremacy over the individual.

3. Germany. Within a few months after _Adolph Hitler_ was elevated to the chancellorship in 1933 he wiped out the last vestiges of democracy, substituting dictatorial rule through his _National Socialist,_ or _Nazi,_ Party. Like fascism, nazism elevated the state above the individual, as well as appealing to German racial prejudice by advocating the persecution of Jews and Catholics. Both systems were intensely nationalistic, advocating the right of expansion at the expense of weaker neighbors.

4. Japan. When the great depression played into the hands of its military leaders, Japan moved toward fascism in the 1930's. Advocating territorial expansion as the only cure for poverty, generals won control of the Cabinet and Emperor, then committed their nation to a program of aggression.

B. The End of Peace.

1. Warfare in China. Japan's expansion began in 1931 with the invasion of Manchuria and the creation of the puppet state of _Manchukuo._ This aggression united dissention-torn China under its leading generalissimo, _Chiang Kai-Shek_. Hence Japan, when she began an undeclared war on that nation in 1937, met strong resistance. For the next decade the two nations fought constantly, with the Nipponese steadily victorious. An incident of the war was the Japanese bombing of an American gunboat, the _Panay_ (1937), an act that aroused resentment but no demand for intervention.

2. Warfare in Africa. In 1935 Mussolini began a war of conquest against Ethiopia. When British opposition prevented the League of Nations from cutting off oil supplies to Italy—which probably would have ended the war—the Italians won an easy victory.

3. Warfare in Spain. A revolution against the Spanish Republican government (1936) was led by General _Francisco Franco_, whose fascist program soon attracted help from Germany and Italy. This foreign aid allowed Franco to win a complete victory.

4. Expansion of Germany. When a plebiscite showed that the people of the Saar Valley favored the move, Germany in 1935 annexed the region; a year later the Rhineland was occupied by force.

C. The American Reaction.

1. Rise of Isolationism. The events in Europe further convinced Americans that the rest of the world was not worth saving. Isolationist sentiment was also fostered by: 1) the great depression, which convinced many that the United States should concentrate on its own recovery; 2) the continued failure of the World War I allies to pay their war debts (see pp. 172-173); 3) the disclosure by a Senate committee under _Gerald P. Nye_ of North Dakota (1934-1936) that during World War I bankers and munitions makers accumulated vast profits. This revelation proved to many people that the United States had been forced into the war by these "merchants of death." By 1937, about 70 per cent of the Americans believed that their country should not have entered World War I.

2. Neutrality Legislation. Isolationist sentiment was mirrored in a series of congressional acts designed to prevent American involvement in future wars:

a. THE JOHNSON ACT (1934) forbade debt-defaulting nations to market their securities in the United States.

b. THE NEUTRALITY ACTS (1935-1937). This group of laws: 1) laid an embargo on the shipment of all munitions, arms, and implements of war to belligerents; 2) provided that all indirect war materials (steel, cotton, food, etc.) must be handled on a "cash and carry" basis—that is, they must be taken from the United States on the ships of a belligerent and paid for in cash; 3) forbade American travel on belligerent ships; and 4) denied belligerents the right to float loans in the United States.

c. MEANING OF NEUTRALITY LEGISLATION. Congress hoped that these acts would prevent the United States from becoming involved in future wars as it had in World War I. They were based on the assumption that _economic,_ rather than idealistic, motives had been responsible for past participation. This represented a reversal of the traditional American stand for freedom of the seas.

3. Presidential Policy. Roosevelt had no sympathy for the neutrality acts, believing instead that the United States could remain at peace only by helping prevent the outbreak of a major war in Europe. As an advocate of _collective security,_ he favored cooperation with the democracies to check and restrain the dictatorships before they became strong enough to bid for world power.

a. THE QUARANTINE SPEECH (1937). In an important address in Chicago, Roosevelt compared world lawlessness to a physical disease and urged the international quarantine of aggressors as the only means of preserving peace. The unfavorable reaction convinced the President that he could not muster support for such a program at that time.

b. NAVAL EXPANSION. Sure that the United States would eventually become involved in the war that was then starting, Roosevelt in 1934 asked Congress to enlarge the fleet to its full strength under the Washington and London treaties (see p. 171). After Japan and Italy refused to accept further naval limitations (1936), he requested a billion-dollar naval-building program (1938). The bill was passed after a long debate.

c. USE OF THE NEUTRALITY ACTS. Roosevelt used the acts whenever possible to punish attacking nations and aid attacked nations. In the Italian-Ethiopian War (1935) he applied the acts, knowing that Italy could purchase arms from the United States while Ethiopia could not. In the Sino-Japanese War (1937), on the other hand, he refused to invoke the laws, allowing the Chinese to continue arms purchases. The embargo was also applied during the Spanish Revolution (1937), despite objections from liberals who wished to aid the Loyalists as Germany and Italy were aiding Franco.

d. ACTION AGAINST JAPAN. The President showed his displeasure with Japan by announcing (July, 1939) that in six months the United States would abrogate a 1911 treaty between the two powers which guaranteed reciprocal trading rights. In effect this prevented Japan from buying gasoline, scrap iron, and other materials needed for her war on China.

III. THE APPROACH OF WAR, 1939-1940.

A. Outbreak of the War in Europe.

1. Expansion of Germany. In 1938 Hitler's troops added Austria to the Third Reich. Hitler then demanded the *Sudetenland,* an adjacent portion of Czechoslovakia inhabited largely by Germans. Although the Czechs were ready to fight, England and France accepted the *Munich Pact* (1938) in which the Sudetenland was surrendered to Germany in return for a promise of no future aggression. The failure of appeasement was shown in March, 1939, when the Nazis conquered Czechoslovakia and Mussolini's troops overran Albania. The two dictators, in May, 1939, agreed on a ten-year military alliance known as the _Rome-Berlin Axis._

2. End of Appeasement. Germany's annexation of Czechoslovakia showed England and France that the dictators could be stopped only by force. When Hitler was rumored to be planning a move against Poland, they promised that country all possible aid in case of attack. The one additional step necessary for war was taken in August, 1939, when Hitler negotiated a nonaggression pact with Russia, the _Moscow-Berlin Pact._ Thus assured of a peaceful western border, Germany was ready to plunge the world into World War II.

3. The War Begins. Immediately after the Moscow-Berlin Pact was signed, Hitler's troops invaded Poland. England and France declared war on Germany on September 3, 1939. Although both nations mobilized, little fighting took place for the six months that Nazis needed to overrun Poland. In the meantime, Russia annexed the Baltic countries and launched a war of aggression against Finland that lasted until March, 1940.

B. Impact of the War on the United States.

1. Division of American Opinion. With the outbreak of war Americans divided into two camps: 1) the _isolationists,_ whose powerful America First Committee included such influential editors as William Randolph Hearst and Robert McCormick, and such politicians as Gerald P. Nye and Hamilton Fish; and 2) the _interventionists_ whose program of all aid to the Allies "short of war" was sponsored by the Committee to Defend America by Aiding the Allies, which was headed by William Allen White, a Kansas newspaperman. President Roosevelt was an outspoken interventionist, while public opinion polls showed that 70 per cent of the people favored aid for the Allies.

2. Administration Policy.

a. CHANGES IN THE NEUTRALITY ACTS. Roosevelt was legally required to apply the arms embargo to all belligerents, thus cutting off munitions shipments to France and England. He therefore called Congress into special session to amend the laws (November, 1939). After repeated prodding, Congress: 1) repealed the arms embargo but applied the "cash-and-carry" requirement to all commerce with belligerents; 2) continued the prohibition on loans to belligerents; 3) stopped American ships from carrying passengers or materials to warring countries; and 4) banned American travel on belligerent ships.

    b. EFFORTS TOWARD HEMISPHERIC SOLIDARITY. To unite the Americans and guard against the "fifth column" activity of German sympathizers, Roosevelt: 1) issued a call for a meeting of the foreign ministers of the American republics at Panama City (September, 1939). The resulting *Declaration of Panama* established a "safety belt" from 300 to 1000 miles wide around the Americas and warned belligerents against naval action in that area. 2) Called together a second conference of ministers at Havana (July, 1940). The *Act of Havana* forbade the transfer of any European colony in America to a non-American owner. Colonies in danger of falling into unfriendly hands were to be administered jointly by the American republics until final disposition was made. 3) Set up a Joint Board of Defense with *Canada* (August, 1940) to coordinate defense efforts.

    C. The German Offensive in Europe. In the spring of 1940 Hitler launched a *"blitzkrieg"* similar to that used in the conquest of Poland. Using Fifth Columnists and paratroopers to soften resistance, he cut down opponents by giant air attacks, then drove his armies forward behind tanks and mechanized infantry. The Allies could not stem this well-geared assault. Denmark and Norway fell in April, 1940. A month later the Netherlands and Belgium succumbed. France capitulated in June, shortly after Italy entered the war. By summer, only England held out against the Nazi juggernaut.

    IV. THE UNITED STATES ENTERS THE WAR, 1940-1941.

    A. Preparation for War. The Nazi blitzkrieg convinced even isolationists that the United States must improve its defenses against an attack that now seemed probable.

    1. Military Preparedness. During the summer of 1940 Congress appropriated $13,000,000,000 for the army, navy, and air force, levying new taxes to meet part of these expenditures. A *Selective Service Act* (September, 1940) required the registration of all men between twenty-one and thirty-five years of age. Of these, 800,000 were drafted for a year of training. Before they were released, the law was stiffened to require eighteen months of service and the registration of all between the ages of eighteen and forty-five.

2. Industrial Mobilization. The *Office of Production Management* (O.P.M.) was set up to put the nation's economy on a war footing. *William S. Knudsen,* a business executive, was placed in charge. At the same time the President sought to unite both parties behind the defense effort by adding two Republicans to his cabinet, *Henry L. Stimson* as Secretary of War, and *Frank Knox* as Secretary of the Navy.

3. Naval and Air Bases. In September, 1940, the President obtained from England ninety-nine-year leases on eight naval and air bases, scattered from Newfoundland to British Guiana, giving in return fifty over-age destroyers.

B. The Election of 1940.

1. The Candidates. The *Republicans* nominated *Wendell L. Willkie* of New York, a utility magnate and outspoken advocate of aid to England. The platform also favored support for Britain short of war, as well as national defense and most of the domestic reforms secured by the New Deal. The *Democrats* broke with precedent to nominate *Roosevelt* for a *third term.* The platform was almost identical with that of the Republican party, differing only in praising rather than condemning the past domestic achievements of the New Deal.

2. The Election. In a vigorous campaign Willkie praised most of the New Deal measures, but condemned the administration's waste, bureaucracy, dictatorial powers, and persecution of business. He also saw the *third term* as a step toward totalitarianism. Roosevelt refrained from campaigning until the last weeks of the election, allowing his record to speak for itself. This proved acceptable to the voters, who returned him to the White House with 449 electoral votes to 38 for Willkie. The Democrats also increased their majorities in both houses of Congress.

C. The End of Neutrality.

1. The Lend-Lease Act (March, 1941). Passed after a long debate, this allowed the United States to lend, lease, or otherwise transfer to nonaggressor nations any military equipment necessary for their preservation. Huge appropriations during the next months permitted mountains of goods to reach England. The United States was, in the President's phrase, the *"arsenal of democracy."*

2. The Greenland Base. In April, 1941, the anti-Nazi Danish minister to the United States granted American forces military bases on the Danish island of Greenland. This moved the American line of defense one step nearer the war zone.

3. The Atlantic Charter.

a. RUSSIA ENTERS THE WAR. After overrunning the Balkans during the spring of 1941, Hitler suddenly attacked Russia on June 22, 1941. This added another powerful nation to the anti-Nazi bloc, for while Stalin had shown no intention of attacking Germany during the period of the Moscow-Berlin Pact, he had been arming his country. Driven back during the summer and fall, the Russian armies stiffened during the winter of 1941-1942 and began to regain lost ground.

b. STATEMENT OF OBJECTIVES. To offset criticism of their partnership with totalitarian Russia, and to clarify their war aims, Roosevelt and Prime Minister _Winston Churchill_ of England issued the _Atlantic Charter_ (August 14, 1941). This stated that: 1) neither nation sought territorial gains; 2) both would respect the rights of all peoples to choose the form of government they wished; 3) both would cooperate in securing for all states access to the world's raw materials; 4) both would encourage international cooperation to secure just labor standards and social security; 5) both were committed to win for all people freedom from fear and want; 6) both favored the unrestricted freedom of the seas; and 7) both sought the disarmament of aggressor nations as a step toward permanent peace.

4. *The Battle of the Atlantic.* Heavy losses suffered by freighters carrying lend-lease supplies to England caused many Americans to demand that the United States provide convoys. The President, still reluctant to start a "shooting war," instead dispatched naval and air units to Iceland (July 7, 1941) to "patrol" the North Atlantic. They were ordered to report German submarines to the British, but not to fire themselves. When an American destroyer, the *Greer,* was attacked (September 4, 1941), Roosevelt ordered the navy to shoot on sight. In October another destroyer, the *Reuben James,* was torpedoed with a loss of seventy-six men. An outraged Congress on November 17, 1941, ordered the arming of merchant ships and the repeal of all neutrality legislation that required them to remain outside the war zone.

5. *The Attack by Japan.*

a. Japanese-American Relations, 1939-1941. Since September, 1939, when Japan formed a ten-year alliance with Germany and Italy, the three totalitarian powers had operated together. This *Rome-Berlin-Tokyo Axis* endangered the United States after July, 1941, when the Japanese occupied French Indo-China, thus menacing the Philippines as well as British and Dutch possessions in southern Asia. In retaliation, all of Japan's assets in the United States were frozen. Prolonged discussions followed, as the American government sought to persuade the Japanese to evacuate Indo-China and Premier Tojo prepared for the attack that was already planned.

b. The United States Enters the War. The attack came on *December 7, 1941,* when Japanese planes swooped down on the naval base at *Pearl Harbor* in the Hawaiian Islands. Taken without warning, the Americans were unable to defend themselves; nineteen ships were sunk or put out of action. A day later Congress recognized the existence of a state of war between the United States and Japan. Germany and Italy declared war on America a few days later.

V. ISOLATIONISM vs. INTERVENTIONISM. Could the United States have avoided involvement in World War II? Was the course that it followed suitable for the nation in the case of future European wars? Those questions must be answered in appraising the New Deal's foreign policy.

A. The Isolationists' Argument. Isolationists believed that economic forces plunged the United States into World War I. Hence they reasoned that if no similar stake in an allied victory was developed during the European phase of World War II, participation could be avoided. This was the purpose of the neutrality acts. In passing them, isolationists failed to recognize that wars were fought for ideological as well as material motives. The American people were willing to enter World War II not to save their dollars, but to save democracy and to preserve their nation's sovereignty.

B. The Interventionists' Argument. Interventionists held that the United States could not stay out of any major European war. Peace, they said, could be preserved only if the nonaggressor nations banded together to suppress aggressor nations in their infancy, thus nipping any possible war in the bud. This required a degree of international cooperation that the Americans were not ready to accept in the 1930's. Their aloofness allowed Germany, Italy, and Japan to gain so much strength that a major conflict was needed to defeat them.

C. Conclusion. The history of the period demonstrated the correctness of those who argued for collective security. Even though protected from economic losses by the neutrality laws, the American people were wholeheartedly behind England from the beginning. So intense was their ideological conviction that they were ready for war before the President or Congress, should war prove necessary to save Britain. World War II taught the United States that it could never know peace in a war-torn world.

ADDITIONAL READING

The biographies of FDR listed in Chapter XIII have much information on his foreign policy. Among specialized studies, the best are Robert H. Ferrell, *American Diplomacy in the Great Depression* (1957), which is thorough, and Allan Nevins, *The New Deal and World Affairs* (1950), which is brief. An excellent account is in James M. Burns,

Roosevelt: The Soldier of Freedom (1970). George Kennan, *American Diplomacy, 1900-1951* (1951), is an able interpretation; economic forces are stressed in Lloyd C. Gardner, *Economic Aspects of New Deal Diplomacy* (1964). E. O. Guerrant, *Roosevelt's Good Neighbor Policy* (1950), is favorable; David Green, *The Containment of Latin America* (1971), argues that the motivation underlying the Good Neighbor policy was economic expansion. A competent biography of Roosevelt's secretary of state is Julius W. Pratt, *Cordell Hull* (1964). The most thorough discussion of events leading to World War II is in William L. Langer and S. E. Gleason, *The Challenge to Isolation, 1937-1940* (1952), and *The Undeclared War, 1940-1941* (1955). A brief survey, designed for general readers but authentic, is John Wiltz, *From Isolation to War, 1931-1941* (1968); also authentic is T. R. Fehrenbach, *F.D.R.'s Undeclared War, 1939 to 1941* (1967). Herbert Feis, *The Road to Pearl Harbor* (1950), is a balanced treatment. Works on isolation include William Cole, *America First* (1953), Selig Adler, *The Isolationist Impulse* (1957), and especially Manfred Jonas, *Isolationism in America, 1935-1941* (1966). A sympathetic but sound survey of Roosevelt's role in both the coming and the progress of World War II is Robert A. Divine, *Roosevelt and World War II* (1969).

~~~~~~~~~~~~~~~~~~~~~~~~~~~~~~~~

CHAPTER XV

World War II
and Its Aftermath
1941-1960

~~~~~~~~~~~~~~~~~~~~~~~~~~~~~~~~

⦅ TOTAL WAR AND THE EMERGING COLD WAR

World War II brought the realities of modern warfare closer to the American people than any previous conflict. The vast number of men involved, the regulatory measures that governed the economy, and the terrifying implications of the atomic bomb all affected every man, woman, and child in the land. Nor did Americans retreat into a shell of isolationism once the war was won. Convinced at last that only collective world security could maintain peace, they helped form the United Nations, which promised a better world than the League of Nations that followed World War I. Yet scarcely had this peace agency been established when harmony was threatened by division of the globe into two hostile camps, one looking to the United States for leadership, the other to Russia. As these two nations and their allies maneuvered for power, sought to enlist the support of smaller countries, and built ever more competitive weapons for nuclear attack and defense, the resulting "Cold War" threatened to lead the world into a global conflict that would dwarf even World War II.

I. THE UNITED STATES IN WORLD WAR II.

A. The Period of Defeat, 1941-1942.

1. Japanèse Victories in the Pacific Area. Japan won a series of spectacular victories during 1941 and 1942. The British naval base at Singapore, the Netherlands East Indies, Burma, Guam, Wake Island, and Hong Kong, all surrendered, allowing the Nipponese to concentrate their attack on the Philippines. There outnumbered Americans made a valiant stand on the _Bataan Peninsula_ and the island of _Corregidor_ before capitulating. Their commander, General _Douglas MacArthur,_ was ordered to Australia before the Philippines fell. Turning next to the _Aleutian Islands,_ the Japanese held Attu and Kiska by the end of the summer, 1942. By that time they had occupied a million square miles of territory.

2. German Victories in Europe. Hitler's troops pushed back the Russians during the summer of 1942, while his air force pounded England mercilessly and his submarines sank hundreds of American freighters. The Allied road back was a hard one, but their offensive began in the fall of 1942.

B. The War in Europe, 1942-1945.

1. The African Campaign. The Allied offensive in Europe began in November, 1942, when troops under General _Dwight D. Eisenhower_ overran French Morocco and Algeria, then turned against the large German force in _Tunisia_. This force surrendered in May, 1943, with a loss of 200,000 men killed or captured.

2. The Italian Campaign. With North Africa won, Eisenhower's forces invaded Sicily (July, 1943). Mussolini fell from power during the conquest of the island, allowing the Italian king to appoint a government that willingly surrendered to the Allies. German soldiers in Italy were not willing to capitulate, however, and some of the bitterest fighting of the war took place before June, 1944, when Rome fell. The nonfascist government that took control of Italy became a cobelligerent of the Allies.

3. The War Against Germany.

a. PREPARATIONS FOR A SECOND FRONT. After winning air supremacy by the beginning of 1943, the Allies were free to attack Germany with British bombers and American flying fortresses. From that time on, mass bombings of industrial centers softened Hitler's war machine. Germany was further weakened when its drive against Russia was stopped at _Stalingrad_ (1942). By 1944 the Russians had driven the Nazis from their soil and freed Finland, Rumania, Bulgaria, and large sections of Poland.

    b. OPENING THE SECOND FRONT.

    ı. _The Battle of France._ On _June 6, 1944,_ an Anglo-American force under General _Dwight D. Eisenhower_ and General Sir _Bernard Montgomery_ landed on the Normandy coast. Two million American troops who had been waiting in Great Britain were poured through this opening during the summer of 1944 to drive the Germans back across France. Paris was liberated on August 25, 1944, just after another landing was made on the Mediterranean coast. By November the last Nazi had been driven from French soil. A "Free French" committee under General _Charles de Gaulle_ took over the government of the liberated nation.

    ıı. _The Battle of the Bulge._ A final German counter-offensive began in December, 1944, in the Belgium-Luxembourg sector. The Allied troops were thrown back almost to the sea, but rallied to regain lost ground by the end of January, 1945. Principally responsible for Allied success was the Third Army under General George S. Patton.

    c. THE BATTLE OF GERMANY. The Russian winter offensive began in January, 1945, when five huge armies moved into Germany from the east. By March 1 they were thirty miles from Berlin. Anglo-American armies from the west crossed the Rhine on March 7, 1945, and six weeks later joined with the Russians at the Elbe. As Hitler and his top officials committed suicide or went into hiding, Germany surrendered unconditionally on _May 8, 1945._

C. The War in the Pacific, 1942-1945.

    1. Beginning of the Pacific Offensive. Americans began the attack in the Pacific area during the summer of 1942 when the Japanese were checked, if not defeated, at the naval battles of _Coral Sea_ and _Midway._ In August, 1942, _Guadalcanal Island_ in the Solomon Islands was invaded; nine months later the _Aleutians_ were freed. Admiral _Chester W. Nimitz,_ commander of the Pacific fleet, was free to plan the offensive against Japan.

2. The Approach to Japan. American strategy called for a direct advance on Japan, with the more important Japanese-held islands captured and the others by-passed. _Saipan_ in the Marianas fell in June, 1944, and nearby Guam a month later. From airstrips on these islands superfortresses began bombing the Japanese mainland 1500 miles away. To shorten this distance the tiny volcanic island of _Iwo Jima,_ lying half-way between Guam and Tokyo, was captured after bitter fighting in March, 1945. The next jump was to _Okinawa,_ less than 400 miles from Japan; that island succumbed in June, 1945. After that bombers roared over the Japanese mainland almost constantly.

3. The Return to the Philippines. Following the same tactics of capturing some bases and by-passing others, General Douglas MacArthur's forces advanced northward from the south Pacific, landing on _Leyte Island_ in October, 1944. The landing was covered by naval forces under Admiral _William Halsey,_ who fought one of the war's decisive engagements in the _Battle of Leyte Gulf._ After conquering outlying islands, the Americans landed on the main island of _Luzon_ in January, 1945. Bitter fighting continued during the next months.

4. The War in China. The Chinese continued their heroic resistance, although they were crippled by lack of supplies after the closing of the _Burma Road_ by the Japanese in 1942. A token American air force under General _Joseph W. Stilwell_ gave some aid to Chiang Kai-shek, but not until January, 1945, was a new road, the _Ledo Road,_ opened between India and China. Properly supplied at last, the Chinese armies began driving back the Japanese invaders.

5. Final Conquest of Japan.

a. THE ATOM BOMB. The final blow necessary to force the Japanese to surrender was delivered in August, 1945, when atomic bombs were dropped on _Hiroshima_ and Nagasaki, two towns. The total destruction caused by America's terrifying new weapon not only hastened the end of the war but brought home to millions the realization that another world war would destroy civilization.

b. Japanese Surrender. Russia's declaration of war against Japan (August, 1945), coupled with fear of further atomic bombing, forced Japan to bid for peace. Delegations from the two nations signed the surrender terms on _September 1, 1945,_ Japan capitulating unconditionally.

D. The War on the Home Front.

1. Industrial Mobilization. The unity of opinion that followed the sneak attack on Pearl Harbor allowed the all-out war effort to surpass that of World War I. Industrial production was managed by a _War Production Board_ (W.P.B.) under _Donald M. Nelson_ which set prices, assigned quotas, converted factories to war tasks, and built $20,000,000,000 worth of new plants. The result was a staggering increase in the volume of production, which was valued at nearly $200,000,000,000 by 1944. To ration scarce peacetime goods and keep prices down, an _Office of Price Administration_ (O.P.A.) was given authority to fix prices and allot civilian supplies (1941). Similarly a _War Labor Board_ (W.L.B.) pegged wages, while unions enforced a no-strike pledge so successfully that industrial disputes all but disappeared. This remarkable teamwork won the _"battle of production"_ and allowed the United States to support an armed force of 12,000,000 men and women.

2. Financing the War. The United States spent $300,-000,000,000 during the war. Most of this sum was raised by borrowing; bonds of every size were sold so successfully that by 1945 the national debt reached $252,000,000,000. Taxes were also increased to unprecedented levels, particularly income taxes, which after 1943 were collected at the source rather than at the end of the year. These, together with corporation taxes, excess-profits taxes, and luxury taxes, allowed the United States to pay 40 per cent of its war costs from taxation, a higher figure than ever before.

3. Civilian Liberties in Wartime. The government imposed fewer restrictions on personal rights than in World War I. Only the Japanese-Americans were treated badly. Thousands of Nisei who lived near the Pacific coast were moved inland to relocation camps where they could be watched, even though they showed every evidence of loyalty.

II. EVOLUTION OF THE UNITED NATIONS.

A. Allied Cooperation in Wartime.

1. Military Conferences. The leaders of the three Allied powers, Franklin D. Roosevelt, Winston Churchill, and Josef Stalin, met regularly to work out military strategy and plan the peace. At the *Moscow Conference* (October, 1943), they agreed on plans for a second front and pledged themselves to establish an international organization of peace-loving nations when the war was over. At the *Cairo Conference* (November, 1943), they agreed to continue fighting until Japan was expelled from China. At the *Teheran Conference* (November, 1943), they settled details of the second front, while Stalin accepted the principle of continued Russian collaboration with the two western' powers after the war.

2. Conferences on Postwar Problems. Delegates from the Allied nations met in May, 1943, to create the United Nations Relief and Rehabilitation Administration (*U.N.R.R.A.*) to speed economic reconstruction when the war was over. In July, 1944, the *Bretton Woods Conference* drew up plans for an International Bank for Reconstruction and Development to help stabilize the world's currencies with the return of peace. The *Dumbarton Oaks Conference* (October, 1944) drafted tentative proposals for a United Nations charter.

B. The Election of 1944.

1. The Candidates. The *Democrats,* recognizing the popular demand for Roosevelt's continued leadership during the closing years of the war, renominated the President for a fourth term. *Harry S. Truman* of Missouri, a party regular, was named vice-presidential candidate. The *Republicans,* rejecting Wendell Willkie for his liberal views, nominated *Thomas Dewey* of New York.

2. Results of the Election. The two candidates agreed in their support of the New Deal domestic program and foreign policy. Dewey based his campaign on the need for a change, while Roosevelt capitalized on his success in the war and the fact that his experienced leadership was essential for an enduring peace. The voters returned the President with an electoral vote of 432 to 99.

C. The Yalta Conference (January, 1945). This was the most important of the wartime conferences of the three Allied leaders. Roosevelt felt that his task was to win Stalin to the principle of a United Nations, thus preventing a return to the "world communist revolution" program of the past. To achieve this he made certain concessions:

1. Concessions to Russia. These included: 1) three Russian votes in the Assembly of the United Nations; 2) the veto power over acts of the United Nations for members of its Security Council; 3) territorial concessions in eastern Poland; and 4) dominance over Manchuria.

2. Concessions from Russia. Russia promised in return: 1) democratic governments for Poland and Yugoslavia; 2) support for the United Nations; 3) to enter the war against Japan after the close of the war in Europe. Military leaders at the time agreed that this last concession was worth any sacrifice.

3. Postwar Plans. The Yalta delegates also agreed: 1) that Germany should be divided into four military zones under England, France, Russia, and the United States, with Berlin an international area; 2) to call a conference of delegates to meet at San Francisco in April, 1945, to draft a charter for the United Nations.

D. The San Francisco Conference (April, 1945). Despite the tragic _death of Roosevelt_ on April 12, 1945, delegates drafted the charter of the United Nations.

1. Organization of the United Nations.

a. GOVERNMENTAL ORGANIZATION. The United Nations was composed of: 1) an _Assembly_ of from one to five delegates from each member nation who would vote as a unit; 2) a _Security Council_ of five permanent members (England, France, China, Russia, and the United States) and six members chosen by the Assembly for two-year terms. No decision of the Security Council became binding without the concurrence of the five major powers; 3) a _Secretary-General_ chosen by the Assembly to coordinate the branches of the United Nations; and 4) an _International Court of Justice_ of fifteen justices meeting at the Hague to settle disputes between nations.

THE STRUCTURE OF THE UNITED NATIONS

GENERAL ASSEMBLY

Up to five delegates from each of all the member nations, but only one vote for each nation. Its duties are to discuss any questions within the scope of the Charter, and submit recommendations to members or to the Security Council.

SECRETARIAT

Secretary General at head, includes research, administrative staffs, reports to Assembly, Security Council.

SECURITY COUNCIL

Eleven members—the Big Five permanent, other six elected for two-year terms by Assembly. It investigates international disputes, takes action against aggressors if necessary.

ECONOMIC & SOCIAL COUNCIL

18 members elected by Assembly. Studies economic, political problems through commissions, and special agencies below.

INTERNATIONAL COURT

Fifteen members chosen by the Assembly. They meet in permanent session to decide legal disputes which arise between nations.

EDUCATIONAL SCIENTIFIC AND CULTURAL ORGANIZATION

Organized to foster world intellectual cooperation through education, science and culture.

INTERNATIONAL MONETARY FUND

Also part of Bretton Woods plan; to be used by members to help stabilize currencies.

WORLD HEALTH ORGANIZATION

Will serve as research organ and as an information center on world medical developments.

TRUSTEESHIP COUNCIL

Includes Big Five and all nations that administer trust territories, some others elected by Assembly.

ATOMIC ENERGY COMMISSION

Includes eleven members of Security Council plus Canada. Considers problems relating to atomic energy.

MILITARY STAFF COMMITTEE

Composed of Chiefs of Staff of the Big Five. Under Council, advises on armed forces placed at disposal of U.N.

CONVENTIONAL ARMAMENTS COMMISSION

Explores the possibilities for general disarmament and suggests stages by which it can be accomplished.

FOOD AND AGRICULTURAL ORGANIZATION

Research and study organization; endeavors to raise world food and nutrition standards.

INTERNATIONAL LABOR ORGANIZATION

Includes labor-management delegates; to raise world employment, welfare standards.

INTERNATIONAL CIVIL AVIATION ORGANIZATION

Deals with the complex economic and legal problems in commercial air transportation.

INTERNATIONAL BANK

Established by the Bretton Woods agreement. Provides loans for reconstruction and development.

INTERNATIONAL REFUGEE ORGANIZATION

Being established. Successor to UNRRA. Will care for refugees; resettle displaced persons.

INTERNATIONAL TRADE ORGANIZATION

Set up to promote world trade, reduce tariffs, eliminate restrictions.

UNIVERSAL POSTAL UNION

Established in 1874 to reduce costs; increase efficiency of international mail service.

INTERNATIONAL TELECOMMUNICATIONS UNION

Established in 1932 to reduce costs; increase efficiency of international telephone, telegraph, radio services.

Graphics Institute for The New York Times

b. MINOR AGENCIES. Subsidiary agencies created by the Charter included: 1) an *Economic and Social Council* of eighteen members to deal with a variety of international problems such as the narcotics trade and postwar reconstruction: 2) a *Trusteeship Council* to supervise colonial possessions taken from Germany and Japan; 3) the United Nations Educational, Scientific, and Cultural Organization (*U.N.E.S.C.O.*) to stimulate international educational and cultural progress.

E. Achievements of the United Nations.

1. The East-West Division. The Assembly and Security Council met first at London in 1946, and subsequently in New York, which was selected as the permanent headquarters. The early meetings showed a division into two blocs, one dominated by Russia, the other by the United States. This was so complete that few decisions could be reached in the Security Council; Russia, which was outvoted by the western bloc, used the veto power thirty times in the first three years. To save the situation, a *Little Assembly* was formed of one delegate from each nation. Its decisions, reached by a two-thirds vote, did not have the force of law but registered world opinion.

2. Settlement of Disputes.

a. PALESTINE. A special committee of the United Nations recommended (August, 1947) that Palestine be divided into three states, one Arab, one Jewish, and one the independent city of Palestine. Although this pleased neither Jews nor Arabs, England announced that it would give up its mandate over the area in May, 1948. Hence the Jews proclaimed the independent state of *Israel.* A war with the Arabs that followed was settled by a United Nations mediator, Dr. Ralph Bunche of the United States.

b. ATOMIC ENERGY CONTROL. The United Nations in January, 1946, created an *Atomic Energy Commission* to recommend means of international control of this weapon. It soon found itself deadlocked between plans already devised by the United States and Russia; the former wanted an international commission to control atomic energy, with the unrestricted right to inspect all nations; the latter desired an international agreement to abandon atomic warfare, an agreement enforceable only by each nation. When these two points of view proved irreconcilable, nothing was accomplished. Again in 1949, when scientists reported the explosion of an atomic bomb in Russia, the United States offered its plan, but with no results.

III. THE FIRST TRUMAN ADMINISTRATION, 1945-1949. Truman was elevated to the presidency by the death of Roosevelt on April 12, 1945.

A. Domestic Problems.

1. Military Demobilization. After the defeat of Japan, pressure for the return of all overseas troops was so great that the United States was faced with the danger of having insufficient soldiers to occupy the defeated countries. Hence the first *peacetime draft* (May, 1946), allowed the conscription of men over eighteen for one year. The returning soldiers were aided by a *G. I. Bill of Rights* (June, 1944) which provided veterans with: 1) unemployment insurance of $20 weekly for fifty-two weeks; 2) government-guaranteed loans for business or home-building purposes; and 3) free education in colleges or vocational schools.

2. Economic Demobilization. The industrial transition to a peacetime economy was planned by the *Office of War Mobilization and Reconversion* (O.W.M.R.) which had been set up in 1944.

a. INFLATION. Price controls maintained by the O.P.A. grew unpopular with peace, especially as many Americans believed with the National Association of Manufacturers that inflation could best be combatted by allowing free competition to force prices to their natural levels. Congress reflected this view when it extended the life of the O.P.A. (1946) but with such limited powers that Truman vetoed the bill. Actually the end of price control sent prices skyrocketing; by December, 1946, the consumers' index was 31.7 per cent higher than a year before. Prices continued to rise for two more years before production caught up with demand.

b. THE LABOR PROBLEM. Strikes multiplied after the war as workers sought to retain the high wages obtained by overtime work. As a result, new wage schedules calling for increases of about eighteen cents an hour were adopted by most major industries. During the next two years _second round_ and _third round_ increases were also obtained. A fourth round wage boost was denied in 1949 when a Presidential Fact Finding Board headed by Dr. Carroll R. Daugherty recommended a company-supported pension plan rather than an increased salary for steel workers. When management rejected this proposal, steel and coal strikes followed. Before the end of 1949, however, major companies had capitulated and granted modified pension plans. The new pattern for labor stressed eventual _security_ rather than immediate higher wages.

c. The Racial Problem. During the war a _Fair Employment Practices Committee_ (F.E.P.C.) protected workers from discrimination because of race, color, or creed. A bill to make the _F.E.P.C._ permanent was advocated by both parties in 1944, but when such a measure was introduced in Congress during 1945 it was talked to death by a filibuster of southern congressmen.

3. The Eightieth Congress.

a. The Election of 1946. The congressional elections of 1946 gave Republicans a majority in both houses as voters, rebelling against wartime controls and taxes, turned out the party in power. This gave the Republicans their chance to develop a reconversion program.

b. Economy Measures. A _tax bill_ (1947) substantially reduced taxes, especially in the upper income brackets. This was vetoed by Truman, who held that an unbalanced budget would result. Congress sustained the veto by a narrow majority.

c. The Taft-Hartley Act (1947). This Republican attempt to deprive labor of some of the power gained during the New Deal: 1) banned the closed shop, which forbade the hiring of nonunion men; 2) permitted employers to sue unions for broken contracts or damages inflicted during strikes; 3) forced unions to abide by a sixty-day "cooling-off period" before striking; 4) required unions to make public their financial statements; 5) forbade them to contribute to political campaigns; 6) ended the "check-off system" in which the employer collected union dues; and 7) required union leaders to swear they were not communists. Denounced by labor as a "slave bill," the measure was passed over Truman's veto.

B. Foreign Problems.

1. Underlying Factors. Foreign policy after 1945 was shaped by the conflict with Russia. Convinced that the Soviets had returned to their prewar policy of fomenting world communist revolution, the western powers adopted a *"get tough" policy* designed to restrict communism to the U.S.S.R. and its satelite states: Poland, Bulgaria, Rumania, Yugoslavia, and Czechoslovakia. In turn Russia withdrew behind an *Iron Curtain* that hid her actions and motives from the western world. The resulting war of nerves—the *cold war*—affected every phase of foreign policy.

2. Drafting the Peace Treaties.

a. THE POTSDAM CONFERENCE (July, 1945). Stalin, Truman, and Clement L. Attlee, representing the newly elected Labour government of England, agreed on the administration of defeated Germany. They decided that policy would be determined by an *Allied Control Council* of American, English, French, and Russian generals who would administer the four military zones into which the country had been divided at the Yalta Conference. They further agreed that peace treaties should be drafted with the minor enemy powers before those with Germany and Japan.

b. TREATIES WITH MINOR POWERS. The task of drafting treaties with Finland, Hungary, Bulgaria, Rumania, and Italy was entrusted to a *Council of Foreign Ministers* representing England, Russia, and the United States, with France participating in the Italian settlement. This Council called together delegates of all twenty-one Allied nations for a peace conference at Paris in May, 1946. The resulting treaties, which were signed in February, 1947, deprived all five defeated countries of territory, assessed heavy indemnities, and stripped away their military power.

c. TREATIES WITH GERMANY AND JAPAN. By the time the minor treaties were completed, the breach between the United States and Russia was so wide that no effort was made to draft treaties with Japan and Germany.

3. Occupation of Enemy Territory.

a. TRIAL OF THE WAR CRIMINALS. In 1945 the leading Nazis still alive were brought before an international military tribunal at _Nuremberg_ to stand trial for beginning the war and employing inhuman tactics during the fighting. So effective was the prosecutor, Justice _Robert H. Jackson_ of the United States Supreme Court, that eleven were executed and eight imprisoned. Similar trials in Japan resulted in the execution of Premier Hideki Tojo and six others, with prison sentences for a large number. Minor war criminals were tried during the next years.

b. MILITARY OCCUPATION OF GERMANY. Members of the Allied Control Council failed to cooperate in administering Germany. After repeated bickering, the United States, England, and France united their three zones into a unit popularly known as _Trizonia_ (1946), while Russia continued to administer its zone independently. This division led to an open break (1948) when the Russian representative withdrew from the Allied Control Council in a dispute over currency problems, then ordered a blockade of Berlin. As 2,000,000 Germans in the western zone of Berlin were threatened by starvation, the Allies developed the _air lift,_ shuttling in food and supplies by cargo plane. Not until May, 1949, was the blockade lifted on the promise of a complete discussion of the whole problem by the Council of Foreign Ministers. With this tense situation resolved, the people of western Germany drafted plans for a federal republic, based on democratic principles and with provisions for the admission of new states from the Russian zone whenever they wished to join. Thus the framework was laid for a German republic.

c. MILITARY OCCUPATION OF JAPAN. Although an _Allied Council_ was set up in Tokyo with delegates from the United States, Russia, China, and England, the actual administration of Japan was entrusted to the country's conqueror, General _Douglas MacArthur._ Under his direction a democratic diet was elected (April, 1946) to draw up a constitution similar to that of the United States. This document called for the dissolution of large landed estates, as well as of industrial and banking monopolies. Although the new constitution pointed the way toward eventual reform, it failed to improve Japan's acute economic crisis, or to resolve the conflict between Russia and the United States which prevented the drafting of a permanent peace treaty. In 1950 American troops still occupied Japan, and American supplies were still essential to its economy.

4. Relations with Former Allies in the Orient.

a. RELATIONS WITH CHINA. A strong communist movement that had been suppressed during the war challenged the Nationalist government of Chiang Kai-shek as soon as Japan was defeated. The United States sent General *George C. Marshall* to China (December, 1945) in a futile effort to secure peace, but he returned after a year with little good to say for either the Nationalists or the Communists. From that time on the United States followed a hands-off policy. By 1950 the Communists had conquered most of China and established a communist state in close cooperation with Russia. On January 5, 1950, the President announced that the United States would not aid the Chinese Nationalists in their last stronghold on Formosa.

b. RELATIONS WITH KOREA. An independent Korea was agreed upon at the Cairo Conference (1943). At the end of the war Russia and the United States divided the country into two halves for military occupation. By 1948 two governments had formed, a Korean People's Republic in the Russian zone, and a Republic of Korea in the American zone. Tension between the two reflected the tension between eastern and western worlds.

5. Relations with Europe.

a. EXPANSION OF RUSSIAN INFLUENCE. Communist minorities in France, Italy, Turkey, and elsewhere gained strength amidst the economic chaos following the war, creating the impression that Russian influence would soon extend over all Europe. President Truman decided on a showdown in Greece, where a conservative government installed by England was being resisted by liberals and communists. When England withdrew its garrisons in 1947 the United States made Greece its frontier against Russia.

b. THE TRUMAN DOCTRINE (March, 1947). In asking

Congress for American aid for Greece and Turkey, Truman laid down the doctrine that "it must be the policy of the United States to support free peoples who are resisting attempted subjugation by armed minorities or by outside pressure." He stated that this "should be primarily through economic and financial aid which is essential to economic stability and orderly political processes." The support given the _Truman Doctrine_ by both parties originated the _bipartisan foreign policy_ that prevailed through 1950.

c. THE MARSHALL PLAN (June 5, 1947). Secretary of State _George C. Marshall,_ in a commencement address at Harvard, stated that as a stable European economy was needed to maintain democratic institutions, the United States was willing to aid any country that was willing to cooperate for its own recovery. The result was the _European Recovery Plan_ (E.R.P.) for the rehabilitation of Europe, displacing the U.N.R.R.A. (see p. 214).

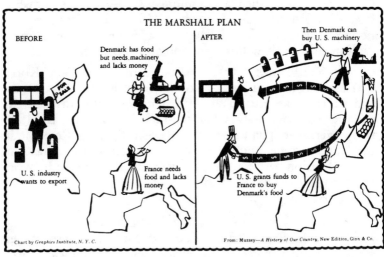

THE MARSHALL PLAN

BEFORE — AFTER

Denmark has food but needs machinery and lacks money

Then Denmark can buy U. S. machinery

U. S. industry wants to export

France needs food and lacks money

U. S. grants funds to France to buy Denmark's food

Chart by *Graphics Institute, N. Y. C.*   From: Muzzey—*A History of Our Country,* New Edition, Ginn & Co.

d. OPERATION OF THE E.R.P. Sixteen European nations drew up plans for economic recovery (July, 1947) that called for nearly $20,000,000,000 in American aid. In April, 1948, an initial grant of $5,000,000,000 was voted by Congress, which also established the _Economic Cooperation Administration_ (E.C.A.) under _Paul G. Hoffman_ to administer the program. In their eagerness to obtain E.R.P. funds the European nations rejected communist bids for power in elections. Thus the Marshall Plan proved effective in confining communism behind the Iron Curtain. Recovery was slow, however, with the prospect that E.R.P. aid would be needed well into the 1950's before Europe's economy was stabilized.

IV. THE SECOND TRUMAN ADMINISTRATION, 1949-1953.

A. The Election of 1948.

1. Party Divisions. The *Democratic Party,* almost certain of defeat after the reversals suffered in 1946, renominated *Truman* without enthusiasm and pledged both repeal of the Taft-Hartley Act and adoption of a civil rights program (see below). *Thomas E. Dewey* of New York was named the *Republican* candidate on a platform favoring a "minimum" amount of governmental control over business. Two splinter groups showed their dissatisfaction with the major parties by nominating candidates. Conservative Southerners, resentful of the Democrats' civil rights stand, formed the *Dixiecrat Party* with Governor J. Strom Thurmond of South Carolina as its nominee. Liberals fearful that Truman's "get-tough-with-Russia" policy would lead to World War III banded together as the *Progressive Party* under Henry A. Wallace.

2. Results of the Election. The Republicans, convinced that Truman's unpopularity assured his defeat, campaigned half-heartedly and at an emotional level holding little appeal. Truman, on the other hand, staged a vigorous battle which so captured the popular imagination that he snatched victory from defeat. In a major political upset, he was elected with 304 electoral votes to 189 for Dewey. The Dixiecrats won 39 electoral votes in the deep South, while the Progressive Party, which was discredited by communist support, polled only a million popular votes and no electoral votes.

B. The Truman Domestic Program.

1. Governmental Reorganization. From the time he entered the White House, Truman worked effectively to streamline the government's administrative machinery. In 1947 he consolidated the offices of Secretary of Navy and Secretary of War into a *Secretary of Defense;* at the same time he named a bi-partisan commission under ex-president Herbert Hoover to suggest other changes. When the *Hoover Commission* reported in 1949 a Congressional Reorganization Plan was adopted which authorized the President to carry out its recommendations. During the next months numerous bureaus and agencies were consolidated, and the post office reformed. The people also ratified the *Twenty-second Amendment* to the Constitution (February, 1951), limiting presidents to two terms.

2. The Fair Deal Program. Truman's progressive program made little headway in the Eighty-first Congress (1949-1951) where it met consistent opposition from Republicans and conservative Southern Democrats. His efforts to repeal the Taft-Hartley Act (see p. 220) and to secure enactment of a national health insurance program both failed. Congress, however, did amend the *Fair Labor Standards Act* (see p. 191) to raise minimum wages from forty to seventy-five cents an hour, alter the *Social Security Act* to increase by 10,000,000 the number of workers eligible for benefits (August, 1950), and adopt a National Housing Act (July, 1949), alloting federal funds to assist cities in slum clearance and the erection of low-cost housing. An *Agricultural Act of 1949* promised continued government support for commodity prices up to 90 per cent of parity, with parity based on prices between 1939 and 1949.

3. Civil Rights Program. A distinguished Commission on Civil Rights appointed by Truman recommended: 1) a federal anti-lynching law; 2) the abolition of poll-tax requirements for voting; 3) the federal enforcement of laws forbidding discrimination in hiring or segregation of races on busses and trains; and 4) a law requiring nondiscrimination as a condition for all federal grants-in-aid for housing or education. When this forward-looking program was laid before Congress, southern legislators threatened a filibuster. An administrative bill to allow a majority (rather than two-thirds) of the Senate to limit debate was defeated by an alliance of Republicans and Southern Democrats, ending hopes that the civil rights program could be adopted.

4. End of Fair Deal Program. Republican gains in the 1950 elections reduced Democratic majorities in the Eighty-second Congress (1951-1953) to the point that Truman abandoned all efforts to carry out his Fair Deal program during his last two years in office.

C. The Truman Foreign Program.

1. The Cold War in Europe.

a. CREATION OF THE GERMAN REPUBLIC. With hopes of a united Germany dissipated by the continued "cold war" between Russia and the United States (see pp. 221-225), a _Federal Republic of Germany_ was created in May, 1949, under the supervision of the Allied High Commission. Russia answered by setting up the German Democratic Republic of East Germany under its control.

b. THE NORTH ATLANTIC TREATY. Fearful lest these frictions lead to war despite the efforts of the United Nations, the Senate in June, 1948, authorized the President to develop collective defense arrangments with friendly powers. The result was the _North Atlantic Treaty_ (April, 1949), in which twelve western nations: 1) agreed that an attack on one would be considered an attack on all; and (2) bound themselves to use force to maintain the security of the North Atlantic area. A year later the _North Atlantic Treaty Organization_ (NATO) was created to integrate western Europe's military forces under one commander, _General Dwight D. Eisenhower_.

c. THE POINT FOUR PROGRAM. Acting upon a recommendation in Truman's 1949 inaugural address, Congress in 1950 made the first of several appropriations designed to make technological and scientific information available to underdeveloped nations. This aid was designed to strengthen such areas economically and make them less susceptible to communist infiltration.

2. The War in Asia.

a. AMERICAN INTERVENTION IN KOREA. In June, 1950, open warfare in Korea began between the Russian-dominated Korean People's Republic (north of the 38th parallel) and the American-backed Republic of Korea (see p. 223). As the North Korean troops, apparently well supplied from Russia, advanced rapidly southward, fear mounted that docile acceptance of the situation would encourage communist aggression in Berlin, the Philippines, and the area south of Communist China. Hence the United Nations Security Council adopted a resolution urging member nations to furnish South Korea with assistance. Two days later (June 27, 1950), Truman ordered air and sea forces into action, at the same time instructing the American fleet to repel any attack on Formosa by Communist China. These forceful moves were almost universally praised by Congress and the people as necessary to halt the advance of world communism.

b. COURSE OF THE KOREAN WAR. When token aid proved ineffective in stopping the North Korean armies, a United Nations army was created under the American, General Douglas MacArthur. As this gained strength, largely in the form of troops sent by the United States, the tide was turned in September, 1950. By the end of November, MacArthur's forces had driven northward across the 38th parallel, only to be turned back there by an army of Communist Chinese troops that had been concealed in the mountains. A brief retreat was followed by a long stalemate. Impatient with inaction, General MacArthur issued a series of belligerent statements demanding the right to reinvade North Korea. Truman, fearful lest these demands precipitate a full-scale war with Communist China, removed MacArthur from his command (April, 1951), at the same time opening truce talks with the North Koreans.

c. THE TRUCE NEGOTIATIONS. Truce negotiations dragged on through the summer and autumn of 1951 with little progress reported on the two areas of disagreement: location of the truce line and procedure for the exchange of prisoners. The continued fighting to little apparent purpose turned American opinion against the war and against the Truman administration which was blamed for failure to settle the conflict.

D. Impact of the Korean War on the United States.

1. The Loyalty Program. The Korean War, following on the "cold war," made Americans increasingly aware of threats to their national security, and particularly from native communists. These fears were seemingly given tangible basis when *Alger Hiss*, a former state department employee, was convicted of giving a self-confessed ex-communist "courier" several top-secret documents (January, 1950). Congress reflected public alarm when it passed the *McCarran Internal Security Act* (September, 1950), requiring the registration of all communist-front organizations with the Attorney-General and forbidding aliens who had been communists to enter the United

States. At the same time the older Smith Alien Registration Act (1940) which forbade any person to teach the desirability of overthrowing the government by force, was used to convict eleven members of the Communist Party. When the Supreme Court upheld their conviction (June, 1951), they began serving terms up to five years. This encouraged an outburst of state laws inflicting "loyalty oaths" on workers or providing for the investigation of "subversives." The leader of this "red hunt" was *Senator Joseph R. McCarthy* of Wisconsin whose indiscriminate and reckless accusations popularized the term "McCarthyism" as a synonym for the repression of civil liberties.

2. Mobilization of the Nation.

a. INDUSTRIAL MOBILIZATION. Economic policy during the Korean War was based on the assumption that World War III could be prevented by strengthening the United States and its allies to the degree that the Soviet Union would not dare risk aggression. Congress implemented this policy by appropriating $24,937,000,000 for defense and $10,065,000,000 for foreign aid (September, 1950). To turn this money into armaments, an Office of Defense Mobilization was created under Charles E. Wilson of the General Motors Company.

b. THE THREAT OF INFLATION. With increased employment and a decline in the production of civilian goods, prices started upward. To check this trend, Truman created the Office of Price Stabilization (OPS) and the Wage Stabilization Board. Opposition to wage and price controls was so strong that both measures proved ineffective. Instead the inflationary spiral was to curve upward for at least a decade.

E. The Election of 1952.

1. Decline in Democratic Popularity. Despite the nation's prosperity, the Democrats lost favor as the election of 1952 approached. This was due to: 1) the unpopularity of the Korean War; 2) the revelation of certain "Truman Scandals" involving bribery and "fixers" in the Reconstruction Finance Corporation, the Internal Revenue Bureau, and the Department of Justice; 3) the disclosure by the Senate *Kefauver Committee* of a link between criminal elements and the Democratic machine in several large cities; and 4) the government's seizure of the steel mills to insure continued military production during the 1952 strike, giving rise to the charge of dictatorship against the President.

2. The Party Conventions.

a. THE REPUBLICAN CONVENTION. Factions representing the conservative neo-isolationism of _Senator Robert A. Taft_ and the liberal internationalism of _General Dwight D. Eisenhower_ struggled to control the Republican convention when it met at Chicago in July, 1952. The latter triumphed when Eisenhower was nominated on the first ballot, with Richard M. Nixon of California as his running-mate. The platform pledged continued support to the policy of collective security, but promised to end the "negative" policy of containment for communism. Its domestic planks approved most Fair Deal measures, but favored tax reduction, removal of economic controls from business, and the substitution of state for federal management of health insurance and civil rights.

b. THE DEMOCRATIC CONVENTION. With Truman not a candidate, a battle for the nomination was waged by Senator Estes Kefauver of Tennessee and _Governor Adlai E. Stevenson_ of Illinois, with the latter victorious on the third ballot. The platform defended the Roosevelt-Truman record, promised repeal of the Taft-Hartley Act, and pledged aid to farmers and small business men.

3. Outcome of the Election.

a. THE EISENHOWER VICTORY. Although Stevenson conducted a vigorous campaign marked by speeches clothed in faultless prose and sparkling with wit, he had little chance against Eisenhower's popularity. The latter devoted his relatively few speeches to attacking the "corruption and inefficiency" of Truman, and pledged himself if elected to visit Korea to bring a speedy end to the war. He won 55.1 per cent of the popular vote, and 442 electoral votes to only 89 for Stevenson. The Republicans also won control of the House by a margin of 221 to 212, and of the Senate by a one-vote majority.

b. REASONS FOR REPUBLICAN VICTORY. The voters' decision to overthrow the party that had been in power since 1933 was based on: 1) a desire to repudiate "Trumanism" which had become associated with corruption and inefficiency; 2) dislike of the Korean War which was costing the nation heavily in lives and money; 3) a popular suspicion that Democrats were "coddling" communists in government posts; 4) the feeling that it was "time for a change"; and 5) Eisenhower's personal popularity.

V. THE EISENHOWER ADMINISTRATIONS, 1953-1961.

A. Inaugurating the Republican Program.

1. The Eisenhower Program. In a dramatic gesture, the President devoted his entire inaugural address to foreign policy. Holding to the internationalism of Roosevelt and Truman, he pledged American cooperation with other powers to "remove the causes of mutual fear and distrust among nations," at the same time denouncing appeasement. In later messages he outlined a *foreign policy* that: 1) promised continued aid to America's allies; 2) pledged continuation of the Reciprocal Trade program and other stimulants to international exchange; 3) repudiated agreements with governments that permitted the "enslavement" of peoples. His *domestic program* promised: 1) tax reductions after the budget was balanced; 2) the extension of social security to additional millions; 3) changes in the Taft-Hartley and McCarran acts; and 4) the abolition of all controls over wages and prices. This program more closely followed those of the New and Fair deals than it did that of conservatives within his own party. The most influential member of his *cabinet* was the Secretary of State, *John Foster Dulles,* to whom was entrusted virtual control over foreign policy. When Congress created the *Department of Health, Education and Welfare* the President named as its head Mrs. Oveta Culp Hobby.

2. Fulfilling Campaign Pledges. Eisenhower's popularity was great enough to win from Congress several measures to which he was committed: 1) the abolition of wage and price controls; 2) a slight reduction in the budget and the number of federal employees; 3) a lowering of taxes on the upper-income brackets; and 4) a Tideland Oil Bill (May, 1953), which handed over to coastal states rights to offshore oil for exploitation by private interests rather than the federal government. On the *foreign front,* Eisenhower's program was aimed at ending the Korean War. A three-day visit to the battlefields by the President (December, 1952) failed to break the deadlock in truce negotiations, but the *death of Joseph Stalin* (March 5, 1953) forced Russia to relax world tensions until the power structure was recast within the USSR. In this mood, communist negotiators in Korea finally backed down in their demand that all prisoners be returned by both sides. On July 27, 1953, a truce was signed that allowed prisoners unwilling to return to their native countries to be handled by representatives of neutral nations.

B. The Eisenhower Domestic Program.

1. The "New Republicanism." The President's honeymoon with his party ended with the death of Senator Robert A. Taft in July, 1953. Although more conservative than Eisenhower, Taft had held Republican congressmen in line to support administration measures. With his death opposition to the presidential program mounted among conservative Republicans and Southern Democrats; support came largely from Northern Democrats and a smaller number of liberal Republicans. The *Congressional Elections of 1954* actually strengthened the President's hand by returning Democratic majorities in both houses, 48 to 47 in the Senate and 232 to 203 in the House.

2. Public versus Private Power. Although supporting a "partnership" between business and the government, the administration alarmed conservationists and public power advocates by turning over many power sites in the West to private corporations. He also supported the *Dixon-Yates contract* (June, 1954) which authorized the building of a private power plant at West Memphis, Arkansas, to supply power needed by the Tennessee Valley Authority for use in producing atomic materials. Opposition forced cancellation of the contract a year later. On the other hand the President approved a congressional measure authorizing construction of the *St. Lawrence Seaway* (May, 1954) although public power would be generated at several of the dams. He also vetoed a bill that would have exempted natural gas producers from direct federal regulation February, 1956).

3. Farm and Labor Legislation. Declining farm income after the Korean War posed a major political problem. When a Democratic measure to continue 90% parity payments on base crops was vetoed by the President, an administration-backed Agricultural Act of 1956 (May, 1956): 1) introduced the *"soil bank"* to pay farmers for removing marginal lands from cultivation; and 2) raised price supports to 82.5-85% of parity on basic crops. Organized labor fared better, largely by capitalizing on its own unity. Wage increases were negotiated yearly in most major industries; in June, 1955, the United Auto Workers won an additional victory when the Ford Motor Company accepted the principle of the "guaranteed annual wage." Similar contracts were later negotiated with other firms geared to seasonal production. Labor's most significant gain came with the merging of the two largest unions as the *American Federation of Labor* and *Congress of Industrial Organizations* (December, 1955) with a membership of 15,000,000.

4. The Eisenhower Legislative Record. Among significant measures secured by the President during his first administration were: 1) a three-year extension of the Reciprocal Trade Agreements Act (May, 1955); 2) a revision of the *Fair Labor Standards* Act raising minimum wages to one dollar an hour; 3) a measure providing for federally supported public housing (August, 1955); and 4) a multi-million dollar *highway construction program* financed by an increase in gasoline and trucking taxes (June, 1956). He failed to win approval for: 1) statehood for Hawaii and Alaska; 2) an expanded public housing program; 3) federal aid for school construction; 4) a federally supported public health plan; and 5) a civil rights act that would guarantee political and social equality to all citizens.

5. The Desegregation Issue. In May, 1954, the Supreme Court held that *segregation of white and Negro children in state schools was in violation of the 14th amendment;* it later ruled that once a "reasonable start" had been made toward desegregation, a period suitable to the "public interest" would be allowed before complete integration. Under these mandates, integration began in border-state schools, despite occasional flare-ups of violence engineered by racists. In the Deep South opposition to the court ruling was so great that Virginia, Alabama and Georgia moved to abolish public schools rather than allow a mingling of the races.

C. The Eisenhower Foreign Program.

1. The Cold War in Europe. Despite the calmer international atmosphere after the death of Stalin, the United States continued to strengthen its defensive alliances with European nations. The Paris Agreement (October, 1954) gave West Germany its sovereignty and admitted the new nation to NATO with a contribution of 500,000 troops. In May, 1955,

Russia suddenly agreed to a peace treaty with Austria. These indications of allied solidarity and USSR reasonableness encouraged Eisenhower to call a "summit meeting" of the heads of state of Russia, England, France, and the United States at Geneva in July, 1955. His plan for general disarmament including the exchange of blueprints and aerial inspection was well received, although later discussion revealed that the United States and Russia were still poles apart. Hope for the future was strengthened by signs of discontent in the USSR satellite nations; demonstrations in Poland (Ocotober, 1956) resulted in lessened Russian controls there, although an uprising in Hungary (October-November, 1956) led to such savage retaliation that world opinion turned against the Soviets to a degree unknown since World War II.

2. The Cold War in Asia. The American program in the Far East suffered a setback when a nineteen-nation Geneva Conference (April-July, 1954) ended the seven-year war in Indochina by granting the northern half of that country to a communist government. To prevent further deflections of this nature, the Eisenhower government organized the _Southeast Asia Treaty Organization_ (SEATO) as a counterpart of NATO (November, 1954). Communist China answered by announcing that eleven American airmen forced down within that country had been sentenced to long prison terms and by preparing for an all-out attack on the Nationalist Chinese stronghold of Formosa. Eisenhower promptly secured from Congress authority to use armed force to defend Formosa and neighboring islands (January, 1955). This threat forced Communist China to release the American airmen and to announce its willingness to discuss the whole status of the Formosa Straits (April, 1955).

3. The Cold War in the Middle East. The Middle East flared into conflict when Britain and the United States withdrew their offer to aid Egypt's president, _Gamal Abdel Nasser,_ construct the Aswam Dam on the Upper Nile (July, 1956), a step prompted by Nasser's purchase of arms from Russian satellite nations. When Nasser answered by seizing the Suez Canal, the neighboring state of Israel invaded the Egyptian Sinai Peninsula (October, 1956). Britain and France ordered both nations to cease fighting; when Egypt refused that country was invaded on October 31. The United Nations, urged on by the

Eisenhower government, called for an immediate cease fire and organized a task force to occupy the disputed territories as the invading armies withdrew. This force assumed control on November 30 as the British, French, and Israeli troops left Egypt's soil. To prevent Russia from capitalizing on this disturbance, Eisenhower in January, 1957, asked Congress for authority to: 1) use American forces to aid any middle eastern country desiring help against aggression from "any nation controlled by international communism" (the *Eisenhower Doctrine*); and 2) allot funds to strengthen the economy of such nations. At the same time the President threw his weight behind efforts to force Israel to relinquish the Gaza Strip which its troops still occupied, even to siding with the Asian-Arab bloc within the United Nations in demanding the application of sanctions against that country (February-March, 1957). This pressure forced Israel's withdrawal on March 1, 1957, ending this period of crisis.

D. Launching the Second Eisenhower Administration.

1. The Election of 1956. Eisenhower suffered a heart attack in September, 1955, but recovered sufficiently to be renominated by the Republicans in 1956, with Richard Nixon again his running-mate. The Democrats again nominated Adlai Stevenson with his principal rival for the nomination, Estes Kefauver of Tennessee, as his vice-presidential candidate. Both platforms promised progressive domestic legislation and a continued international approach to world problems. The threat of a Middle Eastern War so increased Eisenhower's popularity that he received 457 electoral votes to only 74 for Stevenson. Again the Democrats captured control of both houses of Congress, with a majority of 49 to 47 in the Senate and 233 to 200 in the House.

2. Growth of Opposition to Administration. The President enjoyed no honeymoon period with Congress as he had four years before. Liberals opposed: 1) his Middle Eastern policies which were held partially responsible for war there; 2) the "Einsenhower Doctrine" with its "blank-check" authority to use armed force in a manner that might precipitate war; and 3) his alliance with the Asian-Arab bloc against Israel. Conservatives voiced opposition to: 1) his $71.8 billion budget, the largest in peacetime history; 2) his insistence on federal aid for school construction; and 3) his proposal to change the

Walter-McCarran Immigration Act (January, 1957), to allow the admission of more immigrants and to base quotas on the 1950 census rather than earlier enumerations.

E. Foreign Policy in the Second Administration.

1. Continuation of the Cold War. *Nikita Khrushchev,* who in 1955 won the power struggle that followed Stalin's death, temporarily lessened world tensions by talking of "peaceful coexistence" and creating the impression that only his predecessor's madness had accounted for USSR aggression. Time soon showed that Russian policy had not changed and that Khrushchev was as ruthless as Stalin in furthering his ambitions without actually precipitating war.

2. The Armaments Race.

a. NEW WEAPONS AND SPACE EXPLORATION. Both Russia and the United States regularly tested improved atomic weapons despite protests from neutral nations; the United States in 1954 added the lethal hydrogen bomb to its arsenal. Both also experimented with intercontinental ballistic missiles carrying atomic warheads capable of striking a target 5,000 miles away. A new dimension to warfare was added in October; 1957, when the USSR placed the first earth satellite (named *Sputnik*) in orbit. America's first satellite, Explorer 1, was launched in January, 1958; a year later the nation began training seven astronauts in expectation of an attempt to send man into space. Regular satellite launchings by both nations followed. The United States also pioneered the development of nuclear-powered submarines that could launch atomic weapons from beneath the sea. This armament race reversed a trend apparent in 1957 when defense spending was limited to $38 billion a year; by 1961 the defense budget had climbed to $43 billion.

b. ATTEMPTS AT DISARMAMENT. In March, 1957, a United Nations Disarmament Commission with delegates from the United States, Russia, England, France, and Canada met at London. Preliminary talks showed an East-West division over a comprehensive inspection system to detect the secret production or testing of nuclear weapons, nor did continuing talks by an enlarged commission at Geneva a year later bridge the gap. The USSR gained a propaganda advantage by announcing the end of bomb testing(March, 1958); the United States and Britain suspended testing on October 31. In June, 1960, a Russian plan for virtually complete disarmament was submitted

to the Geneva session, but this was rejected by the western
bloc as it contained no inspection procedure. Hopes for the
end of the arms race seemed dim.

3. Early Lessening of Tensions. During 1958 the USSR:
1) signed with the United States an agreement to increase
cultural, technical, and educational exchange, thus opening a
crack in the Iron Curtain; and 2) proposed settlement of
the German problem by demilitarization of the entire city
of Berlin and partial demilitarization of all West Germany
(January, 1959). In effect Russia was willing to make some
concessions on Berlin in return for a slightly weakened West
Germany. A meeting of foreign ministers of England, France,
Russia, and the United States to consider this proposal ended
in deadlock (March-April, 1959). At its close Secretary of
State Dulles resigned, and died six weeks later of cancer.

4. Proposed Summit Meetings. Hopes for more effective negotiations at the summit were increased when Khrushchev
accepted Eisenhower's invitation to visit the United States in
September, 1959. In a hectic tour (September 15-27), he saw
much of the country and conferred at length with the President.
A meeting of the heads of state of the four western powers
(England, France, West Germany and the United States) in
Paris (December 19-21, 1959) officially invited Khrushchev to
attend a Summit Conference in Paris in May, 1960. This
collapsed before it began when an *American U-2 spy plane* was
brought down in Russia (May 5, 1960). Khrushchev, already
in Paris, announced that he would not meet with the United
States until Eisenhower pledged an end to espionage flights and
apologized for his "aggressive" tactics. The President agreed
to end such flights, but refused to apologize. On a subsequent
tour of the Far East (June, 1960), he was hailed as a hero in
neutralist countries but opposition was so great in Japan that
his visit there was cancelled. Relations between the USA and
the USSR were as tense at the end of his administrations as
at the beginning.

5. The Cold War in the Middle East. Periodic outbreaks
in the Middle East required the use of the "Eisenhower Doctrine." In April, 1957, the Mediterranean fleet was sent to stand
by should an uprising in Jordan get out of control. After a
similar revolution in Lebanon, American marines were landed
(July, 1959) to aid the pro-western government. Russia accused

the United States of aggression, and demanded a special session of the UN Assembly to act on the problem. When this authorized needed action to keep the peace in both Lebanon and Jordan, United States forces were withdrawn (October, 1959).

6. The Cold War in the Far East. A threatened Chinese Communist invasion of Formosa in the fall of 1958 led to an announcement by the United States that it would defend Quemoy and other Nationalist Chinese offshore islands. At the same time pressure was brought on the Formosa government to announce that it would renounce the use of force in any possible return to the mainland (October, 1958). This eased tensions, but shelling of Quemoy continued. In August, 1959, the pro-western Laos government reported guerrilla attacks from Communist China and North Viet Nam. This rebellion forced the government from power (August, 1960), but the neutralist government that replaced it continued under attack. Reports of a new invasion from North Viet Nam led to a shift of the United States Pacific fleet to the vicinity (January, 1961). Jungle fighting continued indecisive there, and the United States seemed reconciled to accepting a neutralist government for Laos.

7. The Cold War in Africa. In June, 1960, Belgium freed its Congo colony, which became a new trouble spot as native leaders struggled for power. Premier Lumumba with USSR backing and President Joseph Kasavubu with the support of the western powers, proved unable to stop a bloody civil war, forcing a United Nations task force to intervene in July, 1960. A troubled peace was restored briefly in September, 1960, when an army strong man, Colonel Joseph Mobutu seized control of the country, but the continued presence of Belgium troops enflamed rebellious elements. A new crisis was engendered in February, 1961, with the assassination of Lumumba. Russia's threat of intervention was firmly resisted by both the United States and the United Nations.

8. The Cold War in Cuba. The success of *Fidel Castro's* revolution against the dictator Fulgencio Batista (early 1959), brought the Cold War to America's doorstep. Castro quickly alienated American opinion by the ruthless slaughter of his enemies, by refusing to call popular elections, and by his nationalization of a billion dollars worth of property owned by

United States firms. When the Eisenhower administration retaliated by cutting back its sugar imports from Cuba by 700,000 tons, Castro signed trade agreements with Russia and other communist powers (February-December, 1960). These assured the marketing of the Cuban sugar crop as well as loans and credit up to $350,000,000 for the industrial development of the island. President Eisenhower met this threat by: 1) announcing that under the Monroe Doctrine the United States would meet any attempt of international communism to dominate any regime in the hemisphere with force (July, 1960); 2) sending naval units to aid Guatemala and Nicaragua when governments there were threatened by Castro-type revolutionaries (November, 1960); and 3) *breaking off diplomatic relations with Cuba* (January, 1961), when Castro demanded the reduction of the American embassy and consular staffs on the island to eleven persons.

F. Domestic Policy in the Second Administration.

1. The Political Scene. Dissatisfaction with the administration's record in the Cold War, combined with continuing concern over mounting prices, inflation, and the farm problem, lessened Republican popularity. Confidence in the government was also weakened when Eisenhower's principal advisor, Sherman Adams, was proven guilty of using his influence to benefit a Boston industrialist named Bernard Goldfine. A minor recession in 1958 was also blamed on the party in power. In the *Congressional elections* of that year the Democrats made impressive gains, winning 64 seats in the Senate to 34 for the Republicans, and 283 to 153 in the House.

2. Labor and Farm Problems. Eisenhower's efforts to end accumulation of farm surpluses by lowering price supports and abolishing certain crop allotments (1958) failed to win congressional approval. Instead the farm program of price supports and soil bank were continued without substantial modification. Two laws to provide additional regulation for labor unions were introduced: 1) the Kennedy-Ives Bill requiring unions to report their finances and elect officers democratically was defeated in the House (1958); and 2) the *Landrum-Griffin Bill* (1959) was adopted. This forced unions to report their membership and finances, outlawed secondary boycotts and organizational or recognition picketing, and granted greater authority to state regulatory agencies. It was vigorously denounced by organized labor.

3. Progress in Civil Rights. The spirit of "McCarthyism" declined rapidly following the death of the senator in May, 1957. The new atmosphere was reflected in a series of notable court cases in 1957 and 1958: 1) reversing a contempt of Congress conviction of a former communist who refused to reveal names of associates; 2) ruling that the Smith Act outlawed the advocacy of communism only as a concrete action aimed at the overthrow of the government and not as an "abstract doctrine;" 3) holding that the army could not dishonorably discharge a soldier for past subversive activities; 4) outlawing the government's security-risk program in defense plants for not allowing accused persons to confront witnesses; and 5) ruling that passports could not be denied a citizen because of his beliefs or associations. Two congressional measures also strenghened civil liberties: 1) the *Civil Rights Act of 1957* creating a *Commission on Civil Rights* to investigate the denial of voting privileges because of race, color, or religion and empowered to initiate injuction proceedings in federal courts to assure equal rights at the polls; and 2) the *Civil Rights Act of 1960* providing for the punishment of anyone guilty of threats or force designed to frustrate the Commission's rulings and setting up procedures to restore the vote to persons disenfranchised because of color, race, or religion. In May, 1960, the Attorney General invoked the Civil Rights Act in demanding voting records of four southern counties where no Negroes were registered to vote.

4. The Segregation Issue. School integration made steady but slow progress, with each new school year the occasion for racial flare-ups. In September, 1957, efforts of the *Little Rock,* Arkansas, school board to enroll nine Negro children in the city's schools were frustrated when Governor Orval E. Faubus called out the National Guard to enforce the state's segregation laws. When a court order forced the guardsmen to withdraw, rioting so endangered the Negro children that they were removed for their own safety. President Eisenhower then called the National Guard into federal service to support the Supreme Court's decision. In November, 1960, mob violence broke out in New Orleans when four Negro children were admitted to the schools. Firm action by local authorities kept the mob under control, and while most white pupils temporarily withdrew, integration was under way. Similar occurrences marked the entrance of two Negro pupils into the University of Georgia in January, 1961. Despite these gains, only six per cent of the South's Negroes attended integrated schools in 1960. A new form of protest against segregation began in February, 1960, with Negro "sit-ins" at restaurants which discriminated against non-whites. By August lunch counter segregation had ended in 69 southern communities.

5. The Legislative Record. Among the more important measures adopted by Congress during the second Eisenhower administration were: 1) an immigration bill (September, 1957), authorizing the admission of an additional 60,000 persons yearly; 2) a series of public housing bills in 1957, 1958, and 1959 appropriating sums of from $1.8 billion to $1 billion for construction; 3) A $1.8 billion road construction bill (April, 1958) designed as an antirecession measure; 4) measures increasing postal rates and federal employee salaries (May, 1958), and boosting government salaries an additional 7½ per cent (July, 1960); 5) an increase in old age and retirement benefits under the Social Security Act to be financed by an increase in payroll taxes by one-quarter of one per cent; 6) Bills _admitting Alaska_ (July, 1958) _and Hawaii_ (March, 1959) _to the Union;_ and 7) _a National Defense Education Act_ (August, 1958) providing loans and graduate fellowships for students and teachers. The Senate also moved to check fillibusters by agreeing (January, 1959), to end debate by a two-thirds vote of all members present and voting rather than a vote of two-thirds of the total membership.

6. Politics and the Election of 1960. During the 1960 congressional session the political ambitions of both parties doomed all chances of important legislation. Four issues divided the parties: 1) a Democratic-sponsored amendment to the Fair Labor Standards Act to increase the minimum hourly wage from $1 to $1.25 by 1963; 2) a bill backed by labor and liberal Democrats to provide medical care for the aged through the Social Security Act; 3) an expanded public housing program; and 4) a School Aid measure alloting $1.8 billion over two years for new school construction and teachers' salaries. All were defeated in Congress, but Senator John F. Kennedy, who had supported all and sponsored two, was able to capitalize on their rejection in his forthcoming campaign.

VI. A DIVIDED WORLD FACES THE FUTURE.

A. The American Position. Underlying the world role assumed by the United States after World War II was the same sense of mission that had drawn the nation into that struggle, but it was now altered to contain "International Communism" rather than Hitlerism. To protect its own bastion from the communist doctrines radiating from the USSR, America felt compelled to extend pressures—bolstered now by military aid— over the entire world, seeking to strengthen smaller countries by "foreign aid" designed to build economic stability, provide them with munitions, and join them into alliances such as NATO and SEATO. This policy operated effectively in Europe, Asia, the Middle East, and in the African countries committed to "Free World" doctrines; but in other nations such as Korea, the armed intervention needed to prevent communist expansion not only cost the United States heavily in men and resources, but also threatened to cause a global confrontation leading to world war. Equally dangerous was the growing international image of the United States as a meddler in the internal affairs of other nations, often with the result that despite the opposition of their subjects, dictatorial governments were sustained simply because they opposed communism.

B. Hope for the Future. By the end of the Eisenhower administration, two alterations in the world's power structure promised some hope for continued peace: 1) the elevation to USSR leadership of Nikita Khrushchev and his successors, all of whom proved willing to lessen tensions between the two super-powers so long as the security of Russia and its satellite countries was not threatened; and 2) the rise to major status of China, now equipped with nuclear weapons and strongly opposed to the policies of both Russia and the United States. This tended to upset the "balance of power" situation that had existed so long as only two major nations sought to convert the world to their own ideologies, and thus it made a confrontation less likely. President Eisenhower's successors faced a world where global peace was within reach, but one more major war was to be fought before that goal could be approached.

ADDITIONAL READING

Competent modern surveys of America's military role in World War II are Basil Collier, *The Second World War: A Military History* (1967), which stresses the European scene, and Charles B. MacDonald, *The Mighty Endeavor: American Armed Forces in the European Theater in World War II* (1969). The first study to explore American life and thought during the war is Richard Polenberg, *War and Society: The United States, 1941-1945* (1972). Excellent on the origins of the United Nations is Robert A. Divine, *Second Chance: The Triumph of Internationalism During World War II* (1967); William L. Neumann, *After Victory: Churchill, Roosevelt, Stalin, and the Making of Peace* (1969) is a competent survey of peacemaking. The best general treatment of the Truman administration is Barton J. Bernstein, ed., *Politics and Policies of the Truman Administration* (1970); equally excellent on surveying the intrusion of a social issue into the political arena is William G. Berman, *The Politics of Civil Rights in the Truman Administration* (1970). Truman's foreign policy and the beginnings of the Cold War may be studied in Gabriel Kolko, *The Politics of War: The World and United States Foreign Policy, 1943-1945* (1968), which holds to the New-Left view that the war was initiated by American economic desires; and Lloyd C. Gardner, *Architects of Illusion: Men and Ideas in American Foreign Policy, 1941-1949* (1970), which is somewhat less critical of the United States. The biography of the Secretary of State from 1949 to 1953 also is useful: Gaddis Smith, *Dean Acheson* (1972). The first history of the Korean war based on primary sources is J. Lawton Collins, *War in Peacetime: The History and Lessons of Korea* (1969). A detailed examination of the decision-making process that led Truman to enter the war is Glenn D. Paige, *The Korean Decision* (1968), while Ronald J. Caridi, *The Korean War and American Politics* (1968), deals largely with Republican opposition to the war. Also concerned with the impact of the Korean and Cold wars on internal history is Richard M. Freeland, *The Truman Doctrine and the Origins of McCarthyism* (1972). Herbert S. Parment, *Eisenhower and the American Crusades* (1972), pictures an able but not exceptional president. Louis L.

Gerson, *John Foster Dulles* (1967), is more a summary than a critical analysis of the career of Eisenhower's Secretary of State; while Michael A. Guhin, *John Foster Dulles: A Statesman and His Times* (1972), does not quite succeed in upholding a favorable estimate.

CHAPTER XVI

America's Global Mission: Climax and Decline
1960-1969

⟨⟨THE COLD WAR AND THE NATION'S WORLD ROLE

During the immediate post-World-War-II years the United States, irrevocably committed to the Truman and Eisenhower doctrines, relentlessly pursued its self-assumed tasks of guarding the "Free World" from the forces of "International Communism." This policy reached its logical climax during the 1960s when Presidents Kennedy and Johnson accelerated an internal conflict within South Viet Nam into a devastating war that involved 542,500 American troops and cost more than 50,000 American lives. As the Viet Nam War seemed destined to continue for decades with neither antagonist capable of a decisive victory, a ground-swell of opposition mounted at home, manifested in civil disorders, confrontations between "peace marchers" and authorities, and mounting unwillingness of congressmen to vote funds to continue the conflict. These pressures led President Johnson to initiate the negotiations that finally culminated in a cease-fire during the early days of President Nixon's second administration. This apparently presaged changing American opinion on the nation's global role; increasingly the people seemed determined to put their own house in order whatever the fate of distant nations. President Nixon's successful efforts to restore more cordial relations with Russia and China symbolized not a new isolationism, but an emerging cooperation between the three major powers, and with it a gradual diminution of the Cold-War tensions that had disturbed the world for generations.

I. THE KENNEDY-JOHNSON ADMINISTRATION, 1961-1965.

A. The Election of 1960.

1. The Party Conventions. Senator John F. Kennedy of Massachusetts, who bested Senator Hubert Humphrey of Minnesota in seven state primaries, was nominated on the first ballot by the Democrats, with Senator Lyndon B. Johnson of Texas as his running mate. Vice-president Richard M. Nixon similarly dominated the Republican convention, and was nominated on the first ballot. Henry Cabot Lodge of Massachusetts, former ambassador to the United Nations, was named his vice-presidential candidate. Both party platforms pledged continued acceptance of the nation's international obligations, a strong defense program, and support for civil rights, although the Democratic platform was slightly more outspoken on the latter issue.

2. Outcome of the Election. A recession that slowed the national economy in the autumn of 1960 aided the Democrats, who attacked Eisenhower's "tight-money policy." They also charged that the United States had fallen behind Russia in military might and prestige. One highlight of the campaign was a series of four nationally televised debates between the candidates; these helped make Kennedy known to millions of voters who were already familiar with Nixon. Kennedy was victorious, but by one of the narrowest margins in history. Only 119,450 popular votes separated the two candidates, but Kennedy won 303 electoral votes to 219 for Nixon. Fourteen "Dixiecrat" electors from the lower South voted for Senator Harry F. Byrd of Virginia. Democratic majorities in Congress were reduced, with 64 to 36 seats in the Senate and 261 to 176 in the House.

B. The Kennedy Domestic Program.

1. Inauguration of the Kennedy Government.
Kennedy's carefully selected cabinet included Dean Rusk as Secretary of State and Robert S. McNamara, president of the Ford Motor Company, as Secretary of Defense. His non-cabinet appointments included such outstanding men as Adlai Stevenson as ambassador to the United Nations. The President's *inaugural address* was notable for its lucid rhetoric and moving phrases. Devoted to a general discussion of the world role of the United States, it pledged firmness against the nation's enemies but promised every effort to break the Cold War impasse. "Let us," President Kennedy said, "never negotiate out of fear. But let us never fear to negotiate."

2. The Attack on the Recession. Before Kennedy's legislative program could be launched, he had to end domination of the House Rules Committee by a coalition of conservative Republicans and Southern Democrats which had long prevented progressive legislation from reaching the floor. When Congress met in January, 1961, Speaker Samuel Rayburn maneuvered its members into enlarging the committee from 12 to 15, allowing the appointment of liberal Democrats. Goaded on by the President, Congress in the spring of 1961 quickly adopted a series of anti-recession measures: 1) a bill extending unemployment benefits to 39 weeks; 2) a Depressed Areas Bill permitting grants and loans to cover the cost of public projects in areas of persistent unemployment; and 3) a law raising the minimum wage from $1 to $1.25 over two years and extending minimum-wage benefits to an additional 3.6 million workers, largely in retail trade. By executive order the President: 1) created a food-stamp plan to distribute surplus agricultural goods in depressed areas; 2) ordered a speedup in letting government contracts, and 3) cut FHA mortgage rates to stimulate home building. Alarmed by the continued deficit in balance of payments and the shrinking of the gold reserve to the lowest point since 1939 (under 16 billion dollars), he: 1) reduced the value of duty-free goods of returning travelers from $500 to $100; 2) cut government spending abroad; and 3) expanded credit facilities available to American exporters to encourage sales overseas.

3. Expansion of the "New Frontier"

a. PRESIDENTIAL LEADERSHIP. President Kennedy brought to office a theory of dynamic leadership which contrasted with that of President Eisenhower. He believed the President should persuade Congress to adopt a broad program aimed at elevating living standards, improving educational facilities, providing for the conservation of natural resources, and strengthening the nation's world position. In all he sent twenty-five messages to the first session of Congress (January, 1962), and only slightly fewer to the second (January, 1963). These outlined his *"New Frontier."* They included: 1) a health and medical-care program for persons over sixty-five to be financed from social security taxes; 2) an education bill appropriating $5 billion over five years to be spent on new schools and teachers' salaries; 3) a progressive reduction of income and corporate taxes to stimulate the national economy; 4) the creation of a Domestic Peace Corps; and 5) the use of all "moral authority" to hurry complete integration in the South.

b. PARTIAL ACCEPTANCE OF THE "NEW FRONTIER." Congress adopted several of the Kennedy proposals for social legislation, but rejected three of his most important measures. Those adopted were: 1) a Housing Act (June, 1961) authorizing 30-35 year loans for moderate-income housing, funds for urban renewal, and grants for recreational and historical conservation; 2) a law extending social security benefits to an additional 4.4 million persons (June, 1961); 3) a bill to tighten controls over the manufacture and distribution of drugs (October, 1961); 4) an act requiring equal pay for equal work for both sexes; 5) an offer of federal funds to states on a matching basis to provide better facilities for medical education (September, 1963); and 6) legislation appropriating $329 million to launch a four-year program to aid the mentally retarded. Rejected by Congress were: 1) a Federal Aid to Schools Bill providing federal grants for school construction and teachers' salaries (August, 1961), which was defeated in part because of a conflict over the use of such funds for parochial schools; 2) a Medicare bill providing hospital and nursing benefits for persons over sixty-five through social security taxes (July, 1962); and 3) a cut in corporate and income taxes (September, 1963) which lost when conservatives demanded a reduction in spending to match the reduction in income.

c. THE AGRICULTURAL PROGRAM. President Kennedy hoped to reduce the ever-mounting agricultural surpluses by: 1) distributing excess foods to needy people throughout the world through a _Food for Peace_ program; and 2) imposing more rigid crop and acreage controls. Congress passed: 1) an Emergency Feed-Grains Bill (March, 1961), requiring 20% acreage reductions in return for support equal to one-half the value of the non-produced crops; and 2) the Agricultural Act of 1961 (August, 1961), establishing a wheat-control program with supports conditional on 10% acreage reductions. When a bill requiring greater acreage reductions was defeated (June, 1962), Congress adopted a compromise bill extending existing wheat and grain programs for one year (September, 1962). A further extension for two years was provided in May, 1963.

4. The President and the Business Community. Kennedy in April, 1962, denounced the United States Steel Company for raising prices after a wage settlement in which government pressure had prevented substantial wage increases for workers. The steel company was forced to rescind its increase, but the business community strongly resented Presidential interference with the price structure. One result was a sharp decline in the stock market, wiping out $20 billion in profits in one day (May 28, 1962). Business leaders also protested the Kennedy budgets, which rose from $84.2 billion in fiscal 1962 to $92.5 billion in fiscal 1963 and $98.8 billion in fiscal 1964. On the other hand, the business community approved the President's handling of a controversy between the railroads and the railroad unions. The Supreme Court ruled (March, 1963) that railroads could end "featherbedding" by making work rules reducing the number of jobs. When a railroad strike threatened (August, 1963), Congress hurriedly passed a measure requiring the arbitration of principal issues. The arbitration board ruled (November, 1963) that about 90% of the diesel locomotive firemen's jobs be eliminated by attrition and assignment to other tasks, and that local arbitration determine the size of train crews.

5. The Civil Rights Conflict.

a. EXTENSION OF CIVIL RIGHTS MOVEMENT. The conflict over segregation continued, with integrationists aiming their attack at segregated restaurants, transportation facilities, and schools. They also tried to force local officials to register Negro voters. "Sit-in" demonstrations forced a number of restaurants to provide service to both races; "freedom riders" also invaded segregated areas in buses, waiting rooms, and public parks. Southern racists resisted so strenuously that rioting broke out in, a number of cities. The President responded by sending troops to Montgomery, Alabama (May, 1961) and Birmingham, Alabama (May, 1963), and to other trouble spots. Leadership in this drive was assumed by _Dr. Martin Luther King,_ head of the Southern Christian Leadership Conference, whose determined pleas for nonviolent protest won him the Nobel Peace Prize (December, 1964). Steady but slow gains were registered; thus in Birmingham demonstrations resulted in an agreement between Negro and business leaders that desegrated numerous facilities, provided jobs for Negro workers, and created a bi-racial committee on race relations (May, 1963). Demonstrations against _de facto_ school segregation in northern cities focused attention on the lack of equal opportunity in housing that was common everywhere in the United States.

b. PROGRESS IN SCHOOL DESEGRATION. The conflict over school desegregation reached a climax in Mississippi and Alabama after other states had accepted at least token integration. In Mississippi, Governor Ross Barnett (September, 1962), and in Alabama, Governor George C. Wallace (September, 1963), personally resisted efforts of Negro students to enter the state universities even though armed with court orders. In each instance rioting broke out, in which deaths occurred, but the students were enrolled after federal intervention. By the end of 1963, token integration had been achieved in all states, with 1,129 of the 3,053 school districts in the southern and border states accepting Negro pupils.

c. THE GOVERNMENT AND CIVIL RIGHTS. President Kennedy sought to lessen disorder and hurry integration by proposing a _Civil Rights Act_ (June, 1963). This: 1) guaranteed all citizens equal access to all public accommodations; 2) authorized federal suits to force school integration; 3) provided for the elimination of discrimination on all projects aided by federal funds; and 4) established a Community Relations Service to mediate in tense racial situations. Congress failed to pass the measure, which was blocked by Southerners and conservatives who held that the "public accommodations" section invaded the right of individuals to use private property as they wished. One step toward eliminating discrimination in voting was taken with the ratification of the _24th amendment_ to the Constitution (January, 1964) outlawing the poll tax as a requirement for voting in presidential or congressional elections.

6. The Supreme Court. Two major decisions stirred controversy: 1) a ruling that nonsectarian prayers in public schoolrooms violated the First Amendment (June, 1962); and 2) a decision that the Constitution prohibited the required recitation of the Lord's Prayer or verses from the Bible in public schools (June, 1963). Pressure mounted for congressional action or an amendment to the Constitution to negate these rulings, but without immediate result.

C. Foreign Policy of the Kennedy Administration.

1. Strengthening the Free World. A major long-term objective of the Kennedy administration was the economic and social rehabilitation of nations that might through poverty drift into the communist orbit. To this end the President: 1) continued the foreign aid program, with appropriations of $3.9 billion in 1961 and 1962, and $3 billion in 1963; 2) created a _Peace Corps_ (March, 1961) to send volunteers into underdeveloped countries to aid in improving social and economic conditions and education; 3) signed, with 19 other American nations, the Declaration of Punta del Este (August, 1961), creating the _Alliance for Progress_ through which the United States would funnel nearly $20 billion into Latin America over a ten-year period to stimulate programs of economic and social reform; and 4) gave strong support to creating a _Euro-_

pean Common Market. This was designed to unite six European nations into a European Economic Community, with tariff walls between these nations eliminated and a common external tariff agreed upon. To fit the United States into this new order, the President proposed a *Trade Expansion Act* (passed October, 1962) which gave him power to: 1) reduce or increase customs duties by as much as 50%; and 2) reduce or eliminate tariffs on commodities traded largely by the United States and common market countries. Kennedy's plans suffered a set-back when France vetoed Great Britain's entry into the European Economic Community (January, 1963), and at the same time rejected Anglo-American proposals for a North Atlantic Treaty Organization nuclear force.

2. The Arms and Space Race.

a. EARLY FAILURE OF DISARMAMENT PROGRAMS. Russia abruptly violated the three-year moratorium against above-ground nuclear testing (August, 1961), conducting more than fifty tests in the next few months. As a result, President Kennedy was forced to order underground testing resumed (September, 1961), and in November, 1961, ordered a renewal of above-ground testing unless the USSR desisted. This began in April, 1962, as neutral nations denounced both the United States and Russia for contaminating the atmosphere. Efforts of a British-American-Russian team in Geneva to agree on a formula for nuclear disarmament failed (January, 1962). In March, 1962, a seventeen-nation Disarmament Conference convened at Geneva under UN auspices to seek a means of drafting a world-wide permanent test-ban; its members were unable to reach an agreement that year or during a later meeting in 1963.

b. PROGRESS TOWARD AMERICAN-SOVIET AGREEMENT. Undeterred by these setbacks, President Kennedy in June, 1963, announced that the United States would conduct no more above-ground nuclear tests so long as other nations did not. At the same time, negotiations were resumed with Russia and Great Britain for a permanent end to testing; the result was a *Nuclear Test-Ban Treaty* that banned all nuclear tests save those underground (signed August, 1963; ratified September, 1963). Eventually 31 other nations signed the treaty.

France refused to do so. At the same time a series of agreements between the US and the USSR eased Cold War tensions: 1) a three-year agreement to cooperate on nuclear research for peacetime purposes (May, 1963); 2) an agreement to open a "hot line" to provide direct communication between Washington and Moscow (June, 1963); and 3) an agreement to work together in launching and maintaining weather and communication satellites (September, 1963). In October, 1963, the President announced that the United States would sell $250 million worth of surplus wheat to Russia.

c. RIVALRY IN OUTER SPACE. Russia scored a victory in the space race when Major Yuri A. Gagarin became the first man to orbit the earth in a space vehicle (April, 1961); in August, 1961, another manned USSR spacecraft made 17 trips around the globe in 25 hours. The first United States astronaut to orbit the globe was Colonel John H. Glenn (February, 1962). Other orbital flights followed, but not until May, 1963, did the United States send an astronaut through 22 orbits. Americans outclassed Russians in other space probes, the most spectacular, a satellite flight near Venus (December, 1962) and the landing of a rocket on the moon after it had transmitted thousands of remarkable close-up pictures (July, 1964). Numerous other satellites were launched by both nations for space exploration and communication.

3. The Cold War in Europe. Premier Khrushchev (June, 1961) renewed his threat to sign a separate peace treaty giving East Germany control of access routes to Berlin. The United States answered by preparing for war; Russia backed down before this show of force but insisted that a separate peace treaty might be signed at any time. Within Berlin the flow of refugees from East to West Germany grew to such proportions that a wall was built by the East Germans (August, 1961). This *Berlin Wall* became a symbol of the division between East and West, and stirred western emotions as escaping Germans were shot while trying to reach freedom. President Kennedy visited Germany in June, 1963, to pledge continuous American support for unification.

4. The Cold War in the Far East.

a. LAOS. In June, 1961, President Kennedy and Premier Khrushchev agreed on independence and neutrality for Laos, ending fighting that had gone on since communist guerrilla bands invaded from China and North Viet Nam in 1959. An international conference at Geneva (May, 1961—June, 1962) finally agreed on a Laotian government under three leaders representing the US, USSR, and neutralist positions. Fourteen nations subsequently signed a Geneva accord guaranteeing the country's neutrality (July, 1962). Laos remained a trouble spot, however. Communist troops from there invaded Thailand (May, 1962), forcing the United States to send troops and planes to that country's aid. Factional conflicts also continued within Laos; hopes for peace were shattered when a cease-fire in the spring of 1963 was followed by the outbreak of more fighting during the summer.

b. SOUTH VIET NAM. The United States accepted neutrality for land-locked Laos, but was pledged to protect the pro-western government of South Viet Nam. Troops were sent there (May, 1961) to train fighters for use against the communist guerrilla units constantly infiltrating from North Viet Nam. Matters worsened in November, 1963, when the government of President Ngo Dinh Diem was overthrown, launching a period of conflict between Buddhist and Christian partisans that was marked by the frequent overthrow of governments. Resistance to the Viet Cong was weakened by these internal conflicts, allowing communist forces to occupy more and more of the country's territory. By the end of 1963, 105 Americans had been killed there.

c. INDONESIA. Indonesian troops with communist equipment attacked the Dutch-held colony of West New Guinea in 1962. President Kennedy succeeded in arranging a meeting between the two nations (August, 1962), which provided for the UN to administer West New Guinea until May, 1963, when it would become part of Indonesia. During 1963, Indonesia strongly opposed incorporation of British Borneo into the new Federation of Malaysia, but did not resort to arms.

d. CHINA. Communist China threatened world peace by invading northern India (October, 1962), claiming that the occupied territories were part of Tibet. As Prime Minister Nehru sought help from other powers, the poorly prepared Indian army was pushed back. Russia, the United States, and Great Britain rushed munitions and fighting planes to the front, dramatizing the growing break between China and the USSR. After a few weeks the Chinese withdrew, leaving the West mystified as to the purpose of the invasion.

5. The Cold War in Africa. Conflict was centered in two areas: 1) Algeria, in rebellion against France since 1954, accepted a truce offer from President de Gaulle (March, 1962) which assured a plebiscite on independence. Despite bloody opposition from the French Secret Army (OAS), the Algerians voted overwhelmingly for independence, which was granted on July 3, 1962. 2) The Congo, in turmoil since its independence was granted by Belgium in 1960, was plunged into a new civil war when the rich Katanga province demanded status as a separate nation. When the former premier, Patrice Lumumba, was assassinated while reportedly escaping from Katanga officials (February, 1961), the USSR seized the excuse to denounce UN intervention. The UN, with strong support from the United States, countered by voting to use force to keep peace in the Congo. Fighting between UN and Katanga troops continued until December, 1961, when a settlement was reached bringing Katanga into the central government. UN troops kept peace in the Congo until June, 1964, when their withdrawal touched off a series of retaliatory attacks by rebel bands. In November, 1964, a joint Belgian-United States striking force intervened to rescue 2,000 white hostages held by the rebels, but only after many had been killed.

6. The Cold War in Cuba.

a. BAY OF PIGS INVASION. Relations between Cuba and the United States disintegrated rapidly after diplomatic relations were severed during the Eisenhower administration. Fidel Castro's trade with Russia, and his announced determination to bring "socialism" to the island, brought tension to a climax. This was reached when more than 1,000 anti-Castro

Cuban exiles who had been trained in Central America with the tacit assistance of the United States, *invaded Cuba at the Bay of Pigs in April, 1961*. When the people failed to rise as hoped, the invasion was repulsed and most of the invaders captured. They were later released in return for private donations of food and medical supplies (December, 1962). World opinion strongly condemned the United States for what seemed an attack on a weaker neighbor.

b. THE CUBAN BLOCKADE. Trade with Cuba allowed Russia to send that country long-range bombers and nuclear missiles. When these were detected by aerial reconnaissance, President Kennedy (October, 1962) ordered a complete blockade of the island and warned that any ship carrying offensive weapons would be turned back. In the face of this strong stand and unanimous western opinion supporting the United States, Premier Khrushchev was forced to order removal of all offensive weapons from Cuba. Troops remained, but continued pressure from President Kennedy forced Russia to announce (March, 1963) that all would shortly be withdrawn.

D. Assassination of the President.

On November 22, 1963, while driving through Dallas, Texas, on his way to deliver a speech, *President Kennedy was assassinated*. Lee Harvey Oswald, the pro-Castro Marxist charged with the crime, was immediately arrested, but was killed a day later by a former nightclub operator named Jack Ruby. Vice-president Lyndon B. Johnson, who was sworn into the presidency at once, named a seven-man commission under Chief Justice Earl Warren to investigate the assassination. After an exhaustive study, the *Warren Commission* reported (September, 1964) that Oswald, "acting alone and without advice or assistance," was the assassin, and that neither he nor Ruby was part of "any conspiracy, domestic or foreign," to kill the President. As the nation and Western World mourned, Ruby was convicted of murder and sentenced to death (March, 1964), but appealed on the grounds of temporary insanity. The appeal was eventually upheld (October, 1966), but Ruby died of natural causes on January 3, 1967, before final settlement of his case. Many refused to accept the Warren Commission Report, arguing that a single bullet could not have killed the President and wounded Governor John B. Connally of Texas, and that other assassins were involved. The controversy reached its height in 1966 with the publication of William Manchester's *The Death of a President* and numerous volumes attacking the report.

E. The First Johnson Administration, 1963-1965.

1. Launching the Johnson Program. In a notable address to Congress (November, 1963), President Johnson announced his intention to carry out the Kennedy Program, including a strong civil rights act, tax reduction, and measures to aid education. In his first state-of-the-union message (January, 1964) he announced a *"war on poverty"* which included aid for the depressed areas of the Appalachian Mountain system, youth-employment legislation, a broadened food-stamp program for the poor, a National Service Corps similar to the Peace Corps to operate within the United States, improved unemployment insurance, and other social measures.

2. The Attack on Discrimination and Poverty.

a. THE CIVIL RIGHTS ACT OF 1964. President Johnson's adroit political manipulation wrung from Congress a measure (June, 1964) that outlawed discrimination in all public accommodations, schools, employment, and voting. The constitutionality of the disputed *public accommodations section* was upheld by the Supreme Court in December, 1964 (Heart of Atlanta Motel v. United States).

b. THE ECONOMIC OPPORTUNITY ACT, designed to offer job-training and employment to the underprivileged, provided 1) for a Domestic Peace Corps to operate in poverty areas; 2) for a Job Corps to offer work-training programs for the unskilled; and 3) created an Office of Economic Opportunity to supervise the "war on poverty."

c. OTHER SOCIAL MEASURES. In other measures designed to provide better living conditions for the people, Congress adopted: 1) a Food Stamp Plan (August, 1964) which placed on a permanent basis the distribution of surplus food to needy families; 2) an Urban Mass Transportation Act (July, 1964) authorizing federal loans to states to develop urban transportation systems; and 3) several conservation bills, including a Wilderness Act (September, 1964) establishing a national wilderness preservation system and withdrawing an initial 9.1 million acres of forest from exploitation. The President also won from Congress a decrease in personal and corporate income taxes of $11.5 billion annually (February, 1964) as a device to stimulate the economy.

3. The Problem of Reapportionment. In two important decisions the Supreme Court ruled: 1) that congressional districts within each state must be substantially equal in population (Wesberry v. Sanders, February, 1964); and 2) that both houses in bicameral state legislatures must be _apportioned on a basis of population,_ thus upsetting the "little federal system" used in many states where one house was apportioned on a geographic basis (Reynolds v. Sims, June, 1964). The effect was to force many rurally dominated legislatures to reapportion in a manner that would allow city dwellers just representation. Republicans made repeated attempts to negate the decision through a constitutional amendment, but without success.

4. Foreign Policy of the First Johnson Administration.

a. RELATIONS WITH RUSSIA. Relations with Russia grew steadily more harmonious partly because Red China's aggressive attitude drove the USSR toward a rapprochement with the West. Both the US and Russia radically reduced military spending and the production of fissionable material for nuclear weapons (January and April, 1964). They also signed an agreement to expand cultural, educational, scientific, and technical exchanges. The ousting of Premier Khrushchev (October, 1964) failed to alter this trend as his successors, Leonid Brezhnev and Aleksei Kosygin, continued to follow his program.

b. CONFLICT IN SOUTH EAST ASIA.

i. _The War in South Viet Nam._ As the unstable government of South Viet Nam proved incapable of checking the attacks of South Viet Nam communists (Viet Cong) and guerrilla soldiers from communist North Viet Nam on villages throughout the land, President Johnson gradually accelerated American military aid. During 1964 personnel from the United States increased from 16,000 to 22,000. A major crisis occurred when North Viet Nam patrol boats attacked American destroyers in the international waters of the Gulf of Tonkin. In retaliation the United States bombed that country's gunboat bases and oil storage tanks.

II. *Laos and Cambodia.* Laos continued to be torn by internal conflict, further disturbing the equilibrium of Southeast Asia. Tensions were increased with the charge by South Viet Nam that neighboring Cambodia was harboring Viet Cong insurgents. As President Johnson's first term ended there were no indications of peace or stability for the region. Matters worsened after October, 1964, when Red China exploded its first nuclear bomb.

c. RELATIONS WITH EUROPE. France sought to strengthen its leadership position in Europe by: 1) becoming the first major ally of the United States to recognize Red China (January, 1964); 2) persuading the European common-market nations to refuse tariff reductions sought by the President; and 3) successfully opposing American efforts to create a multilateral naval force armed with nuclear weapons. In November, 1964, the United States signed a military pact with West Germany authorizing the purchase of American arms.

d. RELATIONS WITH LATIN AMERICA. President Kennedy's Alliance for Progress faltered during 1963 as opposition mounted in Brazil and other South American nations. During 1964 two incidents hurried this trend: 1) a dispute over flying the United States flag in the Canal Zone caused the Republic of Panama to break off diplomatic relations (January, 1964), and demand renegotiation of the treaty that gave the United States sovereignty over the zone. Relations were resumed in April, 1964, and in December President Johnson announced that the negotiation of a new treaty had begun, at the same time saying that the United States would build a second sea-level canal through another country. In the treaty that was finally drafted (September, 1965) the two nations agreed to operate the canal jointly, but that sovereignty over the Canal Zone rested in Panama. 2) A minor dispute with Cuba erupted when Castro's government cut off the water supply at the American naval base at Guantanamo Bay (February, 1964). The United States answered by building its own plant to convert sea water.

F. The Election of 1964.

1. Background of the Election. Two scandals threatened the President's popularity on the eve of the election: 1) Robert G. (Bobby) Baker, secretary of the Senate majority, was charged by an investigating committee with soliciting illegal campaign funds; and 2) Walter Jenkins, long-time aide to President Johnson, was forced to resign following his arrest on a morals charge.

2. The Nominating Conventions. The Republicans, meeting in San Francisco (July, 1964), rejected the bids of a liberal (Governor Nelson A. Rockefeller of New York) and a moderate (Governor William W. Scranton of Pennsylvania) to choose as their standard bearer a self-proclaimed conservative, Senator _Barry M. Goldwater_ of Arizona who promised voters "a choice, not a echo." His running mate was Representative William E. Miller of New York. In a lacklustre campaign that alienated many middle-of-the-road Republicans, Goldwater attacked the low moral tone of the nation and the lack of an aggressive foreign policy. The Democrats _nominated President Johnson_ by acclamation, with Senator Hubert H. Humphrey of Minnesota as his vice-presidential candidate. They campaigned vigorously, stressing Senator Goldwater's conservative record which included votes against social security, the civil rights acts, federal aid to education, and the nuclear test-ban treaty.

3. Outcome of the Election. Goldwater was repudiated by one of the most decisive margins in history. Johnson amassed 42,672,220 popular votes to 26,860,314 for his opponent, and an electoral vote of 486 to 52. Goldwater carried only his native Arizona and five states in the deep South attracted by his stand against civil rights. Democrats also gained 38 seats in the House and added two to their lopsided majority in the Senate.

II. THE SECOND JOHNSON ADMINISTRATION, 1965-1969

A. Program for a "Great Society." In a series of messages to the new Congress (January, 1965), President Johnson outlined plans for a *"Great Society"* program and asked for one of the most extensive series of new laws since the New Deal. These included: 1) free medical care for the aged; 2) repeal of the section of the Taft-Hartley Act which authorized state right-to-work laws forbidding compulsory unionization; 3) increased aid to education; 4) extension of the minimum wage to an additional 2 million workers; 5) revision of the immigration laws to eliminate the national quota system and the ban against Orientals; 6) aid to the eleven Appalachian Mountain states where 15% of the workers were unemployed; 7) measures to eliminate air and water pollution; 8) creation of a cabinet post on urban affairs; 9) inauguration of a program to develop high-speed railroad transportation; 10) establishment of a National Foundation for the Arts; and 11) a plan for the beautification of America to assure a "green legacy" for the future. The President also urged a cut of $1.5 billion in excise taxes to help spur the economy.

B. The War in South Viet Nam.

1. Stabilizing the South Viet Nam Government. South Viet Nam's war effort had long been handicapped by divisions within the government; when President Johnson began his second term Buddhists and Catholics were in open conflict. In June, 1965, a military junta named Air Marshal *Nguyen Cao Ky* as premier, bringing a degree of stability. When Buddhist opposition continued, Ky announced a general election for a constituent assembly that would draft a constitution and restore civilian government (April, 1966). The promise of an orderly election was shattered when Ky announced (May, 1966) that the army would refuse to allow any neutralist or procommunist elected to take his seat. This touched off an armed rebellion led by Buddhists and members of the National Liberation Front (NLF), the political arm of the Viet Cong, which centered at Da Nang where 75 persons were killed, in addition to nine monks who protested by burning themselves to death. The insurrection was finally crushed (June, 1966) and elections held (September, 1966). Despite Viet Cong harassment and a boycott by the NLF, 80% of the eligible voters chose 108 delegates who drafted a constitution calling for universal suffrage, a bicameral legislature, and a premier and cabinet appointed by the president. This was promulgated on April 1, 1967, and an election set for September 3. Ky was a leading candidate for president, but was challenged by _Nguyen Van Thieu_ and forced by the military junta to accept the second spot on the ticket. Ten non-military candidates challenged the junta slate. The _Thieu-Ky ticket won with 35%_ of the votes cast, while the "peace" candidates garnered 27%. On October 31, 1967, Thieu became president, ending four years of army rule.

2. Accelerating the Military Effort.

a. COMMITMENT OF AMERICAN TROOPS. Unstable governments in South Viet Nam contributed to a series of military setbacks that brought the Viet Cong close to victory. Rather than allow a communist triumph, President Johnson _ordered the bombing of staging areas_ and other strategic points in North Viet Nam where Red troops were dispatched southward (March, 1965). When this failed to turn the tide he ordered American marines to guard the strategic air field at Da Nang (April, 1965), and a month later _sent army units into battle_ as troops, not under the guise of "advisors." During the next year air raids against North Viet Nam were extended to fuel storage installations on the edge of heavily populated centers such as Hanoi and Haiphong. At the same time, the American ground force was rapidly increased, reaching 190,000 troops by the end of 1965, 380,000 by the end of 1966, 480,000 by the end of 1967, and 525,000 by 1969.

b. THE MILITARY RECORD. Heaviest fighting for these soldiers was centered in the area just below the Demilitarized Zone (DMZ) between North and South Viet Nam, but guerrilla warfare extended over the nation and even penetrated the outskirts of Saigon. General William C. Westmoreland's "search and destroy" tactics used against the Viet Cong and infiltrating North Vietnamese fighters were supplemented by a "pacification" program to pacify village after village. By the end of 1967 the military estimated that 65% of the South Vietnamese were living in government-controlled areas. These optimistic estimates were shattered by the _Tet Offensive_—named for the lunar Tet holidays (January-February, 1968). In ten days of intense fighting the communists attacked all major points, including Saigon and 35 other cities, killing 14,000 civilians.

Although eventually driven off, their success led many to question whether the United States was winning the war. By the end of 1968 Americans killed passed the 30,000 mark, while war costs were over $2 billion a month.

3. Opposition to the Viet Nam War. Americans increasingly questioned the war after mid-1965 when air strikes against North Viet Nam were costing lives and United States troops were assigned a major role in fighting. Peace marches, picketing the White House, and ceremonies in which draft cards were burned became increasingly common, especially after June, 1966, when targets near Hanoi and Haiphong were bombed, with many civilian casualties. Protests were centered within the President's own party, with Senate Majority Leader Mike Mansfield an outspoken foe of indiscriminate bombing. In October, 1967, 30 members of the House appealed to the President to halt the attacks on North Viet Nam, while 54 Senators urged him to ask the UN to take any action needed to end the fighting. On nearly all college campuses military recruiters and interviewers for the Dow Chemical Company, manufacturers of napalm, were picketed or assaulted.

4. Administration Peace Efforts.

a. DEFINING THE WAR AIMS. As the nation and world increasingly questioned America's role in Viet Nam, the President sought to define the war's purposes in a series of statements and conferences: 1) in January, 1966, he declared that a "a just nation cannot leave to the cruelties of its enemies a people who have staked their lives and independence on our solemn pledge;" 2) meeting with Premier Ky in Hawaii, the President issued a joint "Declaration of Hawaii" (February, 1966) which called for the defeat of the Viet Cong, the eradication of social injustice in South Viet Nam, and the establishment there of a true democracy; 3) at the Manila Conference (October, 1966) the United States, Australia, New Zealand, the Philippines, Thailand, and South Korea pledged the removal of all allied forces from South Viet Nam within six months after North Viet Nam withdrew its forces; and 4) at a meeting at Guam (March, 1967), President Johnson and the South Vietnamese government pledged perpetual adherence to the civilian government of that country.

b. THE QUEST FOR PEACE. In April, 1965, President Johnson announced terms acceptable to the United States for an honorable peace, at the same time pledging $1 billion in economic aid for Southeast Asia when the war was over. From then on periodic bombing halts sought to lure the North Vietnamese into negotiations. The first (December-January, 1967) was accompanied by a diplomatic move in which the United States urged 115 nations to pressure North Viet Nam for peace, but Hanoi refused to meet American negotiators until all bombing ceased. The President responded (September, 1967) by stating that the United States was ready to abandon its raids at any time the North Vietnamese were willing to begin productive discussions, providing they did not take advantage of the lull to build up their military position. This proposal was also rejected (October, 1967). In November, 1967, Secretary of Defense Robert S. McNamara resigned, to be replaced by Clark M. Clifford, who was less inclined to insist on total victory; in July, 1968, General Creighton W. Abrams replaced Westmoreland as commander of the American forces, with an announced strategy of increasing the military strength of the South Vietnamese who would eventually assume greater responsibility for the war.

c. BEGINNINGS OF PEACE NEGOTIATIONS. As opposition to the war mounted within the United States, pressure grew to end the bombing of North Viet Nam as the only means of drawing Hanoi into negotiations. On March 31, 1968, President Johnson dramatically announced the *end of all bombing save in a small area just north of the DMZ,* at the same time revealing that he would *not be a candidate for reelection* in 1968. North Viet Nam had no choice now but to begin negotiating, but haggled for weeks over a site for the talks before agreeing on Paris (May, 1968). Negotiations began on May 13, 1968, but disputes over procedural matters delayed serious discussion of the issues until October, 1968. When these were settled, President Johnson proclaimed a total halt to all bombing north of the DMZ (October 31, 1968), as serious talks were to begin between Saigon, Hanoi, the United States, and the NLF. President Thieu further delayed by refusing to allow his diplomats to attend any meetings where the NLF was considered a separate entity. When, after 25 days, Thieu backed down, negotiations were again delayed by a dispute over the shape of the table to be used; Hanoi and the NLF wanted a four-sided table which would place all parties on an equal basis; South Vietnam insisted that this would constitute tacit recognition of the NLF. A compromise arrangement ended this dispute in January, 1969, allowing the discussions to begin. In the meantime fighting continued, with the Viet Cong mounting several major attacks during the summer of 1968, although none as serious as the Tet offensive.

C. World Relations of the Second Administration.

1. International Role of the United States. The United States expenditures in Viet Nam, which sent military budgets soaring from $46.9 billion in 1965 to $72 billion in 1969, together with the unpopularity of the war, lessened congressional interest in overseas involvements. Appropriations for foreign aid declined from $3.2 billion in 1965 to $1.9 billion in 1969, a sum $1.3 billion less than that asked by the President. Congress did extend the Food for Peace program (October, 1966) but specified that nations failing to initiate programs to feed their own peoples could be denied aid until they did so. India, which was receiving 20,000 tons of American grain daily, was refused supplies briefly in 1967. When internal revolutions paralyzed Nigeria and the Congo (1966-1969) the United States showed no inclination to become involved.

2. Relations with the Near East. The delicate balance in the Near East was upset (May, 1967) when Israel warned of retaliation against border raiders from Syria and Lebanon. President Gamal Abdel Nasser of Egypt seized this opportunity for a showdown, demanding the withdrawal of the UN Peace-Keeping Force then occupying the disputed Gaza Strip and the mouth of the Gulf of Aqaba. When Nasser announced that the gulf was closed to Israeli shipping, President Johnson denounced the Arab blockade of this international waterway as illegal. Neither the United States nor other maritime powers was willing to test the blockade, leaving Israel with no commercial access to the Red Sea. Hence that nation struck back on June 5, 1967, when its planes destroyed the entire 450-plane air force of the United Arab Republic on the ground. In the *Six-Day War* that followed, the Israeli army swept across the Gaza Strip and the Sinai Peninsula to the Suez Canal, destroying an Arab army of 100,000 men. At the same time, forces occupied the old city of

Jerusalem, seized all Jordanian territory west of the River Jordan, and captured heights twelve miles within Syria that had been used to bomb Israel territory. Fighting ended on June 10 when both sides accepted a cease-fire proposed by the UN. Despite pressure from the United States and UN, Israel showed no inclination to relinquish its conquests, and on June 28 formally annexed the old city of Jerusalem. Border raids from Jordan and Lebanon were soon resumed, reaching a climax in December, 1968, when Arab terrorists bombed an Israeli commercial plane. In retaliation an Israel commando force raided a Lebanese air field, destroying about half the nation's commercial planes. With Russia rearming the United Arab Republic and the United States providing Israel with fifty more fighting planes, peace in the Near East seemed a distant prospect in 1969.

3. Relations with the Far East. Antagonisms between Red China and the United States over the Viet Nam War prevented any significant moves toward greater understanding. President Johnson made a tentative peace gesture (July, 1966) by stating that the United States sought "conciliation," not conquest, in Asia, and by urging China to seek a better understanding of the outside world. Two events offset this effort: 1) the United States in 1966 and 1968 successfully blocked the admission of mainland China into the UN; and 2) in January, 1968, North Korean naval forces captured the United States intelligence ship *Pueblo* with its 83 crew members, claiming that it was within the twelve mile limit and using listening devices to spy on military installations. The United States admitted that the vessel was equipped with electronic listening devices, but insisted that it was outside North Korea's territorial waters. Negotiations for release of the *Pueblo* crew continued until December 23, 1968, when all were returned save one who was killed in the capture.

4. Relations with France and the USSR. France continued to disrupt the harmonious western Europe planned by the United States when President *Charles de Gaulle withdrew his armies from the North Atlantic Treaty Organization.* (July, 1966). By contrast, relations with the USSR improved steadily as Russia sought friends in the face of China's menacing power. President Johnson *opened the door for cooperation in a major speech* (October, 1966), in which he: 1) urged the removal of nonstrategic items from the list of products barred from shipment to eastern Europe; 2) reviewed the possibility of easing the Polish debt to the United States by the expenditure of accumulated Polish currency; and 3) favored the liberalization of rules for American travel in communist countries. This invitation to better understanding was followed by: 1) an agreement for direct air service between Moscow and New York (November, 1966), with the first flight in July, 1968; 2) an international treaty prohibiting the placement of nuclear arms or mass-destruction weapons in orbit around the earth or on celestial bodies; and 3) a *Nuclear Non-proliferation Treaty,* agreed upon in conversations between the President and Premier Kosygin when the latter visited the United States during the Arab-Israel crisis, and signed by the USSR, the United States, and 58 other nations (July, 1968). Only France and Red China refused to participate in an agreement that bound non-nuclear powers to receive no weapons from nations which possessed them and were promised in return the full use of atomic devices for peaceful purposes. The drift toward greater USSR-US cooperation was halted when 200,000 troops from *Russia and five Warsaw Pact countries invaded Czechoslovakia* to repress the liberal reforms instituted there by the government of Secretary Alexander Dubcek (August, 1968). This suppression, reminiscent of the invasion of Hungary in 1956, turned western opinion against the USSR and ended the growing rapprochement with the United States. As a result the Senate refused to ratify the Nuclear Non-proliferation Treaty until after President Johnson left office.

5. Relations with Latin America. Latin American friendship toward the United States suffered when a *civil war broke out in the Dominican Republic* (April, 1965). President Johnson ordered *marines to invade the country,* holding that American lives were in danger and that communists controlled the rebel party—a charge that was denied. By May 3, 30,000 American troops were battling the insurgents. Peace missions sent by the Organization of American States and the UN arranged a truce on May 21, allowing an Inter-American Peace Force to take over while the controlling military junta and the rebels settled their differences. Withdrawal of American troops began on June 28, 1965. This use of force alarmed all Latin America, nor was tension decreased when Congress, over the

President's opposition, adopted a resolution endorsing unilateral force by any one country in the hemisphere to prevent communist aggression (September, 1965), or when the President declared in a speech in Mexico City that "despots are not welcome in this hemisphere." Stability in Latin America prevented further incidents during the Johnson administrations, but diplomats feared that further unilateral action by the United States would precipitate trouble.

D. Domestic Policy of the Second Johnson Administration.

1. The "Great Society" Program.

a. THE YEAR OF ACTION : 1965. During the first year of his second term, President Johnson enjoyed unprecedented success in winning Congressional approval for his legislative proposals. These included: 1) an Appalachia Bill appropriating $1.1 billion to aid the distressed Appalachian Mountain area; 2) an *Elementary and Secondary Education Act* (April, 1965) providing $1.3 billion to aid primary and secondary schools in areas where at least 3% of the children could be classified as "needy;" 3) a Higher Education Act (November, 1965) creating a program of federally financed scholarships for college undergraduates; 4) a bill establishing the National Foundation of the Arts and Humanities to provide financial means for cultural development; 5) a *Medicare Bill* offering basic hospital care for 60 days to all over 65, with supplementary benefits in the way of physician's and surgeon's fees for those paying a small sum (July, 1965); 6) amendments to the Social Security Act to provide for increased contributions from employers and employees on a rising scale to reach 11% of salaries up to $6,600 by 1987; 7) an *Omnibus Housing Bill* (August, 1965) authorizing grants and loans to municipalities for low-cost housing and the *payment of rent subsidies* to landlords of low-income families; 8) amendments to the *immigration laws eliminating the national quota system,* but limiting immigration to 20,000 yearly from any one nation, 120,000 from the western hemisphere, and 170,000 from the rest of the world (October, 1965); and 9) a Highway Beautification Bill allotting federal funds to states for elimination of billboards, junk yards, and other unsightly objects (October, 1965). In addition Congress doubled appropriations for the

President's anti-poverty program (September 1965), and created the cabinet post of *Secretary of Housing and Urban Development* (September, 1965). President Johnson named to this post Robert C. Weaver, the first Negro to hold a cabinet position. Only two recommendations of the President were ignored by Congress: 1) alteration of the Taft-Hartley Act to eliminate sections favorable to the open shop; and 2) home rule for the District of Columbia.

b. THE YEAR OF DECLINE: 1966. As pressures and divisions stemming from the accelerating Viet Nam War absorbed attention and divided the people, Congress showed less willingness to support the "Great Society" program. Instead, a series of measures were adopted designed to protect the people from illicit actions by industry: 1) a Water Quality Act setting in motion a federal antipollution program designed to diminish the pollution of waterways (October, 1965); 2) a bill setting standards for automobile exhaust systems that would lessen air pollution (October, 1965); 3) an Automobile and Road Safety Act requiring manufacturers to build safer cars and creating a National Traffic Safety Agency to encourage the states to adopt highway safety standards under threat of losing national funds for highway construction; 4) a *Truth in Packaging Act* forcing producers of food and drugs to label their packages clearly and accurately; 5) a Cold War GI Bill of Rights extending educational, housing, health, and job benefits to veterans who had served 180 days or more in the armed services since the end of the Korean War; and 6) a *Demonstration Cities Bill* allotting $1.4 billion for a joint federal-local rebuilding of the slum sections of some 60 representative cities. Congress also provided adequate funds to continue the anti-poverty programs ($1.75 billion), college aid ($3.6 billion), and elementary and secondary school aid ($6.2 billion).

2. *The Elections of 1966.* The congressional elections were influenced by 1) the Viet Nam War; and 2) rising prices. Inflationary pressures based on heavy expenditures in Viet Nam and the mounting national debt caused living costs to spiral during 1966, driving housewives to stage strikes against supermarkets in protest. Interest rates also rose sharply, acting as a curb on needed new building. Voter dissatisfaction was expressed at the polls, where *Republicans captured eight new governorships,*

and gained 47 seats in the House and three in the Senate. Democrats retained control of both houses of Congress but by smaller majorities, while Republician governors now controlled half the states. The elections elevated to national stature Governor George W. Romney of Michigan and Governor Ronald Reagan of California.

3. The Civil Rights Controversy. Civil rights and "law and order" transcended other issues during the last years of the Johnson administrations. Both were linked with the Viet Nam War, for protesters held that the $30 billion spent yearly on that conflict could improve the lot of Negroes and wipe out the urban ghettos that bred crime.

a. VOTING RIGHTS ACT OF 1965. A principal objective of civil rights leaders was the achievement of equal access for all persons to the ballot box in southern states that had used discriminatory "literacy tests" to restrict voting to whites. A series of marches organized by the Reverend Martin Luther King, chairman of the Southern Christian Leadership Conference, in behalf of this reform reached a climax when marchers bound from Selma, Alabama, to the state capital at Montgomery were forcibly stopped by state police who injured 78 persons. National indignation sent 25,000 persons from all the nation to repeat this march, this time peacefully (March 21-25, 1965). This same spirit influenced Congress to adopt the administration-sponsored *Voting Rights Act* (August, 1965) which *suspended literacy tests for voters* and authorized *federal registration* in districts where discrimination had been employed. At the same time school integration was moving slowly; by the end of 1967 only 16% of the Negro children in the South were attending integrated schools.

b. CHANGING CHARACTER OF BLACK DEMANDS. By 1966 younger leaders were challenging the non-violence program of Martin Luther King and others who had dominated the civil rights movement. Led by Stokely Carmichael and Rap Brown of the Student Nonviolent Coordinating Committee (SNCC), they advocated excluding whites from the movement and building a Negro power base so strong that it could not be denied. They held that Negroes should isolate themselves from whites and control their own communities because all whites were fundamentally "racist" and could not be relied on to advance the interests of the blacks. Some extreme leaders advocated violence as the only means of winning Negroes their due. These views were directly the opposite of those of Martin Luther King and other prior leaders who advocated integration of Negroes into the national society. They were also opposed by the powerful National Association for the Advancement of Colored People (NAACP) which continued to advocate cooperation with whites and the end of discrimination. This division hindered the civil rights movement, partly because of the fragmentation of Negro leadership, partly because the demand for "Black Power" helped create a strong white "backlash."

c. RIOTING IN THE CITIES. Violence in the black ghettos of large cities further hindered the civil rights cause. The _Watts Riots_ in Los Angeles (August 11-16, 1965) involved as many as 10,000 Negroes who roamed the streets for six days, looting stores, burning buildings, and committing assaults. In all, 35 persons were killed, 1,032 injured, and $40 million in property destroyed. An investigating committee reported (December, 1965) that the riots were rooted in poverty, unemployment, poor schooling, and hatred of the police as symbols of authority. A year later riots ravaged the Negro section of several cities, reaching a climax in Chicago (July, 1966), where Martin Luther King was staging a series of marches to protest segregated housing. Again in 1967 rioting reaching a scale unknown in America's 20th century in Newark (July 12-18) and Detroit (July 23-30). In each city state and federal troops were required to restore order. The summer of 1968 witnessed only one major riot, this in Cleveland where 11 persons were killed. A Special Advisory Committee on Civil Disorders, named by the President to probe the reasons for racial unrest (July, 1967), reported that racist attitudes among whites were basically responsible and that a changed national psychology was needed as well as specific reforms.

d. THE CIVIL RIGHTS ACT OF 1968. White reaction to Negro rioting doomed President Johnson's attempt to secure new civil rights legislation in 1966 and 1967, but the situation changed in April, 1968, when Martin Luther King was assassinated during a visit to Memphis. His death touched off a period of rioting and looting in 168 cities, but also touched the conscience of the white community. Six days later Congress adopted the _Civil Rights Act of 1968_ which opened 80% of the nation's housing units, including many privately owned homes, _to buyers or renters without discrimination_ by authorizing any person denied housing because of race or color to file a complaint with the Department of Housing and Urban Development. Judicial support for this stand was assured when the Supreme Court (June, 1968) held that the Civil Rights Act of 1866, based on the 13th amendment, "bars all racial discrimination, private as well as public, in the sale or rental of property."

4. The "Law and Order" Issue.

a. EFFECT OF COURT DECISIONS. Lawlessness in cities increased rapidly, due partly to racial conflict, partly to a mounting protest against the existing power structure by students and Negroes, partly to a growing crime rate. Public opinion associated this with a series of Supreme Court decisions aimed at assuring justice to all classes of citizens: 1) Gideon v. Wainwright (1963) ruled that the state must provide free counsel for a defendant who could not afford a lawyer; 2) Escobedo v. Illinois (1964) ordered that a defendant had a right to a lawyer during questioning by police; and 3) _Miranda v. Arizona_ (1966) held that a suspect must be informed of his right to remain silent, his right to counsel, and told that anything said might be used against him; that in case of a confession the prosecution must prove that the suspect knowingly waived his rights to silence; and if a suspect "in any manner" indicated that he wished to remain silent the questioning must end. Police officials complained that these decisions would render most confessions inadmissible as evidence and make punishment for crimes more difficult. Antipathy to the "Warren Court" for these rulings emerged when Chief Justice Earl Warren resigned (June, 1968). The attack on his appointed successor, Justice Abe Fortas, was so violent in congressional committee that President Johnson was forced to withdraw his nomination (October, 1968), leaving Chief Justice Warren still on the bench.

b. ATTEMPTS AT GUN CONTROL. The administration responded to the "law and order" issue by proposing an anticrime bill (February, 1967) that would: 1) control the interstate shipment of guns; 2) restrict the use of electronic wire tapping and eavesdropping devices; and 3) allot federal funds to help states and communities update their law enforcement agencies. Congress refused to act on this measure, influenced partly by the million-member National Rifle Association which opposed all gun control laws. The Omnibus Crime Bill finally adopted (June, 1968) bore little relation to the administration measure and was signed reluctantly by the President.

c. STUDENT PROTESTS. The impression of a lawless society was accentuated by a new student militancy that spread across most of the nation's colleges and universities. This stemmed from: 1) Negroes who demanded a "black studies program" that would stress the Negro's role in history; 2) the use of "Student Power" to demand a share in controlling the nature of courses taught, and in the selection of teachers; and 3) mounting protests against the Viet Nam War in the form of marches and rallies at many schools. Student demonstrations reached their most dangerous form at Columbia University (June, 1968), and San Francisco State College (December, 1968) when rioting and property destruction forced the temporary closing of both institutions.

5. The Legislative Record, 1966-1969. Popular and congressional dissatisfaction with both growing disorder and the Viet Nam conflict, together with narrower Democratic majorities after the 1966 elections, ended President Johnson's hopes of continuing his "Great Society" program. Congress refused to consider administration measures designed to deal with poverty, open housing, political campaign financing through federal funds, gun control, and the protection of consumers. It did adopt: 1) an act continuing the Elementary and Secondary Education program through 1969 and 1970 with an appropriation of $9.3 billion (December, 1969); 2) a Public Broadcasting Act (November, 1967) creating the nonprofit Corporation for Public Broadcasting to improve the quality of television broadcasting; 3) a Home Ownership Act appropriating $5.3 billion for a three-year program to provide 1,700,000 living units for low-income families (August, 1968); and 4) a measure to observe four national holidays—Washington's Birthday, Memorial Day, Veterans' Day, and Columbus Day—on Mondays. Congress also enacted a series of laws designed to provide consumer protection, including a Meat Inspection Bill requiring states to enforce adequate inspection standards, and a *Truth in Lending Act* forcing lenders to provide accurate information on the cost of credit purchases (May, 1968). The congressionally proposed *25th amendment to the Constitution* was ratified in February, 1967, providing for presidential succession in case of the death or resignation of the President, and establishing a procedure through which a vacant vice-presidency could be filled by presidential nomination and confirmation by both houses of Congress.

6. Economic Problems. Inflationary pressures stemming from the heavy Viet Nam War expenditures created two major problems:

a. THE GOLD DRAIN, 1966-1969. When England devalued its pound (November, 1967) international bankers began a run on gold dollars, reducing the nation's gold supply by $1 billion within six months. This drain forced the United States to ask Great Britain to close its gold market (March, 1968), at the same time inviting the Gold Pool nations to a monetary conference to consider the world's money problems, and wringing from Congress a law reducing the amount of bullion needed as backing for paper dollars. The International Conference aided the United States by adopting a two-price system for gold, using the established price of $35 an ounce to settle international exchanges between the Gold Pool nations, but allowing speculators to trade the metal at a price set in the open market. This decision basically altered the international monetary system that had operated since 1934.

b. INFLATION AND DEFICIT. As the yearly deficit showed no signs of diminishing and inflation drove prices higher, President Johnson asked Congress for a *10% surtax on personal and corporate income taxes* (August, 1967). Congress refused to grant this unless the President agreed to reduce expenditures by $6 billion, largely in civil areas. With this agreement, the tax bill was adopted (June, 1968), imposing additional taxes retroactive to April 1, 1968. Congress used this opportunity to cut budgets for the Medicare and Alliance for Progress programs drastically, and to slash funds for the Educational and Cultural Exchange Program so ruthlessly that the "Fulbright Program" for the exchange of scholars between nations was virtually ended for the first time since 1946 (September, 1968). As a result of the tax surcharge and economy measures, President Johnson was able to report (January, 1969) that the nation would have a $3.4 billion surplus in its current budget and that in 1968 it enjoyed a favorable trade balance for the first time since 1957.

7. The Space Program. In a series of manned space flights, Russian and American astronauts circled the earth for increasingly extended periods as both nations prepared for an eventual flight to the moon or beyond. In December, 1965, the American Gemini 7 made 206 circuits and maneuvered within a few feet of another space capsule to demonstrate the feasibility of a rendezvous. Russia landed the first unmanned craft, the Luna 9, on the moon (February, 1966), a feat duplicated by the United States in June with its Surveyor 1. Thousands of pictures taken by this space craft and by others that orbited the planet showed the surface to be hard and capable of sustaining a manned landing; one, Surveyor 5, carried a chemical laboratory that found the soil to be largely basaltic rock. Other satellites were placed in orbit to observe the weather and for communications and observation purposes; rockets were also sent past Mars and Venus to photograph those planets. The United States achieved the most spectacular space flight when three astronauts in an *Apollo 9 space capsule orbited the moon six times,* photographing its surface and the earth, before returning to a safe splashdown in the Pacific (December, 1968). This flight captured the world's imagination, representing as it did man's first venture beyond his own planet.

III. VIET NAM: DEATH BLOW TO DEMOCRATIC ASPIRATIONS.

No single act in American history more effectively doomed a President to mounting criticism than did President Johnson's decision to commit the nation's military forces to a victory in South Viet Nam. History may well reverse the immediate verdict of the people and conclude that the country's decade-long involvement and staggering expenditures in lives, money, and prestige were justified to check the spread of communism in South East Asia and hence throughout the world. Whatever the judgment of the future, the acceleration of the war effort accomplished three ends that the President could never have foreseen: 1) it dangerously polarized American society, pitting young against old, class against class, liberal against conservative, in confrontations that stirred such emotions that national cohesion seemed doomed for many years; 2) it checked the trend apparent under Presidents Truman and Kennedy to inaugurate legislative programs designed to bridge the gulf between rich and poor not only economically but also socially; and 3) it reversed a trend toward global commitment on the part of the American people dating back at least to World War II. This reversal was to be accentuated during the next years as Johnson's successor finally ended the Viet Nam War; with a troubled peace achieved at last, Americans seemed content to resist further involvement in distant lands and to look for global harmony through international agreements rather than clashing arms.

ADDITIONAL READING

A sympathetic analysis of American foreign policy during this period is Seyom Brown, *The Faces of Power: Constancy and Change in United States Foreign Policy from Truman to Johnson* (1968). A collection of essays admirably summarizing the emergence of the Cold War is Lloyd C. Gardner, ed., *The Origins of the Cold War* (1970); John L. Gaddis, *The United States and the Origins of the Cold War, 1941-1947* (1972), is another judicious survey that disputes New Left historians who place primary blame on the United States. This view is even more strongly upheld in Robert J. Maddox, *The New Left and the Origins of the Cold War* (1973) and Lisle A. Rose, *After Yalta* (1973). The major revisionist work stating the Leftist position is Joyce and Gabriel Kalko, *The Limits of Power: The World and United States Foreign Policy, 1945-1954* (New York, 1972). Walter LaFeber, *America, Russia and the Cold War, 1945-1966* (1967), is also revisionist but judicious. The Kennedy administration is covered in the fifteen essays in Aida Donald, ed., *John F. Kennedy and the New Frontier* (1966), and there is a sympathetic description of his economic policies in Jim F. Heath, *John F. Kennedy and the Business Community* (1969). Aspects of the Kennedy foreign policy are described in Jack M. Schick, *The Berlin Crisis, 1958-1962* (1971), and William D. Rogers, *The Twilight Struggle: The Alliance for Progress and the Politics of Development in Latin America* (1967). The importance of the civil-rights issue in domestic politics is shown in such books as Archibald Cox, *The Warren Court: Constitutional Decision as An Instrument of Reform*

(1968), Gary Orfield, *The Reconstruction of Southern Education: The Schools and the 1964 Civil Rights Act* (1969), and Numan V. Bartley, *The Rise of Massive Resistance: Race and Politics in the South During the 1950's* (1969).

Chapter XVII

The Limits of
Presidential Power:
The Nixon-Ford Years
1969-1977

❡ EXECUTIVE VERSUS LEGISLATIVE AUTHORITY

Future historians, looking back on the administrations of Richard M. Nixon and Gerald Ford, may conclude that their single most important contribution was to focus national attention on the degree of authority allotted to the President and Congress by the Constitution. Underlying the conflict between the two agencies was President Nixon's personal belief in his mission to resolve international conflicts; the delicate negotiations he was conducting, he felt, required unlimited authority over both domestic and foreign affairs, even to the extent of violating the civil rights of individuals and refusing to obey congressional edicts. Congress vigorously disagreed, with Republicans joining the Democratic majority to dispute Nixon's concept of an "imperial presidency." In the end, the President's ambitions were shattered by the scandal that drove him from office, giving Congress an opportunity to re-assert its rights. It did so with such vigor against Nixon's successors—the Republican Gerald R. Ford and the Democrat Jimmy Carter—that the stalemate between the executive and legislative branches threatened governmental functioning during the late 1970s, and was far from resolved as the nation approached the end of the twentieth century.

I. ELECTION VICTORIES

A. The Election of 1968

1. Choosing the Candidates. Senator Eugene McCarthy of Minnesota announced (November, 1967) that he would oppose President Johnson for the Democratic nomination, promising an immediate withdrawal from the Viet Nam War. His strong showing in early presidential primaries led Senator Robert F. Kennedy of Massachusetts to announce his candidacy as another peace candidate. When *Johnson announced his withdrawal* from the race (March 31, 1968), his support went to Vice-President *Hubert H. Humphrey* who formally agreed to run in late April. The principal Republican contenders were *Richard M. Nixon* and Governor Nelson Rockefeller of New York. A third party, the *American Independent Party,* was largely the creation of former Governor *George C. Wallace* of Alabama, who campaigned vigorously attacking big government and lawlessness. Before the nominating conventions met, Senator *Kennedy was assassinated* by an Arab Nationalist, Sirhan Sirhan (June, 1968). As the nation mourned, Congress adopted a mild *gun-control law,* forbidding the interstate mail-order sale of certain types of hand guns, but efforts to include the registration of firearms were defeated.

2. The Nominating Conventions

a. THE REPUBLICAN CONVENTION. Richard M. Nixon entered the party's convention at Miami with a strong delegate lead and was *nominated on the first ballot,* with Governor Spiro T. Agnew of Maryland as his running-mate.

b. THE DEMOCRATIC CONVENTION. *Hubert H. Humphrey*'s pledged delegates were enough to assure his nomination, but followers of two "peace candidates," Senator *Eugene McCarthy* of Minnesota and Senator *George McGovern* of South Dakota staged a strong battle, aided by supporters of the late Robert F. Kennedy. In this tense atmosphere Mayor Richard J. Daley of Chicago, fearing trouble from peace demonstrators, turned the convention city into an armed bastion. The defeat of the "peace candidates" and the refusal of the convention to adopt a platform plank pledging the "unconditional end of all bombing" in

North Viet Nam, touched off demonstrations both in and out of the convention. As millions watched on television, police clubbed protestors indiscriminately; an investigating commission later censored "police ferocity" and spoke of a "police riot." This disorder, combined with the deep rifts within the party, sent its two candidates, _Hubert H. Humphrey_ and _Senator Edmund S. Muskie_ of Maine into the campaign with the party's popularity at a low ebb.

3. Outcome of the 1968 Election. Nixon, refusing to take a stand on Viet Nam or other vital issues, confined his campaign to stock speeches on law and order. Humphrey, by contrast, campaigned vigorously, and gained support rapidly. In the end _Nixon won a narrow victory,_ polling 31,085,267 popular votes to 30,760,301 for Humphrey and 9,674,802 for Wallace, and winning the electoral vote of 32 states. Humphrey carried 13 states, largely in the Northeast, and Wallace 5 in the deep South. Republicans gained five governorships, five seats in the Senate, and four in the House, although both branches of Congress remained Democratic, the House with 243 Democrats and 192 Republicans, the Senate with 58 Democrats and 42 Republicans.

4. Inaugurating the New Government. Nixon's most prominent cabinet members were William P. Rogers, an old friend with little international experience, as Secretary of State and Melvin R. Laird, a Wisconsin congressman, as Secretary of Defense. The naming of two Harvard professors, _Henry A. Kissinger_ and Daniel P. Moynihan, as special advisors on foreign and domestic policy indicated that the President intended to shape policy personally with the aid of experts rather than rely on his cabinet. Kissinger replaced Rogers as Secretary of State in August, 1973. Nixon's inaugural address (January 20, 1969) was cast in lofty spiritual tones but suggested no basic changes in foreign or domestic policy.

B. The 1970 Elections

1. The Chappaquiddick Affair. Senator Edward M. Kennedy of Massachusetts, a potential Democratic presidential candidate, was threatened with political eclipse in July, 1969, when his car fell from a bridge on Martha's Vineyard, drowning a twenty-eight year old secretary, Mary Jo Kopechne. Mystery surrounding the incident and his failure to report the accident for ten hours forced Kennedy to offer his resignation as senator, but pressure from his constituents changed his mind.

2. Outcome of the Elections. In a campaign notable for Vice-President Agnew's scoring of "radical liberals," the Republicans gained two seats in the Senate and lost nine in the House, a _better-than-usual showing_ for the party in power. The Democrats, however, gained eleven governorships (for a total of twenty-three), an important advantage when redistricting followed the Census of 1970.

C. The 1972 Election

1. Choosing the Candidates. Senator _George S. McGovern_, who began campaigning as a peace candidate as early as January, 1971, won so decisively over Senator Edmund S. Muskie of Maine in the primaries that he entered the Miami convention (July, 1972), as a heavy favorite. His principal conservative opponent, Governor George C. Wallace of Alabama, dropped from the race after being crippled by an assassin's bullet (May, 1972). Both Muskie and Senator Hubert H. Humphrey challenged McGovern for the nomination, but changed methods of selecting delegates that provided ethnic and age balance favored _McGovern who was nominated_, with Senator Thomas F. Eagleton of Missouri as his running mate. _Nixon and Agnew were renominated_ by the Republicans (August, 1972) without serious opposition.

2. The Rival Platforms. The gap between McGovern's liberalism and Nixon's conservatism was made clear in the platforms. _Democrats supported:_ 1) federal regulation of wages and prices; 2) an "immediate withdrawal from Viet Nam" once prisoners of war were returned; 3) bussing to achieve school integration; 4) a national health insurance program; 5) decreasing America's military establishment in Europe; 6) amnesty for those who had refused military service in Indochina; and 7) support for public housing, welfare, and tax reform. _Republicans favored:_ 1) an end to all controls over the economy; 2) a gradual withdrawal from Viet Nam after a cease-fire had been signed; 3) no school bussing to achieve racial balance;

4) a health program financed by employees and employers rather than the government; 5) maintaining American forces in Europe at "adequate strength;" 6) no amnesty for those refusing to serve in Viet Nam; and 7) decreased federal spending for housing, welfare, and other social services.

3. The Campaigns. When Eagleton revealed that he had earlier been hospitalized for "nervous exhaustion" and had received electric shock therapy, public doubts forced McGovern to replace him as vice-presidential candidate with Sargent Shriver of Massachusetts, a strong campaigner (August, 1972). This cost the Democrats heavily, as did McGovern's indecision on welfare policy. McGovern campaigned widely on the issues of Viet Nam and Republican business favoritism, while Nixon relied on a few televised addresses, creating the image of a statesman rather than a politician. He was aided by "Democrats for Nixon," organized by John B. Connally of Texas, who was later to switch parties.

4. Outcome of the 1972 Election. Nixon was swept into office in one of the *most decisive landslides in history,* with 45,767,218 popular votes to 28,357,668 for McGovern. His electoral vote majority was 521 to 17, with the Democrats carrying only Massachusetts and the District of Columbia. Voters, however, *denied Nixon the "New American Majority" he asked in Congress;* Democrats increased their majority in the Senate to 57-43, and maintained a House majority of 255-179.

5. Emerging Republican Conservatism. With this mandate, Nixon revealed a new conservatism, using his inaugural address to urge Americans to "ask not just what will government do for me, but what I can do for myself." In a series of messages to Congress he asked the *end of the "Great Society"* program by reducing expenditures and shifting social responsibility to the states and local communities. This was to be done by: 1) ending programs to aid the hard-core unemployed, students, small businessmen, and the mentally ill; 2) dropping projects for urban renewal and Model Cities; 3) phasing out federal aid for hospital construction, milk for children, and community health centers; and 4) cutting farm support in half. The refusal of the Democratic Congress to accept this program, and its insistence on lessening military involvement in Indo-china, set the stage for a series of legislative-presidential con-flicts that slowed progress during the Nixon-Ford administra-tions.

6. Assertion of Presidential Authority. Without con-sulting Congress, Nixon elevated four conservative cabinet members to posts as *"White House Consultants"*: Treasury Secretary George P. Schultz to advise on economic affairs, Sec-retary of HEW Caspar Weinberger on human resources, Agri-cultural Secretary Earl L. Butz on natural resources, and Secretary of HUD James T. Lynn on community development. These four, with Roy L. Ash, Director of the Office of Man-agement and Budget, Kissinger, and Nixon's two personal aides —H. R. Haldeman and John Ehrlichman—were designated a *"Super Cabinet"*, thus degrading other cabinet members. This assertion of administrative authority widened the breach with Congress, which felt that it should speak for the people.

II. DOMESTIC POLICY UNDER NIXON, 1969-1973

A. Relations with Congress.

1. The Nixon Program. Nixon's basic purpose was to *shift economic burdens to the states and social responsibility to individuals.* To this end he favored: 1) an overhaul of the welfare system; 2) strengthening state and local governments by sharing federal funds with them; and 3) reorganizing the federal government for greater efficiency. This program largely failed because: 1) Democratic congresses that saw the govern-ment as an agency for social reform strongly disagreed with Nixon's purposes; and 2) the President's preoccupation with foreign affairs during his first term and with the Watergate scandals during his second.

2. Important Legislative Measures. Despite the conflict between President and Congress a number of laws altering the social and economic climate were passed during the Nixon-Ford administrations, although *Nixon vetoed 15 congressional mea-sures and Ford 49.* Among the measures adopted were: 1) bills to create an independent agency to administer the postal service and another, The National Railroad Corporation (AMTRAK) to use federal funds to rejuvenate and operate railroad passenger trains; 2) an Omnibus Crime Bill inflicting the death penalty on all convicted of fatal bombings; 3) a *"Campaign Spending Bill"* setting limits on campaign expenditures, requiring the reporting of major contributions, and providing for public financing in national elections; 4) a *"Product Safety Law"* establishing a commission to set and enforce safety standards for consumer products; 5) a "Pension Reform Bill" setting up a federally operated insurance corporation to protect the retirement benefits of 23 million employees from mismanagement or bankruptcy; and 6) a "Credit Discrimination Law" forbidding discrimination in providing credit because of age, color, sex, religion, or national origin. Congress also created an Energy Research and Development Administration with an initial grant of $5.7 billion to develop nuclear, solar, and geothermal sources of energy (1976).

3. Executive-Congressional Differences. Congress repeatedly challenged Nixon's concept of an "imperial presidency" by over-riding his vetoes. Important laws enacted in this way included: 1) granting *voting rights to eighteen-year-olds;* 2) allotting $24.6 billion over three years to end water pollution in lakes and streams by financing sewage-disposal systems; 3) appropriating $1.3 billion for hospital construction, $5.15 billion for school and college teaching improvements, $1.3 billion for hospital construction, and $4.4 billion to improve schools in slum areas; and 4) *limiting the President's war-making powers* (November, 1973) by requiring that he report to Congress within 48 hours after committing troops to a foreign conflict. Congress also refused to adopt several measures recommended by the President, including: 1) allotment of funds to develop a supersonic plane (SST); and 2) alteration of the welfare system through a family-assistance plan. Congressional assertiveness was also shown by laws expanding the role of the legislative branch in budget-making, and requiring the release of funds impounded by the President after appropriation by Congress.

4. Basis for Future Conflicts. In an important measure, Congress adopted several *major changes in its own procedures,* reducing the importance of seniority in committee assignments and allowing younger, more liberal congressmen a larger voice in legislation. (December, 1974). As these took effect, the gulf between the legislative and executive branches seemed certain to widen.

B. Relations with the Supreme Court.

1. Creating the "Nixon Court." *Warren E. Burger,* a Circuit Court judge with a strong "law and order" record, *was named chief justice* when Earl Warren retired (June, 1969). The resignation of Justice Abe Fortas (May, 1969) allowed an additional appointment, but Nixon's first two nominees, Clement F. Haynsworth and G. Harold Carswell, were rejected by the Senate because of mediocre records. His third nominee, Harry A. Blackmun, another "strict constructionist," was confirmed without dissent (May, 1970). When John M. Harlan and Hugo L. Black resigned two additional judges reflecting the President's conservative viewpoint were named (September, 1971): Lewis F. Powell, Jr. and William H. Rehnquist. The retirement of liberal Justice William O. Douglas after ·36½ years on the bench (October, 1975), allowed President Ford to name John P. Stevens, a moderate who had served on the Court of Appeals.

2. Persistence of the Liberal Tradition. Despite Nixon's efforts to reverse the liberal trend of the "Warren Court," his new appointees did not embrace "strict construction" completely. That this was the case was shown in such decisions as those that: 1) applied the one-man, one-vote rule to school board elections; 2) *upheld equal pay for women;* 3) required construction unions to maintain racial balance in their membership; 4) held that *capital punishment* as practiced under arbitrary and "freakish" state laws *violated the 8th amendment;* 5) declared unconstitutional state laws barring welfare to persons with less than one year of residence; 6) ruled that only thirty days residence in a state qualified a newcomer for the franchise; 7) denied the federal government's right to wiretap radical groups without a prior court order; 8) restricted the rights of juries to define obscenity in terms of their local standards; 9) decided that *states might not prevent a woman from obtaining an abortion* during the first six months of her pregnancy; 10) allowed the use of federal funds for elective abortions; and 11) ruled that states might not make the death penalty mandatory for persons convicted of killing a police officer.

3. The New "Strict Construction." On the other hand the court: 1) ruled that *local communities could adopt their own definitions of obscenity* in barring books or films; 2) held that loyalty oaths opposing the violent overthrow of the government were legal; 3) struck down provisions of the Federal Election Commission Act limiting spending by and for candi-dates in congressional or presidential elections, but upholding the public financing of federal elections and limits on contributions; 4) ruled that the *death penalty was not a cruel and unusual punishment* and could be imposed so long as judges and juries received adequate information for determining whether the penalty was pertinent to the case; 5) decided that spanking school children did not constitute a cruel and unusual punishment; 6) *reversed a ten-year trend toward expanding the constitutional right to privacy* by holding that states could prosecute persons for committing homosexual acts even if performed in private between consenting adults; and 7) ruled that *states might refuse to give public funds for elective or nontherapeutic abortions.*

C. Slow Progress Toward Integration.

1. The Courts and Integration. Integration was both hurried and slowed by Supreme Court Decisions. Those speeding integration included: 1) denying the government's request to delay school integration in Mississippi by *ordering an end to segregation there "at once,"* thus abandoning the prior formula of "with all convenient speed;" 2) specifically *declaring bussing an acceptable means of achieving racial balance* in the schools; 3) holding that blacks who had been denied jobs in violation of the Civil Rights Act of 1964 must be awarded retroactive seniority if they could prove they had been denied work because of racial discrimination; and 4) ruling that private nonsectarian schools could not exclude black children because of race. Decisions contrary to expanded civil rights were: 1) a decision that a proposed merger of Richmond's predominantly black schools with those of white suburbs was unconstitutional; 2) overthrew an Indianapolis desegregation plan requiring bussing between the city and white suburbs unless it could prove that segregation was "intentional;" and 3) holding that seniority systems that perpetuated past racial discriminations were not necessarily illegal.

2. Growing Opposition to Integration

a. ADMINISTRATIVE OPPOSITION. President Nixon's reluctance to hurry integration was shown by: 1) a warning to HEW officials to delay pressure on Austin, Texas, to implement a proposed bussing program; 2) a message _urging Congress to outlaw bussing_ as a means of achieving racial balance while appropriating funds to improve schools in poorer neighborhoods; and 3) supporting a bill (eventually killed by a Senate filibuster) to restrict cross-town bussing of school children.

b. PUBLIC OPPOSITION. Popular opposition to forced integration was accentuated by a series of spectacular court cases related to black militancy: 1) the acquittal on conspiracy charges of the "Chicago Seven" who had been arrested during the rioting at the 1968 Democratic convention; 2) the trial and acquittal of the "Soledad Brothers," three blacks accused of murdering a guard during an attempted break-out at the Soledad Correctional Facility of California after allegedly having been supplied with guns by Angela Davis, a black militant and Communist supporter; and 3) the trial of the "Black Panthers," members of a Negro militant group, on bombing charges in which they were found not guilty. These trials, associating civil disorders with blacks in the popular mind, helped to polarize society on the subject of disintegration. Hence attempts at new bussing programs stirred opposition and street fighting in Boston in 1974 and in Boston and Louisville in 1975. Boston's violence forced the courts to place certain schools under federal receivership to prevent the beating and harassment of black students (December, 1975).

3. Rise of Indian Militancy.
The desire for cultural identity that underlay many black protests also inspired native American militants to demand a new role in white society. This rebellious spirit sparked several incidents: 1) 600 Indians calling themselves the "Trail of Broken Tears" occupied Washington offices of the Bureau of Indian Affairs in November, 1972, to

protest the mistreatment of their ancestors and their own neglect by the BIA; 2) some 200 members of the American Indian Movement (AIM) occupied the town of Wounded Knee, South Dakota, in February, 1973, in a siege that lasted seventy days before a cease–fire was agreed upon.

D. Success of the Space Program

1. The Moon Landings. President Kennedy's ambition to place a man on the moon before the end of the 1960s was realized when *Neil A. Armstrong,* commander of a three-man Apollo 11 crew, *set foot on lunar soil* on July 20, 1969. Other moon-shots followed (November, 1969 to December, 1972) to explore the surface in special cars, bring back soil samples, and leave scientific equipment. All flights were televised over much of the world. The dangers and vast expenditures involved in manned flights, contrasted with the unmanned USSR Luna rocket landings that returned with surface samplings at one-sixth the cost, convinced the government to end the program after the Apollo 17 flight (December, 1972).

2. Expanded Space Exploration. Instead funds were employed on less spectacular scientific projects, including: 1) launching numerous satellites to photograph mineral deposits, weather formations, and soil areas; 2) a "Skylab" in which three astronauts spent 28 days (May, 1973), and were later replaced by other crews who stayed aloft for 59½ days (Summer, 1973) and 84 days (Winter, 1973-1974); 3) a program that allowed the US Apollo and the USSR Soyuz spacecrafts to link 140 miles above the earth in a gesture of good will (July, 1975); 4) a series of unmanned rocket flights to explore the solar system including a rocket placed in orbit around Mars (November, 1971), and 5) landing two space ships on Mars to analyze earth samples and radio back information on the prospect of life there—with negative results (July-September, 1976).

E. The Continuing Economic Crisis.

1. Unsettling Factors. The monetary problems that triggered a series of crises during the Nixon-Ford administrations were due to: 1) inflationary pressures stemming from heavy military expenditures in Viet Nam and elsewhere, leading to spiraling prices and wages; 2) a continued dollar drain to support large military establishments in Europe and Asia; and 3) a mounting trade deficit as imports exceeded exports due in part to the popularity of cheaper Japanese and European products, but largely to the *inflated oil prices with which Arabian producing countries retaliated for American support to Israel* in its 1973 "October War." The US trade deficit rose from $6.4 billion in 1972 to $4.5 billion in the single month of February, 1978. These pressures led to a succession of *"dollar crises"* as speculators in world markets showed lessening confidence in the economy by exchanging dollars for other currencies, driving the price of the dollar downward.

2. Increase in Deficit Spending. Despite Nixon's pledges to cut expenses and balance the budget, both *Nixon and Ford increased expenditures and deficits,* with budgets of $200.8 billion in fiscal 1971, $304.4 billion in 1975, $384.2 billion in 1977, and $459.4 billion in 1978, with a deficit of $57.7 billion. At the same time inflationary pressures drove the price index into double-digit figures by 1973, when the index rose at an annual rate of 22.8%. Unemployment also increased steadily, to more than 8% of the work force by the end of 1976. The combination of inflation, unemployment, and deficit spending lessened confidence in the economy and weakened the value of the dollar in foreign markets.

3. Attempts to Right the Economy.

a. RELIEF MEASURES. A series of depression-like relief measures designed to reduce unemployment were adopted by the Nixon-Ford administrations: 1) a Public Works Program (August, 1971) authorizing $2.5 billion for public building over two years; 2) a Public Service Act (July, 1971) granting $2.5 billion to create 150,000 to 200,000 jobs with state and local governments; 3) an emergency housing bill to stimulate the ailing construction industry by federal guarantees of builder loans at 7.5% (Summer, 1975); 4) appropriations of $15.6 billion in 1976 to provide low interest for various housing agencies; and 5) a $22.8 billion tax cut (April, 1975, extended June, 1976) assuring rebates of $200 to $400 to taxpayers to stimulate buying. Congress also passed over President Ford's veto: 1) a $45 billion appropriation for health, welfare, and manpower programs (January, 1976), and 2) an additional $3.95 billion for public works programs.

b. ATTEMPTS TO CONTROL INFLATION.

I. *Wage and Price Controls.* Under a congressionally adopted Economic Stabilization Act, President Nixon announced Phase I of an anti-inflation program with a *90-day freeze on all wages and price increases* and a $4.7 billion cut in federal expenditures (August, 1971). Phase II (October, 1971), provided for: 1) wage and price increases only if offset by improvements in productivity; 2) a Cost of Living Council to serve as an enforcement agency; and 3) commissioners to serve as watch-dogs over prices, wages, and corporation profits. Phase III (January, 1973) removed all mandatory wage and price controls except in such "problem areas" as food, health care, and construction in the hope that management and labor would impose voluntary restraints. When this failed, mandatory price freezes were resumed (June, 1973) for 60 days except on rents and unprocessed foods. Phase IV (July, 1973) replaced the price freeze with a mixture of mandatory and voluntary controls but with limits on beef prices retained. *Nixon's vacillating policies contributed to a serious recession* in 1974, but President Ford refused to impose mandatory controls, appealing to self discipline and introducing WIN (Whip Inflation Now) buttons for workers and management to wear.

II. *The Problem of Shortages.* The faltering economy was plagued by shortages which required 1) export restrictions on feed-grain, edible oils, livestock feed, and edible fats (June, 1973), and 2) export quotas on wheat and soybeans (October, 1974). These tended to drive prices still higher.

4. Grappling with the "Dollar Drain."

a. THE PROBLEM OF ENERGY. The *Arab oil embargo* imposed by Arab countries during the 1973 Egypt-Israel War and the *quadrupled oil prices* charged from that time on upset the American economy and revealed the need to conserve energy and to increase domestic production. Congress and President Ford proposed conflicting solutions, with 1) Congress favoring price controls, rationing and conservation of energy resources, and 2) the President calling for higher gasoline prices to curb use. This impasse doomed any constructive energy program. Ford raised the duty on imported oil by $2 a barrel (May, 1975), but withdrew this increase when Congress adopted the *Energy Policy and Conservation Act* (December, 1975) allowing gasoline prices to rise up to 10% at the discretion of the President. The problem of adequate energy remained one of the nation's most pressing needs.

b. MEETING THE ATTACK ON THE DOLLAR. Even before the energy crisis skyrocketed unfavorable trade deficits, the dollar had fallen to dangerous lows in relation to foreign currencies. Nixon's *"The Economic Policy"* (NEP) attempted to remedy the situation by *freeing the dollar from its convertability into gold* and allowing it to establish its own value in relation to other currencies, at the same time imposing a 10% surcharge tax on all imports. This triggered foreign resentment and such increased dollar-dumping that the U.S. announced a *devaluation of the dollar* by 8.5% (December, 1971) and removal of the 10% import surcharge. When this failed to halt the decline, a further 10% devaluation followed (February, 1973), but with little effect. Unfavorable trade balances and a declining dollar value continued to pose problems through the Nixon-Ford administrations.

F. The Constitutional Rights Issue

1. Privacy versus National Security. A series of revelations during and following the Nixon-Ford years showed that the *threat to national security* raised by anti-Viet Nam War militants had allowed the *government to invade the constitutionally guaranteed rights of many citizens*.

a. REVIVAL OF INVESTIGATIVE AGENCIES. The Subversive Activities Board, defunct for twenty years, was revitalized (summer, 1971) with authority to investigate individuals or organizations suspected of subversive activities and "list" those found to have "sympathetic association" with such groups.

b. EXECUTIVE PROGRAMS. The White House actively engaged in illegal information seeking by: 1) between 1969 and

1971 tapping the telephones of newspaper reporters and government officials to find those guilty of leeking confidential information; a Senate committee later (December, 1974) absolved Secretary of State Kissinger of such activity; 2) seeking to involve the FBI and CIA in a program of wire tapping and burglary against militant organizations that the President suspected of threatening national security; and 3) when FBI director J. Edgar Hoover refused, creating a _Special Investigations Unit_ ("The White House Plumbers") under the supervision of Nixon's personal aid, John Ehrlichman, to use any needed techniques to secure evidence against persons or groups believed to threaten the national government. These tactics continued to be employed even after June, 1972, when the _Supreme Court specifically forbad the bugging of private telephones_ without a prior court order. Later congressional investigators also found that both the _FBI and the CIA had conducted wire-taps, mail inspection, and even burglary_ to spy on citizens, using techniques that were "painfully unlawful and constituted improper invasions upon the rights of Americans."

c. FOREIGN ROLE OF THE CIA. A Senate Select Committee on Intelligence (November, 1975) found that during the past decade the CIA had 1) ordered the _assassination of Fidel Castro_ of Cuba and Patrice Lumumba of the Congo, and 2) that others including Rafel L. Trujillo of the Dominican Republic and Ngo Dinh Diem of South Viet Nam had been killed in coups known to have been encouraged by US officials.

2. The "Pentagon Papers" Case. Publication of a secret document on behind-the-scenes decision making during the Viet Nam War was announced by the New York _Times_ and other newspapers. An injunction sought by the Justice Department to prevent publication as harmful to American diplomatic interests (June, 1971) was denied by the Supreme Court on the grounds that prior censorship violated the First Amendment, but _Daniel Ellsberg,_ a former Defense Department employee who had helped compile the report and provided extracts to the press in hopes that their appearance would shorten the Viet Nam War, was indicted on charges of violating the Espionage Act (June, 1971). Before his trail ended it was revealed that _CIA agents had burglarized the office of Ellsberg's psychiatrist_ searching for evidence against him (May, 1973), and a mistrial was ordered. A similar mistrial following the arrest of another anti-war protestor, the Reverend Philip Berrigan, when it was shown that the FBI had paid $9,000 to a witness to testify against him (April, 1972).

3. Attempts at Reform. Following guidelines suggested by Congress, President Ford announced (February, 1976): 1) a reorganization of the FBI and CIA with *rigid restrictions on their use of electronic or physical surveillance;* and 2) a three-man committee to monitor the agencies. Ford also asked Congress for authority to permit the use of electronic devices for intelligence purposes after prior court authorization, and to make illegal any disclosure by a former employee of means used by the agencies to gather information. The Senate assumed a watch-dog role when it created (August, 1976) a permanent 15-man committee to oversee CIA activities and help control its expenditures.

III. WATERGATE AND THE DOWNFALL OF NIXON

A. Origins of the Watergate Scandal

1. The Watergate Break-In. Five of seven persons *arrested when breaking into the Democratic Headquarters* in *Washington's Watergate Apartment complex* (June, 1972) to retrieve electronic listening devices planted there in an earlier burglary pleaded guilty after testifying that they could not remember who paid them. One of the remaining two, *James W. McCord,* a former CIA agent employed by the *Committee for the Re-election of the President* (CRP) after being found guilty (March, 1973) told Judge John J. Sirica of the US District Court: 1) that the five had been pressured into pleading guilty by prominent Republican officials who promised them $1,000 a month for all time spent in jail; 2) that several had perjured themselves; and 3) that many responsible for the Watergate break-in had not been identified. Judge Sirica imposed heavy penalties on those who confessed (40 years and $50,000 fines) to encourage them to testify. One who refused to testify, G. Gordon Liddy, finance counsel for the CRP, was sentenced to 20 years and fined $40,000.

2. Investigations Begin. Congressional investigations were broadened to include related activities of the CRP when legal proceedings against _Robert L. Vesco_ for allegedly looting a mutual fund of $224 million revealed that _he had given the CRP $200,000_ in April, 1972, after the campaign contributions law required the reporting of all gifts over $100. Former _Attorney General John Mitchell_ of the CRP and Maurice Stans, its financial agent were charged in the New York court with: 1) aiding Vesco in an unsuccessful attempt to squash his looting of the fund, and 2) accepting the $200,000 gift in return. Both were later found innocent of these charges (April, 1974). Investigators also explored the large sums accepted by Nixon from Charles G. (Bebe) Rebozo, a wealthy financier, and from the government to improve his estates at San Clemente, California, and Key Biscayne, Florida, and the $576,000 tax deduction that he claimed for donating his pre-presidential papers to the National Archives.

3. The Presidential Response.

a. CLAIM OF EXECUTIVE PRIVILEGE. In a televised address (April 30, 1973) in which he claimed executive privilege but announced that he had conducted his own investigation, Nixon: 1) announced that Attorney General Kleindienst and his two personal aids, _H. R. Haldeman and John Ehrlichman who had been accused of paying the Watergate burglars had resigned;_ 2) that he had dismissed John W. Dean III, his personal counsel, who had allegedly reported falsely to the White House concerning responsibility for Watergate; and 3) that he would continue his fair and impartial investigation with Archibald Cox as special prosecutor in charge under Elliot Richardson who replaced Kleindienst as Attorney General.

b. CHANGED PRESIDENTIAL ATTITUDES. Continuing pressure from investigators forced Nixon to abandon his role as "Imperial President" and make important changes in his administrative staff: 1) _abolishing the "Super Cabinet"_ with a corresponding shift in power to the regular cabinet and Congress; and 2) reshuffling administrative posts by elevating James R. Schlesinger to become Secretary of Defense, William E. Colby, a professional, to be director of the CIA, and Clarence M. Kelley, Kansas City police chief, to be director of the FBI (May, 1973).

B. Congressional and Judicial Investigations

1. The Senate Investigation. A _Select Committee on Campaign Practices,_ formed by the Senate with Senator Sam Ervin of North Carolina as chairman, began _publicly televised hearings_ on the Watergate break-in in May, 1973. Such witnesses as former White House Attorney John W. Dean III testified: 1) the CRP had used a $1 million fund to employ such agents as G. Gordon Liddy to spy on Democrats and disrupt their 1972 campaigns; 2) that former Attorney General John Mitchell had paid major sums to Liddy and others; 3) that _Mitchell and other high officials were aware of the break-in_ and assisted in an attempted cover-up; and 4) that John Ehrlichman, the President's assistant, was also involved. Dean's testimony revealed that many of the _President's conversations with his aides had been recorded and preserved on tapes._ Dean also swore that _Nixon had known of the break-in and cover-up,_ but the testimony of H. R. Haldeman denied this.

2. The Presidential Tapes. Both the Senate Committee and Special Prosecutor Archibald Cox secured court subpoenas ordering Nixon to release the tapes (July, 1973). Nixon defied the courts, _claiming executive privilege_ under his primary obligation to the nation's security, and insisted that they contained nothing pertinent to the investigations. When the US District Court ruled that _executive privilege could not be invoked in cases involving possible criminal conduct,_ the President appealed to the Circuit Court which also held that the President "is not above the law's commands" and ordered him to surrender the tapes to Judge Sirica's court. Again Nixon refused, proposing instead to _submit summaries of pertinent sections,_ to be verified by Senator John H. Stennis, a conservative Democrat.

3. The Constitutional Crisis. When Special Prosecutor _Cox rejected this solution_ and announced that he would ask the courts to cite the President for contempt, _Nixon ordered his immediate dismissal._ Both Attorney General Elliot Richardson and Deputy Attorney General William Ruckelshaus _resigned rather than carry out this order._ The President then named Solicitor General Robert Bork as acting Attorney General; Bork immediately fired Cox, completing the _"Saturday Night Massacre."_

4. The Public Reaction. Amidst a clamor of public resentment, the House of Representatives began _investigating means to impeach Nixon_ or remove him from office. Under this threat, the President again reversed himself and announced (October, 1973) : 1) that _he would surrender the tapes_ to Judge Sirica, and 2) name _Leon Jaworski,_ a conservative Texas Democrat, to Cox's position as special prosecutor. This move failed to quiet suspicions when Nixon revealed that nine of the most crucial tapes were missing and that _an 18-minute gap_ existed in an important portion of another (November, 1973).

5. Resignation of the Vice President. Trust in Nixon's administration was weakened when a Maryland grand jury investigating corruption in the state revealed that _Vice President Agnew_ had been charged with _accepting payoffs from contractors in return for favors_ when he was governor. First defying his "prosecutors," Agnew reversed himself when presented with evidence justifying his indictment and pleaded _nolo contendre to a single count of income tax evasion._ He was fined $10,000 and placed on three years probation, at the same time resigning from office. The President named as his _successor House Minority Leader Gerald R. Ford,_ a stalwart Republican better known for his party loyalty than his statesmanship.

C. End of the Nixon Administration.

1. Release of the Disputed Tapes. Continued investigation by: 1) a special Grand Jury, 2) the Judicial Committee of the House of Representatives, and 3) Special Prosecutor Leon Jaworski was climaxed with the _indictment of seven of Nixon's aids_—including H. R. Haldeman, John Ehrlichman, and John Mitchell—for conspiring to obstruct justice (March, 1974). With suspicion that the President was himself involved mounting, Prosecutor Jaworski subpoenaed the remaining tapes held by Nixon (April, 1974). The President retaliated by making public for newspaper publication 1,308 pages of edited transcripts of White House conversations, but refusing to relinquish the crucial tapes demanded. His appeal to the Supreme Court (July, 1974) ended in an _8-0 decision in The United States of America vs. Richard M. Nixon_ which ruled that _executive privilege could not be invoked for withholding information from the courts in criminal cases._

2. Steps Toward Impeachment. The House Judiciary Committee in July, 1974, <u>recommended the impeachment of Nixon</u> on the grounds that he had: 1) obstructed justice, 2) failed to carry out his oath to uphold the nation's laws, and 3) defied legal subpoenas. Six or more Republicans joined with Democrats in voting on each count.

3. The Final Revelations. When Nixon finally bowed to court and public pressure and <u>released the disputed tapes</u> (August 5, 1974) they showed that: 1) he had <u>learned of the Watergate break-in on June 23, 1972,</u> just six days after it occurred; 2) was fully aware at the time that CRP director John Mitchell was involved, together with E. Howard Hunt and G. Gordon Liddy; 3) had <u>helped plan the cover-up</u> that Haldeman suggested, thus engaging in a criminal act to obstruct justice; and 4) sought to prevent the FBI from continuing its investigations of the burglary. The revelation that Nixon had lied in insisting he did not learn of the burglary until March, 1973, convinced his advisors that he faced certain impeachment. This was confirmed when all ten House Republicans who had voted against the charges in the Judicial Committee announced that they would reverse their votes.

4. Resignation of the President. Bowing to pressures within his own party, <u>Nixon decided to resign rather than endure an impeachment trial.</u> He announced his resignation in a televised address (August 8, 1974), still insisting that he was guilty only of faulty judgment. At noon on August 9 he <u>turned the government over to Vice President Gerald R. Ford.</u>

IV. POLITICS OF THE FORD ADMINISTRATION.

A. Initial Presidential Policy

1. Plans of the Administration. President Ford took office determined to make inflation his principal target, and to restore confidence in the government. He selected as his <u>vice president Nelson Rockefeller,</u> a long-time leader of the liberal wing of the Republican Party.

2. The Nixon Pardon. One month after his inauguration, Ford granted a <u>full presidential pardon to Nixon</u> for all crimes "he may have committed or taken part in" (September 8, 1974). He also announced that Nixon would be given full title to all his presidential papers and tapes, but that these would be kept intact for court use. The pardon, granted at a time when the other Watergate conspirators were waiting trial, stirred resentment against Ford and lessened his popularity.

B. The Aftermath of Watergate.

1. The 1974 Elections. Public resentment of the Republican involvement in the Watergate conspiracy and the pardon of Nixon was shown in the November, 1974, elections when the Democratic Party *gained 43 seats in the House of Representatives* and *4 in the Senate.* The Democrats also won 27 governships against only 7 for Republicans. Many of the Democratic victories placed in office young, liberal legislators to replace older conservatives.

2. Fate of the Watergate Conspirators. The trial of the indicted Watergate conspirators before Judge Sirica's US District Court (October, 1974-January, 1975) ended with the *conviction of John Mitchell, H. R. Haldeman, and John Ehrlichman,* as well as lesser conspirators, for conspiracy, obstruction of justice, and perjury. When their appeals were denied by the Supreme Court they began serving sentences of *from 30 months to 8 years in federal prisons.* The Supreme Court also upheld Congress's refusal to release the Nixon papers and tapes to the former President as Ford had promised (June, 1977). In a series of television interviews in May, 1977, Nixon admitted that he "had let the American people down" but refused to admit any criminal or impeachable act. In October, 1977, Judge Sirica reduced sentences of the key figures to from 1 to 4 years, after all expressed regret for wrong doing.

V. FOREIGN POLICY OF THE FORD-NIXON ADMINISTRATIONS

A. Ending the Viet Nam War.

1. Failure of the Paris Negotiations. _Truce negotiations begun in Paris (1969)_ between the United States, South Viet Nam, North Viet Nam, and the National Liberation Front

(NLF, or Viet Cong) revealed an apparently unbridgeable division. North Viet Nam and the NLF demanded: 1) the withdrawal of all US troops by an agreed-upon date, and 2) the exclusion of President Thieu and his government from any provisional government for South Viet Nam. The United States and South Viet Nam insisted on: 1) the simultaneous withdrawal of "major portions" of American and North Vietnamese troops by an agreed-upon date, and 2) internationally supervised elections to choose a provisional South Vietnamese government. Negotiations were complicated by President *Thieu's insistence that all North Viet Nam troops be withdrawn before talks could begin.* In major policy speeches (October, 1970 and January, 1972) President Nixon made important concessions including withdrawal of American soldiers within six months of a ceasefire and release of prisoners (POWs), but these were summarily rejected.

2. Final Military Action.

a. In South Viet Nam. After a major communist offensive in February, 1969, *military action gradually lessened.* By the end of the year the flow of North Viet Nam troops southward had slowed to some 3,000 a month from 10,000 at the height of hostilities.

b. In Laos and Cambodia. *Secret bombing of two neighboring neutral states, Cambodia and Laos,* was ordered by President Nixon in 1969, with a "separate reporting system" to keep news of this aggression from the American people. In a major invasion, 32,000 Americans and 40,000 South Vietnamese entered *Cambodia in an attempt to destroy enemy bases* there (May-June, 1970); a similar raid in Laos aimed at cutting the Ho Chi Minh trail and burning supplies failed when 20,000 South Vietnamese troops operating under an American air umbrella were repulsed after ten days of disaster (February, 1971). American bombing of Cambodia continued until Congress learned (summer, 1973) of the secret attacks. Their response was a *law limiting the power of the President to wage undeclared* war without congressional approval. Vetoed by the President, this was passed over his veto by heavy majorities (November, 1973).

c. IN NORTH VIET NAM. _Bombing of North Viet Nam was resumed_ (December, 1971) on a larger scale than ever before in retaliation for the Hanoi government's failure to halt the shelling of Saigon and cease its troop build-up in the South.

3. Growing Anti-War Sentiment in the United States. The seemingly endless drain of men and dollars bred a mounting anti-war sentiment at home. This was bolstered by:

a. POLITICAL EVENTS IN INDOCHINA. Despite South Viet Nam's supposedly democratic constitution, President Thieu made his views clear by:) barring from his cabinet all Buddhists and representatives of a sizeable portion of the electorate (September, 1969), and 2) forcing three rivals from the ballot in an October, 1971, election to assure a clean sweep at the polls. Similarly in Cambodia Premier Lon Nol suspended the National Assembly (October, 1971) because "the sterile game of democracy" hampered his fight against communism, assuming dictatorial powers in March, 1972.

b. THE ARMY TRIALS. In November, 1970, an army lieutenant, _William L. Calley,_ was tried by a military court for commanding a platoon to slaughter 102 Vietnamese in the _village of My Lai._ Calley was found guilty and sentenced to life imprisonment, but his sentence was later reduced and he was released on bail in 1973 after three years in jail. The trial stirred violent feelings for and against his action, but the nation was shocked by the revelation of American brutality. When several years later the Supreme Court refused to review the Calley case he was transferred to "parole status" and released in April, 1976.

4. The Anti-War Protests.

a. ORGANIZED OPPOSITION. Each escalation of military activity sparked well-organized protest movements including: 1) a "Viet Nam Moratorium" with nation-wide rallies and vigils for peace (October, 1969); 2) a march on Washington arranged by the "New Mobilization Committee to End the War" in which 250,000 protesters converged on the capital (November, 1969), and 3) a similar Washington rally attracting 100,000 to protest the invasion of Cambodia (May, 1970). These and most smaller protest rallies were peaceful, but when militants tried to disrupt the government by blocking traffic (April, 1971), no less than 12,614 were arrested and either jailed or held in stockades for 24 hours.

b. .TROUBLE IN THE UNIVERSITIES. Protesting students at Harvard, Cornell and elsewhere disrupted education by occupying university buildings in sit-ins designed to end military training and gain support for anti-war resolutions. Unrest peaked when the *Cambodia invasion touched off protest meetings in* hundreds of campuses (spring, 1970). Four students at *Kent State University* and two at Jackson State College in Mississippi were killed by guardsmen and police, inspiring protests that closed 448 colleges.

c. EMERGENCE OF VIOLENCE. Extreme militants both in and out of universities resorted to violence in 1969 and 1970 when 4,330 bombs were planted, causing 40 deaths and $21.8 million in property damage. Public resentment against these outrages lessened the public impact of peaceful protests. By mid-April, 1971, however, Nixon's popularity reached an all-time low.

5. Response to the Protesters.

a. CONGRESSIONAL OPPOSITION. Sensing the mounting antipathy to the war, Congress attempted to use its legislative authority to end fighting. In June and September, 1971, the Senate voted to set a date for the total withdrawal of American forces from Southeast Asia, but the effort failed when the House refused to follow. (December, 1971).

b. THE MILITARY RESPONSE. Popular antipathy forced the government to begin a gradual de-escalation of the American war effort. This took the form of: 1) a *"Vietnamization Program"* to shift ground fighting to Vietnamese troops (March, 1969) who supposedly would be able to defend their country by the end of 1970; and 2) the *gradual withdrawal of American forces*. This began in June, 1969, when 25,000 men were returned; by May 1, 1972, the number had been reduced from a high of 542,500 in March, 1969 to 69,000. The President announced at that time the end of withdrawals until: 1) enemy activity slowed; 2) the Vietnamization Program was proven successful; and 3) progress was made in securing the release of American POWs. Australian and New Zealand troops also withdrew in 1972.

6. Final Peace Negotiations.

a. RENEWED MILITARY ACTIVITY. In the largest offensive in four years, communist troops in April, 1972, captured the rich rice province of Bing Dinh, and threatened to cut South Viet Nam in two at its narrow waist. The United States responded with _renewed bombing of Hanoi and Haipong_ (April, 1972), and in May, 1972 announced the _mining of Haipong Harbor_ and other northern ports to stop the flow of military supplies into North Viet Nam. These steps, combined with the few successes of South Viet Nam army, allowed the continued withdrawal of American ground forces. The last _departed in August,_ 1972, although air units continued to operate.

b. PROGRESS TOWARD A CEASE-FIRE. After _30 secret bargaining sessions_ in Paris with North Viet Nam's Le Duc Tho (August, 1969-September, 1972), Nixon's foreign advisor, _Henry A. Kissinger_ announced a _tentative agreement to end the war on_ October 12, 1972. President _Thieu refused to accept_ this and announced his opposition to any agreement that did not: 1) force the immediate withdrawal of all North Viet Nam troops; 2) establish the DMZ as a permanent boundary between the two Viet Nams; and 3) assure the perpetuation of his own government. This ended negotiations, although Kissinger announced on October 26, 1972, that "peace is at hand."

c. RESUMPTION OF WARFARE. When negotiations were resumed (November 20, 1972), the _Hanoi government stiffened its stand,_ demanding: 1) a reunited North and South Viet Nam; and 2) the release of all political as well as military prisoners held by South Viet Nam. Nixon's answer was to order _renewal of the bombing of Hanoi_ on a scale that left a battered city (December, 1972). American losses were high and criticism at home and abroad extensive.

d. THE "END" OF THE VIET NAM WAR. American bombing ended on December 30, 1972, and _secret Paris peace negotia-_

tions between Kissinger and Le Doc resumed on January 8, 1973. An *agreement was finally signed* on January 27 by the four participants, providing for: 1) a cease-fire in Viet Nam to be effective immediately; 2) the withdrawal of all US troops within 60 days; 3) the release of all military prisoners within 60 days; 4) the right of the people of South Viet Nam to decide their own political future; 5) the boundary of the two countries to be the DMZ; 6) the right of Laos and Cambodia to political self-determination; and 7) US aid for Indochina and especially North Viet Nam.

7. Communist Victories in Southeast Asia.

a. CONTINUED MILITARY ACTION. Despite the January, 1973, cease-fire, *heavy fighting continued* as each side accused the other of violating the agreement. Further peace efforts were: 1) An "Act of Paris" (March, 1973) in which twelve nations guaranteed the peace settlement; 2) a second cease-fire (June, 1973) with South Viet Nam ordering its troops to stop shooting and the US agreeing to clear North Vietnamese harbors of mines. The US also agreed to withdraw the last of its troops (March 29, 1973), in return for renewed North Vietnamese promises to release POWs, and to establish a Joint Economic Commission to determine the cost of rebuilding North Viet Nam. President Nixon's promise of $7.5 billion in US aid for this met a cold reception in Congress which finally voted 266-131 to make no such appropriation (May, 1977).

b. TRIUMPH FOR NORTH VIET NAM. War between North and South Viet Nam was *resumed in the summer of 1973* and continued until *April, 1975* when the fall of Qui Nhon and Da Nang signaled the *collapse of South Viet Nam resistance,* with fleeing troops leaving $1 billion in American arms to the at- tackers. President Nguyen *Thieu resigned* on April 21 after denouncing the US as untrustworthy, when Congress refused a presidential request for $972 million to allow South Viet Nam to "save itself." As North Viet Nam troops advanced on Saigon, the National Assembly transferred presidential power to *General Duong Van Minh* (April 27, 1975) who on April 30 announced the *unconditional surrender of South Viet Nam.* Saigon was renamed Ho Chi Minh City by the victors, and in July, 1976,

North and South Viet Nam were officially reunited, with the capital at Hanoi and Pham Dong prime minister. Thousands of refugees sought refuge in the United States. A dispute continued over the return of POWs, but a meeting between commissioners of Viet Nam and the US (May, 1977) agreed that Hanoi would intensify its efforts to identify American POWs and the *US would not veto Viet Nam's entry into the UN.* Viet Nam was admitted in September, 1977, as relations with the US seemed to be returning to normal.

c. WARFARE IN CAMBODIA. American bombing of Cambodia continued after peace in Viet Nam, largely at Nixon's insistence that "dangerous consequences" would follow its end. It only ended on August 15, 1973, when Congress cut off all funding appropriations. Warfare continued there between government forces at Phnom Penh and Khmer Rouge rebels, with the attackers gradually advancing on the capital city, which was placed under siege in January, 1975. The President (February, 1975) asked Congress for $222 million of supplementary aid to check communist aggression there, but was refused. When the old government of General Lon Nol fell and its leader fled the country, a new government of Premier Long Boret *surrendered unconditionally to the communists* (April, 1975). Prince Norodom Sihanouk, who had headed the Cambodian government in exile, returned as head of state. His regime faced a serious problem when a US merchant ship, the *Mayaguez* was charged with violating territorial waters 60 miles off the coast and captured (May, 1975). President Ford branded the seizure an "act of piracy" and ordered a land, sea, and air attack to recover the vessel, with the sinking of three Cambodian gunboats and the loss of 38 American military personnel killed. International opinion generally condemned this over-use of force against a small country.

d. WAR IN LAOS AND THAILAND. The communist victories in Viet Nam and Cambodia were duplicated elsewhere in Southeast Asia. In *Laos* the communist-backed Pathet Lao forces first agreed to a coalition government with the ruling faction (September, 1973) then after further military successes took over the reigns of government, establishing the *People's Democratic Republic* (December, 1975). In *Thailand* a *military* _junto seized control_ (October, 1976) as the Administrative Reform Committee, abolished the Constitution of 1974, and banned all publications. Its authority was cemented a year later (October, 1977) when a second military coup peacefully overthrew the government and assumed control.

B. Relations with the Americas.

1. End of the Alliance for Progress. President Nixon largely ignored Latin America. In a policy statement (October, 1969) he _virtually ended the Alliance for Progress_ by urging South Americans to care for their own social and economic needs without further reliance on the United States.

2. Tarnished Image of the United States. The United States became increasingly unpopular among Latin American people due to: 1) a conflict with Ecuador over fishing rights within the 200-mile zone over which it claimed jurisdiction, leading to suspension of arms sales there; and 2) suspicions that American influence was responsible for the _overthrow_ of the leftist government of _Chili's President Salvador_ (September, 1973). A later Senate investigation concluded that the CIA and the American embassy in Chile had not been directly involved, but had helped create an atmosphere conducive to the event. American unpopularity was shown during an 8-country tour of Latin America by Secretary of State Rogers (May, 1973) who was greeted by anti-American rioting at each stop.

3. Relations with Cuba. As passions bred of the Cuban revolution subsided, an unofficial visit by a group of US senators revealed that Fidel Castro was sympathetic toward the resumption of diplomatic relations (September, 1974). This led to: 1) lifting the ban on trade with Cuba by foreign subsidiaries of American companies although continuing the embargo on direct trade (August, 1975); 2) ending restrictions on American travel in Cuba, as well as Viet Nam and Cambodia (March, 1977); and 3) announcing in June, 1977 that for the first time in 16 years the _US and Cuba would station diplomats in each other's capitals_ as "interest sections," a first step toward resuming formal relations; and 4) drafting a reparation treaty to allow anti-Castro Cubans freer access to the United States (August, 1977).

C. Relations with the Far East

1. Relations with India

a. THE EAST PAKISTAN REBELLION. When President Yahya Khan of Pakistan refused to allow his political rival, Shiek Mujibur Rahman, to assume office after a victory at the polls (March, 1971), Rahman proclaimed the independence of East Pakistan as the Republic of Bangladesh. His ill-equipped troops were decisively defeated by well-armed Pakistani soldiers, sending 12 million Hindu and Moslem refugees from Bangladesh into India.

b. THE INDIA-PAKISTAN WAR. War between India and Pakistan followed (December, 1971), with Indian armies victorious. They withdrew at once after victory was won, at the same time recognizing the Republic of Bangladesh. President Nixon's strong support of Pakistan and his suspension of development loans to India stirred resentment in the United States where public opinion favored Pakistan. The US recognized the Bangladesh government in April, 1972.

2. Relations with China

a. PENETRATING THE BAMBOO CURTAIN. Signs that the People's Republic of China was willing to resume normal relations with the United States were seen when an American ping-pong team with its accompanying journalists was cordially received (April, 1971). President Nixon, who had been secretly signalling China of his willingness to negotiate responded by: 1) easing a 20-year embargo on trade; 2) sending _Kissinger on a secret mission to Peking_ (July, 1971) to arrange a visit by Nixon designed to "normalize relations;" and 3) announcing the willingness of the US to support the People's Republic's admission to the UN providing this did not mean the expulsion of its long-time ally, Taiwan's Republic of China. When the UN acted (October, 1971), the People's Republic was admitted, but the Republic of China was expelled at once.

b. THE NIXON MISSION. _Nixon entered China on February 21, 1972_ to spend eight days in negotiations with Premier Chu En-lai and Communist Party Chairman Mao Tse-Tung. In a joint statement they acknowledged their differing social and global policies but: 1) pledged progress toward normalizing relations, 2) agreed on programs of cultural exchange; and 3) assured their allies that their interests would be protected. The latter statement failed to placate Taiwan which was offended by US acknowledgement of "One China."

c. PROGRESS TOWARD NORMAL RELATIONS. Further steps toward normalizing relations were taken when: 1) the United States and China agreed (March, 1973) to _establish "liaison offices"_ in each other's capitals to perform all save "strictly formal" negotiations; and 2) President Ford made a largely ceremonial visit to Peking (December, 1975). Further negotiations were slowed by the elevation of Hua Kuo-feng to replace Chou En-lai as prime minister (April, 1976), and the death of Mao Tse-Tung (September, 1976), touching off an internal power struggle that absorbed China's energies. Prospects for normal relationships remained strong as China's traditional hostility toward Russia drove it toward friendship with the United States.

3. Relations with Japan. World tensions were eased when Japan-US treaty _returned the island of Okinawa_ to Japan, but allowed the US to retain a naval base there. Okinawa had been a major staging area for air strikes against Korea and North Viet Nam.

D. Relations with Europe

1. Cementing European Alliances. As the Viet Nam War ended, Kissinger turned to repairing the frayed relations with Europe accentuated by that struggle. President Ford continued these efforts when he: 1) visited Europe to assure the NATO nations of the continued American commitment to their security (May-June, 1975), and 2) joined with 35 other nations in signing at Helsinki (July, 1975) a non-binding agreement of "Security and Cooperation" that recognized territorial changes wrought by World War II, pledged inviolable boundaries within Europe, and promised cooperation among all signing nations.

2. Emerging Detente with Russia

a. THE NIXON VISIT. _President Nixon visited Moscow in May, 1972,_ where he and Party Leader Leonid I. Brezhnev agreed on: 1) cooperation in meeting health and environmental problems; 2) future joint space flights; 3) scientific and technical interchange under a joint commission; 4) a joint commission to negotiate trade agreements; and 5) preliminary steps designed to slow the arms race by _freezing offensive missile arsenals at current levels_ for five years while a _permanent Strategic Arms Limitation Treaty (SALT)_ was negotiated.

b. THE BREZHNEV VISIT. In a return visit to Washington (June, 1973), Brezhnev and Nixon agreed on: 1) continued cultural exchange and agricultural research; 2) to begin talks on mutual-troop reduction in Europe; and 3) a declaration of principles designed to speed up SALT negotiations to achieve arms limitation by the end of 1974. These positive steps were threatened by US fears when the USSR announced (August, 1973) the successful testing of multiple independently targeted re-entry vehicles (MIRVs), thus drawing abreast of the US in missile technology.

c. FAILURE TO ACHIEVE ARMS LIMITATION. The second phase of US-USSR _talks aimed at missile limitation (SALT II) began at Geneva_ in March, 1973. Progress remained negligible despite visits of Kissinger and Nixon to Moscow (summer, 1974), and a similar visit by President Ford (November, 1974). The SALT talks continued, but an agreement seemed unlikely by the end of the Nixon-Ford administrations.

d. EFFORTS TOWARD ECONOMIC COOPERATION. Large grain purchases to offset crop failures in the USSR in 1972 and 1975 caused a "grain drain" that skyrocketed domestic prices, causing consumer resentment in the US. Negotiations for an agreement that would stabilize economic interchange began in January, 1975, but were threatened when Russia refused to accept a congressionally-inserted provision linking favorable tariff terms with Russia's relaxing of _restrictions on free emigration._ The impasse was broken (September, 1975) with a five-year agreement for the Russian purchase of 6 to 8 million tons of grain yearly, in return for the American purchase of 200,000 barrels of oil daily.

E. Relations with the Middle East

1. The Turkish-Cyprus Conflict. When Turkey took advantage of a civil conflict in Cyprus to invade that island and establish in its northern portions the Turkish Federated State of Cyprus (February, 1975), Congress showed its disapproval by ordering a six-months ban on all military aid to Turkey. Turkey retaliated by announcing that it would close all military establishments there (July, 1975). Only when Congress voted to ease this embargo were negotiations resumed, leading to an agreement (March, 1976) that reopened the US bases in return for $1 billion in American grants and loans to Turkey.

2. The Israel-Arab Conflicts.

a. GROWTH OF PLO TERRORISM. Irreconcilable Palestinians (Arabs determined to re-occupy Israel and organized as the *Palestinian Liberation Organization*), using Lebanon, Jordan, and Syria as bases, staged repeated raids on Israelis following the 1967 "Six Day War." A brief cease-fire arranged by UN negotiators (August, 1970) collapsed when Israel refused to consider a US-UN proposal to return territories occupied in the war in exchange for permanent boundaries guaranteed by an international peace unit (March, 1971). PLO raiding was intensified after this announcement, reaching a climax during the *Olympic games at Munich* (September, 1972) when 8 Arab guerrillas invaded the Israeli dormitories to *kill two athletes and take nine others captive,* to be killed later. Israel answered with mass raids on PLO camps in Syria and Lebanon.

b. THE "OCTOBER WAR." Mid-east tensions exploded on October 10, 1973 when *Egyptian troops chose a Jewish Holy Day, Yom Kippur, to launch an all-out war*. A hurriedly mobilized Israeli army of 100,000 stemmed the initial assault after Egyptians had established a 103-mile front on the east bank of the Suez Canal and Syrian troops had won strategic sites on the Golan Heights. Eventually Israeli soldiers won a beachhead on the west bank of the canal, capturing the city of Suez and threatening to encircle Egypt's invading force, but they *failed to win a decisive victory* as they had in 1967. Both sides were generously provided with air-lifted weapons, Israel by the United States, Egypt and Syria by the USSR.

c. INTERNATIONAL PEACE EFFORTS. Kissinger, after urging both sides to avoid escalating fighting, conferred with Brezhnev in Moscow on possible peace terms. These were threatened by rumors that Russia was about to respond to Egypt's request for a peace-keeping force by sending its troops to the Middle East, thus upsetting the major power balance there. The United States responded by declaring a "precautionary alert" of its entire military force. The crisis ended when the contestants, the US and the USSR agreed to a _UN Security Council cease-fire on October 28, 1973_, after 18 days of fighting, with a peace-keeping force from the UN as enforcing agent. Kissinger in a whirlwind tour of Egypt, Syria, Jordan, and Israel convinced the combatants to begin peace talks on December 21, 1973.

d. THE OIL EMBARGO. Immediately after the October War, the Organization of Arab Petroleum Exporting Countries (OAPEC), meeting in Kuwait, declared an _oil embargo against the United States_ and most European countries that favored Israel. President Nixon declared an immediate emergency (November, 1973) and urged energy conservation by less driving, cooler homes, and a reduction in speed limits for cars and trucks. Congress responded by declaring a 55 mile-per-hour limit and year-round daylight-saving time. The embargo against all European countries save the Netherlands was lifted in December, 1973, and against the US in March, 1974, but the OAPEC countries at the same time reduced production of oil by 80% and doubled prices.

3. The Quest for a Permanent Peace.

a. ENDING THE OCTOBER WAR. President Nixon visited five middle-eastern countries (June, 1974) to urge agreement on peace terms, promising US military and economic aid in return. His efforts were supplemented by the _"shuttle diplomacy" of Kissinger_ who flew from capital to capital carrying proposals for a settlement that was agreed upon by Israel and Egypt (January, 1974). Under these the Suez Canal was opened in June, 1974. Representatives of Israel and Egypt meeting at Geneva (September, 1975) reached tentative agreement on Israel's return of 1,900 square miles of occupied Egyptian territory in the Sinai Peninsula, to be occupied by a force of 200 American technicians to warn of encroachments. Kissinger's efforts led to an Israel-Syria agreement (June, 1975) to disengage troops in the Golan Heights and exchange prisoners captured in the October War.

b. DETERRENTS TO A PERMANENT PEACE. Efforts to achieve a permanent settlement in the Israeli-Arab conflict were handicapped by: 1) *internal warfare in Lebanon* between Moslems, Palestinian guerrillas, and Christian right-wing Arabs which began in April, 1975, and continued until July, 1976, when with PLO consent 15,000 Syrian soldiers took over peace-keeping duties; 2) *growing support for the Arab position from Third World powers* who dominated the UN Assembly and formally recognized the PLO as representative of the Palestinian people (October, 1974), branded Zionism "a form of racism and religious discrimination" (November, 1975), and suggested a "peace plan" calling for the withdrawal by Israel from all occupied territories and the establishment of a Palestinian state (January, 1976); and 3) continued *PLO raids into Israel from Lebanon or Syria* followed by retaliatory invasions of the borderlands of those nations where Palestinians were encamped. These were climaxed when airborn Israeli commandos invaded Uganda's Entebbe Airport to rescue 103 hostages, largely Israelis, who had been hi-jacked by pro-Palestinian guerrillas, killing 20 Ugandan soldiers (July, 1976).

c. CHANGING ROLE OF EGYPT. Hope for a renewal of the stalled Geneva peace talks was revived when: 1) President Anwar Sadat visited the United States (September, 1975) to urge cooperation between the US, the USSR, and the UN in summoning negotiators; and 2) *ended the treaty of friendship between Egypt and Russia* that had been in force since 1971, signaling a desire for closer cooperation with the US in peace efforts. Despite these developments, mideast peace seemed far away when the Nixon-Ford administrations ended.

F. **Relations with Africa.** Internal and inter-nation conflicts were many among the emerging Third World powers, all involving the US State Department in its role as peace keeper. The most serious developed when Portugal's relinquishment of its colony of *Angola* (November, 1975) began a bitter *war between the People's Republic* of Angola, backed by the USSR, and the *Democratic People's Republic,* supported by the US, western Europe, and China. When the US learned that *3,000*

Cuban troops and advisors were aiding the People's Republic forces Kissinger warned that the United States would not "remain indifferent," at the same time admitting supplying the Democratic People's Republic with $50 million in military aid. This revelation led the Senate to *end all covert funding in the conflict* (December, 1975). The war ended (February, 1976) with the Russian-backed faction victorious, but with guerrilla war continuing.

VI. THE NIXON-FORD YEARS IN RETROSPECT.

Although an appraisal of the Nixon-Ford administrations is impossible until history has arrived at its judgments, there seems little doubt that the verdict of time will show that the two most important developments were: 1) Nixon's establishment of partial detente with the USSR and preliminary diplomatic relations with China, thus taking the first hesitant steps toward the better relations between the major powers necessary for world peace; and 2) his inadvertent shifting of the power balance within the United States by his involvement in the Watergate conspiracy. For the agonies and national trauma of those years: 1) demonstrated the ability of the American constitutional system to affect a transfer of authority without bloodshed or serious disruption; 2) re-affirmed the power of the courts by showing that they could rise above partisan prejudice to defend the Constitution; 3) made clear that "executive privilege" must operate within constitutional limits; 4) checked a trend toward concentration of power in the executive at the expense of the legislative branches; and 5) reversed a movement of both legislature and administration to violate the civil rights of individuals in violation of constitutional protections. The re-asserted power of the legislative branch, however, was to create difficulties for future presidents.

Additional Reading

The most interesting, if unbalanced, treatments of the Nixon Years are found in autobiographies such as Richard M. Nixon, *RN: The Memoirs of Richard Nixon* (1978); Clark Mollenhoff, *Game Plan for Disaster* (1976). The following autobiographies dealing with the Watergate scandal are especially useful: John W. Dean, *Blind Ambition* (1976); Jeb S. Magruder, *American Life: One Man's Road to Watergate* (1974); John J. Sirica, *To Set the Record Straight* (1979). The most accurate account of Watergate is Theodore H. White, *Breach of Faith: The Fall of a President* (1975). Among the lasting books on the Nixon years are: Jonathan Schell, *Time of Illusion* (1976); and Ted Szulc, *Illusion of Peace* (1977). Highly critical but indispensable is William Shawcross, *Sideshow: Kissinger, Nixon and the Destruction of Cambodia* (1979).

CHAPTER XVIII

The Carter Years
1977—1981

The election of a Democratic president in 1976 did not reduce the impact of the Nixon years on the relationship between the legislative and the executive branches of government. Congress continued to assert its authority, with the Democratic majorities in both houses refusing to comply with the President's wishes on legislation, especially since the President had come to Washington as a professed outsider who refused to engage in the politics of presidential leadership. The result was a near-impasse that crippled programs to deal with problems of inflation, unemployment, energy resources, and diplomacy.

I. THE ELECTION OF 1976.

A. Selecting the candidates.

1. The Republican Choice. President Ford's ambitions to succeed himself were threatened when _Ronald Reagan, a leader of the conservative wing of the party,_ announced (November, 1975) that he would challenge the incumbent for the nomination. In the primaries the two candidates divided the spoils fairly evenly. Reagan made a bid for moderate support, but _Ford was victorious on the first ballot_ in the Kansas City convention (August, 1976), with 1,187 votes to 1,070 for Reagan. To court the conservatives, Ford selected as his vice-presidential candidate conservative Senator Robert J. Dole of Kansas.

2. The Democratic Choice. A number of candidates entered the Democratic primaries, but the _voters favored James_

Earl (Jimmy) Carter, a former Georgia governor and avowed "born-again" Christian, whose honesty and criticism of the "Washington Establishment" had wide appeal. He *won on the first ballot* at the New York convention (June, 1976), with 2,238.5 votes to 329.5 for Representative Morris K. Udall of Arizona and 300 votes for Governor Edmund G. Brown, Jr., of California. Carter's choice for a running mate was liberal Senator Walter F. Mondale of Minnesota.

B. The Issues and Outcome of the Election.

1. Republican Pledges. The Republicans promised to: a) attack massive federal funding programs; and b) provide tax reductions for investors and industry.

2. Democratic Pledges. The Democrats promised to: a) lessen defense spending; b) seek gun control to reduce crime; c) support school bussing for racial integration; d) provide tax relief for the poor; and e) restore honesty to government.

3. The Carter Victory. *Carter won a narrow victory* with an electoral majority of 287 to 240, and a popular vote of 40,825,839 to 39,147,770 for Ford. In the congressional races Democrats won 61 seats in the Senate to 38 for the Republicans, and 292 in the House against 143 for Republicans.

II. CARTER'S DOMESTIC POLICIES.

A. Carter's Leadership and Style.

1. The President's Populism. At his inaugural the President stressed his down-to-earth view of the office by *walking from the White House to the Capitol*. He also promised to solicit the views of the people through "town meetings" and radio "call-ins." To win public confidence he asked Congress to enact legislation that required full financial disclosure from all cabinet officers and political appointees.

2. The Cabinet. Only three of Carter's principal appointees were well known: *Cyrus R. Vance* as Secretary of State; *Harold Brown* Secretary of Defense; and *Joseph Califano* as Secretary of HEW. He also named *two women and two blacks to the cabinet*, and *Andrew Young*, another black, was chosen as ambassador to the UN. Bert Lance, the President's Georgia banker who was named to head the Office of Management and Budget, was forced to resign (September, 1977) following charges of improprieties in his banking practices.

3. Use of the Pardoning Power. Ford's first presidential act was to pardon Nixon; Carter's was to *pardon all draft evaders in the Viet Nam War*. He did not pardon deserters (January, 1977).

4. The President and Congress. Carter, who relied on advisers from Georgia, did not make a strong effort to court Congress. He vetoed two measures that were very popular among congressmen: a) a $35.2 billion defense appropriation bill which included $2 billion for a nuclear aircraft carrier that he believed unnecessary; and b) a $10.2 billion Public Works bill which included many dams and water control projects the President thought were too costly. Although the presidential vetoes were sustained (the vote for both measures did not exceed two thirds of the members), Carter lost the support of many congressmen by opposing this legislation.

B. Carter's Economic Program.

1. To Reduce Unemployment. Carter proposed a dual attack on unemployment: a) by stimulating the economy; and b) by establishing the government as the employer of last resort. His *Economic Stimulation Plan* (January 1977) would funnel $31.1 billion of buying power into the economy by: a) a $50 rebate to all payers of 1976 income taxes; b) lowered taxes with a permanent tax cut for the lower brackets; and c) allotting $1.7 billion for job programs. He withdrew the $50 rebate under congressional criticism. Congress passed a $4 billion appropriation for public works to create 1 million jobs. Carter agreed to support a weakened *Humphrey-Hawkins bill* (November, 1977) which Congress passed (October, 1978), in a form that eliminated the provision making the government the employer of last resort. Carter hoped to see unemployment reduced to 3% by 1981. Unemployment fell from 8.1 million when he took office to 5.8 million (October, 1978) but it had risen to 7.5 million (August, 1980) as a result of tight money policies imposed on the administration by increasing inflation.

2. *The Carter Welfare Program.* The President (August, 1977) proposed a complete overhaul of the welfare system to provide: a) work requirements for most welfare recipients; b) higher benefits for the disabled, single parents with children under 7 years, and those physically unable to work; and c) the creation of 1.4 million new jobs by industry and government. Congress did not approve of the plan.

3. *The Carter Social Security Program.* Rising *deficits in the Social Security System* forced Congress (December, 1977) to *triple the taxes paid* by employers and employees to raise $227 billion over ten years. This would *keep the system solvent,* but only if unemployment and benefits did not increase. Mounting unemployment and increased benefits resulting from cost of living adjustments forced Carter to recommend changes (January, 1979): a) eliminate the death benefits; b) phase out survivors' benefits for students between ages 18 and 21 as children of dead or disabled workers; c) repeal minimum benefits for people who paid in less than $100; d) tighten disability rules; and e) provide that pensioners must reach 72 before they could earn money outside the system while still receiving full benefits. Congress was unwilling to accept all of these proposals.

4. *The Carter Tax Program.*

a. SHORT-TERM ACTIONS. An administration proposed bill provided for: 1) the elimination of income taxes for some 3 million low-income families; 2) reduced payroll deductions for 50 million workers; 3) a slight increase in taxes for higher incomes; and 4) simplified income tax forms.

b. LONG-TERM TAX REFORM. Junking his campaign promise of major tax reform, the President proposed (January, 1978): 1) income tax cuts; 2) removal of exemptions for well-to-do taxpayers to raise an additional $16 billion a year; 3) a decrease in corporation taxes by 3% in 1979 and 4% in 1980 to encourage investment; 4) retention of the 10% investment tax credit for industry; and 5) the elimination of specific excise taxes and loop holes. Congress rejected these proposals, and the tax system remained essentially unchanged during the Carter years.

5. Dealing with the Energy Problem.

a. THE PRESIDENT'S PLAN. Carter determined to work toward national energy independence by reducing American dependence on imported oil and converting to coal, nuclear, and solar power. He placed a comprehensive plan before Congress (April, 1977) to: 1) increase gasoline taxes by $.50 per gallon; 2) raise taxes on price-controlled domestic oil until it reached the price of imported oil; 3) impose stiff penalties for cars that exceed mileage limits set by Congress; 4) allow an increase in the price of natural gas but impose federal price control on intrastate as well as interstate sales; 5) provide tax credits for businesses and home owners installing solar heating; and 6) hurry the construction of nuclear power plants. The President also called for the _creation of a Department of Energy._

b. WORLD CONDITIONS AND ENERGY POLICY. Although the nation's demand for oil began to decline, the Organization of Petroleum Exporting Countries (OPEC) raised prices to offset what it claimed was world-wide inflation. But the major cause of soaring prices was the revolution in Iran that reduced the supply of Iranian oil from 6 to less than 1 million barrels a day. The President's hope to overcome the energy shortage by utilizing the growing nuclear energy industry was frustrated by the _first major American nuclear accident at Three Mile Island_ in Pennsylvania (April, 1979), which resulted in a review of existing procedures in nuclear plants and a delay in putting reactors on line.

c. THE ADMINISTRATION'S RESPONSE TO THE ENERGY CRISIS. When gas shortages developed in many parts of the country and the public grew irate because of the fuel allocations established by the Department of Energy, the President drew up a new energy plan (April, 1979). It called for: 1) decontrolling the price of domestic oil by 1981; 2) a _windfall profits tax_; 3) the use of windfall profits tax funds to (a) develop alternative fuels (synfuels), (b) help the poor meet the higher costs of energy, and (c) encourage mass transit systems to reduce reliance on private transportation.

d. CONGRESSIONAL ACTION. Congress responded slowly to the energy problem. It created the Department of Energy, agreed to _decontrol of both oil and natural gas,_ passed the windfall profit tax, and enacted the Synfuel Program (June, 1980). By the close of Carter's term oil prices had stabilized.

6. Inflationary Pressures in the Economy.

a. CAUSES OF INFLATION. Many factors contributed to the persistent increase in the inflation rate during the last two years of the Carter administration: 1) an unfavorable balance of trade in large measure due to enormous increases in imported oil prices; 2) heavy government borrowing to make up for deficits created by heavy payments for governmental services; 3) the decline in the value of the dollar in relation to other currencies; and 4) unrestrained wage and price increases. Initially Carter believed that increased productivity and conservation would bring down prices and slow the rate of inflation. The President opposed mandatory wage and price controls.

b. CARTER'S ANTI-INFLATION PLAN. Carter unveiled a voluntary program to fight inflation (October, 1978) calling for: 1) workers to accept wage increases of no more than 7% per year for 3 years; 2) companies to hold their price increases to 6.5% per year during the same period; 3) the establishment of a Council of Wage Price Stabilization; and 4) Congress to create a tax adjustment for workers whose wages did not rise to the 7% guidelines. The government would monitor the prices of the 400 largest companies, give no contracts to companies that violated the guidelines, and impose a freeze in the size of the federal work force.

c. SLOWING THE ECONOMY. The Federal Reserve Board, which controls the interest rates of banks, _began tightening credit_ (December, 1978). By March, 1980, the prime rate (the amount the banks charge their best customers) reached more than 20%. Nevertheless, during the last years of the Carter administration the inflation rate stayed at double digit levels. The impact was a sharp drop in housing starts and automobile sales, two business activities that require loans.

III. RELATIONS WITH A TROUBLED WORLD.

A. Relations with Europe.

1. Basis of Carter's Policies. Carter's foreign policy was based on: a) moral persuasion to _win human rights_ for all peo-

ples (February, 1978) ; b) support for Third World peoples seeking self-determination ; c) a continuing effort to limit nuclear proliferation ; d) a humane treatment of refugees. Congress agreed with the President's human rights stand and authorized him to *cut off military aid and bank credits to nations violating the basic human rights to their citizens.*

2. Relations with the USSR.

a. THE SOVIETS AND HUMAN RIGHTS. When the US warned Russia that any attempt to silence a dissident, Andrei D. Sakharov, would conflict with the "international standards of human rights" (January, 1977), the USSR: 1) condemned US *interference in its "internal affairs,"* and 2) warned that continued cordial relations on such a basis would be "unthinkable."

b. PROGRESS TOWARD ARMS LIMITATION. Disagreement over human rights slowed the pace of the negotiations for SALT II, a treaty to supplement the SALT I agreement signed in 1972. When SALT II was signed in Vienna (June, 1979) it called for : 1) no change in the existing arsenals ; 2) control in the size of new missiles ; 3) a limit in the number of rocket launchers ; 4) *parity in the missile power* of the two nations ; 5) and continued negotiations to limit the nuclear arms race. Soviet insistence that no part of the treaty could be amended troubled US senators who feared that the treaty did not provide ways for verifying Soviet reports.

c. THE AFGHANISTAN INVASION. A Soviet inspired coup in Afghanistan (December, 1979) was followed immediately by a Russian invasion, the first such act since the USSR invaded Czechoslovakia in 1968. A guerilla war between the Russians and Afghan tribesmen followed. The President reacted by : 1) withdrawing SALT II from consideration ; 2) imposing a grain embargo of $2.6 billion on the Russians (January, 1980) ; and 3) asking other free nations to join the US in boycotting the Moscow Olympics (February, 1980).

B. Relation with Asia.

1. Viet Nam's Policies. Viet Nam began a systematic program of driving its dissidents, Chinese, and wealthier people out of the country. Its invasion of Cambodia increased the stream of refugees which numbered 550,000 by July, 1979. Carter welcomed some 210,000 of these *"boat people"* by 1980.

2. Carter and China. The *US formally recognized China* (December, 1978) after 30 years of dealing with the government on Taiwan. Carter thus completed a process begun by Nixon in 1972. All of this was possible because of the death of Communist Party Chairman Mao Tse-Tung and a shake-up in the Communist party leadership that brought Deputy Premier Teng Hsiao-p'ing to power. Aware of China's need to modernize and an *opponent of the "cultural revolution"* that had sought to end China's contacts with the West, Teng a) exchanged ambassadors, b) welcomed cultural and economic contacts, c) visited Washington (February, 1979), and d) consented to a compromise regarding the Chinese government in Taiwan. Under the new US policy toward China, US-Taiwan relations became essentially economic rather than diplomatic.

C. Relations with Latin America.

1. The Panama Canal. The US and Panama ended years of negotiations (August, 1977) when Carter and General Torrijos Herrara signed two treaties *to return the Panama Canal Zone to Panama at the end of the century*. They provided: 1) that the US would be primarily responsible for the defense of the canal until the transfer in the year 2000; 2) that the US and Panama maintain the canal's neutrality; and 3) that the US pay Panama $10 million annually for police and fire protection, and another $10 million for operating expenses. Ratification was delayed in the US Senate by right-wing senators who deplored the "surrender" of US property. Former *President Ford and former Secretary of State Kissinger* provided bipartisan support for the treaties and the Senate approved them 68 to 32 (the first in March, 1978; the second in April, 1978).

2. The US and Cuba. The presence of Soviet troops in Cuba, Cuban intervention in Africa and Latin America, and Fidel Castro's repeated verbal abuse of the US strained relations between the US and Cuba despite attempts by Carter to reduce tensions. Relations were further impaired when Castro, believing that there were few dissidents in his country, agreed to allow people to leave his country by airlift to Costa Rica. As thousands of Cubans flocked to leave, Castro insisted that the departees no longer go to Costa Rica, where the refugee flow could be controlled, but directly to their final destinations. He opened the port of Mariel and thousands of Cubans boarded boats for the US. To prove his allegations that only criminals were leaving the country Castro opened Cuban jails and compelled ship captains to take prisoners to Florida. The tide of refugees became almost unmanageable, but the President decided that the US should admit them (May, 1980). Stung by world opinion of what was taking place, Castro, by closing Mariel port, ended the sealift October, 1980).

3. The US and Mexico. Although the US and Mexico are major trading partners, relations between the two nations have not been good. The US has not approved of Mexico's close ties with Castro, Mexican reluctance to control the flow of its migrant labor to the US, and Mexican insistence on high prices for its oil and natural gas exports to the US. Mexico, however, has resented American criticism of its neutralist foreign policy, American mistreatment of its nationals working in the US, American insistence that it determine the condition of trade between the two nations, and, especially, the generally patronizing attitude of the US toward Mexico. A low point in Mexican-US relations was reached (February, 1979) when Carter, during a visit to Mexico, was lectured to by President Lopez Portillo on the shortcomings of US policy. Nevertheless, Carter approved of an agreement to pay more for Mexican than for Canadian natural gas.

D. Relations with Africa.

1. The US and Military Involvement. Carter's policy was not to send US troops (although he would send arms) to Africa. When Zaire reported (March, 1977) that mercenaries, with Russian and Cuban support, had invaded the country from Angola, the US sent only arms. US relations with many black governments was improved by the activities of Ambassador Andrew Young, who was known for his work as a civil rights leader.

2. The US and Human Rights.

a. IN RHODESIA/ZIMBABWE. Because of the long-standing guerilla war between the white minority (250,000) and black majority (6.4 million), the US joined Britain in seeking eventual majority rule. Under the human rights provisions established by Congress, Carter imposed an embargo on white-controlled Rhodesia. Through a step-by-step process, *the British brought about free elections in Rhodesia and majority rule under Robert Mugabe* (March, 1980). The US embargo was lifted.

b. IN SOUTH AFRICA. A US-British plan to aid *South Africa in achieving majority rule* (August, 1977) was rejected by the government of Prime Minister John Vorster who ruled out all prospects of the country's 4.2 million whites sharing power with its 18 million blacks. There has been world-wide criticism of the South African government, a US sponsored arms embargo, and intense opposition to South African participation in international sports. Despite his commitment to human rights, Carter did not sever economic ties with South Africa.

E. Relations in the Middle East.

1. The US and the Israeli-Arab Problem.

a. THE FAILURE OF INITIAL US EFFORTS. Carter sought a *comprehensive solution* by bringing the antagonists to a peace table in Geneva. He proposed (March, 1977) as a basis of discussion that: 1) Israel give back much of the territory it had won in the 1967 "Six Day War"; and 2) Israel be assured "defensible borders." *Both Israel and Egypt rejected the proposal*: President Sadat of Egypt demanding that all of his country's lands be returned; Prime Minister Rabin of Israel objecting to the amount of land he was asked to give up. To break the deadlock, the Carter administration *modified its policy on complete support of Israel* by 1) agreeing in a meeting with Syrian ministers that there must be "a homeland for the Palestinian people" October, 1977), and 2) referring to a joint statement with the USSR suggesting guidelines for a settlement of "the legitimate rights of the Palestinian people" (October, 1977). Secretary of State Vance, however, assured the Israelis that this did not alter our "special relationship" with them. There was some optimism when the Rabin government agreed to resume Geneva negotiations and talk with Arab powers and Palestinians, so long as they were not PLO. But the PLO insisted that they alone could speak for all Palestinians. Hope faded when Rabin was forced out of power and was replaced as prime minister by *hardline*

nationalist Menachem Begin who refused to engage in any conference with the PLO or surrender any territory (April, 1977).
Begin also encouraged the *establishment of new Israeli settlements on the West Bank of the Jordan River.*

b. THE SADAT INITIATIVE. In a surprise move, President
Sadat of Egypt went to Jerusalem (November, 1977) to talk
to Israeli leaders—the first Arab leader to visit the Jewish state.
Sadat was denounced by the PLO, the USSR, and the left-
leaning Arab states of Syria, Iraq, and Libya. Sadat's peace
efforts broke down over disagreements on how much land Israel
should return to Egypt and whether the Palestinians living on
the West Bank and in the Gaza Strip should have "autonomous
self-rule" as Israel insisted or the "right of self-determination"
as Egypt demanded. Israel feared that Sadat's proposal would
lead to a pro-Soviet, militant state headed by PLO leader
Yasser Arafat. Carter's reaction to Begin's policies was evident
by his warm reception of Sadat when he visited Washington
(February, 1978) and was allowed to purchase $3 billion worth
of modern fighter-bombers for Egypt and Saudi Arabia over
Israel's protests. A massive Israeli invasion of Lebanon to
avenge a Palestinian raid on Israel (March, 1978) and Begin's
refusal to make any concessions when he visited Washington
(April, 1978) chilled US-Israel relations.

c. THE CAMP DAVID BREAKTHROUGH. Carter broke the
impasse by inviting Begin and Sadat to his official retreat, Camp
David, for secret negotiations. The resulting *Camp David
Agreement* (September, 1978) consisted of a "Framework for
Peace in the Middle East" establishing procedures for a five-year
program that would allow Israel, Jordan, and the Palestinians
to settle the status of the West Bank and Gaza, and would guarantee the security of Israel; and a "Framework for the Conclusion of a Peace Treaty Between Egypt and Israel" to be
signed within three months. The two powers agreed on major
Israeli withdrawals between three and nine months after the
signing, normalization of relations between the two countries
within a year, and the complete Israeli withdrawal from Egyptian territory within three years. Only the status of the Israeli
settlements in the Sinai remained unresolved.

d. IMPLEMENTING THE AGREEMENTS. The staged withdrawals of the Israelis was planned but there were differences

when the Israelis continued to occupy areas in the disputed West Bank (November, 1978). A Peace Treaty was negotiated (April, 1979) but it left the Palestinian problem unresolved. Begin violated the spirit of the Camp David accords by declaring Jerusalem to be Israel's capital and insisting on additional settlements on the West Bank (August, 1980).

2. The US and Iran.

a. IRANIAN ECONOMIC DEVELOPMENT AND US SECURITY. After the mid-1950s US strength in the Middle East rested on its alliance with Iran. That oil-rich kingdom, dominated by the Shah, Mohammed Riza Pahlavi, became one of the largest suppliers of oil to the United States. With a fortune in oil revenues the Shah set about the modernization of his country, defying its strongly conservative Islamic sects. As a bulwark against Soviet expansion, the Shah maintained the largest and most modern army in the region, almost 500,000 men. Between 1958 and 1978 he bought $36 billion arms from the US. The Shah also spent billions of dollars on the economic development of Iran on the assumption that economic prosperity would bring political stability. It did not. As the Shah denied his people political freedom, drove his enemies into exile, and encouraged or allowed his police to brutalize political opposition, there was repeated evidence of unrest in the country. _Every American President from Eisenhower to Carter supported the Shah because they believed that Iranian military strength and oil were essential to US security._

b. THE COLLAPSE OF THE SHAH. Disorder erupted in Teheran, Iran's capital (September, 1978), and soon raged in other parts of the country. There were strikes in the oil fields, and the Shah pledged democratic reforms (December, 1978) but it was too late. In the face of continued upheaval, the _Shah left the country_ (January, 1979). The Shah's army did not intervene as the weak fledgling government tried to maintain order.

c. THE AYATULLAH KHOMEINI. Following the departure of the Shah, exiled Iranians returned to the country. The most influential was the Ayatullah Khomeini, who returned in February, 1979. Khomeini had been the center for opposition to the Shah because, as a religious leader, he had not sided with any of the Iranian political factions. While Iranian politicians struggled to establish a government, Khomeini *capitalized on the unifying force of religion* to seize true power. His militant clergy and followers, the Revolutionary Guards, began the mass arrest and execution of the Shah's supporters, army officers, and opposition leaders. He became the strongest if not the only force in Iran. The US hoped that a stable government might be formed and warned the USSR not to meddle in Iranian affairs. Khomeini blamed the US for the Shah's policies and denounced the US as an enemy of Islam.

d. THE US EMBASSY SEIZED. Anti-US feeling ran strong among radical Islamic students in Teheran. When the US admitted the exiled Shah for medical treatment, they seized the American embassy and proclaimed the diplomatic and military personnel hostages until the Shah was returned to Iran to stand trial (November, 1979). The students released two black marines and one woman in an obvious move to win sympathy in the US.

e. THE US REACTION. The administration could not deport the Shah or submit to blackmail by the student terrorists. The President and Secretary of State Vance made a conscientious effort to secure the release of the hostages through patient diplomacy. (Six hostages, who had been hidden in the Canadian embassy, were smuggled out of Iran in February, 1980). When diplomatic efforts failed, the President broke off relations with Iran, froze all Iranian assets in the control of American financial institutions, and began planning a military rescue of the hostages. Secretary of State Vance, who disapproved of the plan, resigned after it failed.

f. THE RELEASE. The hostages were released when the President, acting through the Algerian government, agreed to unfreeze Iranian assets. They had been held captive for 444 days.

IV. THE CARTER YEARS IN RETROSPECT.

A. Political Trends.

1. Conservatism. Conservative candidates in both parties were more successful in 1978 and there was widespread dissatisfaction with the effectiveness of government. Carter too had stressed reducing government regulation.

2. Growing Apathy. The percentage of eligible voters who participated in the 1978 election (34%) was the lowest since the war year 1942 (32%). This was a serious blow to incumbents.

B. Economic Trends.

1. Demands for Tax Relief. Although many conservatives had argued for years that taxes were too high, opposition to the growth of taxes was dramatized in California, where *Proposition 13*, a referendum to cut property taxes drastically, won. By 1980 it was evident that tax cuts would be part of both party programs.

2. Inflation. Americans were more concerned with inflation than with taxation as the nation suffered double digit rates in 1978-1980. There were serious doubts, even among liberal economists, about the nation's ability to achieve its social goals in an inflationary period. Carter called on the people to exercise discipline until the economy righted itself.

CHAPTER XIX

Reagan Republicanism
1981—

The election of Ronald Reagan brought to the presidency the first self-professed conservative in many years. Although he began his career as a liberal, rising to the head of the actors' union—the Screen Actors' Guild—Reagan became convinced that government was both too large and too powerful for the good of the American people. He campaigned as a private citizen employed by General Electric to defend his ideas and as a politician he tried to implement his views as governor of California. A politician with a quick wit, Reagan captured the Republican party from eastern moderates who were more sympathetic to social programs and a less aggressive foreign policy. He always demonstrated great courage, even after he was gunned down by a potential assassin.

I. THE ELECTION OF 1980.

A. Selecting the Candidates.

1. The Democratic Nomination. President Carter's determination to succeed himself was challenged by Senator Edward Kennedy, younger brother of the former president. In the primaries, however, because of his judicious handling of the hostage crisis in Iran, the President piled up a commanding lead among the delegates. When the Democrats assembled in New York for their convention (August, 1980), Carter swept to victory with 2,129 votes to 1,146 for Kennedy. He selected Vice President Walter Mondale as his running mate.

2. *The Republican Nomination.* Ronald Reagan who had waged an unsuccessful campaign to unseat President Ford in 1976 was the front-runner among seven serious candidates. Although he seemed to falter briefly in the first primary elections, he quickly proved that he was his party's choice. At the Republican Convention in Detroit (July 1980), Reagan won on the first ballot with 1,939 votes to 37 for John Anderson, and 13 for George Bush. To woo moderate voters Reagan considered offering the vice presidential nomination to former President Ford, but ultimately decided on George Bush, a former member of Congress.

3. *The Anderson Candidacy.* Denied the Republican nomination, John Anderson decided to run as an Independent.

B. The Issues and Outcome of the Election.

1. *The Republican Pledges.* The Republican platform advocated: a) *a tax reduction of 10% a year for three years*; b) elimination of the Department of Education; c) opposition to the SALT II accords; d) opposition to bussing to achieve racial balance in the schools; e) reductions in federal regulations of business to fight inflation; f) equal opportunities for women but not the Equal Rights Amendment; g) a substantial increase in military expenditures; h) support for a constitutional amendment to end abortion; and i) cuts in government welfare programs.

2. *The Democratic Pledges.* The Democratic platform called for: a) support of the Equal Rights Amendment; b) the use of bussing to achieve racial balance in the schools; c) a jobs program for the unemployed; d) support for SALT II; e) closing numerous tax loopholes; f) increased military spending; g) a national health plan; and h) freedom of choice on the abortion issue.

3. *The Anderson Pledge.* As a liberal Republican, Anderson's platform a) supported ERA, b) endorsed the Panama Canal Treaties, c) favored normalization of relations with China, d) urged deregulation of the economy, e) advocated stringent measures to reduce oil dependency, including a heavy tax on gasoline.

4. The Reagan Victory. _Reagan won by a substantial margin_ with a popular vote of 43,201,220 votes to 34,913,332 for Carter and 5,581,379 for Anderson. In the electoral vote Reagan won 486 to Carter's 49. In the congressional races the Republicans scored an upset by capturing the Senate 53 to 46 with 1 Independent and losing the House to the Democrats 261 to 192. But at least 50 of the Democrats were southerners, who often sided with Republicans.

II. REAGAN'S DOMESTIC POLICIES.

A. Reagan's Leadership and Style.

1. The Political President. Reagan, a very shrewd politician, recognized that close cooperation with Congress would be needed to pass his conservative program. He had great personal charm in dealing with Congress and proved remarkably effective in going over the head of Congress by appealing to the people through television. The president also stressed that he kept his word. For example, during the campaign he pointed out that, although he opposed ERA, he would _appoint a woman to the Supreme Court,_ a pledge he honored by nominating Sandra Day O'Connor of Arizona to the bench (July 1981).

2. The Cabinet. The two best known appointees were _General Alexander Haig_, former NATO commander, as Secretary of State, and _Casper Weinberger_, a former Nixon cabinet member, as Secretary of Defense. The cabinet contained 1 black, 1 woman, and 1 person under 40 years of age. It included 11 Protestants and 4 Catholics. The average income of the group was $285,000 per year.

3. Reducing Government. A key figure in the Reagan government was _David Stockman,_ Director of the Office of Management and Budget, who was charged with reducing the function and scope of the government to fit the President's philosophy.

B. The President's Economic Program.

1. The Reagan Budget. The Reagan administration proposed a 1982 budget of $689 billion, about $50 billion below the Carter estimate. This budget included more _money for defense_ (refurbishing the battleship New Jersey) but deep _cuts in social welfare programs_. The bill easily passed both Senate and House with the support of southern Democrats.

2. The Reagan Tax Program. The critical part of the Reagan tax program was the reduction of income tax across the board by 10% a year for three years. Because of delays, this was cut to _5% the first year_ followed by 10% reductions in 1982 and 1983. But the Reagan tax program also was a bonanza to business, which the President felt had too long been severely yoked by federal taxation.

3. Social Security. Continuing concern about integrity of the Social Security Retirement Fund prompted _Reagan to suggest cutbacks_ very similar to those recommended by Carter, but Congress simply refused to act on the president's suggestion and called into question Reagan's campaign promise not to alter the benefits of people currently receiving benefits.

III. THE PRESIDENT'S FOREIGN POLICY.

A. Reagan's Assessment.

1. Continuing Soviet Expansion. The President and Secretary of State believed that US policy should have as its first priority responding to or preempting positions that would lead to _containing the USSR_ when it sought to expand its influence.

2. Human Rights. The President felt that the human rights issue had impaired the U.S. goal of protecting its national interest. He was not prepared to let a human rights issue stand in the way of containing the USSR.

3. The Grain Embargo. Despite the President's hard-line toward the USSR, he yielded to pressure from the Republican dominated farm states and _terminated the grain embargo_ that Carter had imposed after the Soviet invasion of Afghanistan (August 1981).

B. The Middle East.

1. Reagan's goal. The President saw the problem in the Middle East not so much as the explosive issues separating

Israel and its Arab neighbors but how to rally all of the nations in the region against Soviet expansion.

2. Relations with Israel. Shortly after Reagan came to office, sporadic fighting broke out between Palestinians and Israelis along the Lebanese border. The Israelis bombed Lebanon not only because of PLO attacks but to support the Christian Lebanese who were under pressure from a Syrian force and the Palestinians to allow the PLO to function freely in that country. Reagan sent a special envoy, Philip Habbib, to negotiate a cease fire.

3. The Iraq Raid. The problem of the US-Israel relations was clouded when U.S.-built fighter bombers sold to Israel for defensive purposes were used to *destroy a nuclear reactor* under construction in Iraq (June 1981) capable of making materials that could be used to build a bomb because, as Israel warned almost a year earlier (August 1980), it would never allow an Arab country to develop an atomic weapon.

4. US Responses. While the Reagan administration weighed the strength of its responses to Israel's actions, Prime Minister Begin ordered a massive and devastating raid on PLO strongholds in Beirut that killed civilians. The President immediately *suspended shipment of additional F-16* fighter bombers to Israel (July 1981). The embargo was expanded to include F-15 aircraft (August 1981).

5. Cease Fire. *Envoy Habbib* successfully negotiated a cease fire (August 1981), but the future of the truce was doubtful. Begin still demanded that Syrians remove Soviet built missiles from Lebanon, reduce their pressure on the pro-Israeli Christian faction, and stop serious troop movements on its borders.

IV. THE REAGAN PRESIDENCY.

The time period is too short to assess the Reagan administration but clearly the nation's economic future is tied to the President's elimination of a host of social programs created by liberal presidents from Truman to Carter. If the tax cuts, deregulation, and severe cutbacks in social welfare bring a new era of prosperity without inflation (even with heavy military spending), Reagan will have solved a problem that has plagued administrations since the Truman presidency. Failure may have serious social consequence. The President's foreign policy represents a return to the pragmatic programs of the Cold War, when the US had overwhelming military dominance. How the USSR and its allies as well as our friends respond to US efforts to restore that power will set the foreign policy issues of the Reagan era.

Examination Questions

Three types of questions are employed in most American history courses: 1) objective questions, 2) identification questions, and 3) essay questions. These are used by instructors in a variety of combinations. Thus one examination may consist entirely of objective questions; another may combine objective questions and essay questions; still another may employ identification questions and essay questions. Usually students are told in advance the kind of questions that will be asked. If not, they should be prepared to deal with all three types. The examples given below will make this preparation easier.

I. OBJECTIVE QUESTIONS. Objective questions are so named because they can be graded objectively—that is, without resort to any subjective judgment on the part of the reader—and rapidly. Hence they are usually employed in large courses. Four types of objective questions are commonly used: 1) true and false, 2) multiple choice, 3) association, and 4) completion.

A. True or False Questions. As with all objective questions, the true or false questions are distributed to students in mimeographed or printed form. Answers are marked directly on the printed pages, which are then returned to the instructor. In this type the student is required to designate whether a large number of brief statements are true or false. Typical questions of this sort follow:

1. Andrew Johnson broke sharply with Lincoln and worked with radical Republicans in formulating reconstruction policy.

2. The Greenback Party was against inflation and in favor of sound money and the gold standard. **F**

3. The Pendleton Act re-established the free coinage of silver. **F**

4. Josiah Strong's philosophy was based on a strong belief in the destiny of the "Anglo-Saxon race" and the "mission" of America to "civilize" the lesser peoples of the world. **T**

5. The Haymarket riot brought about the downfall of the Greenback Party. **F**

6. The federal government's policy toward the railroads was one of strict control before 1887. **F**

7. The case of *Munn v. Illinois* held a federal income tax unconstitutional. **F**

8. The "long and short haul" referred to the long drive of cattle from Texas to the railroads. **F**

9. The Populist revolt during the 1890's was in reality the forerunner of the progressive movement of the early 1900's. **T**

10. The trend toward the consolidation of industry accelerated during the early years of the twentieth century. **T**

11. The Republican Party became the center of agrarian resistance to the growth of big business following the Civil War. **F**

12. The isolationist Hearst press attacked the McKinley Republicans for playing up Cuban incidents and precipitating a war with Spain. **F**

13. Before becoming President, Woodrow Wilson had served as governor of New York. **F**

14. The progressive measures of the Taft administration outnumbered those of Theodore Roosevelt's administration. **T**

15. W. J. Bryan resigned as Wilson's Secretary of State because he thought the President a pacifist. **F**

16. The Zimmermann note proposed an alliance between the United States and Germany in case of a war with England. **F**

17. The Progressive Party nominated Robert LaFollette of Wisconsin for the presidency in 1912. **F**

18. The Pure Food and Drug Act was passed largely as a result of such books as Upton Sinclair's *The Jungle*. **T**

19. The government's victory in the Northern Securities case was the first of importance under the Sherman Antitrust Act. **T**

20. The Hepburn Act extended the power of the Interstate Commerce Commission over express companies, pipe lines, etc. **T**

21. The Congressional insurgents of 1910-1912 were made up of progressive Republicans who attacked the Old Guard and its point of view. **T**

22. The first successful reduction of the tariff since the Civil War was accomplished during Wilson's first administration. **T**

23. The muckrakers were writers who urged the United States to enter World War I two years before it did so. **F**

24. The chief purpose of the Federal Reserve Act was to provide a flexible banking system to meet the needs of industrialized America. **T**

25. The Clayton Antitrust Act of 1914 was designed to modify the too stringent regulatory features of the Sherman Antitrust Act. **F**

26. The "Roosevelt Corollary" to the Monroe Doctrine stated that the United States should cooperate with Latin America in the interests of hemispheric peace. **F**

27. The Sherman Antitrust Act was designed to break up large combinations in restraint of trade and split them into units that would compete with each other. **T**

28. Successful German propaganda almost led the United States into war with England in 1916. **F**

29. Woodrow Wilson inaugurated a preparedness program to stave off infringement of American neutral rights. **T**

30. The revolution in Russia in 1917 made it easier for the United States to join the Allies. **T**

31. German opposition to Wilson's fourteen points led to their failure as a basis for an armistice. **F**

32. Wilson championed the principle of national self-determination, but exceptions to the principle were made at Versailles. **T**

33. World War I stimulated a vast increase in progressive legislation. **F**

34. The Fordney-McCumber Tariff of 1922 promoted the recovery of world trade following World War I. **F**

35. Our immigration laws passed during the 1920's opened the country's gates still wider to Europe's oppressed. **F**

36. Though the United States did not join the League of Nations, it did participate in many of the League's programs. **T**

37. The chief object of New Deal legislation was to provide relief for the unemployed. **F**

38. New Deal domestic monetary policies were designed to further deflation. **F**

39. The Supreme Court upheld the constitutionality of the National Industrial Recovery Act on the basis of the commerce clause of the Constitution. **F**

40. Wendell Willkie and F. D. Roosevelt differed radically in their attitudes toward international affairs. **F**

41. The "Marshall Plan" provided for extensive military aid to all non-Communist nations. **F**

42. The Commission on Civil Rights named by President Truman proposed enforced nondiscrimination in private housing. **F**

43. The Kefauver Committee revealed the link between crime and the Democratic machine in several large cities. **T**

44. The "Eisenhower Doctrine" allowed the President, without Congressional advice, to use the nation's armed forces in a manner that might precipitate war. **T**

45. Martin Luther King advocated the use of force and violence to achieve rights for blacks. **F**

46. The Warren Commission concluded that the assassination of President Kennedy resulted from an international pro-Communist plot. **F**

47. The Vietcong were guerrilla troops sent into South Viet Nam by the North Viet Nam government. **F**

48. The "Burger Court" refused to issue an injunction to halt publication of the "Pentagon Papers." **T**

49. The Democratic and Republican platforms in 1972 showed but little difference in the governmental philosophy of the two parties. **F**

B. Multiple Choice Questions. In this type of examination the student is confronted with a series of statements, only one of which is correct. He must designate which one. Typical multiple-choice questions follow:

1. The "grandfather clause" (1) determined whether or not you were a Democrat (2) gave the Negro protection at the polls (3) was part of the reform legislation of the Reconstruction period (4) <u>denied Negroes the franchise in the South</u> (5) helped the Republican Party.

2. Immigration to the United States in the 1880's and 1890's originated largely in (1) England (2) Ireland (3) northern Europe (4) southern Europe.

3. The Interstate Commerce Act (1) <u>forbade rate discrimination</u> (2) allocated lands to the railroads (3) provided free passes for Civil War veterans (4) gave the President power to fix railroad rates.

4. The Granger cases (1) authorized Congress to regulate railroads (2) <u>allowed the states to regulate business clothed in a public interest</u> (3) banned the coinage of silver dollars (4) forbade the Grange to set up cooperatives.

5. Granger laws were upheld by the Supreme Court in (1) the Wabash case (2) <u>Munn v. Illinois</u> (3) Minnesota rate case (4) Brief case.

6. The Panic of 1873 was caused by (1) <u>a postwar deflation</u> (2) the financial manipulations of Jay Gould (3) the draining away of the gold reserve.

7. The problem of the surplus revenue became acute in (1) the 1870's (2) <u>the 1880's</u> (3) the 1890's.

8. The Insular cases held that (1) <u>the Constitution does not follow the flag</u> (2) the United States must follow

a policy of isolation (3) all islands adjacent to the United States belong to the United States (4) the Bering Sea is a closed sea.

9. The Open Door Policy involved (1) the observance of Chinese laws by foreigners (2) trade opportunities in Latin America (3) free immigration to the United States (4) <u>equal trading opportunities in China for all nations.</u>

10. The American shift toward internationalism in the late nineteenth century was (1) gradual and unconscious (2) rapid and deliberate (3) <u>the result of the Spanish-American War</u> (4) the result of new imperialistic policies (5) due to the writings of Schurz and Mahan.

11. Which of the following was not in the Omaha platform (1) <u>unimetalism</u> (2) control of railroads (3) direct election of Senators (4) postal savings legislation.

12. The progressive movement was basically (1) revolutionary (2) radical (3) <u>an expression of liberal democracy</u> (4) a partisan approach to social problems.

13. Woodrow Wilson's philosophy was expressed in the term (1) the New Nationalism (2) <u>the New Freedom</u> (3) the New Deal.

14. American intervention in Cuban affairs was based on (1) the Teller Amendment (2) <u>the Platt Amendment</u> (3) the Hay-Herran Treaty (4) the peace treaty with Spain.

15. Theodore Roosevelt made one of his great contributions to the United States in (1) <u>his policy of conservation</u> (2) mediation in the Russo-Japanese War (3) trust busting.

16. Robert LaFollette was (1) a Populist leader (2) a <u>progressive Republican</u> (3) Secretary of the Interior under Taft (4) a Democratic congressman.

17. Muckraker was a term used to designate (1) miners working under ground (2) <u>writers exposing evil conditions</u> (3) isolationists (4) interventionists.

18. Acceptance of the Drago Doctrine by the United States would have led to (1) better relations with Italy (2) the application of the Roosevelt Corollary to the Monroe Doctrine (3) <u>better relations with Latin America.</u>

19. The British black list referred to (1) German lead-

ers (2) German spies (3) members of the German bund (4) firms suspected of trading with the enemy.

20. The Sussex Pledge was made by (1) England (2) Germany (3) Ireland (4) the United States.

21. American soldiers in World War I fought in the battles of (1) Ypres (2) Argonne (3) Caporetto (4) Archangel.

22. The final cause for American entry into World War I was (1) insults to our ambassador in Germany (2) the invasion of Belgium (3) the sinking of American naval vessels (4) the resumption of unrestricted submarine warfare.

23. The Teapot Dome scandal referred to (1) the breakdown of the railroads in 1918 (2) corrupt naval oil leases (3) bribery in connection with the veterans bureau (4) corruption in building the Pacific railroads.

24. The Washington Conference of 1921 (1) established reciprocal trade agreements (2) set up the Pan-American Union (3) gave Korea to Japan (4) limited naval armament (5) proposed a soldiers' bonus.

25. The Dawes Plan (1) scaled down German reparations payments (2) proposed priming the pump for recovery (3) favored reducing tariffs to increase trade (4) reduced the German war debt.

26. The Immigration Act of 1924 established (1) a quota of 3 per cent of each nationality here in 1910 (2) a quota of 2 per cent of each nationality here in 1890 (3) a quota of those who had jobs contracted for in this country.

27. Harding's opponent in the campaign of 1920 was (1) Lansing (2) McAdoo (3) Cox (4) Garner.

28. In respect to political corruption, the Harding administration has often been compared to that of (1) Grant (2) Johnson (3) Arthur (4) Cleveland.

29. The government under Coolidge succeeded in (1) taking the United States into the World Court (2) reducing the national debt (3) passing the McNary-Haugen Act (4) repealing the Eighteenth Amendment.

30. The Good Neighbor Policy had especially to do with

American relations with (1) Canada (2) The Philippines (3) Mexico (4) <u>Latin America</u> (5) Russia.

31. The Neutrality Acts of 1935-1937 were designed to (1) defend freedom of the seas in wartime (2) <u>keep the United States out of European wars</u> (3) define the rights of neutral nations (4) form a union of neutral nations in defense of neutral rights.

32. F. D. Roosevelt proposed to reorganize the Supreme Court because in his opinion (1) it exceeded its rights under the Constitution (2) its Republican members were active in politics (3) it neglected its duties (4) <u>its conservative bias prevented social progress.</u>

33. The Stimson Doctrine proposed (1) <u>nonrecognition of Japanese conquests in Manchuria</u> (2) better relations with Latin America (3) payment of the European war debts (4) naval expansion.

34. The economic collapse that led to a Democratic victory in 1932 occurred (1) 1928 (2) <u>1929</u> (3) 1930 (4) 1931.

35. The New Deal tapered off after (1) the first three months (2) <u>1938</u> (3) the Supreme Court intervened (4) the Republicans gained control of Congress in 1936.

36. The destroyer deal with England gave the United States (1) airplanes 2) <u>naval and air bases</u> (3) control of Iceland (4) safe passage across the Atlantic.

37. The Atlantic Charter resembled (1) the Monroe Doctrine (2) <u>Wilson's Fourteen Points</u> (3) the Neutrality Acts (4) the Good Neighbor Policy.

38. Isolationists in the United States prior to Pearl Harbor belonged to (1) the Republican Party (2) <u>the America First Committee</u> (3) the Fight for Freedom Committee (4) the Ku Klux Klan.

39. American isolationist sentiment favored (1) repeal of the Neutrality Acts (2) lend-lease aid to China (3) <u>the Johnson Act</u> (4) arming of American merchant ships.

40. The Marshall Plan proposed (1) miltiary intervention against the Chinese communists (2) <u>the economic rehabilitation of Europe</u> (3) confining communism to eastern Europe (4) military aid for Greece.

41. The "Eisenhower Doctrine" allowed (1) the export of capital to developing nations (2) <u>the use of American forces in Middle Eastern countries desiring help against Communist aggression</u> (3) the sending of supplies to Israel.

42. The Southern Christian Leadership Conference was formed to (1) aid the presidential campaign of Governor George Wallace (2) aid southern sharecroppers (3) <u>encourage nonviolent protest against racial discrimination.</u>

43. Judge John Sirica presided over the federal court that (1) <u>investigated the bugging of Democratic headquarters in the 1972 election</u> (2) handed down key decisions against racial segregation (3) took a strong "law-and-order" position in an attempt to control crime.

C. Association Questions. A student is confronted with the lists of names, dates, and events, then asked to associate those that are connected or arrange them in proper sequences. The following two examples illustrate this type of question:

1. One term in Group II and one term in Group III are closely associated with a term in Group I. Letter the appropriate terms in Group II and Group III with the letter (a). Proceed through the rest of the question in the same way:

Group I	Group II	Group III
a) Platt Amendment	_b_ Rebates	_e_ Populists
b) Hepburn Act	_f_ Northern Securities case	_i_ W. G. Harding
c) Hay-Herran Treaty	_a_ Cuban independence	_j_ War debts
d) Upton Sinclair	_h_ Civil rights	_a_ Admiral Dewey
e) Crime of 1873	_n_ Jones Act, 1916	_c_ Colombia '
f) T. Roosevelt	_e_ Free silver	_g_ Treaty of Versailles
g) H. C. Lodge	_i_ Oil lands	_f_ Interstate commerce·
h) 14th Amendment	_c_ Panama	_h_ Due process of law
i) Teapot Dome	_k_ Labor rights	_d_ Muckrakers
j) Dawes Plan	_l_ Caribbean	_b_ Great Northern Railroad

k) N.I.R.A.　　　　__d__ Meat inspection　　__l__ Clark Memo-
　　　　　　　　　　　　　　　　　　　　　　　　randum
l) Roosevelt Cor-　　__m__ Japan　　　　　__m__ Manchuria
　　ollary
m) Stimson Doc-　　__g__ League of Na-　　__n__ Tyding-McDuf-
　　trine　　　　　　　tions　　　　　　　　fie Act
n) Philippines　　　　__j__ Reparations　　　__k__ Wagner Act

2. Rearrange each of the following in the order of oc-
currence. Place the proper number in the space at left:

Group I

1. (**2**)　　　1. Pendleton Act
2. (**1**)　　　2. Homestead Act
3. (**3**)　　　3. Dawes Act
4. (**4**)　　　4. Hepburn Act
5. (**5**)　　　5. Norris-LaGuardia Act

Group II

1. (**3**)　　　1. Briand-Kellogg Pact
2. (**5**)　　　2. Atlantic Charter
3. (**1**)　　　3. First Hague conference
4. (**4**)　　　4. London disarmament conference
5. (**2**)　　　5. Wilson's Fourteen Points announced

Group III

1. (**2**)　　　1. Pearl Harbor attack
2. (**4**)　　　2. Stimson Doctrine
3. (**1**)　　　3. Yalta conference
4. (**5**)　　　4. Roosevelt's quarantine speech
5. (**3**)　　　5. Opening of second front

D. Completion Questions. The student is presented
with a number of statements which must be filled in with the
proper date, name, or event. The following examples will
illustrate this type of question:

1. Lincoln's successor __ANDREW JOHNSON__ although he attempted to carry out the basic __RECONSTRUCTION__
policies of the wartime President, lacked the __POLITICAL__
acumen to win Congress to his point of view.

2. Cleveland devoted his entire congressional message in __1887__ to the subject of the __TARIFF__.

3. The __ROOSEVELT__ Corollary to the Monroe Doctrine denied to European nations the right to use force in collecting __DEBTS__ in __THE AMERICAN HEMISPHERE__

4. Henry George's important book, __PROGRESS or POVERTY__, argued in favor of a __SINGLE__ tax on land.

5. Theodore Roosevelt became President on the death of __McKINLEY__ in __1901__.

6. The principal financial measure of Wilson's administration was the __FEDERAL RESERVE ACT__.

7. The leader of the reservationists, __HENRY CABOT LODGE__, was not so much interested in making the __LEAGUE OF NATIONS__ acceptable to the United States but in defeating it entirely for __POLITICAL__ reasons.

8. The __FORDNEY McCUMBER__ Tariff of 1922 and the __SMOOT-HAWLEY__ Tariff of 1930 __RAISED__ levels to the __HIGHEST__ point in history.

9. Relief, __RECOVERY__, and __REFORM__ were the triple purposes of the New Deal.

10. F. D. Roosevelt's Secretary of State, __CORDELL HULL__, worked with the President in carrying out the __GOOD NEIGHBOR__ Policy.

11. The Southeast Asia Treaty Organization (SEATO) was organized by __PRESIDENT EISENHOWER__ as a counterpart to the __NORTH ATLANTIC TREATY ORGANIZATION__.

12. The "Alliance for Progress" was signed by __PRESIDENT KENNEDY__ to funnel funds into __LATIN AMERICA__ to __STIMULATE ECONOMIC AND SOCIAL REFORM__.

13. The Civil Rights Act of 1968 opened __PRIVATE HOUSING UNITS__ to __BUYERS AND RENTERS__ without discrimination.

14. The __DEVALUATION__ of the dollar under President Nixon was designed to improve the __BALANCE OF PAYMENT FIGURES OF THE UNITED STATES__.

15. The "Pentagon Papers" were released for publication by *DANIEL ELLSBERG* in an effort to *HELP END THE VIET NAM WAR*.

II. IDENTIFICATION QUESTIONS.

The student is given a list of names or events, and asked to write a brief note about each. Occasionally a list of well-known quotations is substituted for the names or events. As identification questions are frequently employed to test the student's knowledge of the text or other assigned reading, he should take pains to include in his answer material that could be drawn from those sources only. The answers should be brief and compact, but crammed with information. Typical questions follow:

1. Write brief notes to explain the significance of the following: Henry George, John Fiske, Joseph Pulitzer, Henry H. Richardson, Eugene Debs, Washington Gladden, Edward Bellamy, O. H. Kelley, Lincoln Steffens, John Steinbeck, Eugene McCarthy, William Calley, G. Harold Carswell, Philip Berrigan.

2. Write brief notes on: the Hay-Herran Treaty, Crime of 1873, *Ex Parte Milligan,* Mugwumps, Alabama claims, Greenback Party, Dawes Act, *Looking Backward,* Chautauquas, Venezuela boundary dispute, McNary-Haugen Bill, Wagner Act, Stimson Doctrine, the "New Frontier," Peace Corps, Bay of Pigs, Tet Offensive, Yom Kippur War, Hot Line, Pentagon Papers.

3. Identify as closely as possible and discuss as fully as you can the significance of the following quotations:

(a) "Rum, Romanism, and Rebellion."
(b) "Raise less corn and more hell."
(c) "Liners will not be sunk without warning and without saving human lives, unless these ships attempt to escape or offer resistance."
(d) "It is a condition which confronts us, not a theory."
(e) "Nor shall any state deprive any person of life, liberty, or property without due process of law."
(f) "We are opposed to the free coinage of silver except by international agreement . . . which we pledge

ourselves to promote, and until such agreement can be obtained the existing gold standard must be preserved."

(g) "The Gilded Age."

(h) "Property becomes clothed in a public interest when used in a manner to make it of public consequence and affect the community at large."

(i) "Let us never negotiate out of fear. But let us never fear to negotiate."

(j) "A choice, not an echo."

(k) "Ask not just what will government do for me, but what I can do for myself."

III. ESSAY QUESTIONS.

Essay questions are used more widely than any other type, either by themselves or in connection with objective questions or identification questions. As they are the most difficult kind to answer properly, adequate time should be spent in preparation for them. This time can be used intelligently only when the student realizes the _purpose_ of an essay question.

An instructor who gives properly prepared essay questions is testing his students' ability to 1) _understand_ the material of the course, 2) _organize_ that material intelligently, 3) _select_ the most important events for discussion, and 4) demonstrate _factual knowledge._ If the student will always remember that his grade will depend on all four of those attributes, he should be able to handle the essay question satisfactorily. They should be kept constantly in mind both when studying for an examination or when writing one.

Understanding of the material is the first requisite of a good answer. A penetrating essay on a phase of history cannot be written from memory alone; the student must immerse himself in the material so thoroughly that he completely masters the subject. This is necessary as the essay question usually does not test knowledge already familiar to the student (a chapter of the text or a classroom lecture, for example). Instead it forces him to combine information drawn from several sources, arrange that information in an unfamiliar pattern, and draw conclusions that may be new to him. This requires a thorough understanding of the material.

Organization is equally important. Any intelligent essay must be built upon a carefully planned framework; only then will the events unfold in the logical sequence that gives meaning to the past. No instructor is satisfied with a jumbled mass of information, no matter how exact that information may be. Before starting to write an essay question the student should work out an outline in his mind, or perhaps even jot one down on a blank page of his examination book.

Selection of the material to be included in an essay question tests both the student's intelligence and his familiarity with the subject matter. Any well-prepared person would be able to write for an hour or more on most essay questions. To answer them in the limited time available he must choose only the most essential material, eliminating that which is less important. This requires both a thorough knowledge of the subject and a common-sense ability to distinguish between the essential and the nonessential.

Factual knowledge is also needed for a proper answer to an essay question. Many students on an examination may understand, organize, and select their material well. In that case the instructor is certain to give the highest mark to the one whose essay contains the largest amount of exact information.

With these four points in mind, the student should read carefully the following essay questions, selecting those that fall within the field covered in the portion of the course on which he is to be examined. He will note that some are *general essay questions* covering a wide range of time; these are likely to appear on final examinations. Others are *specific essay questions* dealing with briefer episodes of history. These are used on both final examinations and on the shorter examinations that occur periodically in every course. They have been grouped below to conform to the chapters in this outline.

A. General Essay Questions.

1. Describe the changing relations between business and government, 1865-1916, or 1917-1950.

2. Discuss the decline of laissez faire in America since the Civil War.

3. Consider the history of the tariff, 1865-1900, or 1900-1950, in the light of various factors that have influenced legislation.

4. Describe the changing interpretation of the commerce clause (or the Fourteenth Amendment) in the light of the various factors influencing each change.

5. Discuss the attempts of the federal government to regulate banking (or railroads) from the Civil War to the present.

6. "The almost continuous demand for inflation, growing stronger during the periods of economic depression, has been an outstanding characteristic of American economic history." Discuss fully.

7. Discuss the history of American agriculture from the Civil War to the present in the light of the various factors which influenced it.

8. "Since the Civil War there has never been any real difference between the major parties." Do you agree? Discuss.

9. Account for the rise of minor parties, describe the various types, and show the influence, if any, they have had on American political development.

10. Compare Harding and Grant, and their administrations.

11. As a well-informed citizen, how would you have cast your ballots in 1896, 1916, 1924, and 1932? In each case name the principal candidates and issues involved.

12. How far does American history demonstrate the truth of Madison's dictum that war is the mother of executive aggrandizement?

13. Discuss the meaning of the first section of the Fourteenth Amendment in the light of the leading Supreme Court decisions interpreting it.

14. Account for the changing attitude toward immigration, 1865-1950, and describe the measures adopted by the government as a result.

15. Describe the growth and decline of the American colonial empire, 1865-1950, indicating the factors that have led to each increase or decrease.

16. Trace the history of our relations with Japan since 1900.

17. Account as fully as you can for the shifts in the attitude of the American public toward participation in world affairs since the Civil War.

18. Describe the changes in religious thought and institutions since the Civil War, and account for them.

19. Prepare an outline for a history of literature (or religion, or education) from the Civil War to the present, indicating the social and economic forces responsible for each important development.

20. What concept do you find most useful in interpreting American history since the Civil War: the concept of the frontier, the concept of the section, or the concept of the class struggle?

B. Specific Essay Questions.

I. *Reconstruction, 1865-1877.*

1. "The period of Reconstruction was not a 'tragic era' but a blessing in disguise for the South." Do you agree? Justify your answer.

2. "No president has been so thoroughly misunderstood by his contemporaries as Andrew Johnson." Do you agree? Explain fully.

3. Distinguish between the Lincoln Reconstruction Plan, the Johnson Reconstruction Plan, and the Congressional Reconstruction Plan. Which do you think should have been applied?

4. "The story of the Negro in Reconstruction is not so much a story of the Negro himself as it is the record of the competition of the Southern and Northern whites for the control of a docile race." Discuss fully.

5. Why should the radical Republicans have objected as violently as they did to Johnson's Reconstruction Policy?

6. "The Congressional Policy of Reconstruction was tantamount to a declaration that a successful war, waged for the preservation of the Union, had the legal effect of dissolving it." Explain and discuss.

II. *The Revolution in Economics, 1865-1890.*

1. Discuss the bases for the economic revolution in the United States that followed the Civil War.

2. Why were no transcontinental railroads built before the Civil War, and why did construction proceed so rapidly from that time on?

3. Account as fully as you can for the consolidation of industry in the period after the Civil War and appraise the benefits and evils that resulted.

4. Explain the speed with which the industrial revolution transformed the economy of the United States.

5. How do you account for the close cooperation between government and business in the period between 1865 and 1900?

6. Describe immigration to America, 1865-1900, accounting for each change, and discussing the impact on the United States.

III. *Closing the Frontier, 1865-1890.*

1. "The rapid settlement of the West in the period after the Civil War was a calamity, not a benefit, to the nation." Discuss.

2. "The mining frontier differed from other frontiers in two ways: it moved from west to east, and it engulfed the least attractive areas first." Explain.

3. Had you been in control of the national government, how would you have modified or changed the Indian policy of the period 1865-1890?

4. Discuss the rise and decline of the range cattle industry, accounting for each phenomenon.

5. Was the land system employed in settling the Great Plains satisfactory? If not, how could it have been improved?

6. Account as fully as you can for the late settlement of the Great Plains, and the rapidity of settlement once the process was begun.

IV. *Business and Politics, 1868-1890.*

1. Discuss the influences that made possible the re-establishment of the two-party system in the years 1865-1900.

2. "It is in vain to search the Republican and Democratic national platforms between 1868 and 1896 for any clear-cut antithesis on any real issue." Discuss.

3. Explain the fact that both major parties avoided dealing with the major problems stemming from the industrial revolution.

4. Discuss the sources, growth, and achievements of the movement for civil service reform in the period before 1900.

5. "Cleveland was not a man of great courage or independence of mind; he merely asserted the philosophy of the group which had captured control of the government during the Civil War." Do you agree? Discuss.

6. Name the outstanding events of Cleveland's first administration, and discuss fully any one of them.

V. *The Assault on Laissez Faire, 1868-1890.*

1. Describe the organization, methods, and objectives of the Knights of Labor and the American Federation of Labor, accounting as fully as you can for any differences.

2. "The American Federation of Labor succeeded, if you call it success, only because it was willing to sacrifice the interests of the great mass of American workers." Do you agree? Discuss.

3. Account as fully as you can for the failure of farmers and workers to cooperate in forming a new political party during this period.

4. "The attempt of the federal government to regulate the railroads simply resulted in the substitution of new evils for old ones." Do you agree? Explain.

5. Describe and account for the transition from state to federal control of interstate carriers.

6. Why did the Interstate Commerce Act and the Sherman Antitrust Act fail to accomplish the purposes for which they were designed?

VI. *The Urban Impact, 1868-1890.*

1. Trace the connection between humanitarian striving and the revolution in economics of the post-Civil War era.

2. Describe the effects of the impact of urbanization and new scientific concepts on religion, 1865-1890.

3. How generally was the Gospel of Wealth accepted in the period following the Civil War, and how influential were the writings of those who proposed reform?

4. "Throughout the history of civilization the city, rather than the country, has been the cradle of cultural progress." Explain.

5. Analyze in detail the impact of the machine age on one of the following: literature, religion, or the status of women.

6. Does the term "the Gilded Age" properly characterize the intellectual·and cultural progress in the period 1865-1900?

VII. *The Populist Era, 1890-1900.*

1. Discuss the causes and nature of the agricultural depression, 1870-1896, and describe its economic and political results.

2. In what way did the gold standard figure as an important political question between 1865 and 1900? How, in each case, was the problem solved?

3. Does the record of the Republican Party from 1865-1900 justify its claim to being the sound-money party?

4. Discuss the antecedents and subsequent history of the Omaha platform of 1892.

5. "The capture of the Democracy by the forces of free silver gave the death blow to Populism." Do you agree? Discuss.

6. "It is a mistake to speak of the last decade of the nineteenth century as the 'Gay Nineties.' On the contrary it was a time of sober thought and grim endeavor, filled with the dread menace of class conflict and social upheaval." Discuss.

VIII. *America and the World, 1877-1900.*

1. "Between Fish and Hay a procession of politicians sat at the right hand of American presidents and directed foreign affairs of the nation without plan or purpose." Do you agree? Discuss.

2. How do you account for the growing interest of the United States in the Pacific after the Civil War?

3. Assess James G. Blaine as a diplomat. Do you feel that he deserves to rank among the outstanding secretaries of state?

4. "The Spanish-American War is usually taken as the date for the emergence of the United States as a world power." Amplify or comment on this quotation.

5. Account as fully as you can for the growth of American imperialism before 1900.

6. "The great danger of the Open Door doctrine lies in the inference that it is something for which the United States would or should go to war." Explain and discuss.

IX. *The Progressive Period, 1900-1917.*

1. Assess the factors responsible for the rise of progressivism. Which do you consider most important?

2. Describe the attempts of progressives to democratize, in state and union, the government of the United States. To what extent were they successful?

3. "Theodore Roosevelt was the direct heir and beneficiary of the Populism he had once so bitterly assailed." Discuss.

4. "Despite Roosevelt's skill at grabbing the spotlight, progressivism made greater strides under Taft." Do you agree? Discuss.

5. "Conservatives who thought Roosevelt too radical, and radicals who thought him too conservative, failed to perceive that he sought to hold an even balance between the contending elements in modern society." Explain.

6. Describe and contrast the New Nationalism of Roosevelt and the New Freedom of Wilson, accounting for any differences.

X. *Foreign Policy of the Progressive Period, 1900-1917.*

1. Trace and explain the development of American Caribbean policy, 1898-1917.

2. Do you agree that Roosevelt's action in regard to Panama was "indecent, not to say unwise"?

3. Was "dollar diplomacy" or "canal diplomacy" most influential in turning American interest toward the Caribbean and Central America?

4. Was Wilson's recognition policy toward Mexico justified?

5. Discuss Theodore Roosevelt's relations with Japan and the "Japanese menace," 1900-1908.

6. Were the anti-imperialists justified in maintaining that America's new imperialism reversed the trend toward democracy that had gone on since 1776?

XI. *The United States and World War I, 1917-1920.*

1. Was Wilson's administration neutral?

2. Why did the United States declare war on Germany rather than England?

3. Describe Wilson's efforts as a peacemaker, 1914-1917, and account for America's entry in the war.

4. "Upon Wilson's narrow partisanship may be placed the blame for America's failure to join the League of Nations." Do you agree? Explain.

5. How do you explain the rejection of the Versailles Treaty and the League of Nations by the United States?

6. Was the United States right in refusing to join the League of Nations?

XII. *The Era of "Normalcy," 1920-1932.*

1. How was the postwar spirit of nationalism reflected in the United States?

2. "In both domestic and foreign policy the period from 1920 to 1932 witnessed an almost continuous reaction from the idealism of Wilson." Explain.

3. What did President Harding mean by "normalcy"? To what extent did the Harding-Coolidge era approximate his ideal?

4. "In the quarter-century following American entry into World War I, the quest for security against both outer and inner threats to the country's well-being became, for the first time, a national purpose." Explain.

5. "Under Coolidge and Hoover the United States followed a pseudo-internationalism marred by two principal defects: unwillingness to recognize that disarmament was dependent on political security, and refusal to admit that a country could not profitably export goods without importing them." Explain and discuss.

6. "To all intents and purposes the United States by 1932 had become a member of the League of Nations, the Republican Party to the contrary notwithstanding." How far does the evidence support these assertions?

XIII. *The New Deal, 1933-1941.*

1. "The so-called 'Roosevelt revolution' was not a revolution at all, but rather the culmination of forces at work since 1898." Explain.

2. Do you agree with the statement: "Always, F. D. Roosevelt labored in the spirit of Macaulay's dictum: 'Reform in order to Preserve.'" Discuss.

3. "From the conservatives' point of view, F. D. Roosevelt's greatest sin was the deliberate abandonment of economic individualism." Do you agree? Discuss.

4. Trace the major proposals directed toward farm relief from the era of the Populists to the present.

5. Trace the changing relations between government and business during the administrations of F. D. Roosevelt.

6. Should Congress have accepted Roosevelt's proposal to reorganize the Supreme Court? Why?

XIV. *Foreign Policy of the New Deal, 1933-1941.*

1. Discuss the shift in American public opinion from isolationism to internationalism, 1920-1941, in the light of the various factors that influenced the change.

2. Explain the failure of the "Neutrality Acts" to keep the United States out of World War II.

3. Describe and evaluate the changes in American policy toward Latin America from 1898 to 1941.

4. Describe and contrast American policy toward Europe in the two periods, 1914-1917 and 1939-1941, accounting for any differences.

5. As an informed member of Congress, how would you have voted on the following questions: reciprocal trade agreements, conscription, and repeal of the arms embargo? In each case explain your reasons fully.

6. As an informed voter in 1940, would the "third-term tradition" have influenced you for or against Roosevelt? Why?

XV. *World War II and its Aftermath, 1941-1960.*

1. Would you agree with military strategists that the United States was wise in concentrating its war efforts first in Europe and then in the Pacific, rather than the reverse?

2. Describe and contrast federal attempts to control civilian life in World Wars I and II, accounting for any differences.

3. Contrast the League of Nations and the United Nations as instruments for world peace.

4. Has the United Nations served its purpose as a keeper of world peace? If not, what changes would you propose?

5. Describe and contrast the "Truman Doctrine," the "Marshall Plan," the North Atlantic Treaty Organization, and the "Eisenhower Doctrine" as devices to achieve American objectives in the Cold War.

6. Contrast the concept of the presidency held by Truman, Eisenhower, and Kennedy. Which proved more effective in achieving national and party goals?

XVI. *America's Global Mission: Climax and Decline, 1960-1969.*

1. Describe the "New Frontier" program of President Kennedy and the "Great Society" program of President Johnson, accounting for the successes and failures of each.

2. Account as fully as you can for the differences in civilian reaction to the Korean War and the Viet Nam War.

3. Why was the civil rights program more successful under President Johnson than under Presidents Eisenhower and Kennedy? Describe developments under each president.

4. Would American foreign policy have been vastly different if President Kennedy had not been assassinated? Illustrate your argument with specific examples.

5. Describe and evaluate the changing military strategies used by the United States in the Viet Nam War. Which proved to be the more effective?

6. Did rioting and student militancy prove the most effective means of achieving the ends sought? What other means of protest might have been used?

XVII. *The Limits of Presidential Power: the Nixon-Ford Years, 1969-1977*

1. What factors allowed President Nixon to end the Viet Nam War after President Johnson had failed to do so?

2. Describe the activities of Henry Kissinger as a peace-maker in various parts of the world, accounting as fully as you can for his successes and failures.

3. Did the shift from the "Warren Court" to the "Burger Court" affect a basic shift in the role of the Supreme Court in American Society?

4. Describe President Nixon's handling of the economic problems that beset his administration. Could other policies have been more successful?

5. Describe and evaluate President Nixon's concept of the role of the President in American society, and show how his views influenced his relations with Congress.

6. What strengths and weaknesses in the American governmental system have been revealed in the "Watergate Scandals?"

XVIII. *The Carter Years 1977-1981*

1. Discuss and appraise the impact of President Carter's "human rights program" on American foreign policy.

2. How did the Watergate scandal influence the relations between Congress and the President during the Carter administration? Cite as many specific instances as you can.

3. Describe and contrast the economic policies of the Nixon and Carter administrations, accounting as fully as you can for any differences.

4. Compare and contrast the "shuttle diplomacy" of Secretary of State Henry Kissinger with the techniques of President Carter. Which was more effective?

5. Discuss the long term impact of the oil pricing policies and embargo imposed by the OPEC group. How have American presidents responded?

6. How has inflation brought changes in national policy?

XIX. *Reagan Republicanism, 1981-*

1. How did Reagan's style of dealing with Congress differ from that of Carter? What role do southern Democrats play in the enactment of the President's program?

2. How does Reagan's foreign policy philosophy differ from that of Carter? Compare the two.

3. What social issues, as distinct from political or economic issues, separated Republicans from Democrats in their party platforms in 1980?

Index

Abrams, Creighton W., 260
Abrams v. United States, 166
Act of Havana, 203
Adamson Act, 128
Addams, Jane, 73
Advisory Committee on Civil Disorders, 271
Afghanistan, 320,331
Africa, in World War II, 210; in Cold War, 255, 265; relations under Nixon-Ford, 311; Carter, 322
Agassiz, Louis, 75
Agnew, Spiro T., in 1968 election, 279; in 1970 election, 281; in 1972 election, 281; resigns, 296
Agricultural Adjustment Act, 184, 192, 232
Agriculture, changes in during Reconstruction, 11; on Great Plains, 34-35; effect of closing of frontier on, 39; unrest among farmers, 57-60, 86-96; during World War I, 151; in 1920's, 169-170; New Deal program for, 183-185; 191-192; under Truman, 229; under Kennedy, 249; under Nixon-Ford, 290
Aguinaldo, Emilo, 132-133
Alabama Claims, 45
Alabama Midlands Case, 61
Alaska, purchase of, 44; establishment of government for, 132, 241
Aldrich, Nelson W., 53
Aldrich-Vreeland Act, 126
Aleutian Islands, captured by Japan, 210; recaptured by United States, 211
Algeciras Conference, 138-139
Alliance for Progress, formed, 251-252; abandoned, 305
America First Committee, 202
American Federation of Labor, formation of, 64; influences Progressivism, 116; division of, 190-191, 233
American Independent Party, 279
American Legion, 162
American Library Association, 81
Ames, Oakes, 44
Anarchists, in Haymarket Riot, 63-64; philosophy of, 75
Anderson, John, 329-330
Anderson, Sherwood, 167
Angola, 311, 322
Anthony, Susan B., 78
Anthracite Coal Strike of 1902, 120
Anti-Monopoly Party, 68
Anti-Saloon League, 79
Apache Indians, wars of, 32-33
Appalachia Bill, 264
Arab oil embargo, 310
Arafat, Yasser, 324

Architecture, progress of, 84
Arizona, settlement of, 38
Armstrong, Neil A., 288
Arthur, Chester A., as spoilsman, 47; named as vice-president, 48; as President, 48-49; on tariff, 52
Ash, Roy L., 283
Atchison, Topeka and Santa Fe Railroad, built, 24
Atlantic Charter, 205
Atom Bomb, in World War II, 212
Atomic Energy Commission, 218-219
Attica Prison Riot, 298
Automobile and Road Safety Act, 269

Baker, Robert G., 256
Baker, Newton D., 153
Ballinger-Pinchot Controversy, 123
Bangladesh, creation of, 306
Bank Holiday, 180
Barbed Wire, invention of, 35
Barnett, Ross, 250
Barton, Clara, 101
Baruch, Bernard, 150
Battle of the Atlantic, 206
Battle of the Bulge, 211
Battle of Leyte Gulf, 211
Battle of the Little Big Horn, 32
Battle of Midway, 211
Battle of Wounded Knee, 33
Bay of Pigs, 256
Beecher, Henry Ward, 76
Begin, Menachem, 324, 332
Bellamy, Edward, 74
Bering Sea Controversy, 103
Berlin, conflict over after World War II, 222; wall built, 253
Berrigan, Philip, 293
Beveridge, Albert J., as imperialist, 105-106, 109
Birds of Passage, 17
Black Codes, 6
Black Friday, 43
Black Hills, gold rush to, 30; Indian reservation in, 32
Blackmun, Harry A., 285
Black Monday, 245
Black Panther Trials, 287
Black Powder, 267
Blaine, James G., in 1876 election, 46; in 1884 election, 46-50; as Secretary of State, 54; and Panamericanism, 103-104
Bland-Allison Act, 91
Bliss, Tasker H., 91
Bok, Edward W., 82
Bonanza Farms, 37